ENVISIONING

SCRIPTURE

ENVISIONING

SCRIPTURE

JOSEPH SMITH'S REVELATIONS IN THEIR EARLY AMERICAN CONTEXTS

EDITED BY

Colby Townsend

SIGNATURE BOOKS | 2022 | SALT LAKE CITY

The opinions expressed in this book are not necessarily those of the publisher.

Design by Jason Francis.
The cover image is an engraving of a seed sowing machine from *The Iconographic Encyclopedia of Science, Literature, and Art*, 1851.

FIRST EDITION | 2022

LIBRARY OF CONGRESS CATALOGING-IN-PUBLICATION DATA

Names:	Townsend, Colby, editor.
Title:	Envisioning scripture : Joseph Smith's revelations in their early American contexts / edited by Colby Townsend.
Description:	First edition.	Salt Lake City : Signature Books, 2022.	Summary: "The first fifty years of United States history was a period of seemingly endless possibility. With the birth of a new country during the age of revolutions came new religions, new literary genres, new political parties, temperance and abolitionist societies, and the expansion of print and marketing networks that would dramatically change the course of the century. Envisioning Scripture: Joseph Smith's Revelations in Their Early American Contexts brings together ten essays from leading scholars on the history of early American religion and print culture. Covering issues of gender, race, prophecy, education, scripture, real and narrative time, authority and power, and apocalypticism, the essays invite the reader-scholar, student, etc.-to expand their knowledge of early Mormon history by grasping more fully the American contexts that Mormonism grew out of." —Provided by publisher.
Identifiers:	LCCN 2022005279 (print)	LCCN 2022005280 (ebook)	ISBN 9781560854470 (paperback)	ISBN 9781560854180 (ebook)
Subjects:	LCSH: Smith, Joseph, Jr., 1805-1844.	Church of Jesus Christ of Latter-day Saints—Sacred books.	Church of Jesus Christ of Latter-day Saints—Doctrines.	Revelation—Church of Jesus Christ of Latter-day Saints.	Revelation—Mormon Church.	Mormon Church—Sacred books.	Mormon Church—Doctrines.
Classification:	LCC BX8621 .E58 2022 (print)	LCC BX8621 (ebook)	DDC 289.3/2—dc23/eng/20220218

LC record available at https://lccn.loc.gov/2022005279
LC ebook record available at https://lccn.loc.gov/2022005280

CONTENTS

EDITOR'S INTRODUCTION

The long eighteenth century, roughly spanning 1660 to 1830,[1] was a period of intense social, political, and historical upheavals.[2] Besides the series of wars, dramatic changes in politics, and shift away from monarchies and the *ancien régime* within the transatlantic world, this period includes the rise and development of the novel,[3] the Enlightenment,[4] technological and social developments that enabled far more people than ever before to engage directly with print culture,[5] and the development of national and regional identities in the new United States.[6]

It was also a period, as recent scholarship has shown, that, contrary to previous assumptions, saw a turn toward—not away from—religion. As Isabel Rivers states, "Seventeenth- and eighteenth-century English society and culture was essentially religious in its institutions, practices

---

1. I follow the general field of eighteenth-century studies for these dates. Cf. Claude Rawson, *Satire and Sentiment, 1660–1830: Stress Points in the English Augustan Tradition*, new edition (New Haven, CT: Yale University Press, 2000).

2. Lloyd Bowen and Mark Stoyle, eds., *Remembering the English Civil Wars* (New York: Routledge, 2022); Rachel Hope Cleves, *The Reign of Terror in America: Visions of Violence from Anti-Jacobinism to Antislavery* (Cambridge: Cambridge University Press, 2009); Julia Swindells, *Glorious Causes: The Grand Theatre of Political Change, 1789 to 1833* (Oxford: Oxford University Press, 2001); Jonathan Sperber, *Revolutionary Europe, 1780–1850* (Harlow: Longman, 2000).

3. Michael McKeon, *The Origins of the English Novel, 1600–1740* (Baltimore: Johns Hopkins University Press, 1987).

4. Jonathan Israel, *A Revolution of the Mind: Radical Enlightenment and the Intellectual Origins of Modern Democracy* (Princeton, NJ: Princeton University Press, 2010).

5. Elizabeth Eisenstein, *The Printing Press as an Agent of Change*, 2 vols. (Cambridge: Cambridge University Press, 1979); Judith A. McGaw, *Most Wonderful Machine: Mechanization and Social Change in Berkshire Paper Making, 1801–1885* (Princeton, NJ: Princeton University Press, 1987).

6. Stephanie Kermes, *Creating an American Identity: New England, 1789–1825* (New York: Palgrave Macmillan, 2008); Sam Haselby, *The Origins of American Religious Nationalism* (New York: Oxford University Press, 2015).

and beliefs, and … writing on religious subjects dominated the publishing market."[7] Europe and the Americas experienced an explosion of new religious groups, charismatic leaders, and prophets during these years, and these new religious movements took full advantage of everything that print had to offer.[8] Educated and uneducated, rich and poor, it did not matter; all one needed toward the end of the century was an understanding of how print networks functioned, and virtually anyone could get their idea for a book onto paper, into the hands of a printer, and have their manuscript printed, bound, and ready for sale in a matter of months.[9]

For many new religious movements during and toward the end of the long eighteenth century, like Mormonism, this also meant initially taking advantage of print networks outside of one's religious circles. The cost of publishing could be prohibitive depending on the project. This forced people working on large print runs, like Mormon Church founder Joseph Smith (1805–44), who chose to do 5,000 copies of The Book of Mormon, to find a sponsor or financial backer. Martin Harris stepped in to subsidize publication and mortgaged part of his farm. If this printing situation had remained the same for future publications, the Mormons likely would not have been able to thrive. Within only a couple of years of proselytizing, Smith and his associates had found a small handful of converts who had previously worked as printers of local newspapers. This created new networks of print within early Mormonism that were far more cost effective. Smith relied on these networks going forward to get his revelations, translations, hymns, and other materials in print and into his followers' hands during the remainder of his life.

As the study of religion and literature receives renewed attention by scholars of the eighteenth and nineteenth centuries, it seems appropriate to bring some of this attention to the growing field of Mormon

---

7. Isabel Rivers, "Religion and Literature," in *The Cambridge History of English Literature, 1660–1780* (Cambridge: Cambridge University Press, 2005), 445.

8. See the essays in Andrew Crome, ed., *Prophecy and Eschatology in the Transatlantic World, 1550–1800* (New York: Palgrave Macmillan, 2016). See also Jonathan Sheehan, *The Enlightenment Bible: Translation, Scholarship, Culture* (Princeton, NJ: Princeton University Press, 2005).

9. Ann Fabian, *The Unvarnished Truth: Personal Narratives in Nineteenth-Century America* (Berkeley: University of California Press, 2000); Karen A. Weyler, *Empowering Words: Outsiders and Authorship in Early America* (Athens: University of Georgia Press, 2013).

studies. The literature produced by Joseph Smith Jr.—and that is precisely what the texts are that he produced, literature—has also received renewed attention in non-Mormon studies journals and academic presses. The work of both Liz Fenton and Jared Hickman in getting early Americanist colleagues to join in incorporating The Book of Mormon into the study of early American literature recently brought about the publication of a large volume of essays on the topic.[10] It is crucial for the continued study of both early Mormonism and early American religious and literary history that both groups, scholars studying early American topics more broadly and those studying Mormonism specifically, engage with one another even more directly.

In recent decades scholarship on American literature, religion, and politics has seen an explosion of interest in incorporating Mormon subjects in the stories that scholars tell. Scholars of early American literature and religion have explored the ways that The Book of Mormon takes up theories about the origins of the Native Americans,[11] persistent ideologies of ancient "white" Americans,[12] race in early America,[13] and other aspects of print culture that were pervasive during the late eighteenth and early nineteenth centuries. Publications within Mormon studies have similarly grown, as more and more scholars have engaged the field and attempted to help it transform into a larger area of academic inquiry. Scholars may write to their own audiences depending on the venue and their chosen interlocutors, but expanding the circle of conversation partners within Mormon studies to include scholars who do not engage directly in Mormon studies only helps the field to grow larger and more rapidly.

This volume aims to provide a series of essays that invite scholars

---

10. Elizabeth Fenton and Jared Hickman, eds., *Americanist Approaches to* The Book of Mormon (New York: Oxford University Press, 2019).

11. Matthew W. Dougherty, *Lost Tribes Found: Israelite Indians and Religious Nationalism in Early America* (Norman: University of Oklahoma Press, 2021); Elizabeth Fenton, *Old Canaan in a New World: Native Americans and the Lost Tribes of Israel* (New York: New York University Press, 2020).

12. Edward Watts, *Colonizing the Past: Mythmaking and Pre-Columbian Whites in Nineteenth-Century American Writing* (Charlottesville: University of Virginia Press, 2020).

13. Peter Coviello, *Make Yourselves Gods: Mormons and the Unfinished Business of American Secularism* (Chicago: University of Chicago Press, 2019), 135–170; Max Perry Mueller, *Race and the Making of the Mormon People* (Chapel Hill: University of North Carolina Press, 2017), 31–59.

and readers in Mormon studies to engage in these broader conversations. Nine of the ten essays in this volume were originally written for and published in academic journals that have audiences from several fields outside of Mormon studies.[14] Three of the essays are not about Mormonism at all but provide crucial information about print culture and female authorship, the development of biblical translation and interpretation in the Stone–Campbell movement, and gender and prophecy in the first few decades of US history.

I owe large debts to several people for helping to bring this volume together. Without the support and encouragement of Signature Books, this volume never would have happened. I am especially grateful to the contributors in the volume for allowing me to bring them together in this collection. I invited each of them either to revise their original essays or to leave them the way they were originally printed. Several of the authors decided to make revisions, some small and some large, to their essays, and some of the changes are more obvious than others. I also appreciate the different presses that granted permission to reprint the essays. Mark Thomas helped to raise funds to pay for the reprinting of a few of the essays. The work collected in this volume has changed the way that I understand and perceive early Mormonism and its place within early American literary and religious traditions. I hope that they will do similarly for you.

---

14. The exception is William Davis's essay.

ONE

WRITING RELIGIOUS EXPERIENCE
WOMEN'S AUTHORSHIP IN EARLY AMERICA

CATHERINE A. BREKUS

In 1755, a small tract was published in Boston with the title *The Nature, Certainty, and Evidence of True Christianity, In a Letter from a Gentlewoman in New-England, to Another Her Dear Friend, in Great Darkness, Doubt and Concern of a Religious Nature.* The author was Sarah Osborn, a schoolteacher from Newport, Rhode Island, but in accordance with the conventions of her day, she was identified only as an anonymous "gentlewoman." As a note on the title page explained, "Tho' this letter was wrote in great privacy from one friend to another; yet on representing that by allowing it to be printed, it wou'd probably reach to many others in the like afflicted case, and by the grace of God be very helpful to them; the writer was at length prevailed on to suffer it—provided her name and place of abode remain concealed." Whether the Reverend Thomas Prince, who arranged for the letter's publication, or Samuel Kneeland, the publisher, wrote this explanation, readers were encouraged to imagine a humble, self-denying woman who had not wanted to publish her letter, but who had finally "suffered" it because of her compassion for others in spiritual distress. As a further frame for her words, the title page included a brief citation to a passage from 1 Corinthians: "But God hath chosen the foolish things of the world to confound the wise; and God hath chosen the weak things of the world to confound the things which are mighty." Since Osborn never referred to this biblical text in her letter, it is likely that either Kneeland or Prince decided to include it, perhaps as a defense against possible critics. At a time when very few women dared to publish their words, they wanted readers to know that even the weak and the foolish—or in Osborn's case, the female—could offer insight into "the nature, certainty, and evidence of true Christianity."[1]

Many women in early America wrote letters, poems, and diaries, but only a few ever saw their work in print. Publishing was almost entirely a masculine enterprise. According to Charles Evans's indispensable guide to early American publishing, there were approximately 15,429 works published in America between 1639 and 1776, but women wrote only sixty-eight of them. (The number sixty-eight does not include titles that were published more than once: for example, Mary Rowlandson's frequently reprinted narrative of her Indian captivity.)[2] If we eliminate works by French or English writers that were reprinted in America, the number shrinks to thirty-five. Since many books available for sale in the colonies were imported from England, the number of female-authored books in circulation was much higher than these paltry numbers suggest, but as Sarah Osborn must have realized, she was a rare phenomenon: an American woman who was a published author.[3]

Ministers were closely involved in publishing these books, and in many cases they seemed less interested in affirming women's religious authority than in shoring up their own. They used women's writings to

---

1. Sarah Osborn, *The Nature, Certainty, and Evidence of True Christianity* ... (Boston: Samuel Kneeland, 1755), title page. On Thomas Prince's involvement in the publication of Osborn's letter, see Samuel Hopkins, *Memoirs of the Life of Mrs. Sarah Osborn* (Worcester, MA: Leonard Worcester, 1799), 157. The titles of the works cited in this essay are reproduced as they were printed; I have not attempted to standardize them according to contemporary style guides.

2. *Early American Imprints, Series I: Evans, 1639–1800* (Readex Corporation), accessed at the University of Chicago Library, Sep. 1, 2011. Mary White Rowlandson, *The Sovereignty and Goodness of God, Together, with the Faithfulness of His Promises Displayed; Being a Narrative of the Captivity and Restoration of Mrs. Mary Rowlandson* (Cambridge, MA: Samuel Green, 1682).

3. Counting the number of books written by women and published in America is complicated. The Evans collection includes a category entitled "women as authors," but it includes many books that were about women but not written by them. The Evans list is significantly larger than mine because I have omitted books like *The Declaration, Dying Warning and Advice of Rebekah Chamblit. A Young Woman Aged near Twenty-Seven Years, Executed at Boston September 27th. 1733* (Boston: S. Kneeland and T. Green, 1733). (This book was supposedly a transcription of her confession.) I have chosen to count only first editions because some books, especially Mary Rowlandson's narrative, were published in multiple editions. I have also not included titles that included extracts from women's writings: for example, Cotton Mather, *Memorials of Early Piety. Occurring in the Holy Life and Joyful Death of Mrs. Jerusha Oliver. With Some Account of her Christian Experiences, Extracted from her Reserved Papers: And Published, for the Service of Christianity* (Boston: T. Green, 1711).

strengthen religious institutions, to provide models of self-effacing piety for others to emulate, and to reinforce restrictive ideas about gender.[4] But a close look at these sixty-eight titles reveals that despite their small numbers and their emphasis on feminine humility, they also provided a compelling justification for women's right to make their voices heard in the public sphere. Almost all of the women who published books in early America focused on Christian themes, and they defended their decision to appear in print by emphasizing their personal experience of God's grace. Though they did not realize the radical potential of their language, their appeal to experience laid the groundwork for the expansion of women's authorship in the late eighteenth and nineteenth centuries, the defense of women's religious leadership, and the rise of feminist theology.

Congregationalist and Quaker women dominated the list of female authors in America before the Revolution. While Congregationalist women published twenty-six books between 1678 and 1776, meaning that they were responsible for 38 percent of all the titles written by women, Quaker women published eleven (or 16 percent). Despite their theological differences, both Quakers and Congregationalists preached a heart-centered religion that emphasized the importance of personal experience. Although they never encouraged women to publish theological treatises or grand narratives of providential history, they believed that women's personal stories of sin and salvation could serve as valuable models of piety for other Christians, especially women. After reprinting Martha Gerrish's religious letters, the Reverend Nathaniel Appleton exclaimed, "May the lovely Exemplar here bro't into the publick Light, meet with a just Reception and some happy imitations; particularly among the *Daughters of Zion; That they themselves may become the Epistles of Christ; written not with Ink, but with the spirit of the Living God, not in Tables of Stone, but in fleshly Tables of the Heart!*" Gerrish had been a "shining Example to her Sex."[5]

---

4. On the institutional reasons for publishing women's writings, see Christina Maria Devlin, "Piety Promoted: Female First-Person Narratives in Eighteenth-Century Quakerism and Methodism" (PhD diss., University of Chicago, 2001).

5. Nathaniel Appleton, *The Christian Glorying in Tribulation from a Sense of its Happy Fruits. A Discourse Occasion'd by the Death of that Pious and Afflicted Gentlewoman, Mrs. Martha Gerrish ... To Which are Annexed Some of Mrs. Gerrish's Letters* (Boston: J. Draper for J. Edwards and H. Foster, 1736), no page number; emphasis in original.

Before 1700 only three books by American women found their way into print: Ann Bradstreet's *Several Poems Compiled with Great Variety of Wit and Learning*, Mary Rowlandson's *Sovereignty and Goodness of God*, and Sarah Goodhue's *Copy of a Valedictory and Monitory Writing*. When Ann Bradstreet's brother-in-law arranged for her poetry to be published in England in 1650 (without her permission), he included an elaborate preface apologizing for the book. Assuring his readers that she had not forsaken her family responsibilities to write, he explained, "These Poems are the fruit but of some few houres, curtailed from her sleep and other enjoyments." As literary critic Elaine Showalter has pointed out, "No fewer than eleven men wrote testimonials and poems praising her piety and industry, prefatory materials almost as long as the thirteen poems in the book."[6]

There were many reasons for the scarcity of women authors in early America. Besides being less literate than men, women were discouraged from "meddling" in the masculine world of theology, politics, and law. John Winthrop, the first governor of Massachusetts Bay, explained one woman's mental illness as the result of too much "reading and writing": "For if she had attended her household affairs, and such things as belong to women, and not gone out of her way and calling to meddle in such things as are proper of men, whose minds are stronger, etc., she had kept her wits." Although women were encouraged to read the Bible and to write devotional diaries, they were not supposed to seek public recognition, and those who dared to publish their writings instead of keeping them private were subjected to withering criticism. "Your printing of a Book, beyond the custom of your Sex, doth rankly smell," a New England minister wrote to his sister in England in 1650. Even Cotton Mather, who praised female devotional writers for their piety, insisted that the best women writers were "Patterns of *Humility*." In his words, "They have made no Noise; they have sought no Fame."[7]

6. See the Preface to Ann Bradstreet, *The Tenth Muse Lately Sprung Up in America* (London: Stephen Bowtell, 1650). Ann Bradstreet, *Several Poems Compiled with Great Variety of Wit and Learning* (Boston: John Foster, 1678). Mary Rowlandson, *Sovereignty and Goodness of God* (Cambridge, MA: Samuel Green, 1682), and Sarah Goodhue, *The Copy of a Valedictory and Monitory Writing, Left by Sarah Goodhue* (Cambridge, MA: n.p., 1681). Elaine Showalter, *A Jury of Her Peers: American Women Writers from Anne Bradstreet to Annie Proulx* (New York: Knopf, 2009), 3.

7. James Kendall Hosmer, ed., *Winthrop's Journal, "History of New England," 1630–1649* (New York, C. Scribner's Sons, 1908), 2: 225. *The Copy of a Letter Written by Mr.*

Unlike the Puritans, the Quakers allowed women to serve as minis-ters or, in their language, "Public Friends," and they gave women more religious authority than any other denomination in early America. Be-cause of their belief that all people have a spark of divinity with them, an "inner light" that connects them to God, they argued that women as well as men could serve as public witnesses to God's grace. One histo-rian has estimated that there were "thirteen hundred to fifteen hundred women ministers active in the transatlantic Quaker community during the first three-quarters of the eighteenth century."[8] Yet even Quakers were anxious about publishing women's writings. When a group of Quakers decided to reprint the memoir of Elizabeth Stirredge, a British woman who had served as a "Public Friend" in the early years of the faith, they seemed as skittish as Ann Bradstreet's supporters more than seventy-five years earlier. Besides including testimonials from three men who had known her, they also reprinted a recommendation from her Quaker meeting signed by six more. All nine of these men assured readers that Stirredge had been "An Honest Sincere Tender Hearted Zealous Woman for God" who had never wanted to be famous. De-spite her gift for "Verbal Testimony," she had been "backward to appear therein, except she found it was immediately required of her." In other words, she spoke publicly only when God absolutely demanded it.[9]

The number of female-authored books grew in the first four de-cades of the eighteenth century, with eight more titles published before 1740. Seven of them focused on religious topics, and as before, they were usually prefaced by a male testimonial or apology. As the editor of Sarah Fiske's *Confession of Faith* (1704) explained, "Tis not with a design to blazon the Fame and Reputation of any Person, that this is now presented to the Publick View."[10] Since Fiske's writings were published after her death, the editor's apology seems extreme (a dead woman could not take pride in her "fame"), but he seems to have been

---

Thomas Parker (London, 1650), 13. Cotton Mather, *Awakening Thoughts on the Sleep of Death* (Boston: Timothy Green, 1712), iv.

8. Rebecca Larson, *Daughters of Light: Quaker Women Preaching and Prophesying in the Colonies and Abroad, 1700–1775*, 1st ed. (New York: Knopf, 1999), 63.

9. Elizabeth Stirredge, *Strength in Weakness Manifest in the Life, Trials and Christian Tes-timony of That Faithful Servant and Handmaid of the Lord, Elizabeth Stirredge* (Philadelphia: Samuel Keimer, 1726), iv, xii.

10. Sarah Fiske, *A Confession of Faith: or a Summary of Divinity Drawn Up by a Young Gentlewoman, in the 25th Year of Her Age* (Boston: B. Green, 1704), i.

genuinely concerned about tarnishing her character. Since the greatest sign of a woman's virtue in early America was anonymity, any attempt to gain public recognition seemed morally suspect.

Besides these eight titles, Congregational ministers also published several funeral sermons that included extracts from women's writings—six in all before 1740. For example, in 1711 Cotton Mather commemorated his sister's tragic death in childbirth by publishing *Memorials of Early Piety Occurring in the Holy Life and Joyful Death of Mrs. Jerusha Oliver.* Hoping to encourage "Younger Persons of the Female Sex" to become more pious, Mather selected "extracts from her reserved papers" that demonstrated her Christian humility. According to Mather, Jerusha had been so afraid of telling a lie that she "began a Custom she never left off; to avoid Positive Expressions, but rather to say, I think, or it may be, or 'Tis likely; even in things that she was most assured of." Encouraging other women to follow her example, he advised them to cultivate the virtues of modesty and deference. Mather also preached a funeral sermon for Elizabeth Cotton praising her as a "Mother in Israel" who had been an admirable wife, mother, and neighbor. By reprinting extracts from her letters and diaries, he hoped to illustrate her heartfelt devotion to God. "LORD, I desire no *other portion* than *thee*," she testified. "I will *be satisfyed in my* GOD!"[11]

As these examples suggest, women's writings were rarely published without a minister's or husband's support and approval, and they often appeared posthumously. For example, both Sarah Goodhue's *Copy of a Valedictory and Monitory Writing* and Mary Mollineux's *Fruits of Retirement: or Miscellaneous Poems, Moral and Divine* were published after death, and neither woman seems to have anticipated that her words would ever become public.[12] Rather than simply reprinting women's writings in their entirety, men often edited them to suit their own agendas. When Walter Wilmot published extracts from his deceased

---

11. Mather, *Memorials of Early Piety* (Boston: T. Green, 1711), 4. Cotton Mather, *Ecclesia Monilia. The Peculiar Treasure of the Almighty King Opened; and the Jewels that are Made up in it, Exposed. … Whereof one is more Particularly Exhibited, in the Character of Mrs. Elizabeth Cotton, Who Was Laid up a Few Days Before. And Certain Instruments and Memorials of Piety, Written by that Valuable and Honourable Gentlewoman* (Boston: Daniel Henchman, 1726), 24, 37–38; emphasis in original.

12. Goodhue, *Copy of a Valedictory and Monitory Writing.* Mary Mollineux, *Fruits of Retirement: or Miscellaneous Poems, Moral and Divine* (Philadelphia: Samuel Keimer, 1729).

wife's writings, he arranged them under his own headings—for example, "Of the universal Depravity and Corruption of humane [sic] Nature"—rather than her own, removing her reflections from their original context. His voice, not hers, dominates the text. Similarly, when Ebenezer Turell published a tribute to his late wife, Jane Colman Turell, he decided to publish many of her father's letters of advice to her as well as her own letters and poems. "O I hope God means of his free Grace to make you a holy and happy woman," the Reverend Colman wrote, "a gracious Wife, Mother, and Mistress in your House, a Blessing in your Place, and blessed forever." Oddly, the book contains as much material about Colman as it does about his daughter.[13]

Since both Quaker and Congregationalist leaders were concerned about passing on their faith to the next generation, they were particularly interested in publishing women's personal writings about the duty of Christian motherhood. Elizabeth Stirredge's memoir was addressed to her children, and in her first paragraph she expressed "a great Concern upon my Spirit, for my Children, that are coming up after me, that they may not be forgetful of keeping the right way. ..."[14] Troubled by declining church membership rates in the early eighteenth century, Congregational ministers worried that religious fervor was on the wane, and they pointed to covetousness, gambling, drinking, theft, slander, and sexual licentiousness as symptoms of religious decline. Despite their tendency to exaggerate the sinfulness of their age, they were genuinely concerned that parents were failing to raise Christian children. "Nothing is more Threatening to the Welfare of a People, than to have their *Young Ones* generally *Ignorant, Irreligious, Disorderly*," Benjamin Wadsworth warned. "When it is so, it looks as tho' Iniquity would soon abound, to the pulling down [of] heavy Judgments." Since ministers often attributed children's vices to parental neglect, they were anxious to find examples of loving, pious mothers who taught their

---

13. Ebenezer Prime, *A Sermon Preached in Oyster Bay Feb. 27, 1743–4: At the Funeral of Mrs. Freelove Wilmot, Consort of the Rev. Mr. Walter Wilmot ... To Which is Added an Appendix Containing Extracts from Her Private Papers* (New York: J. Parker, 1744), 62. Benjamin Colman, *Reliquiae Turellae: Two Sermons Preach'd at Medford, April 10, 1735 ... the Lord's Day after the Funeral of his Beloved Daughter Mrs. Jane Turell. To Which are Added, Some Large Memoirs of her Life and Death, by her Consort, the Reverend Mr. Ebenezer Turell* (Boston: S. Kneeland and T. Green, 1735), 90.

14. Stirredge, *Strength in Weakness*, 1.

children to fear God and to honor their parents. When the Reverend Nathaniel Appleton published his funeral sermon for Martha Gerrish, he included lengthy extracts from her letters to children, nieces, and nephews. Writing to a daughter who had not yet become a full church member, Gerrish warned her, "Let me tell you,—that while you live in the Omission of any Duty, you have no Room to expect a Blessing: God will turn a deaf Ear to all your Cries; you are Expos'd to His Wrath. ..."[15] The Reverend Appleton could not have said it better, which may have been part of the reason why he decided to publish her words.

From reading the few women's books that were published in America before 1740, one might imagine that all Christian women were self-effacing, moral, and devoted to raising Christian children—and this may have been part of the reason that these particular titles found their way into print. It is unlikely that Cotton Mather would have decided to publish extracts from Elizabeth Cotton's diaries if she had sounded arrogant or had questioned women's subordination to men. Even Martha Gerrish, who seems to have had a sharp tongue, earned praise for her "sincerity" and "modesty." Despite admitting that "Her natural Temper was something quick, and not so inclined to Patience," Appleton emphasized that God's grace had "usually" enabled her to cultivate "*a meek and quiet Spirit.*" When she was afflicted with a chronic illness that robbed her of the ability to walk, she had responded with remarkable "submission."[16]

Yet not all women's writings could be fitted into a paradigm of female humility, and it is possible that readers found other meanings in them. Although the title page of Elizabeth Stirredge's memoir promised that it would focus on "her pious care and counsel to her children," the full text also included stories about her experiences as a female minister. Remembering the evening that a Quaker man ordered a group of female ministers to "go home about their Business, and wash their

15. Benjamin Wadsworth, "The Nature of Early Piety," in *A Course of Sermons on Early Piety* (Boston, 1721), 29; emphasis in original. Nathaniel Appleton, *The Christian Glorying in Tribulation from a Sense of its Happy Fruits. A Discourse Occasion'd by the Death of that Pious and Afflicted Gentlewoman, Mrs. Martha Gerrish ... To Which are Annexed Some of Mrs. Gerrish's Letters* (Boston: J. Draper for J. Edwards and H. Foster, 1736), 66. See also Mather, *Ecclesia Monilia*, 36–40. On fears about the "rising generation," see Richard P. Gildrie, *The Profane, the Civil, and the Godly: The Reformation of Manners in Orthodox New England, 1679–1749* (University Park: Pennsylvania State University Press, 1994), 85–109.
16. Appleton, *The Christian Glorying in Tribulation*, title page, 31–32.

Dishes, and not go about to preach," Stirredge criticized him for valuing worldly conventions more than divine inspiration. Later, when she herself was ordered to "keep silence," she retorted, "I do not know whether ever the Lord may open my Mouth again; but if he do, and unloose my Tongue to speak, I shall not keep silent."[17] Portraying herself as an "instrument" of God, Stirredge insisted that she had been divinely inspired.

There was a small increase in the number of women's writings published during the Great Awakening in New England, the emotional revivals that took place during the 1740s. In comparison to the years between 1730 and 1740, when only three women's books were published, another ten found their way into print between 1740 and 1750. Since three of these books were published posthumously and six were reprinted from England, this number does not reflect an upsurge in women seeking publication, but rather a new interest among publishers in providing female models of piety during the revivals. The public was so hungry for individual religious narratives that publishers saw an opportunity to make a profit, and besides reprinting Puritan texts, they seem to have deliberately sought out women's devotional writings. Elizabeth White's narrative, which was first published in London in the seventeenth century, was reprinted in Boston in 1741, and Elizabeth Bury's diary, first published in London in 1720, was reprinted in Boston in 1743. Two of Elizabeth Singer Rowe's books, *The History of Joseph* and *Devout Exercises of the Heart*, both popular in evangelical circles in England, were published in 1739 and 1742. (Rowe had died in 1737.)[18]

All of these books were widely read during the revivals, and although we do not know why readers were attracted to them, they probably would not have become popular if not for their reassuring emphasis on women's modesty. According to the Reverend Isaac Watts, Elizabeth Rowe's writings were a model of "self-Abasement and holy Shame," and Anne Dutton belittled her writings as "the Lispings of a *Babe*." Even though she was an accomplished woman who may have

---

17. Stirredge, *Strength in Weakness*, title page, 57, 93.
18. Elizabeth White, *The Experiences of God's Gracious Dealing with Mrs. Elizabeth White* (Boston: S. Kneeland and T. Green, 1741). Elizabeth Bury, *An Account of the Life and Death of Mrs. Elizabeth Bury* (Boston: D. Henchman, 1743). Elizabeth Singer Rowe, *The History of Joseph. A Poem* (Philadelphia: B. Franklin, 1739); Elizabeth Singer Rowe, *Devout Exercises of the Heart in Meditation and Soliloquy, Prayer and Praise* (Boston: J. Blanchard, 1742).

authored as many as fifty different publications, she portrayed herself as "weak" and even infantile. Rather than defending her intelligence, she asked her readers, "Who knows but the Lord may ordain *Strength* out of the Babe's mouth? And give you a Visit *Himself*, by so weak a *Worm*, to your strong Consolation?"[19] Other women's books were similarly self-effacing. For example, Elizabeth Bury denigrated herself as "polluted," a "poor, weak, wandering Child" and "a poor, weak, unworthy, defiled Child."[20]

Although men also emphasized their sinfulness, this language was strongly gendered. When the famous evangelist George Whitefield looked back at his childhood, he remembered "such early Stirrings of Corruption in my Heart, as abundantly convince me that *I was conceived and born in Sin*—That in me dwelleth no good Thing by Nature." Yet when Whitefield's narrative of his religious experience is placed next to women's accounts, his humility sounds comparatively mild. Whitefield described himself as a "poor soul" only once, and he never portrayed himself as "weak." (The word "weak" appears only twice in his narrative, once in a quotation from the poet Joseph Addison, and once when he was describing his debility after an illness.)[21] It is hard to imagine him apologizing for his writings in the same way that women apologized for theirs. When Sarah Osborn published her *Nature, Certainty, and Evidence of True Christianity*, she described herself as "a poor nothing Creature," "utterly unworthy," and "vile," and she explicitly denied being motivated by "Self-confidence, Pride, Ostentation, or vain Glory." Often she wrote in the passive voice. "God *caus'd my Heart to go out after Him*," she explained.[22]

---

19. Anne Dutton, *A Letter to such the Servants of Christ, Who May have any Scruples about the Lawfulness of PRINTING any thing written by a Woman* (London: J. Hart, 1743), reprinted in *Selected Spiritual Writings of Anne Dutton: Eighteenth-Century, British-Baptist, Woman Theologian*, ed. JoAnn Ford Watson (Macon, Georgia: Mercer University Press, 2006), 3: 257; emphasis in original. See Stephen J. Stein, "A Note on Anne Dutton, Eighteenth-Century Evangelical," *Church History* 44, no. 4 (Dec. 1975): 485–91.

20. Elizabeth Bury, *An Account of the Life and Death of Mrs. Elizabeth Bury, Who Died, May the 11th 1720. Aged 76. Chiefly Collected Out of Her Own Diary. Together with Her Elegy, by the Reverend Dr. Watts*, 4th ed. (Boston: Green, Bushell, and Allen, 1743), 123, 96, 63.

21. George Whitefield, *A Brief and General Account of the First Part of the Life of the Reverend Mr. George Whitefield* (Boston: S. Kneeland & T. Green, 1740), 2; emphasis in original. He described himself as a "poor soul" on p. 10.

22. Osborn, *The Nature, Certainty, and Evidence of True Christianity*, 3, 4, 13, 5; emphasis in original.

10

Osborn clearly believed that a "feminine" voice was supposed to sound humble and self-denying, but at a time when very few women ever saw their names in print, it would be a mistake to underestimate the importance of her letter being published. Anyone who read her book was encouraged to believe that a "gentlewoman from New England" should be regarded as a model of true grace. Osborn portrayed her story as valuable, indeed priceless, because it offered insight into the meaning of a Christian life.

The Congregationalists who were most active in publishing women's works during the 1740s (and throughout the rest of the eighteenth century) belonged to the evangelical wing of the denomination. As ministers argued over whether the revivals of the Great Awakening were a "genuine work of God" or a dangerous outbreak of "enthusiasm," they also clashed over women's right to testify about their religious beliefs publicly, either in person or in print. Ironically, the theologically liberal wing of the denomination tended to be the most socially conservative, and ministers like Charles Chauncy insisted that "*it is a shame: for* WOMEN *to speak in the church.*"[23] In order to discredit the revivals, they claimed that "irrational" women had disrupted church services by weeping loudly, falling into fits, and even interrupting their ministers during worship. In contrast, the theologically conservative wing of the denomination identified women's fervor as a sign of the presence of the Holy Spirit. If not for the support of Thomas Prince, the influential editor of *The Christian History*, a periodical about the revivals, Sarah Osborn's book never would have been published.

Although evangelicals emphasized women's secondary status in the order of creation, no other religious group in pre-Revolutionary America did more to support women's authorship. (The first African Americans and Native Americans to become published authors were also evangelicals, including Phillis Wheatley, Samson Occom, Olaudah Equiano, James Albert Ukawsaw Gronniosaw, and John Marrant.)[24]

---

23. Charles Chauncy, *Enthusiasm Described and Cautioned Against* (Boston, 1742), quoted in *The Great Awakening: Documents Illustrating the Crisis and its Consequences*, ed. Alan Heimert and Perry Miller (Indianapolis: Bobbs-Merrill, 1967), 241; emphasis in original.

24. Phillis Wheatley, *Poems on Various Subjects, Religious and Moral* (Philadelphia: Joseph Crukshank, 1786). Olaudah Equiano, *The Interesting Narrative of the Life of Olaudah Equiano, or Gustavas Vassa, the African, Written by Himself* (New York: W. Durell, 1791), James Albert Ukawsaw Gronniosaw, *Narrative of the Most Remarkable Particulars in the Life of*

On one hand, Jonathan Edwards warned women not to act too "masculine" or assertive, and he insisted that "it's against nature for a man to love a woman as wife that is rugged, daring, and presumptuous." In 1741 he presided over a church council that admonished Bathsheba Kingsley, a woman from Westfield, Massachusetts, for claiming to be "a proper person to be improved for some great thing in the church of God; and that in the exercise of some parts of the work of ministry." Describing her as a "brawling woman," Edwards complained that she had "cast off that modesty, shamefacedness, and sobriety and meekness, diligence and submission, that becomes a Christian woman in her place." Yet Edwards also praised women for their devotion, and in his *Faithful Narrative of the Surprising Work of God*, he portrayed a young woman named Abigail Hutchinson as "a very eminent instance of Christian experience." Elevating her as a model for others to emulate, he claimed that "she had many extraordinary discoveries of the glory of God and Christ."[25]

Seventeen (or 31 percent) of the women's books published between 1740 and 1776 were written by "evangelicals" who claimed to have been "born again" during a personal conversion experience. Evangelicalism was a new kind of Protestantism that emerged during the 1730s and 1740s in response to political, economic, and intellectual transformations that were transatlantic in scope, including the development of political liberalism, the flourishing of religious toleration, and especially the currents of thought that we now identify as the Enlightenment. As recent historians have argued, the Enlightenment not only took place *against* Protestantism, but *within* it, and just as liberal Protestants were inspired by new ideas about human goodness, divine benevolence, and free will, evangelicals were deeply influenced by the Enlightenment

James Albert Ukawsaw Gronniosaw, an African Prince, Written by Himself (Newport: S. Southwick, 1774). Samson Occom, *Divine Hymns, or Spiritual Songs* (Portland: Thomas Clark, 1803). John Marrant, *A Sermon Preached on the 24th Day of June 1789* (Boston: Thomas and John Fleet, 1789). See also Joanna Brooks, *American Lazarus : Religion and the Rise of African-American and Native American Literatures* (New York: Oxford University Press, 2003).

25. The "Miscellanies," Entry Nos. a–z, aa–zz, 1–500, *The Works of Jonathan Edwards*, Vol. 13, ed. Thomas A. Schafer (New Haven, CT: Yale University Press, 2002), 20. "Advice to Mr. and Mrs. Kingsley," Jonathan Edwards Papers, Andover Newton Theological School, Newton Centre, Massachusetts. Jonathan Edwards, *A Faithful Narrative of the Surprising Work of God*, in *The Works of Jonathan Edwards*, Vol. 4, ed. C. C. Goen (New Haven, CT: Yale University Press, 1972), 199, 194.

emphasis on first-hand experience as the basis of knowledge.[26] "All our knowledge is founded" on *"Experience,"* John Locke wrote. If the Enlightenment was an "Age of Reason," it was also an "Age of Experience," and Enlightenment thinkers insisted that knowledge must be based on empirical proof rather than clerical authority or inherited tradition.[27]

This emphasis on experience was not new, and as historians Bernard McGinn and Susan Schreiner have shown, it had deep Christian roots stretching back to Bernard of Clairvaux and the Protestant reformers. But under the influence of the Enlightenment, the language of experience became more widespread and gained a veneer of scientific authority.[28] Unlike earlier Protestants, who had been hesitant to appear too confident about their salvation (lest they be guilty of pride), the new evangelicals of the eighteenth century claimed that they could empirically feel and know whether they had been spiritually reborn. *"How do I know this God is mine; and that I myself am not deceived?"* Sarah Osborn asked. "By the Evidences of a *work of grace* wrought in my Soul." Many evangelicals claimed to know the exact moment, down to the day and the hour, when they had been born again. Ironically, evangelicals defended their faith against the skeptical and liberal strains of the Enlightenment by appropriating an enlightened language of experience, certainty, evidence, and sensation as their own. "Every

---

26. D. W. Bebbington, *Evangelicalism in Modern Britain: A History from the 1730s to the 1980s* (Boston: Unwin Hyman, 1989); D. Bruce Hindmarsh, *The Evangelical Conversion Narrative: Spiritual Autobiography in Early Modern England* (New York: Oxford University Press, 2005). Catherine A. Brekus, "Sarah Osborn's Enlightenment: Reimaging Eighteenth-Century Intellectual History," in *The Religious History of American Women: Reimagining the Past*, ed. Catherine A. Brekus (Chapel Hill: University of North Carolina, 2007), 108–41. Mark A. Noll, *The Rise of Evangelicalism: The Age of Edwards, Whitefield, and the Wesleys* (Downers Grove, IL: InterVarsity Press, 2003). See also David Hempton, *Methodism: Empire of the Spirit* (New Haven, CT: Yale University Press, 2005), 52. Frederick A. Dreyer, *The Genesis of Methodism* (Bethlehem, PA: Lehigh University Press, 1999). Brian Stanley, "Christian Missions and the Enlightenment: A Reevaluation," in *Christian Missions and the Enlightenment*, ed. Brian Stanley (Grand Rapids, Michigan: Eerdmans, 2001), 1–21.

27. John Locke, *Essay Concerning Human Understanding* (1690; rpt. London: Awnsham and J. Churchill, 1706), Vol. 1, 51; emphasis in original. Roy Porter, *The Enlightenment*, 2nd ed. (New York: Palgrave, 2001), 2.

28. Bernard McGinn, "The Language of Inner Experience in Christian Mysticism," *Spiritus: A Journal of Christian Spirituality* 1, no. 1 (2001): 156–71. Susan Elizabeth Schreiner, *Are You Alone Wise?: The Search for Certainty in the Early Modern Era* (New York: Oxford University Press, 2011), 209–60.

Day's Experience confirms my Faith," Elizabeth Rowe wrote, " and brings a fresh Evidence of thy goodness. Thou hast dispell'd my Fears, and to the Confusion of my spiritual Foes, hearken'd to the voice of my Distress." Searching for proof that Christianity was true, she found it in "every day's experience."[29]

Because of their belief in the inner light, Quakers had emphasized the importance of a personal encounter with God ever since their founding in the seventeenth century, and they, too, believed that their experiences could offer insight into the nature of God. When Sophia Hume, the most celebrated Quaker female author in eighteenth-century America, published her *Caution to Such as Observe Days and Times*, she mixed her admonitions against "drunkenness, oaths, profaneness," and "debaucheries of all kinds" with personal reflections on her life. Because she wanted her readers to know that her authority came from the indwelling of the Holy Spirit, she declared, "I speak what I know experimentally."[30]

Today the word "experience" has become such a common part of our language that we may find it difficult to hear its revolutionary cadences. We tend to use the word "experience" as a synonym for individual subjectivity, and we describe our experiences in the same way as our "feelings"—as interior and private. Indeed, modern-day scholars of religion have criticized an emphasis on "the experiential dimension of religion" because personal experience is "inaccessible to strictly objective modes of inquiry."[31] But in the eighteenth-century, the word "experience" had a more scientific connotation, and Enlightenment thinkers believed that by scrutinizing human experience they could make new discoveries about the world. Inspired by scientific and technological advances, they insisted that empiricism would liberate people from blind devotion to the past. All ideas had to be subjected to the test of experiment and observation.

---

29. Osborn, *Nature, Certainty and Evidence*, 4. Rowe, *Devout Exercises*, 140.

30. Sophia Hume, *A Caution to Such as Observe Days and Times* (Newport: Solomon Southwick, 1771), 9.

31. Robert H. Sharf, "Experience," in *Critical Terms for Religious Studies*, ed. Mark C. Taylor (Chicago: University of Chicago Press, 1998), 95; and Wayne Proudfoot, *Religious Experience* (Berkeley: University of California Press, 1985). For an overview of historical controversies over "religious experience" in America, see Ann Taves, *Fits, Trances, and Visions: Experiencing Religion and Explaining Experience from Wesley to James* (Princeton, NJ: Princeton University Press, 1999).

Neither Quakers nor evangelicals wanted to be "liberated" from the Christian tradition, but they, too, believed that first-hand experience could offer rational evidence about the universe. Like scientists who adopted the Newtonian method in order to verify their findings, they often described their faith as "experimental": it could be validated by concrete, measurable experience. According to Sarah Gill, whose husband published her writings posthumously, she had been "experimentally convinced" of the justice of hell.[32]

Between 1750 and 1776, when there was a sudden spike in the number of self-identified "daughters of liberty" writing about politics, forty-six more books by women were published, not including reprints, and more than half of them focused on religious topics. Although the number forty-six may sound small, it represented a sharp increase from the past. For the sake of comparison, it is notable that twice as many female-authored books appeared during these twenty-six years than in the entire history of American publishing prior to 1750. Most striking, even though ministers continued to publish posthumous collections of women's writings, growing numbers of women dared to publish their work while they were still alive. Before 1740, 42 percent of women's books were published posthumously, but between 1750 and 1776 that number decreased to 26 percent. A few even refused to hide their names behind a cloak of anonymity. When Sophia Hume published her first book in 1748, she identified herself only with her initials, but in 1771 she allowed her name to appear in capital letters on the title page. Even more daring, Martha Brewster announced both her name and her place of residence on the title page of her *Poems on Divers Subjects*, a collection of religious poetry. Breaking with older conventions of female modesty, she proudly advertised that the book had been written "by Martha Brewster, of Lebanon."[33]

Like earlier female authors, most of these women justified their right to appear in print by appealing to their religious experience. In a book of poems honoring George Whitefield, Jane Dunlap used her

---

32. Sue Lane McCulley and Dorothy Zayatz Baker, eds., *The Silent and Soft Communion: The Spiritual Narratives of Sarah Pierpont Edwards and Sarah Prince Gill* (Knoxville: University of Tennessee Press 2005), 25.

33. Hume, *An Exhortation to the Inhabitants of the Province of South Carolina*, title page; and Hume, *A Caution to such as Observe Days and Times*, title page. Brewster, *Poems on Divers Subjects*, title page.

preface to explain how deeply his sermons had touched her heart, and she included a poem about her joy at being born again. Though she apologized for her "homely stile," she claimed that even a woman could teach people about the meaning of a Christian life: "No eloquence does in these lines,/ I'm very sure appear,/ But sacred truths will always shine,/ Tho' in the lowest sphere."[34] In Sarah Osborn's tract, *The Nature, Certainty, and Evidence of True Christianity*, she held up her own religious experiences as a model for what it meant to be born again: she loved holiness for its own sake, she was willing to suffer affliction, and she wanted to do good works. She assured her readers that if they could say the same, then they, too, were on the path to salvation. God revealed himself not only through the Bible, but also through women's personal experiences of his grace.

Perhaps the most remarkable female author in the eighteenth century was Phillis Wheatley, a slave who had been kidnaped from Africa as a child. She published six different titles between 1770 and 1773, including an elegy in memory of the famous evangelist George Whitefield. In order to gain acceptance in the public of letters, Wheatley emphasized the depth of her Christian faith, and in one of her most famous (and controversial) poems, she claimed that her enslavement had been a "mercy" because it had introduced her to Christianity. "'Twas mercy brought me from my pagan land," she wrote, "Taught my benighted soul to understand/That there's a God—that there's a Saviour too: Once I redemption neither sought nor knew." Because she was female, enslaved, and only sixteen when her first book was published, many readers expressed skepticism about her ability to write such sophisticated verse, and her book included a testimonial signed by eighteen of Boston's leading gentlemen, including the governor, swearing that an "uncultivated Barbarian from Africa" had indeed written her own poems. No author female author in early America faced the same degrees of skepticism or hostility, but as Wheatley made clear in her poems, her authority to write came from her rebirth in Christ—in other words, from God himself.[35]

---

34. Jane Dunlap, *Poems, Upon Several Sermons, Preached by the Rev'd and Renowned, George Whitefield, While in Boston : A New-Years Gift* (Boston: Ezekiel Russell, 1771), 19.

35. Phillis Wheatley, *An Elegiac Poem ... On the Death of George Whitefield* (Boston: Ezekiel Russell, 1770); *Poems on Various Subjects, Religious and Moral* (Boston: Cox and Berry, 1773), 18, 8. See also Phillis Wheatley, *To Mrs. Leonard, on the Death of her Husband*

Although Wheatley and other female authors do not seem to have realized it, they stood in a long tradition of Christian women who justified their religious authority on the grounds of divine inspiration, including Hildegard of Bingen, a medieval visionary, and Anne Hutchinson, the "American Jezebel" who claimed to have received revelations from God. Excluded from formal avenues of power, women across the centuries had learned to emphasize the authority of their experience rather than their reason or their education. Yet despite these continuities with the past, the eighteenth century marked a watershed in understandings of "experience." Because Enlightenment philosophers elevated first-hand experience as the only reliable source of knowledge, even more reliable than the Bible, empirical language sounded particularly potent.

Despite their small numbers, women's religious writings seem to have been popular. Sarah Osborn's *Nature, Certainty, and Evidence of True Christianity* was published five different times before her death in 1796, including editions in Boston, Newport, Providence, Danbury (in Connecticut), and even London, and Elizabeth Rowe's *Devout Exercises of the Heart, in Meditation and Soliloquy, Prayer and Praise* was reprinted in sixteen different American editions during the eighteenth century. Female readers seem to have sought out books written by women: for example, Sarah Osborn read Hannah Housman's *The Power and Pleasure of the Divine Life*, and she expressed deep admiration for Elizabeth Bury's heartfelt devotional writings.[36] But men also seemed interested in reading about women's religious experiences. Jonathan Edwards, for example, read the works of Elizabeth Rowe and Hannah Housman, and one of the surviving copies of Sarah Osborn's letter is marked with the signature, "John Perrey,

---

(Boston: s.n., 1771); *To the Rev. Mr. Pitkin, on the death of his lady* (Boston: s.n., 1772); *To the Hon'ble Thomas Hubbard, Esq; on the death of Mrs. Thankfull Leonard* (Boston : s.n., 1773); and *An Elegy, to Miss. Mary Moorhead, on the Death of her Father, the Rev. Mr. John Moorhead* (Boston: William M'Alpine, 1773).

36. Sarah Osborn, Diary, Mar. 10, 1758, Newport Historical Society, citing Hannah Housman, *The Power and Pleasure of the Divine Life: Exemplify'd in the Late Mrs. Housman, of Kidderminster, Worcestershire. As extracted from Her Own Papers* (Boston: S. Kneeland, 1755). Sarah Osborn mentioned Bury's writings in a letter to Joseph Fish, Feb. 4, 1748, American Antiquarian Society, Worcester, Massachusetts, and in her diary for July 17, 1757, Beinecke Rare Book Library, Yale University, New Haven, Connecticut. Elizabeth Bury, *An Account of the Life and Death of Mrs. Elizabeth Bury, Who Died, May the 11th 1720. Aged 76. Chiefly Collected out of Her Own Diary. Together with Her Elegy, by the Reverend Dr. Watts*, 4th ed. (Boston: D. Henchman, 1743).

his Book." We can only imagine what it meant for an eighteenth-century man to search for religious truth in a woman's book, but it seems likely that women like Osborn paved the way for the acceptance of female novelists, poets, and political writers in the late eighteenth and nineteenth centuries. As the American public grew accustomed to seeing the words of Christian women in print, they became more comfortable with the idea of women's authorship in general—provided, that is, that women never forgot Paul's words, "the man is the head of the woman" (1 Cor. 11: 3).[37]

The female authors of the late seventeenth and eighteenth centuries left an ambivalent legacy to future generations of women. Most of them accepted (and reinforced) negative stereotypes of women's frailty and passivity, and despite their obvious gifts, they never defended their religious authority on the grounds of their rationality or their education, but only their experience. Few dared to claim that they were as intelligent or as intellectually curious as men. When the Reverend Ebenezer Pemberton published some of his mother's writings, he took pains to point out that she had not been a scholar: "She read the sacred Pages, and other religious Tracts, not so much to increase her *speculative Knowledge*, and gratify the Inclinations of an *inquisitive Mind*; as to learn the self-denying Mysteries of the Cross of CHRIST. ..."[38] During the nineteenth century, the word "experience" lost some of its power as it became increasingly associated with subjectivity, emotion, femininity, and racial inferiority, and the work of female authors was often devalued on the grounds that they were simply writing about their experience, not the universal human condition. According to stereotypes, white men based their decisions on "reason" while women and African Americans relied on emotion and "experience."

Yet by emphasizing the authority of their personal religious experience, the female authors of the late seventeenth and eighteenth centuries also paved the way for more radical voices. Very few women dared to claim the authority of ministry in early America, but hundreds of evangelical and Quaker women crisscrossed the country as itinerant

---

37. On the female authors whom Edwards read, see Peter J. Thuesen, ed., *Catalogues of Books, The Works of Jonathan Edwards* (New Haven, CT: Yale University Press 2008), 98–103. See the copy of Osborn's *Nature, Certainty, and Evidence* owned by the American Antiquarian Society in Worcester, Massachusetts.

38. Ebenezer Pemberton, *Meditations on Divine Subjects: By Mrs. Mary Lloyd. To Which Is Prefixed, an Account of Her Life and Character* (New York: J. Parker, 1750), 22.

preachers in the late eighteenth and early nineteenth centuries, and they defended their right to preach on the grounds of their personal experience of God's grace. One of the most remarkable was Jarena Lee, an African Methodist who entitled her book, *The Religious Experience and Journal of Mrs. Jarena Lee*. Insisting that God had communicated with her through voices and visions as well as through the Bible, Lee claimed that her religious authority did not come from her education (she had attended school for only three months), but from her heartfelt religious experiences. "By the instrumentality of a poor coloured woman," she explained, "the Lord poured forth his spirit among the people."[39]

By the late nineteenth century, feminist theologians like Frances Willard and Elizabeth Cady Stanton would transform this experiential language into a critique of the patriarchal assumptions undergirding the Christian tradition. In contrast to earlier generations of women, they argued that their distinct experiences as *women*, not simply as Christians, could be an important source for theological reflection, and they insisted that Christian understandings of God had to be reconstructed on the basis of women's as well as men's experiences. "God never discriminates," Elizabeth Cady Stanton wrote in *The Woman's Bible*. "It is man who has made the laws and compelled woman to obey him. The Old Testament and the New are books written by men; the coming Bible will be the result of the efforts of both, and contain the wisdom of both sexes, their combined spiritual experience."[40] Cady was far more radical than earlier women, but she was hardly the first woman in America to treat religious experience as a form of revelation. The discipline of feminist theology was constructed on an assumption that would have been deeply familiar to early American authors like Sarah Osborn and Phillis Wheatley: the assumption that women's experiences could offer insight into the nature of God.[41]

---

39. Jarena Lee, *The Life and Religious Experience of Jarena Lee*, in *Sisters of the Spirit: Three Black Women's Autobiographies of the Nineteenth Century*, ed. William L. Andrews (Bloomington: Indiana University Press, 1986), 45–46. On female preaching, see Catherine A. Brekus, *Strangers and Pilgrims : Female Preaching in America, 1740–1845* (Chapel Hill: University of North Carolina Press, 1998).

40. Elizabeth Cady Stanton, *The Woman's Bible* (1898; New York: Prometheus Books, 1999), 23.

41. For contemporary debates over the usefulness of the category, "women's experience," see Joan W. Scott, "The Evidence of Experience," *Critical Inquiry* 17, no. Summer (1991): 773–97.

Early American women writers could not have foreseen the changes that they would set in motion by justifying their authority on the grounds of their religious experience. Like Sarah Osborn, most of them wanted only to affirm the "nature, certainty, and evidence of true Christianity." But their language of experience, with all of its limitations and possibilities, inspired future generations of women to publish, to preach, and to propose new ways of thinking about God.

TWO

REASSESSING JOSEPH SMITH JR.'S
FORMAL EDUCATION

WILLIAM DAVIS

How much formal schooling did Mormon Church founder Joseph Smith (1805–44) obtain in his youth and early adulthood? Such a question might appear innocuous, but it is fraught with implications that extend beyond a simple historical account of his educational opportunities. The amount (and quality) of Smith's formal education, or rather the various assumptions surrounding his presumed lack of it, has been enlisted by followers and detractors alike in order to frame Smith's life within the narratives of divinely-inspired prophet or deceptive fraud, perhaps most acutely in the context of attacking or defending the origin and authenticity of the Book of Mormon.[1] As Dennis Wright and Geoffrey Wright observe, "Ironically, both perspectives use the Prophet's lack of formal education to strengthen their respective views."[2] Any attempt to isolate the amount of time Joseph may have actually spent in classrooms thus presents a challenge with deeper implications.

---

1. Orsamus Turner's skeptical statement (1851) connects Smith's purported lack of education with one of several authorship theories: "there is no foundation for the statement that their [the Smith family's] original manuscript was written by a Mr. [Solomon] Spaulding, of Ohio … but the book itself is without doubt, a production of the Smith family, aided by Oliver Cowdery" (Dan Vogel, ed., *Early Mormon Documents: Volume 3* [Salt Lake City: Signature Books, 1998], 50–51). (Subsequent citations will use the abbreviation "EMD," followed by volume and page numbers.) By portraying Smith as being "a dull scholar," "lazy, indolent," "illiterate," and "possessed of less than ordinary intellect," skeptics could attribute the existence of the Book of Mormon to some alternative method or source. For "a dull scholar," see Christopher Stafford's statement, and for "lazy, indolent," see the Manchester Residents Group Statement, EMD 2:194, 18. For "illiterate," see Pomeroy Tucker's account, and for "possessed of less than ordinary intellect," see Orsamus Turner's account, EMD 3:93, 49.

2. Dennis A. Wright and Geoffrey A. Wright, "The New England Common School Experience of Joseph Smith Jr., 1810–16," in *Regional Studies in Latter-day Saint Church History: The New England States*, ed. Donald Q. Cannon and Arnold K. Garr, *Regional Studies Series* (Provo, UT: Religious Studies Center, Brigham Young University, 2004), 237.

Furthermore, with the passage of time and the development of traditions, such representations become further entangled in cultural identities, transforming historical speculations into theological propositions that approach canonical certainties, interweaving Smith's humble origins with the cosmologies of either faith or disbelief. These depictions, when further coupled with fragmentary historical records, complicate the process of excavating below the weighted representations in order to determine with any precision what might have actually occurred. Given such circumstances, I attempt to step back from the entangled layers of critical and apologetic modes to reexamine the historical sources and the assumptions underlying competing claims. By retracing the locations and educational practices of the places where Smith lived in his youth and early adulthood, I seek to demonstrate that Smith's formal education was more extensive than passing speculations and shared cultural memory might suggest.

Before embarking on an analysis of Joseph's life in relation to his formal educational opportunities (i.e., time spent in a formal school setting, as opposed to the various and common avenues of informal educational practices in early nineteenth-century America), I want to begin by exploring two important issues that will help to contextualize the interpretation of the incomplete array of historical references that address Joseph's formal education: first, the role of education in the Smith family home, and, second, an analysis of some of the more commonly known statements regarding Joseph's limited education and abilities.

SMITH FAMILY CULTURE AND THE ROLE OF EDUCATION

A review of Joseph Smith Jr.'s common school education necessarily begins with the importance of education within the Smith family home. Though this essay focuses on Joseph's formal schooling, as opposed to domestic education and self-improvement, the role of family culture inevitably constitutes the foundation of early nineteenth-century educational practices. For instance, that his father, Joseph Sr., had been a professional schoolteacher was certainly one of Joseph Jr.'s greatest advantages.[3] So, too, was having a mother, Lucy, who had been raised

---

3. According to Lucy, Joseph Sr. was already teaching school in Sharon, Vermont, when Joseph Jr. was born. See EMD 1:253; Richard L. Bushman, *Joseph Smith: Rough Stone Rolling* (New York: Alfred A. Knopf, 2005), 19. Yet, William Smith described his father's

in a household where her own mother, Lydia Mack, was also a school-teacher.[4] Indeed, Lydia may well have influenced Joseph Jr. directly. Lydia and Solomon Mack lived in Tunbridge, Vermont, where they were in constant close reach of their grandchildren, from the time of Joseph Jr.'s birth on December 23, 1805, to the Smith family's move to Lebanon, New Hampshire, in either 1811 or 1812.[5]

Education was deemed no less important on Joseph's paternal side of the family. In April 1799, Asael Smith, Joseph Jr.'s grandfather, who also lived in Tunbridge, Vermont, wrote a message to his entire family, admonishing them all to live good lives. In his treatise, Asael

---

occupation as a schoolteacher in the years *prior* to Joseph Sr. and Lucy Mack's marriage, stating, "My Father was bourn (and raised principly) in the Town of Topesfield, Mass[achusetts,] his occupation in early life was that of a School teacher[.] he was a man well letter[e]d in our <the> Common branches of our english Studies," later adding, in his chronological narrative, "after <his> Marriag[e] my father engaged in Merchandising" (EMD 1:489). If accurate, William's account indicates that Joseph Sr. began working as a school teacher in his mid- to late-teenage years, when he was still part of the household of his parents (Asael and Mary) in Topsfield, Massachusetts. Tracing Joseph Sr.'s locations, however, would prove challenging: even though he could have worked locally, young teachers often had to find work outside their own long-settled communities, either in neighboring towns or even across state lines. Such youthful schoolteachers were common and had skills ranging from college-trained schoolmasters to those who "came to teaching almost immediately after completing their own elementary education and did not differ so much from some of their older pupils in age, knowledge, or size" (Gerald F. Moran and Maris A. Vinovskis, "Schools," in *A History of the Book in America: An Extensive Republic*, vol. 2, ed. Robert A. Gross and Mary Kelley [Chapel Hill: American Antiquarian Society and University of North Carolina Press, 2010], 298). Charles Monaghan, for instance, describes the early career of teacher and educational book author Lyman Cobb (1800–64), born in Massachusetts and raised in New York, who, "not having much formal schooling himself," began teaching at a common school when he was only sixteen years old. See Charles Monaghan, "Lyman Cobb and the British Elocutionary Tradition," *Paradigm* 27 (2003). The issue of Joseph Sr.'s experience as a school teacher has yet to receive full scholarly attention.

4. A. Gary Anderson indicates that Lydia was "a young schoolteacher and a member of the Congregational church. She was well educated and from a well-to-do religious family. ... Lydia took charge of both the secular and religious education of their eight children" (A. Gary Anderson, "Smith Family Ancestors," in *Encyclopedia of Mormonism*, ed. Daniel H. Ludlow [New York: Macmillan, 1992], 1361).

5. Lydia and Solomon moved to Tunbridge, Vermont, in 1799. See Donna Hill, *Joseph Smith: The First Mormon* (Garden City, NY: Doubleday, 1977), 29. Although the Smith family moved several times from 1805 to either 1811 or 1812, "all the moves were in a tiny circle around Tunbridge, Royalton, and Sharon, immediately adjoining towns, and probably never involved a distance of more than five or six miles" (Bushman, *Rough Stone*, 19). Thus, the Smith children's education in this period would have occurred under the watchful eye of Lydia. For a crucial and detailed historical account of the Smith and Mack families living in this region, see Richard Lloyd Anderson, *Joseph Smith's New England Heritage*, revised ed. (Salt Lake City: Deseret Book Co., 2003), esp. 25–37.

urged his family to educate their children: "Make it your chiefest work to bring them up in the ways of virtue, that they may be useful in their generations. Give them, if possible, a good education."[6] Asael's message came two months after the birth of Alvin Smith, Joseph Jr.'s oldest brother, and may have been inspired by the new generation of grandchildren. Moreover, apart from parents and grandparents, older siblings got involved in the education of younger brothers and sisters.[7] After his training at the prestigious Moor's Charity School, Hyrum, Joseph's second oldest brother, would have been expected to share in the education of his younger siblings. Indeed, Hyrum's commitment to education would result in his becoming both a school trustee and schoolteacher in Palmyra.[8]

This family concern for education thus created a dynamic where the parents and the older children were actively involved in the entire family's instruction. Lucy would recall how she and her husband acted "together in the education and instruction of our children,"[9] and John Stafford (1805–1904), a neighbor to the Smiths in Manchester, New York, remembered how the Smiths "had school in their house, and studied the Bible."[10] Ever since the colonial period, the task of teaching children how to read and write typically began at home, and

---

6. Quoted in Hill, *Joseph Smith*, 23 (spelling and punctuation modernized).

7. For instance, Gordon and Gordon describe the childhood education of Almira Hart Lincoln, who grew up in a home where "the oldest children always tutored the youngest, turning the home into a school" (Edward E. Gordon and Elaine H. Gordon, *Literacy in America: Historic Journey and Contemporary Solutions* [Westport, CT: Praeger, 2003], 83). Education simultaneously involved the inculcation of good moral character "through the processes of imitation and explanation, with adults and older siblings modeling attitudes and behavior and youngsters purposely or inadvertently absorbing them" (Lawrence A. Cremin, *American Education: The National Experience, 1783–1876* [New York: Harper Colophon Books, 1980], 373).

8. Richard Behrens claims that following Joseph Jr.'s leg surgery in the winter of 1812–13, Hyrum became "young Joseph's principal tutor since Joseph could not attend school" (Richard K. Behrens, "Dreams, Visions, and Visitations: The Genesis of Mormonism," *John Whitmer Historical Association* 27 [2007]: 177). In her Smith family history, Lucy mentions how Hyrum "was one of the trustees" in a Palmyra school district (EMD 1:374). After getting married, Hyrum had moved back to the Smith's former residence in the log cabin on Stafford Road in Palmyra; see Bushman, *Rough Stone*, 47. Mrs. S. F. Anderick, a former resident of Palmyra, claimed "Hyrum was the only son sufficiently educated to teach school. I attended when he taught in the log school-house east of uncle's [the Smith's log cabin on Stafford Road]. He also taught in the Stafford District" (EMD 2:208).

9. EMD 1:282.

10. EMD 2:122.

the responsibility belonged chiefly to the mother.[11] And even though Joseph Sr. had been a schoolteacher, the cultural expectation of raising educated, moral, upright children would have primarily fallen to Lucy. As education historian Lawrence Cremin observes, "The new literature on child-rearing involved the vastly expanded responsibilities of the mother," placing special emphasis on raising virtuous and principled citizens.[12] Thus, having both a mother and a father actively involved in his education, young Joseph would have been exposed to greater instructional resources at home than most of his rural peers.

The Smith family's emphasis on the importance of education provides a vital contextual framework for historical inquiry. Though sickness, relocation, and financial exigencies would constrain educational opportunities, Lucy and Joseph Sr. nevertheless engaged in a lifelong effort to provide their children with a solid foundation of instruction. The interpretation of historical accounts, particularly when confronting the lacunae in documentation, should therefore be mindful of Lucy and Joseph Sr.'s efforts and concerns. Interpretations that assume Joseph did not attend school whenever historical documentation is silent run counter to Joseph Sr. and Lucy Mack's conscientiousness and stated efforts to provide their children with a good education. Thus, as a touchstone for the examination of educational practices, the cultural values within the Smith home offer guidance in the exploration of Joseph Jr.'s formal common school education, from youth to early adulthood, from Royalton, Vermont, to South Bainbridge, New York.

REPRESENTATIONS

Furthermore, the survey of Joseph's educational experiences requires an examination of the claims, often inconsistent and contradictory, made about his level of literacy. Such statements, whether favorable or unfavorable, constitute retrospectives deeply informed by his eventual prophetic and miraculous accomplishments. The contextualization of assertions therefore requires the recognition that historical depictions

---

11. Lawrence A. Cremin, *American Education: The Colonial Experience 1607–1783* (New York: Harper Torchbooks, 1970), 128.

12. Cremin, *The National Experience*, 65. Gordon and Gordon add, "the mother's role as primary tutor was of supreme importance. Though the literature of the period spoke of both parents acting as teachers, most books were written for women" (Gordon and Gordon, *Literacy in America*, 83).

of Joseph's level of education rarely, if ever, present uncomplicated or unbiased accounts of Joseph's life, delivered for no other purpose than the enrichment of posterity. Addressing every claim about Joseph's education extends beyond the scope of this essay; nevertheless, in order to emphasize the need to interpret such statements in their cultural context, I will look at two of the most common representational claims that are invoked as evidence of Joseph's lack of education: his wife Emma's assertion that Joseph could not dictate a simple letter, much less a text the size of the Book of Mormon; and Joseph's own statement that his education was limited to the basics of reading, writing, and arithmetic.

In an 1879 interview, Emma (Hale) Smith delivered her opinion on whether or not Joseph could have composed the Book of Mormon by famously declaring, "Joseph Smith ... could neither write nor dictate a coherent and well-worded letter, let alone dictating a book like the Book of Mormon."[13] Emma's statement, some forty years after the event, is often, and unfortunately, interpreted as a literal and objective depiction of Joseph's writing and composition skills. Nonetheless, as his surviving letters, revelations, and journal entries well attest, Joseph could certainly write and dictate coherent letters and intricate texts.[14]

---

13. EMD 1:542. See also, Joseph Smith III, "Last Testimony of Sister Emma," *Saints' Herald* 26 (Oct. 1879): 290.

14. For instance, observe the cohesiveness and sophistication of Joseph's style in the opening section of an October 22, 1829, letter: "Respected Sir, I would inform you that I arrived at home on Sunday morning, the 4th, after having a prosperous journey, and found all well. The people are all friendly to us, except a few who are in opposition to everything, unless it is something that is exactly like themselves. And two of our most formidable persecutors are now under censure and are cited to a trial in the church for crimes, which, if true, are worse than all the Gold Book business. We do not rejoice in the affliction of our enemies but we shall be glad to have truth prevail." I have modernized the spelling and punctuation in order for readers to observe the content and flow of the text, but the emendations also provide an opportunity to address the issue of Joseph's spelling. Joseph's inconsistency in spelling and punctuation reflects prevailing cultural attitudes toward spelling in the early nineteenth century, when writers of every level of educational attainment employed idiosyncratic spelling and punctuation in manuscripts, letters, and other communications. Some scholars point to Joseph's spelling as evidence of his illiteracy, but the use of inconsistent spelling as a measure to evaluate the education level of a nineteenth-century author is a mistake, a fallacy of presentism that imposes a modern "correct spelling" fixation onto historical writings. Similarly, the idiosyncratic use (or lack) of punctuation primarily reflected rhetorical cues for *pronunciation*, rather than strictly grammatical concerns. For further discussion, see, e.g., Carolyn Eastman, *A National of Speechifiers: Making an American Public after the Revolution* (Chicago: University of Chicago Press, 2009), 27; and Jay Fliegelman, *Declaring Independence: Jefferson, Natural Language, and the Culture of Performance* (Stanford: Stanford University Press, 1993), 4–28. For an online review of Smith's

In order to appreciate Emma's claim, we therefore need to reintegrate her comment into the cultural context in which it was given.

Emma's juxtaposition of Joseph's inability to write a "well-worded letter" with the production of a book of over 500 printed pages reveals the assumptions she shared with her audience. Here, she is specifically invoking a parallel with introductory classroom exercises in nineteenth-century education: letter-writing was one of the earliest and most basic composition assignments children encountered at home and at school. By copying and composing short letters, children learned the style and format of basic correspondence, along with the skill of assembling cohesive paragraphs. For instance, one of the most popular letter-writing schoolbooks of the early nineteenth century was Caleb Bingham's *Juvenile Letters* (1803), which consists entirely of short, easy-to-read letters written by fictional children "from eight to fifteen years of age."[15] Thus, Emma's depiction of Joseph's writing ability presents two polar extremes: the expansive Book of Mormon text pitted against a simple "well-worded letter." In other words, in order to emphasize her opinion that Joseph could not have produced the Book of Mormon, Emma declared that Joseph could not compose at the level of a child receiving his first writing lessons in one of the most elementary forms of composition exercises. Emma's hyperbolic statement should be read with the same tone as "he couldn't walk and chew gum at the same time" or, more specifically, "he couldn't compose at the level of *Dick and Jane*, much less write a whole book." Interpreting Emma's description as a literal and objective account of Joseph's actual letter-writing skills is a mistake—one that fails to take into account the context of her statement and the nuance of her thought. At the same time, in spite of her dismissive characterization, Emma's facetious exaggeration need not be interpreted as an intentional misrepresentation. Her comment merely serves to highlight her emphatic belief that Jo-

---

written and dictated materials, see The Joseph Smith Papers, www.josephsmithpapers.org. For the original letter, see "Letter to Oliver Cowdery, 22 October 1829," www.josephsmithpapers.org/paperSummary/letter-to-oliver-cowdery-22-october-1829.

15. Bingham's *Juvenile Letters* (1803) provided examples that taught the "forms" (proper templates and conventions) of letter writing. See Caleb Bingham, *Juvenile Letters; Being a Correspondence between Children, from Eight to Fifteen Years of Age* (Boston: Caleb Bingham, 1803). Even with an intermittent education, Joseph would almost certainly have been exposed to introductory letter writing exercises as an extension of his penmanship lessons (see below).

seph could not have created the work without divine assistance.[16] Thus, while Emma's comment provides insight into her beliefs (and sense of humor), a literal interpretation of her assertion obscures Joseph's actual compositional skills.

Joseph's self-representation of his educational opportunities appears in what historian Dan Vogel describes as "the earliest known attempt by Joseph Smith to record a history of his life."[17] Dictated in 1832, the statement reveals how the indigent circumstances of the Smith household "required the exertions of all that were able to render any assistance for the support of the family; therefore, we were deprived of the benefit of an education. Suffice it to say, I was merely instructed in reading, writing and the ground rules of arithmetic, which constituted my whole literary acquirements."[18] While this depiction may initially appear straightforward, several issues require a cautious interpretation of what precisely this statement means. I do not want to minimize the essential claim being made regarding Joseph's childhood opportunities. As this essay hopes to demonstrate, his chances to participate in formal education were limited and intermittent, with few chances to complete a full year of school without significant interruptions. Nevertheless, if we interpret "deprived of the benefit of an education" to mean "entirely denied an education," then Joseph's statement contradicts itself (i.e., if completely deprived, Joseph would not have learned basic reading, writing, and arithmetic skills). Thus, the statement requires further contextualization.

Joseph's description of "reading, writing and the ground rules of arithmetic" invokes a common, formulaic phrase in early nineteenth-century America (indeed, it remains common today, often expressed as "the three R's"), which operates as a shorthand depiction of the most basic, fundamental level of education that early Americans hoped to achieve. Gideon Hawley, the first New York Superintendent of Common Schools, invoked this formula in the process of working

---

16. Later in the same interview, Emma states, "my belief is that the Book of Mormon is of divine authenticity—I have not the slightest doubt of it. I am satisfied that no man could have dictated the writing of the manuscripts unless he was inspired. ... It would have been improbable that a learned man could do this; and, for one so ignorant and unlearned as he [Joseph] was, it was simply impossible" (EMD 1: 542).

17. EMD 1:26.

18. EMD 1:27 (spelling and punctuation modernized).

toward a standardized curriculum in his 1819 publication, *Instructions for the Better Government and Organization of Common Schools*, in which he writes, "[I]n every common school the course of study to be pursued must necessarily embrace *reading, writing* and *arithmetic*. These are the first rudiments of education. ... Reading, writing and arithmetic, as they are the means of acquiring all subsequent knowledge, may justly be considered the necessaries of education. ... Nothing short of these will constitute a common school, or satisfy the lowest requisites of the school act."[19] This phrase expresses the goal of instilling a basic and fundamental level education, but it was never intended as a comprehensive description of all the topics of instruction, training, or materials that children would encounter in common school classrooms.

In the process of obtaining an education, children in New York common schools learned how to read from books of increasing levels of difficulty (primers, spellers, introductory readers, advanced readers), along with studying penmanship, grammar, the basics of rhetoric and composition, geography, history (either as short passages in readers or as separate history books), and other potential subjects, such as surveying (depending on the skills and interests of the instructor). And even though these subjects appear familiar today, the content of the lessons, the manner in which teachers instructed students, and the ways that students demonstrated their knowledge could be very different from modern assumptions. The subject of "grammar," for example, covered a much wider range of topics than the study of sentence structure, grammatical rules, and syntax. Students studying from Lindley Murray's schoolbook on grammar—the most popular grammar book in New York common schools in Joseph's time and location—also learned basic literary figures and rhetorical devices, such as parallelism, metaphor, allegory, "comparison" (simile), metonymy, synecdoche, personification, apostrophe, antithesis, hyperbole, "vision" (imagery, imagination), interrogation, exclamation, irony, and amplification/climax. Grammar also included introductory writing lessons on writing style (purity, propriety, and precision), word choice, accuracy in expression, and clarity, with the King James Bible used as a model of style for "Grave, solemn, and majestic subjects," and "Any composition that rises considerably

---

19. Gideon Hawley, *Instructions for the Better Government and Organization of Common Schools* (Albany: State of New York, 1819), [3] (emphasis in original).

above the ordinary tone of prose."[20] And in terms of pedagogy, the central mode of classroom learning and instruction was primarily by means of oral performance rather than written assignments. Instead of demonstrating their competence about a subject with a written examination, children memorized and performed their knowledge in school exhibitions at the end of each school term.[21]

William Smith, one of Joseph's younger brothers, offered an account that reveals important clues about Joseph's exposure to this more expansive and demanding educational context. Though he wrote his reflections circa 1875, long after the events in question, William's account was based on several years of firsthand experience, having shared the same one-room schoolhouses with Joseph in both Palmyra and Manchester. In an attempt to strike a balance between the popular notion of Joseph's alleged illiteracy and his actual level of education, William provided an eyewitness account of Joseph's common school studies that reveals a variety of classroom subjects within the framework of their shared classroom instruction: "That he [Joseph] was illitterate to some extent is admitted but that he was enterly [entirely] unlettered is a mistake. In Sintax, authography [orthography][,] Mathamatics[,] grammar[,] geography *with other studies* in the Common Schools of his day he was no novis [novice] and for writing he wrote a plain intelegable [intelligible] hand."[22] Contemporary reports regarding common school instruction in New York confirm William's description and offer further details about the schoolbooks used in the counties where the Smith children attended school.

As part of a project to create a uniform level of basic instruction throughout the state, the commissioners of the New York common schools conducted surveys to identify the most prevalent schoolbooks

---

20. Lindley Murray, *An English Grammar: Comprehending the Principles and Rules of the Language*, vol. 1 (United Kingdom: Thomas Wilson & Son, 1808), 449, 464–93, 421–93, 458.

21. See, e.g., Carolyn Eastman, *A Nation of Speechifiers*, 30.

22. EMD 1:486; emphasis and some additional editorial notes added. Joseph also owned several common school textbooks that were published and available during his school years, such as Murray's *Introduction to the English Reader* (1804), Charles A. Goodrich's *A History of the United States of America* (1822), and Thomas T. Smiley's *Sacred Geography* (1824), though we do not know if Joseph used these specific texts during his common school education. For a list of Joseph Smith's books, see H. Michael Marquardt, "Books Owned by Joseph Smith," www.user.xmission.com/~research/about/books.htm.

used in classrooms. Their first survey covered the 1825–26 school year— the same year that Joseph attended his last term of common school in South Bainbridge, New York, while working for Josiah Stowell (more on this later). In that school year, the most widely used classroom texts were Lindley Murray's enormously popular *The English Reader* (used in 434 towns); Lindley Murray's *An English Grammar* (389 towns); Nathan Daboll's *Schoolmaster's Assistant* (an arithmetic; 349 towns); Noah Webster's *The American Spelling Book* (302 towns); the "New Testament (and Bible)" (168 towns); John Walker's *Critical and Pronouncing Dictionary* (133 towns); three geography books by Jacob Willetts, Jedidiah Morse, and William Channing Woodbridge (117, 110, and 108 towns, respectively); and Caleb Bingham's *The American Preceptor* (93 towns). Other popular schoolbooks on the commissioners' list specifically used in Palmyra and Manchester included, among others, Caleb Bingham's *Columbian Orator* (often described as Bingham's "Speaker"; 34 towns), and Ezra Sampson's *Brief Remarker on the Ways of Man* (a reader advocating religious principles for a moral society; 30 towns).[23]

By grouping the schoolbooks together within their respective topics of instruction, the reports also reveal the general subject areas taught in New York common school classrooms. For example, the survey of schoolbooks for the 1828–29 school year offers six broad rubrics that corresponded with the topics of classroom curricula: spelling books, arithmetics, grammars, geographies, dictionaries, and "readers and other books," which included such works as the New Testament, history books, and a surveying manual. For the 1828–29 school year in Ontario County, where the Smith family lived in Manchester, the most popular schoolbooks within these subject areas were Murray's *The English Reader*, Murray's *An English Grammar*, Webster's *American Spelling Book*, Daboll's *Schoolmaster's Assistant*, Woodbridge's *Rudiments of Geography*, Walker's *Critical and Pronouncing Dictionary*, Ezra Sampson's *Brief Remarker*, the New Testament, and an unidentified "History [of the] United States."[24]

Though the reports for the counties of Wayne and Ontario occurred

23. A.C. Flagg, "Annual Report of the Superintendent of Common Schools," Document No. 31, *Journal of the Assembly of the State of New-York, Fifty-Third Session*, vol. 1 (Albany: State of New York, 1830), Appendix. F58-9. All subsequent *Journal* citations will be abbreviated as JA, followed by the session and page numbers.

24. JA 53v1: Appendix F52; see also "Recapitulation," Appendix F56-8.

after Joseph had finished his common school experience in those areas, the inventories of local printers and booksellers indicate that many of the same titles in the commissioners' reports were also part of the educational milieu when Joseph attended school a few years earlier in Palmyra and Manchester. For example, James Bemis, a local publisher in Canandaigua, printed and supplied schoolbooks throughout the region, including such titles as Murray's *English Reader* (first Bemis edition, 1819; second edition, 1820[?]; third edition 1822); an abridgment of Murray's *English Grammar* (1823); Sampson's *Brief Remarker* (1821, 1823); and Thomas Smith's abridgment of John Walker's *Critical Pronouncing Dictionary* (1824).[25] Local bookstores also regularly advertised popular common school texts, such as Palmyra printer and bookseller T.C. Strong's announcement in 1820 of "a general supply of School Books, comprising [Murray's] English Readers, Murray's large and abridged Grammar, do. ["ditto"; i.e., Murray's] Key, Exercise and Introduction [part of Murray's Grammar], Daboll's and Adams's Arithmetics, American Readers [Webster's and/or John Hubbard's], Preceptors and Speakers [most commonly Caleb Bingham's *The American Preceptor* and *The Columbian Orator*]—[Jacob] Willet's Geography and Atlas—Spelling Books, and a general assortment of BLANK BOOKS [for writing exercises, commonplace books, etc.]. Also—Testaments, large and small, BIBLES."[26] Moreover, though the specific schoolbooks might vary from one classroom to the next, the core pedagogical approaches and the general subjects of study that took place in Palmyra and Manchester in the latter half of the 1820s would have been identical to those in the early 1820s, following traditional approaches of instruction that had remained virtually unaltered since the colonial period.[27]

Along with these schoolbooks, many common school teachers also taught subjects that did not have corresponding classroom textbooks for student use, such as composition (short essays or "themes," and a variety of narrative exercises, both written and spoken) and penmanship.

---

25. Douglas C. McMurtrie, "A Bibliography of Books, Pamphlets and Broadsides Printed at Canandaigua, New York, 1799–1850," in *Grosvenor Library Bulletin*, 21, no. 4 [June, 1939]: 79–81, 83, 85, 87, 105.

26. "T.C. St[r]ong ... Books, and Stationary," *Palmyra Register*, May 17, 1820), 4.

27. For a detailed review of education in the colonial period, see E. Jennifer Monaghan, *Learning to Read and Write in Colonial America* (Amherst and Boston: University of Massachusetts Press, 2005).

Awareness of such instruction is critical when attempting to reconstruct a complete picture of Joseph's education. When he attended school, for example, a new approach to composition was sweeping the nation. Packaging traditional writing instruction into a system that shepherded students from introductory to advanced writing skills, educational writer John Walker formulated a method that became "the exemplar for a whole school of composition pedagogy" in his influential work, *The Teacher's Assistant* (1801; first American edition, 1804).[28] Walker's book was a teacher's manual, not a schoolbook, so it would not have appeared on the commissioners' report of classroom texts. Indeed, Walker had admonished teachers, "that it is of the utmost importance that pupils should *not* have this book in their possession."[29] Even so, Walker's system remains relevant to Joseph's educational background, because his own approach to composition mirrored Walker's method.

In brief, Walker's system centrally involved the creation of preliminary outlines for essays (skeletal outlines of "heads," or the main points of written assignments), which students expanded into fully developed compositions. By the time Joseph was attending school, several additional writers of education books had incorporated Walker's method into their own works, such Daniel Jaudon's *The Union Grammar* (1812), John Rippingham's *Rules for English Composition* (1811), and William Russell's *Grammar of Composition* (1823). Thus, the method was readily available in multiple instructional manuals. Notably, Joseph used this same method to compose his 1832 History (a combination of autobiography and early history of the church). Moreover, it is the same writing technique referenced (and used) by Nephi and Jacob in the Book of Mormon (Jacob 1:4).[30] Whether or not Joseph

---

28. For Walker's influence, see Robert J. Connors, *Composition-Rhetoric*, 218.

29. John Walker, *The Teacher's Assistant in English Composition* (Boston: J.T. Buckingham, 1810), xvi, emphasis added.

30. For further information, see William L. Davis, *Visions in a Seer Stone: Joseph Smith and the Making of the Book of Mormon* (Chapel Hill: University of North Carolina Press, 2020), 14–18, 91–92, 122–25. In his excellent study *Joseph Smith: History, Methods, and Memory* (Salt Lake City: University of Utah Press, 2020), Ronald O. Barney argues that Joseph's scribe, Frederick G. Williams, composed the opening portion of the 1832 History (i.e., the majority of the section containing the preliminary outline of heads), rather than Joseph himself. Barney's interpretation relies primarily on the narrative shifts from first person to third person, the perceived "abstruse language" that "likely muddled and confused what J[oseph] S[mith] probably hoped to convey." Moreover, Barney apparently assumes that the preliminary outline was part of the narration itself: when Joseph's handwriting appears at the end of the opening outline, Barney

learned some form of this method in a common school setting remains an open question: even though a teacher could have introduced such writing techniques in the classroom, young students also learned this method in such venues as domestic education or self-improvement

describes how Joseph "broke into the first-person voice *to resume* and conclude his personal narrative" (137, 139; emphasis added). This interpretation, however, is problematic on several levels, including manuscript conventions in preparation for printing, the style of writing for preliminary outlines, and the language of the text. The appearance of Joseph's handwriting, for instance, occurs at the break between the preliminary sketch outline of the account and the beginning of the actual narration. In other words, Joseph was not *resuming* a narrative but *completing the opening outline*, followed by *initiating* the actual narrative. Joseph's writing in the original manuscript clearly indicates this break with a prominent line that separates the end of the outline ("blessings of God to him &c") from the beginning of the narrative on the next line of text ("I was born in the town of Charon [Sharon]"). Joseph's shift from third person (for the outline) to first person (for his narration), coupled with his demarcation between the two sections, follows a standard convention that alerts a potential printer to the separation between a preliminary outline and the main body of the text. See The Joseph Smith Papers, "History, circa Summer 1832," www.josephsmithpapers.org/paper-summary/history-circa-summer-1832/1. Next, the style of the language in the opening outline—a series of "heads" that correspond with the development of the narration which follows—was also a standard convention for such formatting. Contrary to Barney's argument that these "introductory words" are "indistinct and without context," the series of heads do, in fact, map directly onto the narrative that follows, providing readers with guideposts that track the sequence of the main sections of the history. Finally, the specific style of language also points to Joseph's spiritual register. A comprehensive analysis extends beyond the scope of this essay, but one of several examples is the formulaic phrase (embedded in a longer sentence), "all the mighty acts which he doeth in the name of Jesus Ch[r]ist the son of the living God." The core of this phrase originates in the New Testament: "thou art that Christ, the Son of the living God" (John 6:69) and "Thou art the Christ, the Son of the living God" (Matt. 16:16). A common nineteenth-century variant of this core formula adds "Jesus" to the phrase and appears in the 1832 History as "*Jesus* Christ, the Son of the Living God." This phrase, however, is embedded within a larger formula that diverges from common usage, introducing the components of 1) performing religious actions under 2) the auspices and authority of Christ ("*mighty acts* which he *doeth* // *in the name of* // Jesus Ch[r]ist the son of the living God"). The full expression of this expanded formula is rare in nineteenth-century religious communication (particularly among Protestants), with the variant appearing most prominently in a Catholic litany for the "Recommendation of a Soul that is just departing" (see, e.g., Rev. Richard Challenor's apologetic, *The Catholic Christian* [Baltimore: Bernard Dornin, 1809], 164). This unusual variant, however, appears elsewhere in Joseph's dictations, such as the Book of Mormon, "see that *ye do all things in worthiness* [e.g., baptism, taking the sacrament], and *do it* // *in the name of* // *Jesus Christ, the Son of the living God*" (Mormon 9:29) and the Doctrine and Covenants, "*to preach repentance and remission of sins by way of baptism* // *in the name of* // *Jesus Christ, the Son of the living God*" (55:2). Interestingly, Joseph's father often uses the phrase in his patriarchal blessings, suggesting that this variation may have derived from religious conversations within the Smith family household. See, e.g., Joseph Sr.'s patriarchal blessings for Ebenezer Robinson, Julian Moses, Amoranda Murdock, Suke McArthur, Isaac Rogers, and Truman O. Angell in H. Michael Marquardt, ed., *Early Patriarchal Blessings of the Church of Jesus Christ of Latter-day Saints* (Salt Lake City: Smith–Pettit Foundation, 2007), 62–63, 76, 85, 91, 101. In summary, the internal evidence overwhelmingly favors Joseph Smith as the author of the opening outline, which he dictated to Frederick G. Williams.

organizations. Joseph's participation in a juvenile debate society, for example, would be one such venue.[31]

Penmanship is another subject that students often learned without the use of a formal schoolbook. When describing the subjects of Joseph's common school education, William Smith made a direct reference to penmanship when he argued that, "for writing he [Joseph] wrote a plain intelegable [intelligible] hand."[32] Documentary evidence bears out William's claim. Joseph's earliest examples of handwriting openly display a well-practiced skill in the common "round hand" style of the early nineteenth century (expressing connective characteristics of the "running hand" technique, a sub-style of round hand, resulting in a casual cursive appearance). Such internal evidence confirms William's claim and provides strong evidence of formal instruction in penmanship. It should be noted that Philander Packard, a Palmyra common school teacher, who may have instructed the Smith children (see later in the essay), taught the same style of formal round hand in his Palmyra classroom.[33]

The variety of common school subjects taught in Joseph's immediate environment therefore prompts a reevaluation of the historical sources that address his educational achievements. When considering his description of his education being limited to "reading, writing and arithmetic," we must recall that this common phrase, widely used in the period, elides and conceals a rich variety of topics, lessons, and exercises that actually occurred in common school classrooms. Joseph's enlistment of this formulaic phrase therefore functions as a rhetorical device to convey his limited educational opportunities to his readers, without going into the unnecessary detail of outlining every topic, every skill, or every assignment he encountered. Put another way, the rhetorical effect of Joseph's depiction would have been defeated, obviously, if he had said, "I was merely instructed in reading, writing, arithmetic, basic rhetoric, composition, geography and history," though such a catalogue would have more accurately depicted the

---

31. See EMD 3:49–50.

32. EMD 1:486.

33. See Packard's manuscript page beginning with the phrase "Procrastination is a thing," which contains penmanship exercises in formal round hand (Packard, Philander 1797–1857. School Records, 1815–1838, www.catalog.churchofjesuschrist.org/record?id=28b079b2-63b0-48bf-8d09-cb9417d9b4cf&view=summary).

demanding curriculum that he would have encountered in New York common school classrooms.

Finally, Joseph's representation of his educational achievements requires further recognition of how this depiction functions within the context of his entire narrative. Joseph's 1832 history was not an indifferent account of his life. Rather, the account represents his first attempt to construct a narrative that centers on his divine prophetic calling. As Vogel observes, "The History was begun in the midst of challenges to Smith's authority, primarily initiated by Bishop Edward Partridge in Missouri, which evoked Smith's introduction of the office of president of the high priesthood. It is therefore not simply an autobiographical sketch, but an apology setting forth Smith's credentials as leader of the church."[34] As part of this project, Joseph's reference to his humble beginnings, contrasted with his rise to prominence as God's chosen instrument, evokes the commonplace trope of the humble individual who, against all odds, rises to greatness—a popular framework of biographical representations in both secular and religious maelstroms of early nineteenth-century America.[35] Thus, the formula of "reading, writing, and arithmetic," as a representation of the bare minimum level of education one might receive, acts as a counterpoint to the lofty heights to which God would elevate Joseph's life and work. Nevertheless, setting such rhetorical effects aside, we do not receive a detailed account of Smith's educational experiences and are left to wonder about the actual time he spent in school and the lessons he learned. By retracing his life and experiences, this essay therefore aims to further the discussion surrounding Joseph's background, education, and training.

ROYALTON, VERMONT: 1809–11/1812

Junius F. Wells, a member of the Mormon Church who purchased the farm where Joseph had been born, provides the first reference to Joseph's

34. EMD 1:26.

35. This framework remains a popular narrative formula today. For instance, using Abraham Lincoln as a point of reference, biographer Richard L. Bushman situates Smith's life and accomplishments within this same trope: "Reared in a poor Yankee farm family, he had less than two years of formal schooling and began life without social standing or institutional backing. ... Yet in the fourteen years he headed the Church of Jesus Christ of Latter-day Saints, Smith created a religious culture that survived his death ... published the *Book of Mormon* ... built cities and temples and gathered thousands of followers" (Bushman, *Rough Stone*, xx).

earliest formal education. When describing the Smith's family life in rural Vermont, Wells indicates that "during this period, Joseph, Senior, worked on the farm summers, and taught school part of the time winters. His son Joseph attended the school on Dewey Hill, and was taught his letters by Dea[con] Jonathan Kinney, the schoolmaster there."[36] Joseph Jr. was born in Sharon, Vermont, on December 23, 1805. Sometime between the months of March and December in 1808, the Smiths, who had been moving among several locations in the region, relocated to Royalton, Vermont, where they lived for approximately three to four years.[37] The exact length of their stay is uncertain. According to Lucy's account, the Smith family moved out of the area in 1811; according to tax assessment records, however, the move did not occur until sometime between May 1812 and May 1813.[38] In either case, Joseph Jr. would have grown from a three-year-old toddler to a five- or six-year-old child in Royalton, Vermont, prior to the family's relocation.

During that time in Vermont, it was typical for children to start school at the age of four. Ever since the General Assembly of the State of Vermont passed the Act for the Support of Schools in October of 1797, determinations regarding the formation of schools, allocation of funding, and selection of trustees in any given district were made "according to the number of children in such district between the age

---

36. Mary Evelyn Wood Lovejoy, *History of Royalton, Vermont, with Family Genealogies, 1769–1911*, vol. 2 (Burlington, VT: Town of Royalton and Royalton Woman's Club, 1911), 646. Jonathan Kinney Jr. (1790–1851), was a member of the First Congregational Church in Royalton. According to church records, he was elected deacon in 1829 (the writer of his genealogical sketch in *History of Royalton* claims 1833). Junius Wells's use of Kinney's title "Deacon" is therefore anachronistic, as Kinney was not yet a deacon when the Smith family lived in Royalton. Even so, Kinney, who turned twenty during the 1809–10 winter term (the same term Joseph Smith would have been of appropriate age to start attending school), was of the typical age of young schoolteachers at the time, making Wells's claim plausible. For a list of the elected deacons, see ibid., 1:229. For Kinney Jr.'s genealogical sketch, see ibid., 2:844. Wright and Wright refer to him as "Jonathan Rinney," apparently following Donna Hill's use of "Rinney" in her biography of Joseph Smith. Hill does not provide her source, and the variant spelling appears to be either a typo or a transcription error. See Wright and Wright, "New England Common School," 237; and Hill, *Joseph Smith*, 35.

37. The dates throughout this essay are based on Vogel's chronology. See EMD, Appendix B, "Chronology, 1771–1831," 5:377–456.

38. EMD, 5:382. After Royalton, the Smith family moved to Lebanon, New Hampshire. As Vogel indicates, if Lucy's date for the move were 1811, then Joseph Sr.'s name should have appeared on the May 1812 tax assessment records in Lebanon. But it does not appear until the following year in May 1813, suggesting that the Smiths actually moved to Lebanon sometime between May 1812 and May 1813.

of four years and eighteen years old."[39] These ages were based on the *customary* ages of children attending school throughout the state, but they were not the *exclusive* ages of those actually attending classes. In any given district, children might start school earlier than four or attend later than eighteen. Indeed, children throughout New England were known to start school as young as two or three years of age.[40] Nevertheless, in order to have a common standard of funding for all the counties, the state used the census figures and school records to identify the population that customarily attended school and allocated funds accordingly.[41]

That children four years of age, and even younger, attended common schools was not unusual.[42] Throughout the United States in the

---

39. Vermont, *Laws of the State of Vermont; Revised and Passed by the Legislature, in the Year of our Lord, One Thousand Seven Hundred and Ninety Seven* (Rutland: State of Vermont, 1798), 494, 97. The 1797 Act was still in force when the Smith family moved to Royalton. A reprint of the laws appeared the same year they moved into the town; see *The Laws of the State of Vermont, Digested and Compiled*, vol. 2 (Randolph: State of Vermont, 1808), 181–86. See also Wright and Wright, "New England Common School," 243.

40. Memoirist Warren Burton (1800–66) started school at three-and-a-half years old in New Hampshire; New York editor Horace Greeley (1811–72) began school two months shy of his third birthday; social reformer Elizabeth Buffum [Chace] (1806–99) started at two years of age and "could read very well" by the age of three; and Dr. Henry E. Spalding (1843–1912), future president of the Boston Homeopathic Medical Society and the Massachusetts Surgical and Gynecological Society, started school at two-and-a-half years in a farming community after he wandered "into the nearby district school and from that time he was a regular attendant." For Burton, Greeley, and Chace, see Carl F. Kaestle, *Pillars of the Republic: Common Schools and American Society, 1780–1860* (New York: Hill and Wang, 1983), 15. For Spalding, see Rev. D. Donovan and Jacob A. Woodward, *The History of the Town of Lyndeborough, New Hampshire, 1735–1905* (Medford, MA: Tufts College Press, 1906), 858.

41. Specific to Joseph's time in Royalton, local historian Mary Lovejoy asserts that 705 children "between four and eighteen years of age" attended school in the combined districts, in accordance with the Act of 1797. Lovejoy's phrasing for the ages of school children repeats, nearly verbatim, the language of the 1797 Act, without providing details regarding students younger than four or older than eighteen who might have also attended school (the ages were used for funding estimates, not attendance restrictions). The same year, at the start of winter term 1809–10, Joseph Jr. turned four years old and would have been of an appropriate age to attend school (Lovejoy, *History of Royalton*, 1:295–96). For a review of how Royalton residents responded to the Act of 1797, see ibid., 293–94.

42. Citing Kaestle's study in common school education, Wright and Wright observe that very young rural children often attended school with older siblings: "Because there was no standard age for starting to attend school, many two- and three-year-olds were sent to school along with their older brothers and sisters" (Wright and Wright, "New England Common School," 246). See also Kaestle, *Pillars of the Republic*, 15. In his memoir, Rev. Warren Burton, who attended common school in Wilton, New Hampshire, recalled how a young classmate could not answer a question about the alphabet because "he is but two

earliest decades of the nineteenth century, the average starting age for school children ranged from four to five years.[43] And though the determination of such ages may have been arbitrary in each state, they often reflected the circumstances of the population, particularly in farming communities. In rural schools, according to historian Carl Kaestle, children "began at younger ages and enrolled in greater proportions than their urban contemporaries. By the age of four or five, and until the age of about fourteen, most rural children in the North ... attended school at some time during the year."[44] Kaestle further suggests that

---

years and a half old, and has been sent to school to relieve his mother from trouble rather than to learn" (Burton, *The District School As It Was* [Boston: Carter, Hendee and Co., 1833], 48). Even so, Wright and Wright offer a conservative estimate for young Joseph's start: "An exact chronology is impossible, but it appears that Joseph began school in Royalton, Vermont, in 1810" (Wright and Wright, "New England Common School," 238). If this date is true, however, the question arises as to why Joseph's parents held him back from school, in spite of his eligibility to start earlier. Winter terms for common schools in small rural towns in the first decade of the nineteenth century often started on the Monday of the first full week in December. If this were the case for Royalton, winter classes in 1809 would start on Monday, December 4, a little over two and a half weeks prior to Smith's fourth birthday on Saturday, December 23. Thus, the winter 1809 term would have been the age appropriate time for Smith to start. Even if the winter term started earlier, Smith, according to the conventions for reckoning age, was already nearing the end of his fourth year of age at the start of the 1809 winter term.

43. One of the first attempts to provide national statistics on school attendance appeared in Archibald Russell's *Principles of Statistical Inquiry* (1839). Because the data were fragmentary for his study, not only for education but for several other categories (manufacturing, agriculture, occupations, vital statistics, crime, etc.), Russell acknowledges that his essays "do not aspire to the character of a statistical treatise." Russell was a pioneer in social statistics, and this book, in spite of its self-admitted flaws, was nevertheless popular and "earned him widespread recognition in mid-nineteenth century America" (Peter J. Wosh, "Bibles, Benevolence, and Bureaucracy: The Changing Nature of Nineteenth Century Religious Records," *American Archivist* 52, no. 2 [Spring 1989]: 172). In order to determine the number and ages of schoolchildren, Russell turned to state school records, or made estimates based on state censuses and common cultural practices. In his review, Maine and Illinois reported students ranging "between the ages of 4 and 21" and "between 4 and 16 years of age," respectively. All the remaining states, when noted, reported ages between (or within) the range of five and twenty, with the New England states figured between five and fifteen. None of the ranges identify beginning students as being older than five years of age in any of the states included in the survey, suggesting that four and five were typical starting ages throughout early nineteenth-century America. See Archibald Russell, *Principles of Statistical Inquiry; As Illustrated in Proposals for Uniting an Examination into the Resources of the United States with the Census to be Taken in 1840* (New York: D. Appleton & Co., 1839), iii, 217–31.

44. Kaestle, *Pillars of the Republic*, 15. School attendance at three and four years of age was not, however, limited to rural areas. For example, Josiah Holbrook, a Boston-based education reformer and promoter of the early lyceum movement, indirectly reveals the ages of schoolchildren in Boston in a critical essay on formal pedagogical methods in common

"parents who sent very young children to school seem to have done so through a desire to have them out from under foot. ... One can understand the desire of rural mothers with busy work schedules to be freed from the care of toddlers."[45] Thus, basing estimates on the customary ages of school attendance in Royalton, the following scenarios emerge: if the Smiths moved out of town in 1811, as Lucy suggests, Joseph would have been able to attend school for three, possibly four, terms (winter 1809–10, summer 1810, winter 1810–11, and summer 1811); if the Smiths moved in 1812, as tax assessment records indicate, Joseph would have been able to attend five terms (the terms noted above, along with winter 1811–12). Accordingly, if he started school at the same age as his Royalton peers, Joseph could have received either 1.5 or 2.5 years of formal schooling, depending on the date of the Smith family's departure. The point is significant: prior to Joseph's departure from Royalton, he may well have obtained as much, if not more, formal education as historians tend to attribute to his entire lifetime.

WEST LEBANON, NEW HAMPSHIRE: 1811/1812–14/1815

Lucy Smith provides the next reference to her children's formal schooling in her history, *Biographical Sketches* (1853). In 1811, according to Lucy, the Smith family relocated approximately twenty-three miles southeast of Royalton, across the Connecticut River, to the town of West Lebanon, New Hampshire. About the same time, Joseph Jr.'s older brother Hyrum began attending Moor's Charity School, originally called Moor's Indian Charity School, which was located on the same campus as Dartmouth College in Hanover, New Hampshire, approximately seven miles north of the Smith's new home in West Lebanon.[46] Though Moor's Charity

---

schools: "Whoever will look at the nature and course of exercises and management, to which many children are subjected, from the time they enter a school-room *at the age of three or four years*, till they cease their school education, must be convinced that their tendency is to cramp, not to invigorate the faculties, either physical, intellectual, or moral" (Holbrook, "Abuses: Schools," *The Family Lyceum* [1833]: 102, emphasis added).

45. Kaestle, *Pillars of the Republic*, 15–16.

46. In his biography of Hyrum Smith, Jeffrey S. O'Driscoll notes that "documenting Hyrum's presence from school records is difficult. His name cannot be located in the records of 1811, and the rolls for the school years ending in 1812 and 1813 are missing. Records show a 'Hiram Smith' from Lebanon attending the session from August 1814 to August 1815. Hyrum Smith had moved from Lebanon to nearby Norwich, Vermont, by that time, but the record is probably referring to him" (Jeffrey S. O'Driscoll, *Hyrum Smith: A Life of Integrity* [Salt Lake City: Deseret Book Co., 2003], 17–18n26). The records indicate Hyrum

School was technically a separate institution from Dartmouth at the time, the distinction was largely in name only.[47] Hyrum's acceptance would have held the hope of a promising career; and upon the Smith family's arrival in West Lebanon, Lucy indicates that "as our children had, in a great measure, been debarred from the privilege of schools, we began to make every arrangement to attend to this important duty. We established our second son Hyrum in an academy at Hanover; and the rest, that were of sufficient age, we were sending to a common school that was quite convenient."[48] (It should be noted that Lucy's recollection here has minimal bearing on Joseph's education: her statement refers to challenges that occurred previously in Vermont, where Joseph had only recently started school.) Because Lucy did not specifically name the children who "were of sufficient age" to start school in West Lebanon, some historians have assumed Joseph Jr. did not attend school at this time.[49] Nevertheless, children in New Hampshire started school at the same ages children started in Vermont.[50]

---

was a "charity scholar," which meant his tuition and board were covered by annual rental income from lands owned and leased by Moor's and Dartmouth. In his *History of Dartmouth College*, Frederick Chase indicates how Moor's "had thirty scholars in 1780, eighty in 1794, forty-four in the fall of 1813, and sixty-one in the summer of 1814. Of these sixty-one about seventeen were charity scholars, carried upon the Moor's School share of the Wheelock rents" (Chase, *A History of Dartmouth College and the Town of Hanover New Hampshire (To 1815)*, 2nd ed., 2 vols., vol. 1 [Brattleboro, VT: Dartmouth College, 1928], 634).

47. Apart from training ministers for evangelical work among Native American nations, Moor's Charity School was often perceived as a preparatory school for Dartmouth and other institutions of higher learning. The last two years of Moor's curriculum dovetailed with the first year of Dartmouth's curriculum and entrance examinations (such as the study of the Greek New Testament and rhetoric). In terms of institutional identity, the primary reason Moor's Charity School and Dartmouth College were separate institutions in the early nineteenth century related to funding issues: Moor's relied heavily on donations from English and Scottish societies for propagating the gospel among Native Americans, while Dartmouth received state funding. The Scottish and English donors were concerned that funds for Moor's might be diverted to Dartmouth, so the two institutions kept separate financial records in order to maintain their subsidies. Moor's Charity School would eventually be absorbed officially by Dartmouth College in the early twentieth century (John King Lord, *A History of Dartmouth College, 1815–1909: Being a Second Volume of A History of Dartmouth College and the Town of Hanover, New Hampshire, Begun by Frederick Chase*, vol. 2 [Concord, NH: The Rumford Press, 1913], 232–44). See also Chase, *A History of Dartmouth College*, 1:239–48, 588–600.

48. EMD 1:260.

49. Assuming the Smiths moved to West Lebanon in 1811, Bushman, for example, speculates that Joseph Jr. did not attend school but "remained at home" (Bushman, *Rough Stone*, 20).

50. Wright and Wright indicate that "it is apparent from available histories that the schools in Vermont and New Hampshire were similar because of their geographical

Unlike Vermont and New York during this period, New Hampshire based school funding on overall population, rather than census numbers and school records for children within a particular age range.[51] As such, the state did not provide information in its laws reflecting the customary age for children to start school. Even so, memoirists and observers indicate that children in the state began school as early as two to three years of age.[52] During his tours through New England and New York from 1795 to 1816, Timothy Dwight IV (1752–1817), president of Yale College, observed, "In Massachusetts, New-Hampshire, and Vermont, schools are everywhere established. They are often styled parochial schools. … To these little seminaries the children of New-England are universally sent, from two, three, four, and five years of age, to the period in which they have learned to read, write, and keep accounts. … I speak of the common schools only."[53] Within this context, the year the Smith family moved to West Lebanon becomes irrelevant with respect to schooling: Joseph Jr., who turned six in December 1811 and seven in December 1812, would have been old enough—indeed, much older— than children "of sufficient age" to start school in New Hampshire.[54]

The winter of 1812–13 would, however, bring a traumatic interruption to young Joseph Jr.'s formal education. Whether or not he started school that winter term, he certainly would not have finished

proximity and shared history" (Wright and Wright, "New England Common School," 242). Though the Smith family crossed state lines in their move from Royalton to West Lebanon, they remained in the same Upper Connecticut River Valley region.

51. From 1808 through at least 1830, state funding for New Hampshire schools (whether through state taxes, bank taxes, or the state "literary fund") was "divided among the towns in the ratio of representation" (American Education Society, "Common Schools," *The Quarterly Register and Journal of the American Education Society*, [Nov. 4, 1830]: 230–31).

52. Warren Burton (1800–66) and Horace Greeley (1811–72) attended New Hampshire common schools before their fourth birthdays. See fn37.

53. Timothy Dwight, *Travels in New-England and New-York*, 4 vols., vol. 4 (London; Edinburgh: William Baynes and Son; Ogle, Duncan & Co.; H. S. Baynes and Co. [Edinburgh], 1823), 287. Dwight's depiction of common schools as "parochial schools" is part of his wider vision of New England's religious exceptionalism: although common schools were technically nondenominational, they nevertheless served as part of God's teleological plan for New England; thus, all common schools were, to use his term, "parochial schools."

54. As Vogel has noted, Joseph Sr.'s name does not appear on the May 1812 tax assessment records in West Lebanon, suggesting that the family arrived in New Hampshire *after* 1811. Furthermore, according to Jeffrey S. O'Driscoll, Hyrum Smith's "name cannot be located in the record of 1811" for Moor's Charity School, providing additional evidence for the timing of the move. Thus, Joseph Jr. was most likely six years old, soon to turn seven, when he started school in West Lebanon. EMD 5:382; O'Driscoll, *Hyrum Smith*, 17n26.

it. During the winter, a typhoid epidemic "swept through the upper Connecticut Valley and left 6,400 dead in five months."[55] Young Joseph was not spared the fever. The story is well-known: the infection spread through his body, eventually locating in his lower left leg and causing a bone infection. The Smiths summoned medical doctors from Dartmouth and the decision was eventually made to cut the infected bone from Joseph's leg. Though the operation was successful, Joseph remained bedridden for the next several months, waiting for the wound to heal.[56]

Joseph's experience would, of course, affect his formal schooling. His attendance during the winter term 1812–13 would have been abruptly cut short by his infection and surgery. He almost certainly missed the 1813 summer term as well, not only because of convalescing at home but due to a possible trip to Salem, Massachusetts, with his uncle Jesse. "When he had so far recovered as to be able to travel," Lucy recorded, Joseph Jr. "went with his uncle, Jesse Smith, to Salem, for the benefit of his health, hoping the sea-breezes would be of service to him."[57] Thus, for the 1813 school year, Joseph's educational improvement would have been limited to reading books, family devotionals, and domestic education.

Lucy's history suggests Joseph returned to formal schooling in the winter 1813–14, after approximately a full year of recuperation. Immediately following her account of Joseph's surgery, Lucy indicates that, "having passed through about a year of sickness and distress, health again returned to our family" (her 1845 manuscript version reads, "After one whole year of affliction we were able once more to look

---

55. Bushman, *Rough Stone*, 20.

56. Bushman, *Rough Stone*, 21.

57. EMD 1:268. See also Wright and Wright, "New England Common School," 238. Interestingly, Jesse Smith's detailed and precise business ledger, currently in possession of the LDS Church History Library, does not indicate a trip to Salem during the summer 1813. Joseph's trip to Salem, of whatever length and whenever it actually took place, would have offered its own form of practical education. Salem was a major port city of trade: merchant ships brought exotic cargo from all over the world, and its bustling shops were packed with a rich panoply of merchandise and patrons. Yet, such excitement would have been counterbalanced by a hostile British navy patrolling along the seacoast, seizing ships, impressing sailors, and threatening invasion. See Hill, *Joseph Smith*, 36; Dan Vogel, *Joseph Smith: The Making of a Prophet* (Salt Lake City: Signature Books, 2004), 18; Fawn M. Brodie, *No Man Knows My History: the Life of Joseph Smith, the Mormon Prophet*, 2nd ed. (New York: Vintage Books, 1995; repr., First Vintage Books Edition), 8.

upon our children and each other in health").[58] Young Joseph, though continuing to convalesce and recover, was apparently no longer bed-ridden. Thus, from the time of his return until the Smith family's move to New York, Joseph may have experienced one of the longest periods of sustained formal education in his lifetime: because he would remain on crutches until the Smith family's move to New York, Joseph would have been prevented from performing heavy farm labor for the remain-der of the family's stay in the Connecticut Valley, allowing him full participation at school in both winter and summer months.[59] In such a compromised physical condition, school attendance, reading, medita-tion, and domestic chores would have been the extent of his activities.

NORWICH, VERMONT: 1814/1815 TO WINTER 1816–17

Sometime between May 1814 and March 1816, the Smith family moved back across the Connecticut River to Norwich, Vermont, sit-uated approximately two miles west of Dartmouth. The exact time of their arrival is yet again uncertain.[60] Furthermore, records are silent regarding the Smith children's school attendance, though Wright and Wright observe, "When considering this period in Joseph's life, it seems consistent to assume that his mother would have again encouraged him and his siblings to attend public school."[61] During their stay in Nor-wich, the family was plagued with a series of crop failures, which left them destitute.[62] After hearing about cheap land and better farming conditions in western New York, no doubt combined with rumors of the economic potential of the region, Joseph Sr. decided to relocate the

58. EMD 1:268.

59. For Smith's length of time on crutches, see Vogel, *Making of a Prophet*, 18. Bush-man, *Rough Stone*, 21. Hill, *Joseph Smith*, 36. When she recounted the family's move to New York in the winter 1816–17, Lucy mentioned that Joseph "was still lame" (EMD 1:274).

60. According to Vogel, "probably in the late spring or early summer of 1814, the Smiths returned across the Connecticut River to Norwich, Vermont" (Vogel, *Making of a Prophet*, 19). In addition, Vogel notes that tax assessment records indicate the Smiths moved out of Lebanon between May 1814 and May 1815, though he also observes, "exactly when they arrived in Norwich is less clear, although it was certainly before the birth of Don Car-los [one of Joseph's younger brothers] on 25 March 1816." Vogel suggests Lucy may have misremembered the dates of the family's move "or the Smiths may have lived in a remote quarter in or near the town and later moved onto Murdock's property [the rental property the Smiths leased]" (EMD 5:383).

61. Wright and Wright, "New England Common School," 238.

62. See Bushman, *Rough Stone*, 27. Hill, *Joseph Smith*, 37; Brodie, *No Man Knows*, 8–9; Vogel, *Making of a Prophet*, 19–24.

family to Palmyra, New York, a town that would become a stop along the Erie Canal. In late 1816, Joseph Sr. went to Palmyra by himself to make arrangements, while the family packed their belongings and followed after him, apparently in January 1817.[63]

Thus, in terms of formal schooling opportunities, the timing of the Smith family's departure provides a window for their stay in the Upper Connecticut River Valley. From the time the family arrived in West Lebanon, New Hampshire, in 1811 or 1812 to their final departure from the area in the winter 1816–17, Joseph Jr. would have been eligible to attend school for either five or six terms (winter 1811–12, summer 1812, then skipping the 1813 school year, followed by winter 1813–14, summer 1814, winter 1814–15, and summer 1815). Depending again on arrival and departure dates, the amount of eligible formal education for this period would be between two and three school years.

PALMYRA, NEW YORK: 1817–20/1821

The Smith family's move to Palmyra, a journey of about 300 miles, would have taken approximately one month.[64] The move would occur in the middle of the 1816–17 winter term, effectively disrupting the start of the school year, though one account suggests the children attended the latter part of that term after initially getting settled in western New York State. Jacob E. Terry of East Palmyra was one of Joseph's classmates. Vogel observes that if Jacob's sister, Elizabeth, is correct in her memory of the dates and locations where their family lived, as recorded in the *Parshall Terry Family History* (1956), then "this would indicate that Joseph Smith attended school immediately after his arrival at Palmyra sometime during the winter of 1816–1817."[65]

---

63. Vogel observes that Martha Coray, Lucy's amanuensis for her history, wrote in her notebooks, "1816 [1817] moved to ... Palmyra in Jan[uary]" (EMD 5:384).

64. Bushman, *Rough Stone*, 29.

65. By 1819, the Terry family had moved away from Palmyra. If Elizabeth's memory of the dates is inaccurate, then, according to Vogel, "it is possible for Jacob E. Terry to have attended school with Joseph Smith either in the winter of 1816–1817 or 1817–1818" (EMD 3:261). That Lucy and Joseph Sr. would immediately enroll their children in school upon their arrival is consistent with their actions when they arrived in West Lebanon midway through the winter term, when they promptly enrolled their school age children into classes. See EMD 1:260. Enrolling children near or at the end of a term was common in early nineteenth-century America. The ongoing westward migration of families resulted in children constantly arriving at or departing from schools in the middle of school years. Moreover, attending a new school mid-term would not cause a disruption in the continuity of education:

Such partial attendance would not be the last time the children's formal education would be interrupted, particularly because of financial exigencies. Upon their arrival, Lucy records how the Smiths held a family council regarding their "destitute circumstances" and how they "came to the conclusion to unite our strength in endeavouring to obtain a piece of land."[66] This being the case, the children old enough to work likely spent their summers earning money to help the family rather than attending school during the summer terms. Thus, though he had only recently stopped walking with crutches, Joseph probably started working in the summer of 1817. And given the continued financial struggles of the Smith family, Joseph may never have attended another summer term at any common school again.[67]

Insight into the Smith family's financial challenges, particularly in relation to formal education, emerged with the 2008 discovery of Philander Packard's school records.[68] Packard, a school teacher in Palmyra's District No. 1 (the same district in which the Smith family lived), kept a record of tuition payments he received from his students.[69] Instead of entering the child's name, however, Packard listed funds received under the heads of households. "Joseph Smith" appears among them, nestled

---

unlike their modern counterparts, most common school teachers in the early nineteenth century did not use detailed, progressive lesson plans. The basic and comparatively homogenous curriculum of common school instruction simply resulted in new student arrivals being shuffled into appropriate groups for their reading level.

66. EMD 1:276.

67. Christopher Stafford, a neighbor of the Smiths in Manchester, New York, recalled that "Jo was away much of the time summers" (EMD 2:195). Mrs. S. F. Anderick, a neighbor of the Smiths, confirmed Joseph was away "from home much summers. Sometimes he [Joseph] said he had been to Broome County, New York, and Pennsylvania" (EMD 2:210). Vogel notes that Joseph Jr. and his brother Samuel were not listed on the 1820 census, "perhaps because they were hired out in another township" (EMD 5:391). Joseph likely spent his summers performing manual labor on various farms and occasionally acting as a treasure-hunting seer. Prior to hearing about Smith finding the gold plates, for instance, Lee Yost, "a Michigan merchant and former resident of Fayette, New York [a town approximately twenty-four miles southeast of Manchester, New York]," recalled seeing Joseph with a team of treasure hunters searching among Native American ruins on the farm of his wife's grandfather in Fayette (EMD 5:287).

68. Donald L. Enders, "Treasures and a Trash Heap: An Early Reference to the Joseph Smith Family in Palmyra," *Journal of Mormon History* 40, no. 3 (Summer 2014): 201–222.

69. For the boundaries of the nineteen school districts in existence in 1814, see Town of Palmyra, "Town of Palmyra Board Meeting Minutes," Palmyra, New York: Town and Village of Palmyra, 1819, www.palmyrany.com/minutes/TB/1814.pdf.

in a list that includes several of the Smith family's neighbors.[70] And as Donald L. Enders observes, the payments from the Joseph Smith family were the second lowest in the account book, bested in meagerness only by the widow Hannah Hurlbut and her child.[71] The document provides stark evidence of impoverished family circumstances. Nevertheless, it is essential to recognize that Packard's notes are not *attendance* records but running *accounts of payments*. Interpreting the documents as attendance records for poor families is, in fact, highly problematic. Thus, contextualizing Packard's records within New York's common school system is crucial.

Before the Smith family moved to Palmyra, Gideon Hawley, Superintendent of Common Schools for the State of New York, had been mounting an aggressive campaign to provide a common school education to all the children in the state. Since 1812, when New York instituted a statewide common school system, universal access to education had become a social and political priority; and Hawley recognized that children from poor families often could not afford to pay their share of teachers' wages and therefore could not regularly attend school. Hawley thus participated in shaping new laws for the common schools, explicitly giving local school commissioners the power to waive tuition costs for poor families. Encouraged by Hawley's advocacy, the legislature passed "The Act for the Better Establishment of

---

70. The identity of this "Joseph Smith" is not entirely conclusive. While Packard's list includes several of the Smith family's neighbors, suggesting that the "Joseph Smith" entry may very well be Joseph Smith Sr., the criteria establishing the claim can be problematic. Enders argues, "[I]n 1817, the schoolhouse where Philander Packard was teaching … was the only one in the village, standing at East Main and Mill streets. That year, the township (as opposed to the village) had at least eight school districts." While it is literally true that Palmyra did have "at least eight school districts," the total number was actually twenty, significantly altering the perception of the educational landscape of the township (see Appendix B). Furthermore, Palmyra Village had the highest population density in the township and would have required more than one common school to cover the five- to fifteen-year-old population. Enders's assumption that Packard was "the only teacher in the village" further leads him to the conclusion that Packard's forty-three students were the only ones in attendance in the village, while the remaining "seventy-nine (or 65 percent) of the school-age children received no formal instruction during the fall of 1817" (Enders, "Treasures and a Trash Heap," 215). Contrary to this estimate, Palmyra (town *and* village) taught a total of 987 students out of 1,050 total children between the ages of five and fifteen in the 1817–18 school year. Thus, rather than Enders's claim of seventy-nine untaught children in Palmyra village alone, in reality only sixty-three children between five and fifteen years in the town and village *combined* did not attend school during that time (see Appendix B).

71. Enders, "Treasures and a Trash Heap," 212–13.

47

Common Schools" on April 15, 1814, which allowed commissioners and local trustees "to exonerate from the payment of the wages of such teachers, or the residue aforesaid [balance of wages not paid by the state], of such wages, all such poor persons within their district, as they shall think proper."[72] Hawley's strategy proved to be an enormous success. Between the state funding and the waiver of local fees, children from poor families gained access to the same educational opportunities as all other common school students, and overall statewide attendance began to rise significantly in each successive year. In his report to the legislature for the 1819–20 school year, Hawley reveled in the progress of the common school system:

> There is now therefore, reason to believe that the number of children in the state who do not attend any school, and who are not otherwise in the way of receiving a common education, is very small. The public bounty is sufficient to defray the expense of most schools for about three months in the year; and where that is expended in different parts of the year, so as not to defray the whole expense of the school for any particular part, it is understood that in most districts, poor children have been permitted to attend the district school free of expense, under that provision in the [1814] school act which empowers districts to exonerate such children from the payment of teachers' wages.[73]

As Hawley's presentation indicates, payment for common school education came from both public and private sources: state funding covered a portion of the year ("about three months"), while local taxes and assessments made up the difference for teachers' wages. If the local commissioner and trustees deemed a family too poor to pay an assessment (in full or in part), the children would be entitled to attend school either free of charge or at a reduced rate, in accordance with the family's ability to pay. Thus, Packard's school records reveal the families who could afford to pay along with the families who apparently could not. But the point needs to be reemphasized that the accounts do not indicate actual attendance at school. Indeed, rather than providing evidence of the Smith children's lack of attendance, Packard's school record very likely suggests the opposite. Because the "Joseph Smith"

---

72. State of New York, *The Act for the Better Establishment of Common Schools* (Albany: State of New York, 1814), 11.

73. JA 44:556.

family was one of the poorest in the records, they would have been among the most eligible candidates for tuition waivers. And if they did in fact receive full or partial waivers, the Smith children could have been in regular attendance at classes, even though Packard's accounts would show a near absence of payments. The widow Hannah Hurlbut's child, for example, though the least able to pay, with empty column after column of payments received, would nevertheless be entitled to, and may well have been participating in, full and regular attendance over the duration of Packard's accounts. Thus, while Packard's records potentially reveal the indigent circumstances of the Smith family, they do not confirm the actual attendance or non-attendance of the Smith children at school.

The unreliability of Packard's records as attendance records is further complicated by the time period they cover. As Enders observes, Packard's notes cover only the period from September 9 through October 7, 1817, while "the columns are blank after Friday, October 10, possibly because it was harvest time, even though the headings continue through Saturday, November 1."[74] The point is significant: planting and harvest times were the two busiest periods in the life of a farming family. And in the first decades of the nineteenth century, when frontier towns rapidly grew in size and started to become well established, school years often lengthened from shorter periods (roughly five months) to longer sessions (seven to eight months). Such changes resulted in schools commencing winter terms during the fall harvest season. For a poor family like the Smiths, who could not afford to hire additional laborers, the oldest children would likely have stayed home to work on the farm, delaying attendance until after the harvest. Thus, Packard's records are silent on the Smith children's status in the post-harvest winter months. Nevertheless, the records offer, even if indirectly, potential insights into the working and educational lives of the Smith children.

Harvest season did not occur at precisely the same time each year, because of weather conditions and the annual variations for the maturation of crops. Nonetheless, the harvest season in upstate New York for sweet and silage corn, barley, beans, oats, potatoes, and wheat

---

74. Enders, "Treasures and a Trash Heap," 202.

usually finished by the end of October. The exceptions were field corn (dried and hardened, usually for animal feed) and possibly soybeans (an uncommon crop in upstate New York, used for animal feed in this period), for which harvesting usually occurred by the end of November.[75] In terms of scheduling the actual harvest, farmers relied heavily on weather predictions in the yearly almanacs. In 1817, for example (the fall season in which Packard kept his school records), almanacs covering New York, Pennsylvania, and the surrounding states (mostly New England) consistently urged readers to prepare for winter in late November with the anticipation of snow and storms in early December.[76] Whether or not inclement weather actually occurred, farmers would nevertheless have worked to finish harvest before those dates.

Thus, if he were working on the family farm or hiring out to neighbors for the 1817 harvest, Joseph Jr. would likely have delayed attendance at school until the end of October, at the soonest, or the end of November, at the latest. Planting season for the following year would not begin until late March, at the earliest (usually early April), which would result in Joseph attending approximately only four to five months each school year in Palmyra and later in Manchester. This estimate finds indirect support from Lemuel Durfee's account book for 1815–29. After Durfee purchased the Smith family farm on December 20, 1825, the Smiths continued to work the property, while Samuel

---

75. On crops, Bushman notes, "Most farmers planted corn for family and animals on the first cleared land. Wheat followed in the second year, with the possibility of a small surplus beyond the family needs" (*Rough Stone*, 33).

76. For the first week in December, *Smith & Forman's* almanac predicts "Hard [rain?], Snow, with bluster weather" (*Smith & Forman's New-York and New-Jersey Almanac, For the Year of Our Lord 1817* [New York: Smith & Forman, 1816]). Pennsylvania-based almanacs consistently predict "snow" on November 28. See *The New St. Tammany Almanac, For the Year 1817*, (Philadelphia: George W. Mentz, 1816); Joshua Sharp, *Bailey's Rittenhouse Almanac, For the Year of Our Lord, 1817* (Philadelphia: Lydia R. Bailey, 1816); *Poor Will's Almanac, For the Year 1817*, (Philadelphia: Joseph Rakestraw, 1816). "If no signs of storms and winds should fail in this month," warns a Windsor, Vermont, almanac for the start of December, "we shall have enough of it [i.e., if all the predictions for the month come true, the month will be filled with more than enough storms and winds]. High winds with a driving storm" (Truman Abell, *The New England Farmer's Diary and Almanac, From the Year of the Creation, According to Sacred Writ, 5779, and the Christian Era, 1817* [Windsor: Jesse Cochran, 1816]). For the start of December, a Hartford, Connecticut, almanac that "will serve for any of the adjoining States" waxes poetic: "Now frowning winter rears its head array'd in all majestic dread. Now expect foul weather" (A. Allen, *Allen's New-England Almanack, For the Year of Our Lord 1817* [Hartford: Peter B. Gleason & Co., 1816]).

Harrison Smith (Joseph's younger brother) worked for Durfee to pay the rent on the farm. Durfee's account reads, "April, the 16 day, the year 1827, S. Harrison Smith, Son of Joseph Smith, began to work for me by the month. Is to work 7 months for the use of the place where said Joseph Smith lives."[77] This "7 months" span, from April to November, coincides with the regular farming season, from planting to harvest. This then suggests that the Smith children who hired out their labor were working the same yearly schedule as their adult contemporaries, causing them to delay their attendance at school each year.[78]

While the precise details of his school attendance in Palmyra are elusive, Joseph Jr. still managed to appear at school. Several of his former classmates mentioned attending with him during the family's years in Palmyra. William H. Cuyler, a lifelong resident of Palmyra, "attended school with Joseph Smith the Mormon, and his brothers—particularly Alvin [1798–1823] and William [1811–93]."[79] Isaac Butts also "attended school with Prophet Jo" in Palmyra.[80] And Jacob E. Terry of East Palmyra was said to be "a school associate and friend of young Joseph Smith, they being the same age."[81] The Smith family would remain tax-paying residents in the Palmyra school districts from 1817 to late 1820/early 1821, but they were not planning to stay in town indefinitely.

Between April 1819 and April 1820, some of the members of the Smith family moved "into a small log cabin on the property of Samuel Jennings on Stafford Road near the southern border of Palmyra township."[82] This cabin was adjacent to a parcel of land they hoped to purchase for a family farm in the neighboring town of Manchester.

---

77. H. Michael Marquardt, "Historical Setting of Mormonism in Manchester, Ontario County, New York," *John Whitmer Historical Association Journal* 35, no. 2 (Winter 2015): 73 (spelling and punctuation modernized).

78. Apart from Durfee's account book, other indirect evidence suggests the schedules the Smith family followed to balance winter schooling with the months devoted to farm labor. For example, when Joseph established the "school of the prophets," Dean C. Jessee informs us that "the 1835–36 session of the school met between 2 November and 29 March" (Jessee, ed. *Personal Writings of Joseph Smith* [Salt Lake City: Deseret Book Co.; Brigham Young University Press, 2002], 88n31). This span of time coincides with Samuel Smith's work schedule for Durfee, suggesting it was common practice to dedicate seven months of the year to farm work, while devoting the remaining five months to such activities as school attendance.

79. EMD 3:169–70.

80. EMD 2:202.

81. EMD 3:261–62.

82. EMD 5:389.

Though they did not yet own the land, the Smiths were apparently confident enough of its purchase to start developing the property. For approximately two to three years, the Smiths maintained residences on both Main Street and Stafford Road in Palmyra; and the cabin appears to have served initially as an outpost, where family members stayed who were developing the Manchester land.[83] The Smiths would eventually take formal possession of the Manchester property sometime between July 1820 and February 1821.[84] This period therefore marks the time when the Smith family became official residents of Manchester.[85] Whether or not the children started attending school in Manchester at this time, however, is not known.

As of April 1822, the Smiths were still recorded on the Palmyra road list, suggesting that the family had not yet made a full transition to the Manchester farm.[86] Therefore, the children apparently could have attended school in either Palmyra or Manchester during the 1820–21 winter term. These dates provide a framework for Joseph's potential attendance at school in Palmyra. If he started school in Manchester during the same period in which the Smiths took possession of the new farm (1820–21), then Joseph Jr. would have been eligible to attend three winter terms in Palmyra (winter 1817–18, winter 1818–19, and winter 1819–20). If, however, he continued to attend school in Palmyra after the Smiths officially purchased the Manchester property

83. The Smiths are associated with three different locations at this time: the Main Street home in Palmyra, the Jennings cabin in south Palmyra (on the northern border of Manchester), and the adjacent Manchester farm. According to Vogel, the April 1820 Palmyra road list appears to indicate two dwelling locations for the Smith family: "Alvin appears as fifteenth and Joseph Sr., as forty-second on a forty-four-name list, probably indicating that part of the Smith family moved sometime between April 1819 and April 1820 to the south end of Stafford Road." Vogel further adds, "Alvin was apparently on Main Street, perhaps running the family's cake and ale shop, and Joseph Sr. was south on Stafford Road near the Palmyra township line, evidently occupying the Jennings cabin" (EMD 5:389–90). Bushman notes, "The Smiths moved onto their [Manchester] land in stages. Before obtaining title to the land, the Smiths raised a log house adjacent to their prospective purchase on the land of a local merchant, Samuel Jennings, possibly to begin clearing land they intended to buy" (*Rough Stone*, 32).

84. Vogel notes that as of June 22, 1820, "the entire 300 acres of Farmington (now Manchester) Lot 1 is taxed to the heirs of Nicholas Evertson [the owners of the property prior to the Smiths], indicating that the Smiths had not yet contracted for their land" (EMD 5:391).

85. At this time, the Smith farm was technically within the town of Farmington; Manchester had not yet been created. As Vogel notes, the town was divided in 1821 into two townships: the western half continued under the name of Farmington, the eastern portion became Manchester (EMD 5:391–92).

86. EMD 5:392.

(this would assume he traveled back and forth the relatively short distance between Manchester and Palmyra), then Joseph would have been eligible to attend five winter terms in Palmyra (winter 1820–21 and winter 1821–22, in addition to the above mentioned).

MANCHESTER, NEW YORK: 1820/1821–25

At this stage, Joseph's age becomes a factor for consideration. Less than three months after the beginning of the 1820–21 winter term, Joseph turned fifteen years old. According to the New York Act for the Support of Common Schools, passed the previous year in 1819, the local commissioners of common schools distributed state funds "according and in proportion to the number of children, between the ages of five and fifteen years, inclusive, living in each such [school] district."[87] The age range, though arbitrary, nevertheless reflects cultural assumptions about the normative age range of common school students in New York. Therefore, because he turned fifteen on December 23, 1820, Joseph could have dropped out of school at that time, without disrupting social conventions or doing anything unusual in comparison to his peers. Yet, in spite of this option, Joseph nonetheless attended at least one term in Manchester, as attested by Joseph's former classmates in the township.[88] Orrin Porter Rockwell, a well-known Mormon convert

---

87. State of New York, *The Act for the Support of Common Schools; Passed April 12, 1819; With Extracts from Acts Passed March 30, 1820, and March 23, 1821; Also, The Act to Amend the Act for the Support of Common Schools, passed April 17, 1822* (Albany: State of New York, 1822), 9–11.

88. Manchester did not exist until 1821, when it was created out of Farmington (see fn82). To avoid confusion and maintain consistency, however, I refer anachronistically to the Smith's farm in Farmington as being in Manchester; see EMD 5:391–92. Even though members of the Smith family were possibly staying in the Stafford Road cabin in Palmyra as early as 1818 or 1819, Joseph's attendance at a Manchester school in this early period is problematic. The family did not become official residents of Manchester until they formally contracted for their new farm sometime between July 1820 and February 1821; thus, they would not have begun paying taxes or school assessments to Manchester Township until that time (EMD 5:391–92). In order for the Smith children to attend school in Manchester prior to that time, Joseph Sr. and Lucy would have been required to get permission from the trustees of both the Palmyra and Manchester school districts (see EMD 3:258n4, where Vogel indicates, "according to early maps of Manchester, the Smiths' former residence was included in school district 11"). Permissions for families to transfer children from one school district to another (within a township or across township lines) took place during town meetings. Palmyra's minutes in 1815, for example, indicate how "Enoch Saunders is set off from 1st School District in Palmyra with leave to annex himself to Farmington. Parshall Terry is set off from Palmyra with leave to attach himself to Farmington. Isaac Sweezy is set off from

and longtime confidant of Joseph, "was a schoolmate and friend of Smith's" in Manchester.[89] Moses C. Smith, another Manchester classmate (not related to Joseph), was said to have "attended [school] with the Prophet and once they had an altercation."[90] And Samantha Payne, also of Manchester, claimed to have "attended school with [Joseph] for some time."[91] Thus, if he started attending school in Manchester during the first term in which he was eligible as a resident, Joseph would have attended at least the winter 1820–21 term.

A subsequent question then naturally arises: did Joseph stop attending school in Manchester after the 1820–21 winter term or did he continue

---

Palmyra with leave to attach himself to Williamson. Martin Harris [Joseph's early supporter] is set off from School District No. 1 and attached to School District No. 8 in Palmyra." None of the town minutes record the Smith family transferring their children from a Palmyra school district to a Farmington/Manchester district, which strongly suggests the Smith children attended school in Palmyra until the family became taxpaying residents of Manchester between July 1820 and February 1821 (when they could transfer schools without needing permission or being recorded in the town minutes). See Town of Palmyra, "Town of Palmyra Board Meeting Minutes," 1815, www.palmyrany.com/minutes/TB/1815.pdf. While the Manchester trustees could have allowed the Smith children to attend their school, the Smiths normally would have been required to cover all the costs of their children's attendance. The 1822 revision of the common school act of New York indicates, "But if children, not residing in the district, be permitted, by the trustees, to attend their school, as such permission might have been withheld, *it may, and ought, if granted, to be on condition that no part of the public money shall be applied for their benefit*" (State of New York, *The Act for the Support of Common Schools*: 35 (emphasis added)). The Smiths were struggling financially at this time, suggesting the children would have continued to attend school in Palmyra, where they would not incur additional expenses. An exception to this rule would be the case in which neighboring townships shared a school district. Nevertheless, Manchester school district 11 was not a jointly-shared school district with Palmyra. The only school district the two towns shared at this time was Palmyra's District 21, formed on February 14, 1820, which contained Palmyra lots 46, 50, 53, and part of 37 in Township 12, 2nd range, joined together with Manchester (Farmington) lots 25 and 78 in Township 11, 2nd range. See Town of Palmyra, "Town of Palmyra Board Meeting Minutes," 1819, www.palmyrany.com/minutes/TB/1819.pdf. For helpful online maps showing lot numbers, see Dale R. Broadhurst's webpage: www.oliver-cowdery.com/smithhome/smithmap.htm. In summary, the earliest any of the Smith family children could have attended a Manchester school would be the 1820–21 winter term.

89. See Elizabeth Kane's interview, EMD 3:406. Caroline Rockwell Smith, Porter Rockwell's sister, also stated, "I attended school with their [the Smith's] children" (EMD 2:199). Benjamin Saunders, about two years younger than Caroline Rockwell Smith, said, "I knew young Joseph just as well as I did my own brothers. Went to the same school with the younger boys" (EMD 2:137). Though Benjamin's and Caroline's statements do not specifically identify Joseph as a classmate, their observations demonstrate Lucy and Joseph Sr.'s commitment to have all their children educated; therefore, the idea that Joseph would be excluded from such influence and withheld from school seems untenable.

90. EMD 3:258.

91. EMD 2:172.

to participate longer? Again, historical documentation does not provide a clear answer. Nevertheless, a look at the laws governing school funding, coupled with the state's statistics on school attendance, offers further insight and clarification. To begin, in order to determine how much money the state would allocate to each school district, New York's "Act for the Support of Common Schools" in 1819 measured the population of *all* the children "between the ages of five and fifteen years" within every county, regardless of actual attendance. Legislators then used this overall population to determine the amount of money each county would receive. It is important to note, however, that this law did not *restrict* school attendance to children between those ages of five and fifteen; the figures merely provided guidance for funding allocations.[92] Thus, students could attend school at *any* age. The 1822 clarification of the 1819 act states, "In applying the public money, it must always be paid to the teacher on account of his wages. It is not to be distributed among the scholars or their parents; *nor is it to be applied for the exclusive benefit of children between the ages of five and fifteen years*, or of any other particular description of scholars. *All who reside in the district and attend the school, as they may of common right, must necessarily participate equally in the benefit of the public money.*"[93] As such, Joseph could have continued attending common schools for the remainder of his teenage years in Manchester, if he so chose. And whether or not he took advantage of this opportunity, many of his peers did.

According to the annual reports of the New York Superintendent of Common Schools, students throughout the state frequently attended classes at ages younger than five and older than fifteen years. And this was certainly true for Manchester (originally part of Farmington). In the 1821 school year (when Joseph turned sixteen), Manchester/Farmington taught a combined total of 1,051 students. Of these students, 972 were five to fifteen years of age, leaving a remainder of seventy-nine students either younger than five or older than fifteen (7.5 percent of all

92. The state paid teachers a flat rate based on the census numbers and school records of children between five and fifteen within any given school district. Teachers did not receive additional money if more children attended than the census indicated, nor did they receive less if all the eligible children did not attend.

93. State of New York, *The Act for the Support of Common Schools*, 35 (emphasis added). The logistics of tracking a moving population of settlers during a period of intense migration made attendance figures at each country schoolhouse difficult to record. Therefore, in lieu of using actual school attendance records exclusively, state officials also based funding allocations on the more reliable census figures.

students).[94] And the pattern continued for all the years the Smith family resided in Manchester: in the 1822 school year, seventy-four students younger than five or older than fifteen attended (6 percent of the total 1,236 students taught);[95] in 1823, sixty students younger than five or older than fifteen attended (7.8 percent of the total 770 taught);[96] in 1824, 83 students younger than five or older than fifteen attended (9.8 percent of the total 850 taught);[97] and in 1825, the number of students younger than five or older than fifteen jumped to 179 (18.2 percent of the 985 taught, or nearly one in five students).[98]

Joseph's continued presence in school and desire for an education are suggested not only by the presence of other older students in Manchester, but by additional clues. During this same period, for example, Joseph attended a juvenile debating society, likely during the 1821–22 winter when he turned sixteen, which reveals an ongoing, self-motivated desire to improve himself.[99] Tantalizing clues also emerge from his personal library. For example, Joseph owned the Reverend Charles A. Goodrich's schoolbook *A History of the United States* (1822), an advanced school reader that Joseph donated to the Nauvoo Library and Literary Institute on January 31, 1844.[100] First published sometime after March 8, 1822, Goodrich's *History* quickly became popular in common schools and was "reprinted forty times in just ten years; eventually his work sold over 150,000 copies during the decade of the 1840s."[101] Nevertheless, rather than encountering

---

94. The figures are listed under Farmington (Manchester and Farmington had not yet split) (JA 45:632).

95. Though the two towns had technically split by now, Manchester and Farmington filed a joint return for 1822 (JA 45: Appendix A-11).

96. Manchester stopped filing a joint return with Farmington this year, which explains the drop in numbers (JA 47: Appendix A-12).

97. JA 48: Appendix B-13.

98. JA 49: Appendix G-20.

99. H. Michael Marquardt indicates that Orsamus Turner, who provides us with this account, moved away from Palmyra in the summer 1822 (H. Michael Marquardt, *The Rise of Mormonism: 1816–1844* [Longwood, FL: Xulon Press, 2005], 49). Thus, Joseph's attendance with Turner at the debate society likely occurred at the same time as the 1821–22 school winter term, if not earlier (rural debate clubs met most frequently during the winter months, when farm work was minimal). In addition, specifically after January 1822, at least one other "Debating school" formed in the Palmyra area. See Marquardt, *The Rise of Mormonism*, 50n56. Yet, the records for all these clubs are currently lost or unknown.

100. Kenneth W. Godfrey, "A Note on the Nauvoo Library and Literary Institute," *BYU Studies* 14, no. 3 (1974), 1–2.

101. Barry Joyce, *The First U.S. History Textbooks: Constructing and Disseminating the American Tale in the Nineteenth Century* (New York: Lexington Books, 2015), 45. On

this popular text in school, Joseph likely used this schoolbook in one of the several avenues of self-improvement he pursued, such as domestic education or participation with the juvenile debate society.[102]

More directly linked to classroom study, Joseph's copy of Murray's *Introduction to the English Reader* (1804) suggests Joseph's level of common school curriculum and achievement, if he did, in fact, use this specific copy of the book during his common school education.[103] This text was an introduction to (or rather a condensed version of) Murray's *English Reader* (1799), which was one of the most advanced textbooks that youths encountered in common schools. Both texts required a prerequisite sequence of schoolbooks that included primers, spellers, grammars, and other introductory readers. Thus, Murray's *Introduction* not only suggests Joseph's abilities, it also signals the extensive history of educational development needed to acquire the skills necessary to use this book. Joseph's participation in a juvenile debate club and his ownership of Murray's *Introduction* and Goodrich's *History* therefore suggest that Joseph continued—however intermittently—to attend school in Manchester during his later teenage years.[104] In any event, Smith's formal

March 8, 1822, Goodrich submitted his manuscript for copyright to Charles A. Ingersoll, Clerk of the District of Connecticut. See Rev. Charles A. Goodrich, *A History of the United States of America*, 3rd ed. (Hartford: Barber and Robinson, 1823), imprint.

102. Even though we do not have records of the schoolbooks in Manchester classrooms during Joseph's years there (approximately 1822–25), New York common schools rarely used American history textbooks at this time. In the report for the 1825–26 school year, the first year state records identified schoolbooks in common school classrooms, only six towns in the entire state used an American history text, none of them in Ontario, Wayne, or Chenango Counties. See JA 50: Appendix A-9, A-40. While a local Manchester teacher may have adopted Goodrich's *History* during Joseph's attendance at school, it is much more likely that Joseph obtained this book on his own.

103. In my original essay, I misidentified Joseph's text as Murray's *English Reader* (1799). I am indebted to Colby Townsend for providing images of the schoolbook that allowed for the correction of this error. For references to Joseph's books, see John Henry Evans, *Joseph Smith: An American Prophet* (Salt Lake City: Deseret Book Co., 1989), 33, 436; and Marquardt, "Books Owned by Joseph Smith." Whether or not Joseph used this specific copy of Murray's *Introduction* during his common school years remains unknown.

104. In an 1867 reminiscence, Thomas Davies Burrall (1786–1872) of Geneva, New York, claimed that Joseph worked for him as a woodcutter "through the winter in company with some twenty or thirty others, rough back-woodsmen" (EMD 3:363–64). Burrall, however, did not provide a date for his account. He only offered an ambiguous reference: "I knew him [Joseph] well before his book [Book of Mormon] was published" (EMD 3:363). In 1912, Joel H. Monroe (1852/3–1935), a journalist and historian of local New York town histories, *speculated* that this event occurred "from about 1812 to 1820," casting a wide eight-year estimate (*A Century and a Quarter of History: Geneva* [Geneva, New York: Joel H. Monroe; W.F. Humphrey, printer, 1921], 41). Monroe himself, however, was not always sure about the accuracy of his dates. In the

education in Manchester would have ranged from a minimum of one winter term (1820–21) to a maximum of five winter terms (1820–25).

---

preface to his work, Monroe acknowledged that his history was "not free from errors, perhaps glaring ones" and that some of the errors "may be in the names or the dates, or possibly in the matter of detail." Even so, using Monroe's dates for reference, Vogel concludes that "Burrall obviously employed a much older man named 'Joe Smith' and confused him with the Mormon prophet" (EMD 3:363). This interpretation, however, remains problematic. Monroe provides no evidence to support his dates, and his estimate does not align well with contemporary events. Burrall, for example, apparently did not purchase his property until 1814 (see EMD 3:363; Charles F. Milliken, *A History of Ontario County, New York, and Its People*, vol. 1 [New York: Lewis Historical Publishing, 1911], 358). The purchase, moreover, reflected Burrall's effort to make a transition from his career as a real estate lawyer to working on agricultural projects and inventions. Yet, he continued to work as an attorney at least through the end of 1817, before shifting his full attention to agricultural pursuits (see, e.g., "For Sale, Two Hundred Acres," *Geneva Gazette*, Dec. 24, 1817, 4). In 1822, he became a town manager in the Ontario Agricultural Society and was given the honor of addressing the entire organization ("Officers of the Ontario Agricultural Society, Elected Oct. 22, 1822," *Ontario Repository*, Nov. 5, 1822, 2; Thomas D. Burrall, *Address, Delivered Before the Ontario Agricultural Society, at its Fourth Annual Meeting, October 22, 1822* [Canandaigua: James D. Bemis and Co., 1822]; see also Douglas C. McMurtrie, "A Bibliography of Books, Pamphlets and Broadsides Printed at Canandaigua, New York, 1799–1850," in *Grosvenor Library Bulletin*, 21, no. 4 [June 1939]: 83). Notably, the following year, in late 1823, when he started his second term as an officer, Burrall began working with Martin Harris, who had just been elected as one of the two town managers representing Palmyra. These officers and town managers belonged to a small and select group of fifty-four men in all, and Burrall and Harris would most certainly have become acquainted no later than this period. During the same October 1823 county fair, held in Canandaigua, New York, Burrall and Harris both made a big splash. Burrall showcased his popular invention "of a machine for threshing and cleaning Clover Seed," while Harris won several awards for "the best Cotton and Woolen Coverlet" and "the best 20 yards bleached Linen Cloth," among other prizes (see "Farmer's Holiday," *Ontario Repository*, Nov. 4, 1823, 2; "Farmer's Holiday" *Wayne Sentinel*, Nov. 12, 1823, 3; "Officers of the Ontario Agricultural Society," *Wayne Sentinel*, Nov. 19, 1823, 3). The fairs were major countywide events, drawing crowds of all ages and circumstances, and the heightened attention that Burrall and Harris received would have presented an ideal situation for contact with members of the Smith family. Farmers throughout the region gathered to display their goods and produce, while discussing business, visiting family and friends, and sharing news. For laborers seeking work, the annual gatherings were ideal locations to meet landowners and farmers looking for hired hands. Burrall's account thus remains credible, with a possible *terminus post quem* of meeting members of the Smith family in 1822, the year he became a town manager and delivered a prominent speech to the Ontario Agricultural Society, rather than Monroe's guess of "about 1812 to 1820." Moreover, contrary to Monroe's speculations, the historical circumstances in connection with Burrall's account—the transitions in his personal career, his prominent entry into the Ontario Agricultural Society, his acquaintance with Martin Harris, and his fame at the 1823 Canandaigua fair—are more consistent with events in the early to mid 1820s. The claim that Joseph Smith worked for Thomas Burrall also remained part of Burrall family lore. In 1885, Elisha Jenkins Burrall (1827–87), Thomas' oldest son, presented a paper to the Geneva Historical Society, in which he reaffirmed his father's assertion (see "Geneva Historical Society," *Geneva Advertiser*, Jan. 13, 1885, 3). For some of these sources and observations, I am indebted to Dale R. Broadhurst's notes; see www.sidneyrigdon.com/dbroadhu/NY/miscNYS3.htm.

SOUTH BAINBRIDGE, NEW YORK: 1825–26

The final location in this review of Joseph's formal education is South Bainbridge, New York. In October 1825, Josiah Stowell hired Joseph Jr. to work as a scryer for a team of treasure hunters. A few months later, Joseph was arrested and stood trial in Bainbridge on March 20, 1826, accused of being a "disorderly person and an Impostor."[105] According to court documents, Joseph admitted to working for Stowell as a treasure-hunting seer but asserted that the majority of his time was spent working on Stowell's farm "and going to school."[106] Stowell's son, Josiah Jr., corroborated the court record in an 1843 letter, in which he claimed, "I have been intimately acquainted with him [Joseph Smith Jr.]. He then was about 20 years old or there about. I also went to school with him one winter."[107] Another student, Asa B. Searles, also claimed to have attended school with Smith in Bainbridge.[108]

When he started school with Josiah Jr., Joseph was nineteen years old and would turn twenty in the course of the winter term. From a modern perspective, Joseph's advanced age for such instruction might seem awkward, but no doubt his history of intermittent attendance contributed to his desire to participate. The circumstances surrounding his attendance, however, urge caution against the exclusive assumption that Joseph's attendance derived from a desire to fill any potential gaps in his education. For instance, as an older student in Chenango County, Joseph was certainly not alone. The county was consistently one of the highest in the state for teaching youths both younger and older than the statewide category of students "between the ages of five and fifteen years." When he attended school, Smith was one of 238 students who fell outside the range of five to fifteen years, which amounted to 23.3 percent of the total 1,023 students taught. Assuming half of those students were older than fifteen (state statistics group the two age groups together), then roughly 12 percent of the students were older than the five-to-fifteen category. In other words, when Joseph, age nineteen, started the winter term in Chenango County, roughly 12 percent of

---

105. EMD 4:248–49.
106. EMD 4:249.
107. EMD 4:80 (spelling and punctuation modernized).
108. EMD 4:177.

his classmates were also older than fifteen.[109] Josiah Stowell Jr., in fact, who was born on April 16, 1809, was himself sixteen years old when he attended school with Joseph and would turn seventeen before the end of the school year. Thus, Joseph's attendance may reflect his desire to participate in the same activities as his peers as much as a personal desire to improve his education.[110]

Regardless of his reasoning, however, Joseph's time in school would not have been idle, and his age suggests an important role he may have played in the classroom. Older students were regularly enlisted as teaching assistants when the class was separated into groups, according to skill levels. For several years prior to this time, several New York schools were also experimenting with a new form of pedagogy known as the Lancasterian system.[111] In this model, older students, under direction of the schoolteacher, participated in the teaching process by guiding younger students in their exercises. It is possible that Smith may have been acting as a monitor, though the historical record is unfortunately silent on such details. Yet, such participation well may have influenced Joseph's desires to teach: he would eventually instruct members of the "school of the prophets" in grammar as well as teach

---

109. JA 50, vol. 1: Appendix A-13 (only eighteen of twenty-one school districts reported this year). In the 1825 school year, Bainbridge taught 225 students younger than five or older than fifteen (25.3 percent of the total number of students taught). See JA 49: Appendix G-8 (only sixteen of twenty school districts reported this year). In the 1824 school year, Bainbridge taught 248 (26.3 percent of the total number). See JA 48: Appendix B-4.

110. Winter terms took place when the work on farms was at a minimum, and the choice between working in the cold weather on a farm or finding shelter in the local schoolhouse with his new friends may well have influenced Joseph's motivations. Regarding older students attending common schools, Joseph's attendance was not anomalous. For instance, Oliver Culver, a twenty-five-year-old resident near Rochester, New York, was so determined to attend classes that he helped build his local schoolhouse. See Rick Grunder, *Mormon Parallels: A Bibliographic Source* (LaFayette, NY: Rick Grunder Books, 2014), 42.

111. On March 16, 1817, Gideon Hawley, proposed the introduction of the Lancasterian system ("Lancastrian") to selected schools in New York: "it is respectfully submitted, whether the time has not arrived when some provision ought to be made for the encouragement, and gradual introduction into our schools, of the Lancastrian system of education … The great principle, which forms the distinctive character of this system … is a kind of self teaching, which the scholars are made to undergo, by means of monitors selected from themselves" (JA 41:478). The experiment, however, did not last long. In 1844, Samuel S. Randall observed, "[A]fter an ephemeral and sickly existence, these institutions, from which such favorable results were expected, languished, and with few exceptions, disappeared" (*A Digest of the Common School System of the State of New-York* (Albany: State of New York, 1844], 25).

grammar to his family.[112] In any event, the 1825–26 winter term was likely the last time Smith attended class in a common school.

TALLYING THE TIME

Throughout this essay, I have revisited several of the claims and historical accounts regarding Joseph's formal education in an effort to interrogate popular notions regarding his level of literacy. A close examination of the existing evidence confirms that Joseph Sr. and Lucy faced significant challenges in providing a formal education for their children. Frequent relocation, illness, and financial exigencies contributed to a string of interruptions, resulting in gaps and intermittent school attendance over the years. At the same time, however, the historical accounts reflect the family's recognition of the importance of education and a persistent effort to obtain it. And if the available historical references provide relatively accurate representations, then the overall amount of Joseph's formal education requires significant upward revision.

Because the historical record does not precisely identify each and every term Joseph attended school, a number of speculative combinations can be formulated either to expand excessively or minimize unnecessarily the number of his years of formal education. On one hand, we might claim Joseph rarely attended school, regardless of the available evidence. On the other hand, we might claim Joseph attended, in full or in part, every school term that he would have been eligible to attend (excluding, of course, his times of illness and the summer terms when he was likely working), spanning from the 1809–10 winter term in Royalton, Vermont (the term in which Joseph turned four years of age and became eligible to attend school), to the 1825–26 term in South Bainbridge, New York (the last known school term Joseph attended, when he turned twenty years of age). In the latter case, the total number of school terms that Joseph was technically eligible to attend during those fifteen years would have included six full winter terms, six full summer terms, and nine partial winter terms—or approximately ten years of school (see Appendix A for a year-by-year breakdown).

---

112. In his journal entry of November 5, 1835, Joseph records, "[I]n the evening lectured on Grammar" (to the "school of the prophets"). Six days later, he states, "[R]eturned home and spent the evening, around my fire-side, teaching my family the science of grammar." See Dean C. Jessee, *Personal Writings of Joseph Smith*, 101–02, 109.

What Joseph actually experienced in his life, of course, would surely have occurred somewhere in between these two extremes. To that end, this essay attempts to minimize speculation by outlining a scenario of Joseph's participation in formal schooling that is grounded in direct and indirect historical references.

Junius Wells provides the first reference to Joseph's formal education by claiming that Joseph learned his letters from Deacon Jonathan Kinney in Vermont. This requires a minimum of one school term. If we assume Joseph did not begin school until the 1810 summer term (delaying his start until he was four and a half years old), and if we also assume the Smith family moved to West Lebanon in the fall of 1811, then Joseph could have attended school in Royalton for three full terms (summer 1810, winter 1810–11, summer 1811). Yet, this is the same period when Lucy claimed the Smith children had been deprived of the benefit of an education. Therefore, we limit the estimate of Joseph's time to the winter 1810–11 school term.

Next, assuming Lucy's dates, the Smith family moved to West Lebanon in the fall or winter 1811, which would allow Joseph to attend the 1812 school year (winter 1811–12 and summer 1812). As discussed earlier, Lucy stated in her history that all the Smith children who "were of sufficient age" were sent to a local common school. Joseph, who turned six during the 1811–12 winter term, would have been included. This brings the total amount of Joseph's formal education to two winter terms and one summer term, or approximately one and a half school years.

In 1812–13 winter, Joseph fell ill. Though he likely started the winter term, Joseph would have withdrawn early, as the leg surgery and subsequent convalescence would have prevented him from attending school for the remainder of the term. Joseph most likely missed the following summer 1813 term, as well. One year after Joseph's surgery, Lucy stated that everyone in the family returned to health. No longer bedridden, though still lame and using crutches, Joseph would have had the opportunity to return to school and pick up where he left off. Thus, between the first half of the 1812–13 winter term, combined with the latter half of the 1813–14 winter term, Joseph would add the equivalent of one more winter term. This raises the estimated amount of formal education to approximately two school years.

Even though Joseph remained on crutches until the family moved to Palmyra, Lucy's claim that all the children in the family returned to health further suggests that Joseph's condition allowed him to return to school for the remainder of the Smith family's time in the Upper Connecticut Valley. Furthermore, Joseph's continued physical challenges that would instead have prevented heavy farm labor would have allowed him to attend school during the summer terms. Nevertheless, for this estimate, I will *not* include any summer school sessions for this period. Rather, for the sake of argument, this scenario assumes that family exigencies did not permit Joseph to attend during these summers, though he was apparently physically capable to do so. This results in the equivalent of approximately one more year of formal school (winter 1814–15 and winter 1815–16). Joseph's total time in formal school would then be the equivalent of just over three years.

Sometime during winter 1816–17, Lucy and the children spent one month relocating to Palmyra, New York, from Norwich, Vermont. Once the family arrived, Lucy and Joseph Sr. appear to have enrolled the children in school for the remainder of the winter term (February and March). Between starting the winter term in Norwich, withdrawing to prepare for and complete the move to New York, and then finishing the term in Palmyra, the Smith children may have attended between two to three months for the winter 1816–17 term. This estimate limits the school time to the final two months in Palmyra, bringing Joseph's total school time to approximately three and a half years.

Shortly after their arrival in Palmyra, the Smiths held a family council and determined to pool their efforts in an attempt to get established. Therefore, in this scenario we will assume that Joseph, now eleven years old, began to work the same seasonal schedule as an adult, splitting his time between family labors and hiring out to local farms and employers. This also means that from this time forward, Joseph would miss all future summer school sessions. Furthermore, he would start late in every ensuing winter term (thus limiting his time in school to between four and five months per year). We also assume that Joseph worked this same schedule during every subsequent harvest season, both in Palmyra and Manchester. Using the property tax records as a guide, Joseph's partial attendance during the winters would include four months of each winter term in 1817–18, 1818–19, and 1819–20.

This brings to the total time to the equivalent of approximately five years of formal schooling.

Several accounts from former classmates indicate Joseph also attended school in Manchester, which indicates a minimum of one partial winter term (winter 1820–21). During this period, Joseph participated in a juvenile debate club, which reveals his interest in self-improvement—an activity that also suggests continued attendance at school. Furthermore, Joseph's possession of advanced school texts, particularly Murray's *Introduction* and Charles Goodrich's *A History of the United States of America*, alerts us to his level of achievement within the common school system (assuming, of course, that he used these texts during his common school education). Therefore, this estimate proposes that Joseph potentially attended school in Manchester during the 1820–21, 1821–22, and 1822–23 winter terms. This intermittent attendance equates to one school year and approximately four months, raising Joseph's total estimated time in formal school to six years and approximately four months. Finally, this stringent scenario assumes that Joseph did not attend school, in either the winter or summer terms, during the 1824 or 1825 school years. Thus, the last time Joseph attended a common school would be the 1825–26 winter term in South Bainbridge, Chenango County. This final term increases the overall estimated time that Joseph spent in formal education to the equivalent of approximately *seven full school years*—a notable increase to that proposed in previous historical representations, and one that requires the careful evaluation of future historians.

Because of the several gaps in the historical record, this estimate—a *conservative estimate*—can either be increased or decreased, according to any given historian's perceptions and intents. In any case, however, the overall combined effect of historical sources points to a higher amount of Joseph's formal education than is traditionally acknowledged. My aim, however, is not to assert a specific amount of time; other supportable estimates certainly exist. Rather, I want to highlight the implications that emerge when traditions and cultural contexts are brought into discussion with a detailed review of historical evidence: such incongruence, even when resistant to definitive measurements and final authoritative claims, opens windows to neglected historical narratives.

ANOTHER FACET OF JOSEPH'S LIFE

Joseph's transformation from an uneducated farm boy to a prophet of God remains deeply entangled in cultural traditions, religious identification, and the Mormon cosmology of faith. Yet, an excavation below the hagiographical representations reveals a narrative of Smith's life that is equally compelling for its resonance with the individual struggle for respect and self-determination. Regardless of whatever praise or criticism would be heaped upon his memory, Smith rose to prominence through determination, persistent hard work, and systematic self-improvement. Inevitably, Smith's formal study would surely have been complemented by *informal* avenues of education, including instruction at home, reading, attendance at Sunday school, participation in a juvenile debate society, and even his preparations to become a Methodist exhorter.[113] One could argue that Smith, like so many of his ambitious fellow citizens in a striving nation, was above all an autodidact. The story of a young man, struggling against economic disadvantages and intermittent opportunities to attend school, would be inspirational and serve as a model for Mormon ethics of industriousness and productivity, were it not overshadowed by the near-exclusive enlistment of Smith's early life, humble beginnings, and alleged "uneducated" background as evidence of divine manifestations. Neither would Smith be an easy target for critics hoping to portray him as an illiterate farm boy, who duped a bunch of so-called gullible and equally illiterate folk into following him. For below the surface of both idealized and demeaning stories, a persistent pattern of ambitious preparation begins to emerge, revealing the narrative of an individual's yearning to overcome seemingly insurmountable obstacles to achieve a prominent role in public life and religious leadership. Smith's story truly exemplifies the ideological aspirations and ambitions of early nineteenth-century Americans, though the narrative of his self-motivated ascendance has been pushed into the background. It is, however, a story that deserves more nuanced respect, greater attention, and continued research.

---

113. EMD 2:127; EMD 3:49–50.

APPENDIXES

APPENDIX A. Joseph Smith Jr. — Common School Years

School Term	Location	Age (b. 12/23/1805)	Notes
Winter 1809–10 (i.e., the start of the 1810 school year)	Royalton, VT	3 (turns 4 on Dec. 23)	Eligible to attend school
Summer 1810	Royalton, VT	4	Eligible to attend school
Winter 1810–11	Royalton, VT	4 (turns 5)	Eligible; attends a minimum of one school term in Royalton
Summer 1811	Royalton, VT, or West Lebanon, NH	5	Eligible[1]
Winter 1811–12	Royalton, VT, or West Lebanon, NH	5 (turns 6)	Eligible
Summer 1812	Royalton, VT, or West Lebanon, NH	6	Eligible
Winter 1812–13	West Lebanon, NH	6 (turns 7)	Typhoid epidemic; leg operation; winter term interrupted
Summer 1813	West Lebanon, NH (Salem, MA?)	7	Bedridden, convalescing
Winter 1813–14	West Lebanon, NH	7 (turns 8)	Eligible to return to school; on crutches
Summer 1814	West Lebanon, NH	8	Eligible; on crutches, no heavy labor
Winter 1814–15	West Lebanon, NH, or Norwich, VT	8 (turns 9)	Eligible;[2] on crutches
Summer 1815	Norwich, VT	9	Eligible; on crutches
Winter 1815–16	Norwich, VT	9 (turns 10)	Eligible; on crutches
Summer 1816	Norwich, VT	10	Eligible; on crutches
Winter 1816–17	Norwich to Palmyra, NY	10 (turns 11)	The family moves 300 miles; winter term interrupted
Summer 1817	Palmyra, NY	11	Eligible, but likely starts working[3]
Winter 1817–18	Palmyra, NY	11 (turns 12)	Eligible; attends a minimum of one school term in Palmyra
Summer 1818	Palmyra, NY	12	Likely working

School Term	Location	Age (b. 12/23/1805)	Notes
Winter 1818–19	Palmyra, Main Street, and Palmyra, Stafford Road	12 (turns 13)	Eligible
Summer 1819	Palmyra, Main Street, and Palmyra, Stafford Road	13	Likely working
Winter 1819–20	Palmyra, Main Street, and Palmyra, Stafford Road; working Manchester farm (Farmington)	13 (turns 14)	Eligible[4]
Summer 1820	Palmyra, Main Street, and Palmyra, Stafford Road; Palmyra to Manchester (Farmington)	14	Likely working out of town[5]
Winter 1820–21	Palmyra, Stafford Road; Palmyra to Manchester (Farmington)[6]	14 (turns 15)	Eligible; attends a minimum of one school term in Manchester
Summer 1821	Palmyra, Stafford Road;[7] Manchester (Farmington)	15	Likely working; unlikely at school
Winter 1821–22	Palmyra, Stafford Road;[8] Manchester formally separates from Farmington	15 (turns 16)	Eligible
Summer 1822	Manchester	16	Likely working
Winter 1822–23	Manchester	16 (turns 17)	Eligible
Summer 1823	Manchester	17	Likely working
Winter 1823–24	Manchester	17 (turns 18)	Eligible
Summer 1824	Manchester	18	Likely working
Winter 1824–25	Manchester	18 (turns 19)	Eligible
Summer 1825	Manchester	19	Likely working
Winter (1825–26)	South Bainbridge	19 (turns 20)	Attends school

Summary

Minimum number of school terms attended: 4 (one per town: Royalton, Palmyra, Manchester, South Bainbridge)

Number of winter terms eligible for attendance: 15

Number of summer terms eligible for attendance: 6
Equivalency in eligible full school years: 10.5 (approx.)

Notes

1. The precise timing of the Smiths' move to West Lebanon is unknown. Either the Smiths moved between school terms in 1811 or 1812 (not affecting the children's schooling), or they moved at a time that would have partially interfered with the winter term. The move was regional, approximately twenty-three miles, which would have minimized the amount of school time lost.
2. The timing of the seven-mile move to Norwich, Vermont, is unknown. If it occurred during a school term, the impact would have been minimal.
3. Joseph may have started working summers to assist the family.
4. Though the family might have started developing the Manchester farm prior to a formal contract to purchase the land, the Smiths were not yet Manchester taxpayers. The children would likely have continued attending school in Palmyra.
5. Vogel observes that "both Joseph Jr. and Samuel Harrison are missing from the 1820 census, perhaps because they were hired out in another township" (EMD 5:391).
6. Vogel notes, "Joseph Sr. and Alvin contract with Zachariah Seymour for 100 acres of the Evertson land in Farmington [later Manchester]. ... This occurred after Seymour received power of attorney for the land on 14 July 1820 and before 5 February 1821" (EMD 5:391). In terms of schooling, the same date range applies to the earliest timing for the Smith children's eligibility to attend school in Manchester.
7. Vogel notes that Lucy Smith, daughter to Joseph Sr. and Lucy, "is born in Palmyra (NY), perhaps indicating that the Smiths had not yet moved to Farmington" (EMD 5:392).
8. Vogel observes how in April 1822, "Joseph Sr. and Alvin appear on the Palmyra road list, indicating that the Smiths had not yet moved to their Farmington (Manchester) property" (EMD 5:392).

APPENDIX B. Common School Statistics for Palmyra, Manchester (Farmington), and Bainbridge, 1817–26[1]

PALMYRA	1817	1818	1819	1820	1821	1822	1823	1824	1825	1826
School Year	1817	1818	1819	1820	1821	1822	1823	1824	1825	1826
Joseph's Age	11	12	13	14	15	16	17	18	19	20
Overall Students Taught	NA*	987	908	1,100	1,253	1,276	628	690	685	777
Students 5–15 Years	NA‡	1,050	886	1,025	1,048	1,109	552	582	608	687
Students under 5, over 15	NA	NA	22 (2.5%)	75 (6.8%)	205 (16.4%)	167 (13.1%)	76 (12%)	108 (15.7%)	77 (11.2%)	90 (11.6%)
School Districts	NA	18†	20	20	25	22	9	10	10	11
Districts Reporting	NA	NA	16	20	20	21	9	10	10	11
Average Months School in Session	NA	NA	NA	8	5††	7	7	8	8	8

From 1817 to 1823, Palmyra statistics are recorded under Ontario County; from 1823 to 1826, Palmyra statistics are recorded under Wayne County.
*Palmyra did not submit a report for the 1817 school year.
‡Shaded areas indicate Joseph's age group and potential location for school attendance.
†This figure likely indicates the number of school districts that reported, rather than the total number of districts (in 1816, Palmyra created a twentieth school district).[2]
††This figure is likely a misprint.

MANCHESTER (FARMINGTON)*

School Year	1817	1818	1819	1820	1821	1822	1823	1824	1825	1826
Joseph's Age	11	12	13	14	15	16	17	18	19	20
Overall Students Taught	675	984	977	1,215	1,051	1,236	770	850	985	987
Students 5–15 Years	790	852	1,028	1,113	972‡	1,162	710	767	806	821
Students under 5, over 15	NA	132 (13.4%)	NA	102 (8.4%)	79 (7.5%)	74 (6%)	60 (7.8%)	83 (9.8%)	179 (18.2%)	166 (16.8%)
School Districts	18	14†	18	22	21	18	11	12	13	13
Districts Reporting	NA	NA	17	19	14	18	10	12	13	13
Average Months School in Session	NA	NA	NA	7	8	8	7	8	8	8

*1817–21 statistics are for Farmington (Manchester not yet created); in 1822, Farmington and Manchester filed a joint report; 1823–26 statistics are for Manchester.

‡Shaded areas indicate Joseph's age group and potential location for school attendance (statewide inconsistencies in a standard for determining who qualified as a fifteen-year-old means Smith could have been counted in either category for 1821).

†This figure likely represents the number of districts reporting, rather than total number of districts.

REASSESSING JOSEPH SMITH JR.'S FORMAL EDUCATION

BAINBRIDGE, CHENANGO COUNTY

School Year	1817	1818	1819	1820	1821	1822	1823	1824	1825	1826
Joseph's Age	11	12	13	14	15	16	17	18	19	20
Overall Students Taught	642	567	772	744	721	866	838	943	891	1,023
Students 5–15 Years	537	457	607	571	544	699	679	695	666	785
Students under 5, over 15	105 (16.4%)	110 (19.4%)	165 (21.4%)	173 (23.3%)	177 (24.6%)	167 (19.3%)	159 (19%)	248 (26.3%)	225 (25.3%)	238‡ (23.3%)
School Districts	17	17	18	21	18	19	20	19	20	21
Districts Reporting	12	11	16	13	14	17	18	19	16	18
Average Months School in Session	NA	NA	NA	6	8	8	7	7	7	6

‡Shaded area indicates Joseph's age group and location for school attendance.

71

Notes

1. For 1817 statistics, see JA 41:480, 484, 490. For 1818, JA 42:443, 447. For 1819, JA 43:474, 479, 480. For 1820, JA 44:559 [published typo reads 259], 562. For 1821, JA 45:626, 632. For 1822, JA 46: Appendix A-5, A-11. For 1823, JA 47: Appendix A-4, A-12, A-20. For 1824, JA 48:B4, B13, B21. For 1825, JA 49: Appendix G-8, G-20, G-30. For 1826, JA 50, vol. 1: Appendix A-13, A-20, A-27.
2. See Town of Palmyra, "Town of Palmyra Board Meeting Minutes," Palmyra, New York: Town and Village of Palmyra, 1816, www.palmyrany.com/minutes/TB/1816.pdf.

THREE

OPEN CANONS
SACRED HISTORY AND AMERICAN HISTORY
IN *THE BOOK OF MORMON*

ELIZABETH FENTON

The story of Joseph Smith Jr. discovering and translating, through divine revelation, a set of golden plates buried in the forest in upstate New York is by now a commonplace in accounts of the nineteenth-century United States.[1] After all, that story is also the story of the emergence of Mormonism, one of the largest and longest lasting "homegrown" US religions. Far less familiar, to non-Mormons anyway, is the book that resulted from Smith's purported translation process. The bulk of *The Book of Mormon's*[2] narration follows the story of the descendants of Lehi, a prophet who flees Jerusalem with his family prior to the Babylonian captivity. Lehi's son, Nephi, receives a divine vision instructing him to build a ship and migrate to what is now known as the Western Hemisphere. This proposition angers Nephi's brothers, Laman and Lemuel, and in the aftermath of the journey, the family splits into two groups: the Nephites and the Lamanites. *The Book of Mormon* recounts centuries of war between these groups, culminating in a final battle that decimates the Nephites and leaves America to the Lamanites. Within this set of narratives lies another, much briefer account of an earlier westward migration—that of the Jaredites, who relocate to the Americas after the fall of the Tower of Babel described in Genesis. Covering roughly a thousand years and hundreds of characters, *The*

---

1. For a detailed account of Smith's early life and purported discovery of the plates, see Terryl Givens, *By the Hand of Mormon: The American Scripture That Launched a New World Religion* (New York: Oxford University Press, 2002).

2. I prefer to italicize the title of the book throughout this piece because I treat it as a literary text and not as scripture.

Book of Mormon is a sweeping epic in which Israelite families form the foundation of indigenous America.[3]

At the close of *The Book of Mormon*'s main narrative, the sole Nephite survivor, Moroni, is left alone to write the final chapter of his people's history. Despite his willingness, Moroni discovers that his circumstances are not conducive to history writing. "My father hath made this record," he writes, "and behold, I would write it also, if I had room upon the plates; but I have not; and ore I have none, for I am alone."[4] The "plates" in question are an abridged copy of records engraved on sheets of metal (hence Moroni's need for ore), passed down through, and written by, many generations of Nephites. Moroni's father, Mormon, collated and buried the original plates, hiding "up in the hill of Camorah, all the records which had been entrusted to [him] by the hand of the Lord," then instructed his son to write the conclusion of the Nephites' story (529). In attempting to write his portion of the history, then, Moroni endeavors to complete something that has been rendered permanently incomplete. Working with a smaller set of redacted plates, the son undertakes his own engraving with a series of false starts, stops, and abridgments. "Were it possible," he writes, "I would make all things known unto you" (532). The implication, of course, is that the formulation of a complete historical narrative is impossible. Though he is the only voice remaining in *The Book of Mormon*, Moroni highlights his inability to tell the story with which he has been entrusted, making such assertions as "I cannot write them," "I do not write those things," and "I was about to write more, but I

---

3. The theory of Hebraic American origins was by no means new in 1830. Most early writings on the subject, however, specifically linked indigenous Americans to the ten lost tribes of Israel. Smith's text is thus unique, in that it posits an alternate Hebraic origin for indigenous Americans. For more on the myth of the lost tribes, see Zvi Ben-Dor Benite, *The Ten Lost Tribes: A World History* (Oxford: Oxford University Press, 2009). For more on the theory of Hebraic American origins, see Richard W. Cogley's essays, "The Ancestry of the American Indians: Thomas Thorowgood's *Iewes in America* (1650) and *Jews in America* (1660)," *English Literary Renaissance* 35, no. 2 (2005): 304–30; and " 'Some Other Kinde of Being and Condition': The Controversy in Mid-Seventeenth-Century England over the Peopling of Ancient America," *Journal of the History of Ideas* 68, no. 1 (Jan. 2007): 35–56.

4. Joseph Smith, *The Book of Mormon: The Original 1830 Edition* (Berkeley, CA: Apocryphile Press, 2005), 523. All subsequent references are to this edition and appear parenthetically in the text. Although it is customary to cite passages from *The Book of Mormon* using a chapter and verse notation similar to that used for the Bible, the 1830 edition of the book did not break the text into these units. As I am citing a facsimile of that edition, I will use page numbers for my citations.

am forbidden" (533, 539, 567). An ostensible account of the ancient peoples of the Americas, the book presents the compiling of American history as a process fraught with erasure, failure, and loss.

It is fitting that *The Book of Mormon* finishes its tale with the laments of a frustrated historian, because much of the book is preoccupied with the process of compiling and interpreting records. Perhaps the only thing less familiar than the book's narrative is its complex structure. Like the Bible, Smith's book is not a single text but a composite of several books. Unlike the Bible, however, *The Book of Mormon* provides its own manuscript history, often describing the conditions under which it ostensibly is being written. It derives its name from its purported editor, the aforementioned prophet-historian Mormon, who compiled, copied, and abridged accounts from different sets of metal plates. The book asserts that Nephi created two sets of plates—one small, one large—sometime around 600 BCE. These plates contain references to and partial copies of a third set of plates, made of brass, containing the genealogy of Lehi and several books of the Hebrew Bible. According to Mormon mythology, in the fourth century CE, Mormon abridged the large plates of Nephi, added his own commentary, and combined them with the small plates. Moroni later abridged and added the plates of Ether (which tell the story of the Jaredites) to the mix and added his own final commentaries. Smith's "golden bible," then, appears as a translation of a set of plates that are copies of other plates, and even copies of copies in some instances. Plates within plates and writing about writing not only frame but also are an integral component of its action; thus *The Book of Mormon* operates both as a history and as an account of history making.

This essay will treat *The Book of Mormon* not as a history but as a text deeply concerned with the production and preservation of historical documents. Historicist scholarship on the book has situated it, I think appropriately, within the context of both the revivalism of the Second Great Awakening and the dynamic religious cultures at work in the Burned-Over District of pre-Civil War New York.[5] But as Lindsay

5. Jan Shipps, for example, notes that Smith's use of "seer stones" was in step with contemporary "money digging" practices and the region's "folk magic" (*Mormonism: The Story of a New Religious Tradition* [Urbana: University of Illinois Press, 1987], 10). And in his foundational study, Gordon Wood argues that early Mormonism's appeal lay in its reconciliation of "the ecstatic antinomian visions of people with the discipline of a hierarchical

DiCuirci demonstrates, antiquarianism emerged alongside revivalism in pre-1860 United States, and the Second Great Awakening "was just as historical as it was religious in its ideological thrust, for an integral part of American Puritan theology was a belief in God's guiding hand in history."[6] Her study of efforts to reprint Cotton Mather's *Magnalia Christi Americana* aptly shows that the era was as much characterized by what David Van Tassel calls "Documania"—the impulse to compile and preserve records—as it was by the desire to fashion a more authentic Christian experience.[7] Indeed, in the pre-Civil War United States these processes were inseparable. But where the documents produced and preserved by evangelical Protestants and antiquarians aim "to establish a sustaining historical narrative of America's development from colony to nation," *The Book of Mormon* offers a radical revision of American history that presents both documania and the Puritan errand as dead ends. Through its frequent and fraught depictions of record keeping, the book highlights the impossibility of compiling an accurate account of the past even as it offers an alternative history of the Americas. In so doing, I argue, Smith's text not only establishes a narrative precedent for the critique of US Protestantism that would come to form the backbone of early Mormonism but also importantly reframes American Christianity as a cyclical rather than linear phenomenon. Christianity is the ancient if dormant force driving American history, and just as the hemisphere's indigenous inhabitants seem to have forgotten their Christian roots, so too might its European settlers.

Despite its status as the foundational document of one of the nation's most successful, domestically produced religions, *The Book of Mormon* has received relatively little attention from scholars of American religion and culture. Over twenty years ago, Nathan Hatch noted that "for all the recent attention given to the study of Mormonism,

---

church," which made it "a popular version of the elitist churchly reaction to revivalism that began in the second and third decades of the nineteenth century" ("Evangelical America and Early Mormonism," in *Critical Issues in American Religious History: A Reader*, ed. Robert R. Mathisen [Waco, TX: Baylor University Press, 2001], 190).

6. Lindsay DiCuirci, "Reviving Puritan History: Evangelicalism, Antiquarianism, and Mather's Magnalia in Antebellum America," *Early American Literature* 45, no. 3 (2010): 565–92, 572.

7. David D. Van Tassel, *Recording America's Past: An Interpretation of the Development of Historical Studies in America, 1607–1884* (Chicago: University of Chicago Press, 1960), 103.

surprisingly little has been devoted to *The Book of Mormon* itself."[8] With a few notable exceptions, this omission continues. One reason for this may be that the book's actual contents have never been its most important feature within or beyond Mormon practice. As Terry Givens argues: "This American scripture has exerted influence within the church and reaction outside the church not primarily by virtue of its substance, but rather its manner of appearing, not on the merits of what it *says*, but what it *enacts*."[9] Because Mormonism's truth claims rest on the conditions under which Smith produced the book, *The Book of Mormon*'s very existence has seemed perhaps more significant than the stories it tells.[10] But to borrow Paul Gutjahr's phrasing, the "rare ability to influence readers toward radical life change makes *The Book of Mormon*, one of America's first indigenous sacred texts, worthy of thoughtful and prolonged investigation."[11] It, in other words, is a blind spot that American studies must address.

If scholars of American religious cultures have focused on *The Book of Mormon*'s composition and reception, literary critics have ignored the text almost entirely. This may owe to several factors, one of which is undoubtedly the book's claim to sacred status. In the last half-century, Americanist literary criticism has organized itself around a narrative

---

8. Nathan O. Hatch, *The Democratization of American Christianity* (New Haven, CT: Yale University Press, 1989), 115.

9. Givens, *By the Hand of Mormon*, 64.

10. Philip Barlow notes that treatments of the book have tended to focus on Smith's relation to its composition, presenting him as either "a prophet in the most fundamentalist sense," "a charlatan," or "a mentally deranged charismatic" ("Joseph Smith's Revision of the Bible: Fraudulent, Pathologic, or Prophetic?" *Harvard Theological Review* 83, no. 1 [Jan. 1990]: 45–64, 45). As Shipps shows, the division characterizing the reception of Smith's text centers on temporality, because the book's claim to sacred status is inseparable from its claim to ancient origins. Critics "have regarded the book from the first as a nineteenth-century document composed by a nineteenth-century man completely concerned with nineteenth-century matters," while believers deem it "at one and the same time, a nineteenth-century document and an ancient record, a book and more than a book" (28). To treat *The Book of Mormon* as a nineteenth-century artifact is to de facto take a position on its relationship to the divine. This may be another reason why scholars of the nineteenth century typically have shied away from the text—the book itself resists inclusion within the canon of texts from this period, and situating it within nineteenth-century concerns might seem a mark of disrespect as well as disbelief. But I would suggest that, like all complex texts, *The Book of Mormon* certainly can withstand a variety of approaches.

11. Paul Gutjahr, "The Golden Bible in the Bible's Golden Age: *The Book of Mormon* and Antebellum Print Culture," *American Transcendental Quarterly* 12, no. 4 (Dec. 1998): 275.

of secularization, which presents the nation as gradually exchanging faith for reason and embracing Enlightenment modes of epistemology over the course of the nineteenth century.[12] The complementary notions that there is a clear distinction between the "religious" and the "secular," and that the study of literature has shifted from a religious to a secular pursuit, are essential components of the story of the discipline.[13] Within this disciplinary structure, a bible published in the era of Enlightenment seems at best a quaint anachronism and at worst a direct challenge to progressive theories of US history. But as Grant Hardy's excellent work on *The Book of Mormon*'s narrators has demonstrated, literary analysis offers a means of understanding this important work without either falling back on or merely resisting its truth claims. "Adopting a path of narrative interpretation is not to deny the problematic archaeology or anachronisms that can make *The Book*

---

12. As I have noted elsewhere, perhaps the most famous, foundational articulation of this narrative is Perry Miller's essay "Jonathan Edwards to Emerson," which, Joanna Brooks argues, "gave us the gentlest and most elegant way of telling the children that at some point even the best and brightest Puritans could keep it up no longer ... and that it was, finally, really, *okay* because it gave us *literature*" (see Fenton, "The Secularization Narrative and Nineteenth-Century American Literature," in *A Companion to American Literary Studies*, ed. Robert S. Levine and Caroline Levander [Cambridge, MA: Blackwell, 2011]; and Joanna Brooks, "From Edwards to Baldwin: Heterodoxy, Discontinuity, and New Narratives of American Religious-Literary History," *American Literary History* 22, no. 2 [2010]: 426). Susan Griffin brilliantly demonstrates that literary critical reading practices themselves have been structured by religious assumptions about texts and textual meaning in "Threshing Floors: A Response to Joanna Brooks," *American Literary History* 22, no. 2 (2010).

13. Tracy Fessenden recently has argued, "Disinclination to engage religion (except perhaps when it appears in the past, where it belongs) is not incidental to what scholars of literature do ... a byproduct of some much larger and relatively straightforward process called 'secularization,' but instead goes deeply to the making of professional identity" ("'The Secular' as Opposed to What?" *New Literary History* 38, no. 4 [2007]: 632). For a detailed discussion of the secularization narrative in literary studies, see Michael Kaufmann "The Religious, the Secular, and Literary Studies: Rethinking the Secularization Narrative in Histories of the Profession," *New Literary History* 38, no. 4 (2007). The study of secularism as a complex matrix of discourses, structures, and experiences—rather than the mere opposite or absence of religion—is a relatively recent but critical development in the study of culture. Important works on this topic include Talal Asad, *Formations of the Secular: Christianity, Islam, Modernity* (Stanford, CA: Stanford University Press, 2003); Tomoko Masuzawa, *The Invention of World Religions, or, How European Universalism Was Preserved in the Language of Pluralism* (Chicago: University of Chicago Press, 2005); Vincent Pecora, *Secularization and Cultural Criticism: Religion, Nation, and Modernity* (Chicago: University of Chicago Press, 2006); Rajeev Bhargava, ed., *Secularism and Its Critics* (New York: Oxford University Press, 2005); and Michael Warner, Jonathan VanAntwerpen, and Craig J. Calhoun, eds., *Varieties of Secularism in a Secular Age* (Cambridge, MA: Harvard University Press, 2010).

of Mormon difficult to take seriously," he acknowledges, but he also rightly asserts that "non-Mormons who are willing to suspend disbelief long enough to read through the text attentively, on its own terms, may discover something of the literary power and religious vision that make it so convincing to Latter-Day Saints."[14] I certainly agree, and I hold particularly that careful attention to the book allows us to see just how vexed and contested something as ostensibly simple as the story of the origins of American Christianity was in the pre-1860 United States.

At stake in *The Book of Mormon*'s many depictions of vexed history making and textual inadequacy is the broader question of canonicity. As David Holland's work on this subject has demonstrated, *The Book of Mormon* emerged at a time when numerous groups in the United States—from Shakers to Transcendentalists—contested the notion of a closed sacred canon. Smith's text, Holland explains, "repeatedly takes aim at a religious culture that offered a priori resistance to 'more' of God's words," and that it presents itself as "one of many [divinely revealed] books that will ultimately come to light."[15] I concur with Holland's assessment but would contend that *The Book of Mormon*'s challenge to the biblical canon is inseparable from its presentation of an alternate American history. *The Book of Mormon* complicates not only the collection of books comprising the Hebrew Bible and New Testament but also the historical documentation that Smith's contemporaries were compiling to tell the story of US Protestant history. Though they are history's heroes in the Protestant documentation Dicuirci's work has excavated, Anglo-Protestants appear only in the margins of *The Book of Mormon*, and their role in American history is vexed at best. This essay will examine three modes through which Smith's text challenges the idea of a closed canon—historical as well as biblical. The first section examines *The Book of Mormon*'s engagements with biblical texts to show how it complicates the very notion of an ur-text and offers a model of sacred history that depends upon iteration and proliferation. The second section demonstrates that, through descriptions of its own faulty composition process, the book becomes itself an "open" text. In

---

14. Grant Hardy, *Understanding The Book of Mormon* (New York: Oxford University Press, 2010), xviii.

15. David Holland, *Sacred Borders: Continuing Revelation and Canonical Restraint in Early America* (New York: Oxford University Press, 2011),147.

this way, the book offers a radical and capacious picture of canonicity itself, which, I argue in the essay's concluding section, structures the book's history of ancient America. As the text rewrites the story of colonialism, it presents an iterative history at odds with and critical of teleological understandings of American Christianity.

MORMON GRAFTING AND THE OPEN BIBLE

The fifth chapter of the Book of Jacob presents a parable comparing Israel "unto a tame olive tree, which a man took and nourished in his vineyard; and it grew, and waxed old, and began to decay" (131). In an effort to save the tree, the vineyard owner instructs his servant to "go and pluck the branches from a wild olive tree, and bring them hither … and graft them in"; at the same time, the owner proposes to "take away many of these young and tender branches [from the old tree], and … graft them withersoever I will" (131–32). In what follows, the vineyard keeper experiences much disappointment, as the grafted trees produce good and bad fruit alike. In the end, having decided to graft "the branches of the natural tree … into the natural branches of the tree," the owner yields a satisfying crop but promises that "when the time cometh that evil fruit shall again come into my vineyard … my vineyard will I cause to be burned with fire" (137–39). Although Jacob provides an interpretation of the parable that overlays its imagery onto human relations with the divine—"how blessed are they who have labored diligently in his vineyard" (139)— the conceit of grafting structures *The Book of Mormon*'s presentations of history, particularly when it comes to the book's relationship to the Bible. If grafting is the process of inserting or transplanting a piece of one body into that of another in order to form a seamless and indissoluble union, then *The Book of Mormon* both includes "grafts" of the Bible and grafts itself back onto biblical texts. In this way, Jacob's parable offers a framework through which to understand *The Book of Mormon*'s engagements with sacred history. Though the grafting process aims to produce a new whole, it is as an act of laceration as well as repair, highlighting the incompleteness of both its source and its recipient. In this way, it operates as a supplement of the Derridean kind, adding "only to replace," highlighting the very gap it would address, and compensating "for what *ought* to lack nothing at all in

80

itself."[16] Jacob's olive tree thus stands as a figure of impossible unity. Despite a successful attachment of scion to stock, the vineyard keeper looks ahead to the tree's ultimate immolation; the olive tree's status is neither permanent nor secure.

It is important to note that the parable of the olive tree not only describes grafting but also operates as a kind of grafting itself. Jacob's parable iterates a passage from the eleventh chapter of the New Testament Book of Romans, which asks: "For if thou wert cut out of the olive tree which is wild by nature, and wert graffed contrary to nature into a good olive tree: how much more shall these, which be the natural branches, be graffed into their own olive tree?" (v. 24).[17] This is one of *The Book of Mormon*'s many moments of textual time travel. The book dates itself using biblical markers—the Tower of Babel, Babylonian captivity, the birth of Jesus—and its events are presented as synchronous with Christian sacred history. And yet Smith's text often presents biblical language out of this sequence. Jacob's parable, within *The Book of Mormon*'s internal chronology, predates Paul's writing of Romans by nearly 600 years and thus appears as both an impossible citation and a prefiguration. Mormonism's detractors have pointed to these anachronisms as proof of the book's fraudulence, arguing that Smith cribbed from the King James Bible, while believers contend that such moments demonstrate the close relationship between canonical Christian texts and *The Book of Mormon*. What matters for this essay, though, are the ways in which *The Book of Mormon*'s presentations of biblical passages complicate the distinction between source material and copy, between, in other words, the graft and the body to which it is grafted. A citation of Romans that ostensibly predates Paul's birth opens up a space in which it is possible to consider *The Book of Mormon* as the ur-text for the passage, rather than Paul's letter. The parable thus destabilizes orthodox Christian claims about the Bible's originality and completeness, threatening to decenter New Testament writings and replace them with itself.

Many of *The Book of Mormon*'s engagements with the King James Bible take the form of repetition with a difference. The perhaps most

---

16. Jacques Derrida, *Of Grammatology*, trans. Gayatri Spivak (Baltimore, MD: Johns Hopkins University Press, 1998), 145.

17. I use the King James Version of the Bible throughout this essay.

radical of these appears in its story of the brass plates. Lehi's escape from Jerusalem hinges on scenes of what might be deemed antiquarian violence, as he receives a revelation regarding significant historical records. "Laban hath the record of the Jews," Lehi tells his son Nephi, "and also a genealogy of my forefathers, and they are engraven upon plates of brass." The crux of this scene is Lehi's command that Nephi "go unto the house of Laban, and seek the records, and bring them down hither into the wilderness" (9). Initial efforts fail, as Laban refuses Nephi's offer of exchange for "our gold, and our silver, and all our precious things" (11). At this point, documania reaches a fevered pitch. Nephi returns to Laban's house, discovers him in a drunken sleep, and receives a divine command to "slay him, for the Lord hath delivered him into thy hands" (12). On one level, this story is a grafting similar to that of Jacob's parable, because it recalls the well-known biblical tale of David's finding Saul asleep in 1 Samuel. Although the stories end quite differently—David spares Saul, while Nephi decapitates Laban—the similarity of language is unmistakable: David's companion urges him to kill, arguing, "God hath delivered thine enemy into thine hand this day" (1 Sam. 24:8). The repetition of this scene aligns Nephi with David, who holds a prominent place in Christian mythology as both a king of Israel and an ancestor of Jesus. At the same time, in presenting the divine command Nephi executes in the same language as the human suggestion David refuses, *The Book of Mormon* threatens to supplant the story of David with that of Nephi. This moment of iteration, then, carries the trace of the older text while simultaneously over-matching it. In the service of record keeping, Nephi will do what David would not. The brass plates raise the question of gaps in the biblical record through the specter of synchronicity. Ownership of these plates is non-negotiable, because they offer "a genealogy of [Lehi's] fathers; wherefore he knew that he was a descendant of Joseph; yea, even that Joseph who was the son of Jacob, who was sold into Egypt" (15). The grafting achieved in this passage marks the suturing of one family tree into another. The "Jacob" in question is the grandson of Abraham, the Genesis patriarch who receives the divine promise: "I will make nations of thee, and kings shall come out of thee" (Gen. 17:6). Within Christian mythology, Abraham's lineage provides a connective tissue between the Hebrew Bible and New Testament, as "Joseph the husband of Mary, of whom was born Jesus" is a descendant of Jacob's son, Judah (Matt. 1:16). In the scene Nephi describes, Lehi finds that he is descended of Jacob's younger son, Joseph. This discovery retroactively builds the Nephites into the genealogy of Abraham and Jacob, and it invites readers to extrapolate forward and link the Nephites to Jesus. Thus the brass plates graft the texts together through revelations of a shared familial tie. But even as they promise to expand the story of Jacob's family tree, Lehi's plates serve as a reminder that the Bible is vulnerable to supplementation. Though Judah's family line is traced through to its culmination with Jesus, biblical narration does not so thoroughly account for the descendants of Jacob's other eleven sons. While the Bible recounts the history of Judah's line, *The Book of Mormon* provides a simultaneous story of Joseph's descendants, reminding readers that the Bible itself lacks such narration and might, in fact, require more stories to complete its project.

The question of origin and lineage is crucial to texts as well as people in *The Book of Mormon*. In addition to providing a genealogical link between the Nephites and the descendants of Judah, the brass plates operate as an alternative source of "the five books of Moses ... a record of the Jews from the beginning, even down to the commencement of the reign of Zedekiah ... [and] the prophecies of the holy prophets" (15). *The Book of Mormon* describes Nephi copying the text of the brass plates into his own plates, and the resulting text is very similar to that which would have appeared in the King James bibles on nineteenth-century readers' shelves. This is one of the book's most remarked-upon features, particularly its lengthy citations of Isaiah. Smith's text includes over twenty complete chapters of Isaiah, thirteen of which appear consecutively and almost verbatim in 2 Nephi. Mormon scholars have speculated that the brass plates share source materials with the Hebrew Bible—that is, that they are copies of a single set of sacred originals—but the text itself offers no such explanation. And although Lehi predicts that "these plates of brass should ... never perish," they appear only partially and as citations in *The Book of Mormon* (15). The brass plates thus operate as a simulacrum in the sense that they are copies lacking an original, but they are also the missing originals for Mormon's edited copies. Close inspection reveals that the Isaiah found in *The Book of Mormon* is not precisely the same as that in the King James Bible. As John Tvedtnes has noted, "Of the 478 verses in *The Book of Mormon* quoted from the book of Isaiah, 201 agree with the King James reading while 207 show variations. Some 58 are paraphrased and 11 others are variants and/or paraphrases."[18] Critics of Mormonism have pointed to this differently phrased Isaiah as proof that Smith poorly copied the Bible, while Mormon theologians have argued that the differences between Smith's Isaiah and that of the Bible actually demonstrate Isaiah's unity.[19] But I would argue that by offering readers a variant Isaiah that traces to a different origin from the one found in pre-Civil War bibles, *The Book of Mormon* poses a challenge to the very notion of singularity within the sacred canon. With its partial citations, variations, and unknowable source material, the book asks: Which Isaiah is the "real" Isaiah? Its tacit response seems to be: Both.

Through its presentation of variations on biblical texts such as Isaiah, *The Book of Mormon* offers a model of sacred history that centers on iteration and proliferation rather than unity. This is perhaps clearest in its presentation of the Sermon on the Mount. Jesus delivers versions of this sermon in the gospels of Matthew and Luke. In Smith's text, the sermon appears in 3 Nephi, after the resurrected Jesus appears to the Nephites and invites them—as he does Thomas in the Gospel of John—to "thrust your hands into my side, and also that ye may feel the prints of the nails in my hands and in my feet" (477). The 3 Nephi version differs from those in the Gospels, but rather than standing as a mark of difference between *The Book of Mormon* and the Bible, it serves as a reminder that the Bible differs from itself. The sermon occupies a large section of Matthew, but it is scattered throughout Luke, and in Luke, Jesus delivers the sermon's most famous "Beatitudes" section "in the plain" rather than "up into a mountain" (Luke 6:17, Matt. 5:1). The first of those Beatitude blessings offers a useful example of intertextual difference, as it reads "Blessed are the poor *in spirit*: for theirs

---

18. John A. Tvedtnes, "Isaiah Variants in *The Book of Mormon*," in *Isaiah and the Prophets: Inspired Voices from the Old Testament*, ed. Monty S. Nyman (Provo, UT: Brigham Young University Religious Studies Center, 1984), 165–77. It is worth noting that there does not seem to be clear consensus among Mormon scholars on the precise number of Isaiah verses that appear throughout *The Book of Mormon*. This is likely because fragments of hundreds of biblical verses appear in Smith's text, and thus it is not always clear whether a particular phrasing constitutes an overlap in the texts.

19. For an articulation of this theory of Isaiah in *The Book of Mormon*, see Sidney Sperry, "The 'Isaiah Problem' in The Book of Mormon," *Journal of Book of Mormon Studies* 4, no. 1 (1995).

is the kingdom of heaven," in Matthew (5:3), "Blessed be ye poor: for yours is the kingdom of God" in Luke (6:20), and "Yea, blessed are the poor in spirit *which come unto me*, for theirs is the kingdom of heaven" in 3 Nephi (479). These disparities are not merely syntactic; each version bears a blessing contingent upon different factors. Through its presentation of a third, different version of the sermon, 3 Nephi suggests that there is no distinct "Sermon on the Mount." Furthermore, its evocation of the Gospel of John—through the display of Jesus' wounds—reminds readers that John does not contain the sermon in question at all, and neither do the other gospels tell the story of Thomas. A composite of several texts, 3 Nephi forces readers to confront the fact that the synoptic gospels themselves form a composite story. "Open" to each other, they might be open to other texts as well.

If 3 Nephi presents the gospels as interdependent, suggesting an incompleteness that might apply to its own texts, it also evokes a narrative lacuna that neither it nor the Bible ever resolves. As he prepares to depart, Jesus tells the Nephites, "But now I go unto the Father, and also to shew myself unto the lost tribes of Israel" (488). In referencing the lost tribes, *The Book of Mormon* reaches back to the passage in 2 Kings, in which "the king of Assyria took Samaria, and carried Israel away into Assyria" (17:6). From here, the ten tribes all but disappear from the biblical as well as the historical record. In 3 Nephi, however, the lost tribes appear in the present tense, their story running simultaneously with that of the Nephites. *The Book of Mormon* does not tell the story of the lost tribes of Israel. In presenting the resurrected Jesus as traveling back and forth between the Nephites and the tribes, however, it inserts itself into the biblical gap while also suggesting that even more narration will be necessary to produce a full sacred history. Thus, although *The Book of Mormon* time and again suggests that the Bible is not a closed and complete history, it does not merely offer itself up as the final text to complete the sacred canon. Rather, through the highlighting of fissures in sacred history, it challenges the very notion of textual sufficiency— even when the texts in question are divinely inspired.

FAILED ANTIQUARIANISM IN *THE BOOK OF MORMON*

The title page of the 1830 edition of *The Book of Mormon* pronounces the book "an abridgement of the Record of the People of Nephi," but the first

story readers encounter between its pages is not one of ancient civilizations. The book's initial narrative voice is Smith's, and he bears a tale of
antiquarian subterfuge. "I would inform you," he writes, "that I translated
... one hundred and sixteen pages, the which I took from the Book of
Lehi ... which said account, some person or persons have stolen and kept
from me, notwithstanding my utmost exertions to recover it again" (v).
The text thus opens with a gesture of incompleteness: the Book of Lehi is
The Book of Mormon's phantom limb. Its narrative gap never will be rem-
edied, because, Smith asserts, "Satan had put it into [the thieves'] hearts
to tempt the Lord their God, by altering the words ... and ... if I should
translate the same over again, they would publish that which they had stolen, and Satan would stir up the hearts of this generation, that they might
not receive this work" (v). Thus he has been "commanded of the Lord
that [he] should not translate the same over again" (v). Out of Smith's
control and subject to corruption, the Book of Lehi disappears forever.
The Book of Mormon, then, opens with an expression of frustration on
the part of history's compiler. The missing text is an embarrassment and,
even worse, a threat to the book's entire project, which is revealed from
the outset to be the abridgement of an abridgement.

With Smith's preface and Moroni's laments, *The Book of Mormon*
brackets its central story with meditations on the difficulty of pre-
serving history. Smith's account of his thwarted efforts to preserve the
records in his care is not merely a convenient story to explain away a
text that has fallen out of his control. Rather, it offers an interpretive
frame for the book as a whole, as the text is rife with what Robyn Warhol has termed "unnarration," moments in which the narrative voice
foregrounds its inability or unwillingness to describe events.[20] Although
the book mainly consists of stories of the Nephite and Lamanite peoples, another strain in the text is the story of the plates themselves
passing from generation to generation, receiving additional writing as
they change hands. The Book of Jarom, for example, deals almost entirely with the problem of deficient materials. "I, Jarom, write a few
words according to the commandment of my father, Enos," the book
begins. "And as these plates are small ... it must needs be that I write

---

20. Robyn Warhol, "Neonarrative; or, How to Render the Unnarratable in Realist Fiction and Contemporary Film," in *A Companion to Narrative Theory*, ed. James Phelan and
Peter Rabinowitz (Cambridge, MA: Blackwell, 2005).

a little; but I shall not write the things of my prophesying, nor of my revelations" (146). Jarom's descendants follow suit, and the subsequent Book of Omni offers little more than a sequence of unnarrations. "I had kept these plates according to the commandments of my fathers," Omni writes, "and I conferred them upon my son Amaron. And I make an end" (148). Amaron picks up the narration but asserts only, "I, Amaron, write the things whatsoever I write, which are few, in the book of my father" (148). This goes on until Amaleki actually dies while engraving the last of the small plates: "I am about to lie down in my grave; and these plates are full. And I make an end of my speaking" (148–49). Covering hundreds of years and several generations, Omni occupies just a few pages of *The Book of Mormon*, and the stories it tells are of storytellers with little to say.

In 1 Nephi, Jarom, and Omni, the gesture of unnarration often appears as a measure against redundancy, but within the context of *The Book of Mormon* as a whole such assertions of completeness take on an ironic cast. The family genealogy Nephi refuses to narrate is "given in the record which has been kept by my father" (16). Jarom similarly asserts that readers interested in missing narratives "can go to the [large] plates of Nephi" (147). Readers familiar with Smith's preface, however, will know that the record kept by Nephi's father is the stolen Book of Lehi, a text destined to disappear. *The Book of Mormon* does offer readers a version of Lehi's work in 1 Nephi, when Nephi asserts that he will "make an abridgement of the record of my father, upon plates which I have made with mine own hands" (7). Smith's text presents Nephi's version as a fortunate redundancy that makes up for the lost Book of Lehi, but a statement of its lack, its status as "abridgement," accompanies the promise of its reparative value. A similar structure is at play in Jarom's assertion that his people's history may be found on the large plates of Nephi, which readers quickly learn no longer exist. In the book entitled The Words of Mormon—which immediately follows Omni—Mormon narrates his process of compiling the main portions of *The Book of Mormon*, noting that he "made an abridgement from the plates of Nephi" and asserting, "I cannot write the hundredth part of the things of my people" (152). The text to which Jarom refers, then, has been replaced with a partial copy of an absent original produced by an overwhelmed historian.

Beyond presenting the works of individual historians as inadequate,

The Book of Mormon indicates that some of its writings always will be concealed from readers. In a lengthy section of prophecy, Nephi describes the book's public unveiling in what is to him a distant future but to Smith's contemporaries the immediate present. "The Lord God shall bring forth unto you the words of a book ...," Nephi begins, "And behold the book shall be sealed ... But the book shall be delivered unto a man, and he shall deliver the words of the book ... But the words which are sealed he shall not deliver, neither shall he deliver the book" (110).

The prophecy foretells both the emergence and the perpetual obscurity of *The Book of Mormon*. It highlights the fact that the book in question—the golden plates—will never be made fully present to the public. The man will "deliver the words of the book," but the plates themselves will remain unavailable. Pointing to a "sealed" portion of its own contents, the book indicates that crucial information is present within this text but out of its readers' reach. By its own account, then, *The Book of Mormon* is neither a complete account nor even a complete document. Rather, it is a series of incomplete histories, some of which will be revealed only at the end of history itself.

If the issue of completeness hovers at the margins of *The Book of Mormon*'s depictions of failed history writing and biblical contingency, it takes center stage in 2 Nephi, when Lehi has a vision of the biblical Joseph (son of Jacob) predicting the nineteenth-century emergence of *The Book of Mormon*. A "seer will I raise up out of the fruit of thy loins," God tells Joseph, "and unto him will I give power to bring forth my word unto the seed of thy loins" (66). The book is quite clear about the identity of this seer: "his name shall be called after me," Joseph asserts, "and it shall be after the name of his father" (67). This prophecy imbues the name "Joseph Smith Jr." with teleological import by linking Smith to the Nephites and the family of Jesus. But although the "seer" prophecy particularly describes the publication of *The Book of Mormon*, 2 Nephi offers a picture of a sacred canon that is far broader than even the Hebrew Bible, New Testament, and Book of Mormon combined. "I command all men," God insists: "both in the east and in the west, and in the north, and in the south, and in the islands of the sea, that they shall write the words which I speak unto them; for out of the books which shall be written I will judge the world, every man according to their works, according to that which is written" (116).

This is a prophecy of scriptural proliferation on a global scale. The command to "all men" suggests the universal potential for divine revelation, while the passage's referentless pronoun ("they") and passive future construction ("books which shall be written") indicate that more texts will be continually forthcoming from always as-yet-undetermined sources. This is not the story of a single, chosen people producing an eternal and eternally complete scripture. "Thou fool," comes the rebuke, "that shall say: A Bible, we have got a Bible, and we need no more Bible" (115). Whether they wish to be or not, proponents of a closed canon will be subject to judgment "according to that which is written," which might, in the end, turn out to be a great deal of text.

In its explicit rejection of the idea of a whole and intact sacred canon, *The Book of Mormon* posed a direct challenge to traditional Protestant reading practices. The doctrine of *sola scriptura* ("by scripture alone")— belief that only accepted scriptures could form the foundation of true Christian belief and practice—had been (and remains) a central tenet of most Protestant denominations since the Reformation. Embedded within this doctrine was the belief that the *scriptura* in question was already available in its entirety. The sixth article of the 1642 Westminster Confession, for example, asserts:

> The whole counsel of God, concerning all things necessary for his own glory, man's salvation, faith, and life, is either expressly set down in Scripture, or by good and necessary consequence may be deduced from Scripture: unto which nothing at any time is to be added, whether by new revelations of the Spirit, or traditions of men.[21]

It is not surprising, then, that Smith's book appeared to his contemporaries as an affront to both accepted Protestant beliefs and the Bible itself. The 1834 treatise *Mormonism Unvailed* goes so far as to accuse Mormons of declaring the Bible "a dead letter—*so dead* that the belief and obedience of, without the reception of [*The Book of Mormon*], is no longer available to salvation."[22] In this account, addition is tantamount

---

21. G. I. Williamson, *The Westminster Confession of Faith: For Study Classes* (Phillipsburg, NJ: P & R Publishing, 2003), 12. For an explanation of the Westminster Confession's importance to various Protestant denominations, see Holland, *Sacred Borders*, 35–39.

22. Eber D. Howe, *Mormonism Unvailed: Or, A Faithful Account of That Singular Imposition and Delusion, from Its Rise to the Present Time: With Sketches of the Characters of Its Propagators* (Painesville, OH: printed and published by the author, 1834), 117.

to annihilation; the supplement is all poison and no remedy. Smith's text thus offered readers much more than a new set of sacred words. With its gestures of wide-scale scriptural incompleteness supplementation, it presented a new kind of Christian reading in which no single set of texts delimited the borders of the divine.

Beyond its explicit rejections of closed canonicity, *The Book of Mormon* formally resists completion, as Moroni describes his inability to stop writing. The Book of Moroni—the final piece of Smith's text—opens with its eponymous narrator expressing incredulity regarding his own continuing narration. "I had supposed not to have written more," he explains, "but I have not as yet perished ... Wherefore, I write a few more things, contrary to that which I had supposed; for I had supposed not to have written any more" (574). The question of where a sacred text should end, it seems, confounds the writer as much as the reader. And in the end, *The Book of Mormon* leaves off with a gesture of recursion rather than conclusion. "I bid unto all, farewell," Moroni writes,

> I soon go to rest in the paradise of God, until my spirit and body shall again reunite, and I am brought forth triumphant through the air, to meet you before the pleasing bar of the great Jehovah, the Eternal Judge of both quick and dead. Amen (588).

Although that "Amen" suggests an end—a prayer concluded, a truth pronounced—the passage as a whole opens yet another series of intertextual loops. The phrase "paradise of God" iterates Revelation 2:7, in which God promises "to him that overcometh will I give to eat of the tree of life" that resides there. And Jesus stands poised to judge the "quick and dead" in Acts, 1 Peter, and 2 Timothy. Thus even as it offers a terminal statement, Moroni's book performs a doubling back, reaching not only toward a promised millennial end but also, and perhaps more importantly, toward the sacred history upon which it depends but which it also renders incomplete.

OTHER HISTORIES, OTHER AMERICAS

In challenging contemporary notions of biblical canonicity, *The Book of Mormon* also undercuts longstanding notions of providential, Protestant US history. If, as Dicuirci suggests, pre-Civil War antiquarianism confronted the "varied and sometimes competing historical discourses emerging in the nineteenth century concerning colonial New England

and the legacy of Puritanism,"[23] then Smith's text—also ostensibly a record of American history—invites readers to turn away from the Puritan past altogether and consider a different point of origin for American Christianity. Within *The Book of Mormon*, Christianity takes root in the Americas not only before the arrival of Europeans but also, more radically, before the birth of Jesus. In moments of prolepsis similar to those appearances of Pauline language that predate Paul, the Nephites embrace the teachings of Jesus and assume the title of "Christians" in advance of the gospels.[24] The Book of Mosiah, for example, presents the Nephite king Benjamin predicting around 124 BCE that "the Lord Omnipotent ... shall come down from Heaven among the children of men, and shall dwell in a tabernacle of clay, and shall go forth amongst men, working mighty miracles ... and he shall be called Jesus Christ" (160). And in the Book of Alma, supposedly produced around 73 BCE, Moroni prays "that the cause of the Christians, and the freedom of the land might be favored" (351). This is Christianity before Christ; the prophecies of *The Book of Mormon*, unlike those of the Hebrew Bible, are explicit in their designations of the Messiah to come. But more important for this project is the fact that this is also American Christianity without Europe, without colonialism, and especially without Anglo-Protestants.

Within *The Book of Mormon*'s historical framing, indigenous Christianity operates as a residual presence in the Americas, having practically disappeared with the destruction of the Nephites but remaining, if only in latent form, among the Native American descendants of the Lamanites. The civil war that rages throughout the text is part family conflict (as Lehi's progeny turn on each other), part crusade (as their conflict is generally religious), and part race war. Though the Lamanites originally appear, as their Nephite brethren, "white, and exceedingly fair and delightsome,"[25] their fall from divine favor has physiological consequences. "That they might not be enticing unto my people," Nephi explains of the cursed Lamanites, "the Lord God did cause a skin of blackness to come upon them" (73). There is no denying

---

23. Dicuirci, "Reviving Puritan History," 567.

24. I thank Jared Hickman for bringing these passages to my attention.

25. 4 Nephi reiterates this phrasing, noting that "the people of Nephi did wax strong, and did multiply exceedingly fast, and became an exceedingly fair and delightsome people" (515).

the racialized logic of this passage: dark skin operates not only as a mark of communal fallenness but also as a source of human disgust. And yet, though these passages situate *The Book of Mormon* squarely within nineteenth-century discourses of racial hierarchy, it is important to note that Smith's text presents race as a mutable commodity. As Craig Prentiss avows, "Not only could the Lamanites' obedience to God be changed, so too could their relative skin color … Jacob warns the Nephites that should they fail to repent for their sins, the skins of the Lamanites 'will be whiter than yours.'"[26] Thus the status of the Lamanites and their descendants is not fixed for all eternity, and neither is that of their enemies. To acknowledge this aspect of *The Book of Mormon* does not require denial of its vexed racial politics. Rather, it allows for a clearer picture of the book's investment in the presentation of American history as iterative and recursive. The Lamanites' story begins, but does not end, with racial delineation, and the "skin of blackness" that covers them may be removed or transferred elsewhere.

The story of the Lamanites' decline takes on particular significance when Nephi has a vision of their future undoing. "I looked and beheld a man among the Gentiles," he writes, "and he went forth upon the many waters, even unto the seed of my brethren" (29). Latter-day Saints' interpretations of this passage typically identify the "man" in question as Columbus, which makes sense given the events Nephi goes on to predict. "I beheld the spirit of God," he explains, "that it wrought upon other Gentiles; and they went forth out of captivity, upon the many waters" (29). The "other" Gentiles in question are European Protestants, fleeing the corrupting influence of the Catholic Church, which Smith's text refers to as "a great church … which is most abominable above all other churches" (28). Nephi's vision reveals that these people will serve the divine purpose of punishing the Lamanites, who, like the Hebrews of Exodus, are destined to fall from God's favor. "The wrath of God … was on the seed of my brethren," Nephi reports, "and they were scattered before the Gentiles" (29). Here, Puritan settlement of the Americas is not a process through which Anglo-Protestants

---

26. Craig R. Prentiss, "'Loathsome Unto Thy People': The Latter-Day Saints and Racial Categorization," in *Religion and the Creation of Race and Ethnicity: An Introduction*, ed. Prentiss (New York: New York University Press, 2003), 128–29. Another useful account of race in *The Book of Mormon* can be found in Hokulani K. Aikau, *A Chosen People, a Promised Land: Mormonism and Race in Hawai'i* (Minneapolis: University of Minnesota Press, 2012).

assume the role of a new Israel but rather the fulfillment of a prophecy that centers on an alternate imagining of indigenous America. But readers expecting to find that European Christians merely displace the children of Lehi might be surprised to learn that though the Gentiles in the vision "prosper and obtain the land for their inheritance," they also are "white, and exceedingly fair and beautiful like unto [Nephi's] people before they were slain" (29). The iteration of the language is unmistakable. Like the Nephites and Lamanites before them, the Gentiles of Europe are "white, and exceedingly fair." Within the context of Smith's work, such an appearance more often hints at a pending fall from grace than indicates immunity against one. The white Christians who arrive to destroy the Lamanites fall into a recursive historical cycle that predates them and might even outlast them. And Protestantism merely enters a hemisphere where Christianity continually emerges, is forgotten, and is remembered only to be forgotten again.

The Book of Mormon's investment in moving Puritanism even beyond the margins of American history becomes perhaps most apparent in 3 Nephi, when Jesus tells the Nephites, "A city that is set on a hill cannot be hid" (480). This line is not merely a verbatim citation of Matthew 5:14—part of the Sermon on the Mount—it is also a radical subsumption of Puritan history into Smith's alternate account of the Americas. As Sacvan Bercovitch has shown, the image of a "city on a hill" allowed Puritan settlers to "give the kingdom of god a local habitation and a name."[27] Aboard the *Arbella* in 1630, John Winthrop delivered the most famous version of that metaphor when warning the separatists against iniquity: "For we must consider that we shall be as a city upon a hill. The eyes of all people are upon us."[28] Berkovitch notes that Winthrop's "scriptural phrases locate the [separatist] venture within a configuration extending from Ararat, Sinai, and Pisgah to the New World city on a hill, and thence forward ... to Mount Zion of the Apocalypse."[29] Reading the colonial endeavor into scripture allowed the Puritans, and their descendants, to see themselves as operatives

27. Sacvan Bercovitch, *American Jeremiad* (Madison: University of Wisconsin Press, 1980), 40.

28. John Winthrop, "A Model of Christian Charity," in *The Puritans in America: A Narrative Anthology*, ed. Alan Heimert and Andrew Delbanco (Cambridge, MA: Harvard University Press, 1985), 91.

29. Bercovitch, *American Jeremiad*, 8.

within a teleological plan. The image of the city on a hill thus pervades Puritan discourses about the early settlements and their failures. And as John Ernest has shown, this city served as a flexible conceit into the pre-Civil War era: in an 1859 anti-slavery essay, for example, the Reverend Amos Gerry Beman asserts that the "colored race is an element of power in the earth, 'like a city set upon a hill it cannot be hid.'"[30] A figure of "chosenness," the city resonates through claims of American exceptionalism as well as critiques of the nation's failures. In *The Book of Mormon*, however, the people Jesus likens to a city on a hill are not Puritans, and they will not produce the US nation. White Christians have not come to build a city on a hill; they instead have come to destroy one. The Puritan errand stands as the mere fulfillment of a millennium-old revenge prophecy—the destruction of the fallen Lamanites—and the city at the center of divine interest is not Plymouth Plantation but the Nephite stronghold of Zarahemla.

If the city metaphor fails to communicate *The Book of Mormon's* revisionist project, then Jesus' explication of John 10:16 in 3 Nephi makes the decentering of Puritan history explicit. "Ye are they," Jesus tells the Nephite crowd, "of whom I said: Other sheep I have which are not of this fold" (486). For many mainline Christians, John 10:16 marks a moment of opening within the New Testament, creating a space in which non-Jewish subjects also may operate as God's chosen people. But US Protestants hoping to link that expansive notion of chosenness to the Puritan project will find *The Book of Mormon* very disappointing. "They understood me not," Jesus explains, "for they supposed it had been the Gentiles … And they understood me not that I said they shall hear my voice; and they understood me not that the Gentiles should not at any time hear my voice" (486). Smith's text thus disrupts a teleology that runs from the Gentiles of John through the early Christian church and Reformation, and into the settlement of the Americas. Not surprisingly, Smith's text presents itself as the event that will move Anglo-Protestants into the realm of divine interest. "I, Nephi, beheld that [the Gentiles] did prosper in the land; and I beheld a Book; and it was carried forth among them … and it is a record like

30. Quoted in John Ernest, "The Governing Spirit: African American Writers in the Ante-bellum City on a Hill," in *A Mighty Baptism: Race, Gender, and the Creation of American Protestantism*, ed. Susan Juster (Ithaca, NY: Cornell University Press, 1996), 259.

unto the engravings which are upon the plates of brass, save there are not so many" (29). Here, Smith's golden bible enters the arc of sacred and secular American history, converting the Gentiles into Mormons and saving them from the errors of Puritan history.

With its presentation of an alternate Christian history, *The Book of Mormon* lays narrative groundwork for what eventually would become explicit within early Mormonism: the notion that mainline American Protestantisms were dangerous falsehoods. Perhaps the most explicit articulation of this appears in Smith's first vision, a story that did not widely circulate until the 1840s.[31] In this vision, which first appeared in the Latter-day Saints newspaper *Times and Seasons* in 1842, Smith recounts a moment around 1820 when he was unsure of what church to join and thus "retired to a secret place in a grove and began to call upon the Lord."[32] Smith claims that he was visited by two "glorious personages" who "told [him] that all religious denominations were believing in incorrect doctrines ... And [he] was expressly commanded to 'go not after them.'"[33] Here, the revivalism sweeping the United States appears not as a renewal of true Christian enthusiasm but rather a widespread delusion, and the choice between, say, Methodism and Congregationalism is something of a Morton's Fork. As an ostensibly ancient text, *The Book of Mormon* does not engage explicitly with the religious debates of Smith's nineteenth century. Still, its insistence that American Gentiles exist in an "awful state of blindness" and "do stumble exceedingly" indicates a need for large-scale correction. Indeed, when God shows Nephi the future he promises, "I will manifest myself unto thy seed, that they shall write many things ... and after that thy seed should be destroyed ... behold, these things shall be hid up, to come forth unto the Gentiles" (31). *The Book of Mormon* is the antidote to a mistaken Christian tradition, not because it is the final divine word, but because it denies the very possibility of a complete

---

31. For a detailed history of the early circulation of Smith's first vision, see James B. Allen, "The Significance of Joseph Smith's 'First Vision' in Mormon Thought," *Dialogue: A Journal of Mormon Thought* 1, no. 3 (Autumn 1966). Allen notes that early Mormon missionaries did not rely on the first vision when seeking converts, probably because for those who "believed in the authenticity of The Book of Mormon, as well as the other claims of Joseph Smith to divine authority and revelation, the story of the first vision would not have been difficult for them to believe once they heard it" (33).

32. Joseph Smith, "Church History," *Times and Seasons* 3, no. 9 (Mar. 1842): 706.

33. Joseph Smith, "Church History," *Times and Seasons*, 707.

sacred canon. "I beheld other books," Nephi writes, "which came forth by the power of the Lamb" (31). He is not talking about Mather's *Magnalia*. In Smith's America, sacred texts proliferate to correct the errors of Protestantism, and Mormonism triumphs precisely because it marks a moment of opening in which the revelation and production of sacred texts begins anew.

In pushing Puritanism and its heirs to the margins of American history, *The Book of Mormon* creates narrative space in which it becomes possible to imagine the Western Hemisphere as a place where disparate Christian trajectories merge, and American history is recursive and multifaceted rather than linear and singular. The text most explicitly links its ancient American history to that embraced by Smith's contemporaries in 2 Nephi's prophecy regarding the book's rejection by nineteenth-century US Protestants. Correcting those who would assert that "we need no more Bible," this passage speaks directly to the notion of biblical openness that, as Holland shows, lies at the heart of early Mormonism. Only arrogance, the prophecy suggests, would motivate some to set a limit on divinely inspired texts. Equally important, though, is 2 Nephi's assertion that *The Book of Mormon* is a national as well as a sacred text. "Know ye not that there are more nations than one?" Nephi's god asks those who would reject the book. "I speak the same words unto one nation like unto another," the divine insists, "And when the two nations shall run together the testimony of the two nations shall run together also" (115). In this moment, *The Book of Mormon* becomes the site through which two nations—that of the children of Lehi and that of pre-Civil War US Protestants—combine to form a new story of the hemisphere. The book thus presents an opportunity for configuring American history *as* sacred history. The Gentile occupation predicted in 1 Nephi ostensibly sounds the death knell for the Lamanites, but it also forms the basis of a new, Anglo-Protestant nation. But, *The Book of Mormon* suggests, it would be a mistake to imagine the story of that new nation in singular and exclusive terms. Now part of the sacred canon, American history, too, must be open, contingent, and endlessly prone to proliferation.

FOUR

SCRIPTURE, TIME, AND AUTHORITY AMONG EARLY DISCIPLES OF CHRIST

SETH PERRY

God's book is, however, put into the hands of men, as it was first spoken to men; but they have, by some unpropitious cause, been taught not to receive it from God, but from men. They do not consider, that the written book as well as the spoken word, is tendered to us under the stipulations of human language—according to the contract between man and man, touching the value or meaning of the currency of thought: that every word and sentence is to be weighed and tested, by the constitutional laws and standards of the currency of ideas.

—Alexander Campbell, 1835[1]

Biblical primitivism was a hallmark of early-national American protestantism. The period saw a number of groups coalesce around various leaders arguing essentially the same ideas: that the existing churches had departed, in belief and practice, from the ecclesiastical model established by Christ, and that the Bible should be re-established as the sole authority for Christian practice. Two major threads of this movement, led by Barton W. Stone (1772–1844) and Alexander Campbell (1788–1866), united in the early 1830s to form what became known as the Disciples of Christ. Stone and Campbell argued that "priests" and theologians had replaced the simple truths communicated by God with elaborate schemes of their own devising, interspersing human authority between Christians and scripture. Their remedy was a set of twin commitments: to the plain Bible as the proper source of authority for Christian faith and practice, and to the right and responsibility

---

1. Alexander Campbell, *A Connected View of the Principles and Rules by Which the Living Oracles May Be Intelligibly and Certainly Interpreted* (Bethany, VA: M'Vay and Ewing, 1835), 16.

of individual Christians to access that source of authority directly, for themselves. John Allen Gano, who converted to Stone's movement in the 1820s, found the two commitments inseparable, as scripture itself enjoins the individual's capacity and freedom to access its truth: "To the Bible I looked as the polar star to direct me; common sense and all the Scripture with which I was acquainted taught me to join, where I could read, think, believe and obey the Truth for myself, untrammeled by any Creed, Confession of Faith, Church Rules or any other Book or System merely of human invention."[2]

These commitments generated a preoccupation with the Bible's printed form which has been widely overlooked. The tenacity with which Disciples emphasized their allegiance to an idealized Bible has obscured their attention to its physical manifestations and use as printed scripture. For the Disciples, as much as any other group, the timeless authority of the Bible was entangled with the historical contingencies of mere bibles, and the ways in which they dealt with these tensions offer important perspective on nineteenth-century bible culture. Attending to Disciples' negotiation of the material and the abstract with respect to the Bible raises important questions about early-national primitivism itself. Scholars have treated primitivism as an ahistorical impulse—the idealization of the New Testament church as a mythical sacred era outside of time that could be perpetually inhabited. By contrast, I argue here that in seeking to recover that era through historicized understandings of scripture, primitivists like Campbell situated the early church itself firmly within historical, not primordial, time.

Disciples evinced an idealizing abstraction of scripture—they imagined the Bible as an inviolate, timeless source of truth. Stone drew the distinction between theological argument and biblical reliability explicitly: "I pay deference to the judgment of great and pious men who have lived before us, or contemporary with us. But great and good men have differed. Therefore from the Bible I wish to draw my sentiments, and by

---

2. Journal of John Allen Gano, John Allen Gano papers, 1820–1887, University of Kentucky Special Collections, Lexington. For the context of primitivism in the early nineteenth century, see Nathan Hatch, *The Democratization of American Christianity* (New Haven, CT: Yale University Press, 1989), esp. 68–81; Douglas A. Foster, ed., *The Encyclopedia of the Stone–Campbell Movement* (Grand Rapids, MI: Eerdmans, 2012), is an excellent source on the Stone–Campbell movement and its significance in the history of Protestantism in America.

the Bible to have them judged."[3] Here, Stone opposes the complicating disagreements of history—"men have differed"—with the Bible's univocal authority in a perpetual present. Such idealized purity mixes poorly with the necessity of printed texts, though. The granting of revelation might be a divine prerogative, but printing it is definitely human: the idealized Bible can be singular and unchanging in its abstractness, but material bibles are subject to the historicizing and diversifying effects of, among other things, collation, translation, editing, and publishing.

Here, I will investigate early Disciples' approach to the inevitable materiality of scripture through six material artifacts: five editions of the New Testament edited and published by Alexander Campbell between 1826 and 1835 and the personal bible of Thomas M. Allen (1797–1871), a convert of Stone's and a widely-known Disciples minister in Kentucky and Missouri during the 1830s and 1840s. Campbell was a conflicted bible editor: he was fully committed to a belief in the transparent simplicity of scripture, but also convinced that the meaning-making power of a bible's paratextual, extra-scriptural, content was anything but simple.[4] Allen's personal bible, on the other hand—a duodecimo Authorized Version published by Silas Andrus of Hartford, Connecticut, in 1828, now held by the University of Chicago—is covered in handwritten notes, an artifact of an individual reader's efforts to interpret the Bible for himself. Allen's notes demonstrate the layers of paratextual and textual authority that went into reading the "Bible alone," including his use of Campbell's New Testament. Together, these objects are a fascinating window on early Disciples' negotiation of the distance between the ideal Bible and the bibles of material experience, and they shed new light on the conception of historical time that primitivist commitments demanded.

ALEXANDER CAMPBELL AND THE BIBLE'S COMPLICATED SIMPLICITY

Alexander Campbell embodied the Bible-alone ethos in the early-national period.[5] It would be difficult to find a greater obsession with

---

3. Barton W. Stone, *An Address to the Christian Churches in Kentucky, Tennessee, & Ohio on Several Important Doctrines of Religion* (Nashville, TN: M. & J. Norvell, 1814), 5.

4. Gerard Genette, *Paratexts: Thresholds of Interpretation,* trans. Jane E. Lewin. (Cambridge, Eng.: Cambridge University Press, 1997). Throughout this essay "Bible" refers to the idealized, abstract scripture; "bible" to a book.

5. The best recent scholarly study of Campbell's life and work is Peter A. Verkruyse, *Prophet, Pastor, and Patriarch: The Rhetorical Leadership of Alexander Campbell* (Tuscaloosa:

the idealized Bible among his contemporaries. However, Campbell's insistence on the simplicity of scripture was only one aspect of his complicated approach to the Bible as printed word. His very confidence in the unique authority of the Bible and in believers' ability to read, understand, and apply it to proper Christian practice forced Campbell to confront the challenges of its presentation. Although he is remembered for urging the common-sense reading of scripture, close analysis of Campbell's bible-editing work demonstrates that he recognized multiple contingencies leading up to an individual moment of common-sense reading, conditions which had to be met and controlled in order to give the common reader the opportunity to read plainly. These conditions were to be met by an editor who compiled a correct text, presented it in the appropriate manner, and constructed a paratextual apparatus for it—a framework of materials such as prefaces, annotations, and appendices that would assist and encourage reading. Campbell held the Bible in too high esteem not to recognize that the pure access to it he sought for his followers would have to be facilitated by learned mediation, but his insistence on the self-sufficiency of scripture led him to downplay that role even as he found it necessary.

Campbell's New Testament was first published in 1826 as *The Sacred Writings of the Apostles and Evangelists of Jesus Christ, Commonly Styled the New Testament.* It was part of a flurry of more or less unsuccessful challenges to the dominance of the King James Version in the early nineteenth century. Although it is unlikely that *The Living Oracles*, as the volume became commonly known, was ever the most used Bible even among Campbell's own followers, it probably had a wider readership and influence than most alternative translations produced in the early nineteenth century, owing to Campbell's ecclesiastical distribution channels. It was used by Mormon founder Joseph Smith (1805–44) and his associates in Ohio in the 1830s and a critic in Pennsylvania noted its use in preaching there in 1839.[6] By 1842, editions

---

University of Alabama Press, 2005). Thomas Allen has been the subject of a dissertation— Edward Feland Coffman, "Elder T.M. Allen, Pioneer Evangelist: 'The Artillery of Heaven'" (PhD diss., Vanderbilt, 1972)—and a hagiographic monograph—Alvin Ray Jennings, *Thomas M. Allen: Pioneer Preacher of Kentucky & Missouri* (Fort Worth, TX.: Star Bible and Tract Corporation, 1977).

6. For a thorough study of the theological contributions of Campbell's New Testament, see Cecil K. Thomas, *Alexander Campbell and his New Version* (St. Louis, MO: The Bethany Press, 1958).

had been printed in Virginia, St. Louis, Cincinnati, Pittsburgh, and London, and Campbell estimated that about 40,000 copies had been distributed.[7] New editions appeared periodically through the nineteenth century; the work was last printed in 1974.

Although he was a more-than-capable student of Greek (he later translated the book of Acts for the American Bible Union), Campbell did not produce the New Testament translation himself. The primary text for *The Living Oracles* was taken from an 1818 London edition of the New Testament which combined the work of three different translators. The gospels were the work of George Campbell, a Presbyterian divine and a theorist of rhetoric whose work Campbell revered.[8] The epistles were translated by James MacKnight, another Scottish Presbyterian. Acts and Revelation, finally, were taken from Philip Doddridge's *Family Expositor,* dating from the mid-eighteenth century.

Campbell became aware of this version of the New Testament when a printer in New York sent him a prospectus for issuing an American edition. Campbell subscribed for 100 copies, but the project fell through. Having the technical and financial means, he decided to take it up himself, but with important changes. Campbell thought it should sell more cheaply than the New York printer had proposed—that edition was to have been priced, depending on the binding, at $3.00 or $2.50, expensive for a New Testament at a time when the American Bible Society (ABS) was selling them for about twelve cents.[9] Beyond price, Campbell took special care for paratexts and presentation. He thought that the volume ought to include "critical notes and amendments from other translations" and that the text "should appear in another form on the paper."[10]

In the context of Campbell's obsession with "the Bible alone," these concerns are surprising. We might expect a bible produced by such a thoroughgoing primitivist to be, like those of American Bible Society, shorn of the varied paratextual accretions that were attached to bibles in this period. In his own way, Campbell was in fact even more sensitive

---

7. Alexander Campbell, "The Bible Society and the Reformation," *The Millennial Harbinger* (hereafter *MH*) 6, no. 11 (Nov. 1842): 521–22.

8. Verkruyse, *Prophet, Pastor, and Patriarch*, 30.

9. Gutjahr, *An American Bible*, Table 2.

10. Campbell, "Historical Sketch of the Origin and Progress of the New Translation," *MH* 6, no. 3 (June 7, 1832): 268–69.

to what he called the "cluttering" of bibles than the ABS and went even further in stripping human conventions from the sacred text: in his version, he eliminated the chapter breaks and verse numbers that had been standard in English bibles since the Geneva.[11] At the same time, the fourth, and what its editor considered finally complete, edition of Campbell's New Testament contained 125 pages of non-biblical material—a full quarter of the volume. From the perspective of the ABS—always seeking a purity of the text—the addition of extensive "note and comment" was at odds with the impulse to strip the text of human additions. Campbell sought a different sort of purity, though, one which he believed was accessible through, rather than despite, biblical paratexts—a purity of understanding.

Campbell believed that complete understanding of the Bible was both necessary and possible for all Christians. Perspicuity was a requirement of revelation: "when God spoke to man in his own language, he spoke as one person converses with another—in the fair, stipulated, and well established meaning of the terms. This is essential to its character as a revelation from God; otherwise it would be no revelation, but would always require a class of inspired men to unfold and reveal its true sense to mankind."[12] At the same time, Campbell championed a Baconian rationalism which carried with it humanist assumptions regarding history and language. Campbell argued that clarity inheres as a characteristic of scripture. However, he was also bound to observe that revelation came through language—a human institution subject to the vicissitudes of historical change—and through people, historical actors in particular situations. Consequently, a reader's appreciation of the clear meaning of the Bible was historically contingent. Though Campbell is routinely linked to the "common sense" reading of scripture, for him, the exigencies of language and the situational logic employed by the Bible's various authors meant that the sense of scripture was truly "common" only to its immediate, original audiences. All subsequent readers would need to make an effort to learn the art of reading scripture.

---

11. David Daniell, *The Bible in English: Its History and Influence* (New Haven, CT: Yale University Press, 2003), 275; see also Paul Henry Saenger and Kimberly Van Kampen, *The Bible as Book: The First Printed Editions* (London: British Library, 1999).

12. Campbell, *The Christian System*, 3rd ed. (Bethany, VA: A. Campbell, 1840), 15–16.

If words and phrases, and the manners and customs of mankind were un-changeably fixed, or universally the same at all times and in all countries, the art of interpreting would have been still more simple than it is: for so far as it is *artificial*, it is owing to different dialects, idioms, manners, cus-toms, and all the varieties which the ever changing conditions of society have originated, and are still originating. ... The very fact that we have a *written* revelation, that this revelation was first *spoken*, then written, sup-poses that there is somewhere, a native or an acquired art of interpretation; that the persons addressed were already in possession of that art: for with-out such an understanding, there would have been neither wisdom nor benevolence, in giving to mankind any verbal communication from God.[13]

Campbell wrote of what he called the *"understanding distance"*: in order to understand scripture, one must come appropriately close to it, the way one comes within speaking or hearing distance of someone with whom he or she wishes to speak. Campbell was referring to spiri-tual closeness, achieved through faith and humility, but the phrase can also be applied to his sense of that "art of interpretation" which was "native" to the New Testament era and necessarily "acquired" by those of later times.[14] The knowledge required for closing that distance was *philological* and *historical*: neither the original languages of the biblical documents nor the details of life in first-century Palestine were "com-mon sense" to early-nineteenth-century Anglophone American readers.

As a bible editor, then, Campbell sought to close the understanding distance for his readers through translation and historical contextu-alization of the text. In keeping with his democratic sensibilities, Campbell would always argue that editorial mediation was not essen-tial to biblical understanding: theoretically, with enough effort anyone could approach the Bible's original languages and educate themselves about its historical context. The languages were difficult, though, and those historical details were not obvious: they had to be teased out of various sources, clarified, and contextualized by wider learning. The ABS sought a purity of the English Bible text by producing bibles

---

13. Campbell, *Connected View*, 17. Campbell's views on language and the relationship of facts to faith and testimony were heavily influenced by the writings of George Campbell, whose writings on rhetoric Alexander Campbell studied at the University of Glasgow. As noted, Alexander used George Campbell's translation of the gospels in *The Living Oracles*. For a detailed analysis of this influence, see Verkruyse, *Prophet, Pastor, and Patriarch*, 30.

14. Campbell, *Connected View*, 17.

without note or comment, ostensibly leaving each reader to apply her own prayerful efforts in discernment of an English text whose contingency was masked. The purity of understanding that Campbell sought, however, required a thoroughly annotated printed Bible.

Taken to its extreme, Campbell's insistence on historicized reading posited an ideal reader who looked nothing like the average American bible reader of the nineteenth century: a student of Greek who had collated his or her own manuscripts and studied life in first-century Palestine. This idealized potential reader is a scholar, which is an important clue to understanding Campbell's bible-editing and the nature of his claim of authority for the Bible. In short, Campbell saw his editorial work as an exercise in bringing scholarly work on the Bible to "common" readers, not as an exposition of the biblical text. He mediated between scholars and common readers, not between the authors of the Bible and common readers.

BIBLICAL SCHOLARS AND THE "COMMON READERS"

Thomas M. Allen was one of those readers. Born in Virginia in 1797, Allen was converted after encountering the preaching of Barton Stone about 1822 and was active as a preacher himself, primarily in Virginia, Kentucky, and Missouri from the mid-1820s until his death in 1871. Allen was devoted to Stone—his bible records that Stone performed his wedding—and came to know Alexander Campbell when he and Stone came together to form the Disciples of Christ in the early 1830s. Allen was reasonably well known, particularly in Missouri later in his life, and shows up infrequently in the publications of the Disciples of Christ, typically as T. M. Allen.

Though he was as adamant about taking "the Bible as [his] only rule of faith and practice" as any Disciple, the markings in Allen's bible make it clear that he did not read it "alone."[15] The influence of biblical scholarship

---

15. Bible of T.M. Allen, University of Chicago Special Collections, http://pi.lib.uchi-cago.edu/1001/cat/bib/3142074. Allen's bible is a small duodecimo published by Silas Andrus at Hartford, Connecticut, in 1828 from stereotyped plates by J. Howe of Philadelphia. It has been re-bound—the original cover and binding are lost, but the book is otherwise intact. It has Allen's signature in the top left corner of the title page; I have matched it to those on Allen's letters at the University of Kentucky. Likewise, the handwriting and the details of the genealogical material match Allen's. The book's accession record indicates that it came to Chicago from Louisville in 1913 as part of the Reuben T. Durrett collection.

is present all over his bible, both in printed materials that came bound with it and in Allen's handwritten notes evincing his use of other materials. Allen's bible contained a chart between the testaments, for example, one ubiquitous in eighteenth- and nineteenth-century bibles, giving conversion factors for biblical units of length, weight, money, and time. On the page of his bible containing Genesis 6:15, Allen made use of the conversion factors given on the chart to calculate the size of Noah's ark, converting the cubits of God's commandment to English feet and inches. On the last page of Malachi (a common site for bible marginalia, as it typically has a large blank space), Allen wrote in cross references, chapter and verse designations for about twenty verses, connecting them to specific words in Malachi 3:16—such compilations clearly suggest the use of a concordance. Allen made similar lists in a few other places.

Most significantly, Allen's bible heightens the irony of Campbell's editing of the New Testament: in his pursuit of full, direct understanding of the Bible, Allen made extensive use of Campbell's scholarship. At the head of each book of the New Testament, as well as a few of the prophets, Allen wrote in a year and often a place of composition; for the New Testament epistles, he also included the addressee. He also made his own little chart of this information for the New Testament on a back flyleaf. In Allen's day, scholarship was unsettled with regard to the dates of authorship of the New Testament books. For the Gospel of Matthew, for example, scholars posited dates ranging from CE 36 to 64; some German scholars were beginning to suggest, as almost all modern scholars now accept, that Matthew was not the earliest Gospel and that it dates from the last two decades of the first century. Allen was at least somewhat aware of the disagreements with regard to the dates of the New Testament books. His bible contained a chart giving the dates of composition of the New Testament texts compiled by Princeton president John Witherspoon. First printed in 1790, Witherspoon's chart was reprinted in countless nineteenth-century bibles, but by Allen's day it had been superseded by more recent scholarship. Allen ignored Witherspoon's chart. The dates he wrote into his bible instead come from a chart Campbell included in *The Living Oracles*, specifically from the first or second edition.[16]

---

16. All of Allen's years match Campbell's, and no other single source, and their phrasing—"first published in Judea AD 41" for Matthew, for example, comes verbatim from *The*

Thomas Allen was a particularly vitriolic participant in the routine mocking of "DD's" in early Disciples publications—he used "doctor" as an epithet and once suggested that a Presbyterian minister he heard cite Doctor of Divinity Thomas Scott may as well "quote the Pope of Rome" to make his case.[17] Campbell, though, while adamant that explaining the Bible would not require a "class of inspired men," did not deny that it required scholars: he identified the three translators whose work he compiled in *The Living Oracles* as "Doctors" on the title page. Allen's use of *The Living Oracles* demonstrated that while he was avowedly less comfortable with scholarship than Campbell, he nevertheless shared Campbell's commitment to the historicity of scripture. Allen's marginalia indicate that he observed Campbell's oft-repeated first rule of bible reading, which held that when a reader opened a text of scripture, he or she must "consider first the historical circumstances of the book. These are the order, the title, the author, the date, the place, and the occasion of it."[18] This type of historical imagination manifested in Allen's obsessive need to date the New Testament books, as well as in his effort to calculate the size of Noah's ark using the chart in his bible. The chart had an historicizing influence: it allowed Allen to think of the ark as a thing with dimensions, just like a barn or a home. Allen was not going to come upon those details of the Bible which Campbell said were essential on his own, because they were neither present in the text or not readily apparent to common readers of "the Bible alone." The historical and historicizing details that made possible the kind of reading Allen was committed to were provided by the type of authorities he railed against.

THE STAKES OF EDITORIAL AUTHORITY

The acknowledgment that contemporary Bible understanding required instruction—that what was rendered as transparent truth by God now required gloss—was the tension at the heart of early

---

Living Oracles, where it appears at the heading of the "Testimony According to Matthew." ("Testimony," Campbell's term in place of "Gospel," is present throughout Allen's notes, another place where Campbell's influence is plainly evident.)

17. *Christian Messenger* (Georgetown, KY) 4 (Dec. 1830): 279–83; reproduced in Jennings, *Thomas M. Allen*, 203.

18. Campbell, *The Christian System, in Reference to the Union of Christians, and a Restoration of Primitive Christianity* (Pittsburgh, PA: Forrester & Campbell, 1840), 16. See also *Connected View*, 96.

Disciples' wide-ranging engagement with biblical authority. Campbell's work on the New Testament was controversial, beginning at the level of the translation itself. Campbell started with the work of three scholarly translators, and they are credited with the translation on the title page, but he made countless edits to their work. These were enough for his critics to claim that the preponderance of the work was actually his own and that he was passing it off under the names of the three scholars to enhance the text's authority. It is clear from simple comparison that the core of the text was unaltered (as Campbell claimed), but there is also no mistaking the fact that *The Living Oracles* is emphatically "Campbell's New Testament," which is indeed what many people called it.[19]

Despite his historically-grounded approach to language, Campbell had complete confidence that the problems of translation could be overcome. Because the Bible was originally written according to the commonly-accepted language of given places and times, it could be translated by the same principles into the language of a different place and time. "The English, or German, or French 'New Testament,' is as much the word of the Spirit as the Greek original, if that original is faithfully translated."[20] Translations could be faulty, however, in two ways. They could be outdated, owing to "constantly fluctuating" living language, or they could be inherently warped, as a result of translator error, use of flawed manuscripts, or deliberate subterfuge.

Campbell laid all of these forms of error on the King James. While there were many "new" English bibles in America in the early nineteenth century, there was only ever one "old" one, and all promoters of new versions felt the need to position their work against the King James. Directly preceding the first publication of *The Living Oracles*, Campbell ran a series of articles on "the history of the English Bible"

---

19. Beth Barton Schweiger has pointed to the paradox of Campbell's primitivist convictions in an article exploring his obsession with print. Campbell, she writes, "embodied the contradiction of the Protestant preacher and printer, one that lay at the heart of his restorationist doctrine. By directing his reader's attention to the Scriptures, he drew attention to himself as the one pointing to them. By denying the necessity of interpretation, of merely pointing out the plain meaning of the text, Campbell asserted his authority over readers who would apparently recognize the truth only with his help." "Alexander Campbell's Passion for Print: Protestant Sectarians and the Press in the Trans-Allegheny West," *Proceedings of the American Antiquarian Society* (2008), 129.

20. Campbell, *Connected View*, 21.

in the *Christian Baptist*, his magazine at the time, culminating in a piece which argued that the Authorized Version was hopelessly subject to translation errors and deliberate obfuscation. Campbell promised something better: "To remedy those evils, so long and so justly complained of, we have issued proposals for publishing a new translation of the New Testament, made by Doctors Campbell, Macknight, and Doddridge, decidedly the best that has appeared in our language."[21] No one of those translators solved all of the problems, though, and so as a solution to the problems of the King James, *The Living Oracles* was the creation of Campbell's heavy editorial hand.

Campbell's positioning of *The Living Oracles* against the King James continued in the "General Preface" to the work, where he focused on the King James Version's outdated language. Campbell mocked the widespread devotion to King James English as inherently sacred: "Our whole phraseology on religious topics is affected by the antiquated style of the common version. ... This old fashioned style we call '*the sacred style.*'—yet this *sacred* style was the common style in the reign of James."[22] By contrast, his translators—products of late-eighteenth-century England and Scotland—used more contemporary English. At Acts 26:14, for example, Doddridge changed the King James's "kick against the pricks" to "kick against the goads"; "prick" was one of those earthy King James words that later English speakers found out of place in their bibles. Thomas Allen absorbed this change—in an 1838 letter to his friend John Allen Gano, he applied that verse to some people in his own life and used "kick against the goads."[23] This kind of change did not suit everyone, though. The publishers of an 1848 London edition of *The Living Oracles* observed that abandoning *thou*, *thee*, and *thy* for *you* and similar changes had the effect of "robbing the New Testament of its pure old Saxon style, and also of that degree of reverence which so beautifully characterizes the 'Word of

---

21. Campbell, "History of the English Bible—No. IV," *The Christian Baptist* 2, no. 11 (June 6, 1825): 161.

22. Campbell, ed., *The Sacred Writings of the Apostles and Evangelists of Jesus Christ, Commonly Styled the New Testament*, 2nd ed. (Bethany, VA: Alexander Campbell, 1828), 448.

23. Thomas M. Allen to John Allen Gano, Aug. 18, 1838, University of Kentucky Archives. They were not all equal in this respect, though. Campbell complained (with considerable justice) that Doddridge's work was often verbose and clumsy, and comparison shows that he freely edited Doddridge's Acts and Revelation to make them more readable.

God.'" They thought it scandalous to address the Savior as "You" and corrected for Campbell's informality.[24]

Matters of doctrinally-significant translation loomed larger. The most conspicuous idiosyncrasy in terms of word choice in *The Living Oracles* concerns βαπτίζω—"baptizō" and related words. Tradition cited by Campbell held that James I himself had forbade his translators to translate these and other "old ecclesiastical words," committing the cardinal sin, in Campbell's view, of forcing their work to conform to pre-existing doctrinal commitments.[25] The resulting "no-translation" (as opposed to mistranslation), as Campbell called it, prevented English readers from recognizing that Christ mandated believers' "immersion." Campbell's concern for the proper authority for the Bible shone clearly here: "But who said those words were consecrated and ecclesiastical words, which should not be translated? The king and ecclesiastics, whose practice required this pious fraud to justify their kind of baptism, or at least to conceal that their practice was unscriptural." These authorities were, needless to say, insufficient to impress Campbell. Translation must be a disinterested academic exercise. What is notable, though, is that none of Campbell's three scholarly translators used "immerse" for "baptize" as often as he would have liked, which was in every possible instance. Comparison shows that Campbell changed "baptize" and related words to "immerse" throughout the translations. George Campbell, as a Presbyterian, did not use the word in his rendering of the gospels at all; in Alexander Campbell's version of George Campbell's text, it appears so consistently as to refer, rather awkwardly, to "John the Immerser" at every opportunity.

Campbell's assertion of authority over the translation grew in strength over the course of the early editions. The first and second editions contained a lengthy appendix of divergent translations of difficult passages, cross-referenced from the text. This was in the service of transparency—the reader would be able to glean the shades of Greek meaning of a difficult passage without actually knowing Greek,

---

24. Campbell, ed., *The Sacred Writings of the Apostles and Evangelists of Jesus Christ, Commonly Styled the New Testament* (London: Simpkin, Marshall, and Co., 1848), vii.

25. In the November 1, 1824, issue of the *Christian Baptist*, Campbell printed extensive extracts from John Lewis's *A Complete History of the Several Translations of the Holy Bible, and New Testament, into English, both in MS. and in Print*, probably from the 1818 London edition.

through a collation of learned translators' choices. "We have given the most conspicuous place to that version which appeared to deserve it," Campbell wrote, "but as the reader will have both, we have not judged for him, but left him to judge for himself."[26] After the third edition, Campbell went ahead and judged for the reader. He removed the appendix giving the long list of parallel translations and struck the disclaimers from the "General Preface." The appendix for the third edition still included a Table XIV giving "principal Greek terms yet in controversy" and some various translations of them, but even this is omitted from the fourth edition.

The most controversial changes which Campbell made to the work of the three translators stemmed from manuscript issues. None of the three translators had used the Greek New Testament collated by German biblicist Johann Jakob Griesbach, first published 1775–77, which Campbell considered to be the best possible source text. Modern scholars credit Griesbach (1745–1812) with laying the foundations for modern scholarship on the Greek manuscripts of the New Testament.[27] Griesbach traveled extensively to compare extant Greek manuscripts of New Testament texts, and made judgments about the most likely original text based on interpretive principles that took into consideration quotations used by the church fathers and the transmission history of the manuscripts. On the strength of Griesbach's scholarly acumen, Campbell found this work completely persuasive. "The world is, perhaps, more indebted to this learned and distinguished professor and critic, than to any other critic on the long list of collators, interpreters, and editors of the New Testament," he wrote.[28]

In the first and second editions, Campbell wove this critical text into the work of the three translators by italicizing most words and phrases Griesbach deemed spurious. As with the parallel translations, though, Campbell's assertion of authority over spurious passages grew stronger in the later editions, where they were deleted in the body of the text.

---

26. Campbell, ed., *The Sacred Writings of the Apostles and Evangelists of Jesus Christ, Commonly Styled the New Testament* (Buffaloe, Brooke County, VA: Alexander Campbell, 1826), xiii.

27. Bruce M. Metzger and Bart D. Ehrman, *The Text of the New Testament: Its Transmission, Corruption, and Restoration*, 4th ed. (New York: Oxford University Press, 2005), Part II, chap. 4.

28. Campbell, *MH*, extra no. 11 (Oct. 1839): 522.

He deleted most of the passages italicized in the first two editions and removed the italics from those which he kept, removing what had been considered scripture and eliminating the typography through which he had marked some parts of the text as more reputable than others. The deleted passages were noted in a new appendix. The 357 deleted passages were numbered sequentially, as if at some point there was a plan to reference them in the text, but no such references are present in the third and subsequent editions—within the text itself, the questioned passages are silently removed. Campbell viewed this as the apogee of a scholarly approach to scripture, but it incensed his critics and alienated some readers. R. W. Landis, author of the most thorough and most bitter critique of *The Living Oracles*, was rendered speechless: "We cannot trust ourselves to speak the sentiments we entertain of such atrocious treatment of the word of God."[29] In 1827, Campbell reported, with what reads like both exasperation and glee, that a copy of *The Living Oracles* had been publicly burned in Jessamine County, Kentucky.[30]

Many did not find Griesbach's authority as a scholar sufficient to warrant the deletion of material that had been regarded as inspired for centuries. "There can be no doubt," Landis conceded, "that some few errors have crept into the Greek text of the New Testament. But then neither Professor Griesbach, nor any other person, is yet able, from the data which we have, to point them out with sufficient certainty to justify our rejection of any portion of Scripture.[31] Campbell did not deign to defend individual deletions, but his preface to the fourth edition makes a characteristic appeal to scholarly consensus: "Some, indeed, appear to be rejected without a very overwhelming authority; but all, I think, have more than a bare majority of votes regarding both number and character, against their standing in the text."[32]

Campbell presented his treatment of spurious passages as allegiance to the scholarship of Griesbach, but his own judgments loomed large.

---

29. R. W. Landis, "Campbellism," *The American Biblical Repository*, Second Series, no. 11 (Apr. 1839): 318.

30. *Christian Baptist* 4, no. 9 (Apr. 2, 1827): 326. For more on the controversy around *The Living Oracles*, see Gutjahr, *An American Bible*, 105.

31. Landis, "Campbellism," 325.

32. Campbell, ed. *The Sacred Writings of the Apostles and Evangelists of Jesus Christ, Commonly Styled the New Testament*, 4th ed. (Bethany, Brooke Co., VA: M'Vay and Ewing, 1835), Appendix p. 30.

Griesbach, for instance, gives a lengthy footnote on the Markan Coda (Mark 16:9–20, widely thought by modern scholars to be a late addition to the text), but Campbell let it stand without comment.[33] This is possibly owing to the rather ambivalent ending which cutting it off gives to the text—"neither said they any thing to any man; for they were afraid"—or, possibly, because Campbell appreciated the risen Christ's specific endorsement of "immersion" in 16:16.

At the same time, Campbell was willing to eliminate verses that helped his particular theological positions in deference to Griesbach's scholarship. Acts 8:37, the confession of the Ethiopian eunuch, was a text with significance for Campbell's side of the intra-Baptist argument over the terms of believer's baptism. Campbell and like-minded reformers argued that baptism should be granted to anyone making a simple confession of faith, while other Baptists were convinced that the new believer must narrate a conversion experience. In Acts 8:37, Philip's baptism of the eunuch is connected to a simple statement of faith, supporting Campbell's side of the argument: "The eunuch said, See, here is water; what doth hinder me to be baptized? And Philip said, If thou believest with all thine heart, thou mayest. And he answered and said, I believe that Jesus Christ is the Son of God." Griesbach, however, found the verse spurious, and Campbell removed it.

UNBROKEN TIME: THE BIBLE IN/AS HISTORY

Tellingly, Thomas Allen did not follow Campbell in abandoning Acts 8:37. In Allen's Bible, the verse is marked with the curling lines he evidently used to mark passages of particular interest or import, looping brackets which explicitly connect the verse to those before it, rather than cut it off from among them. Beyond that, documentary evidence records that Allen had a particular regard for Acts 8:37. In his journal, John Allen Gano recorded Allen's participation in a moving scene of baptism focused around the exchange between Philip and the eunuch:

> On Lord's day 16th [of September, 1827] Bro Allen again preached and afterward immersed Mrs. Williams, as she came up out of the water her mother (Mrs. Mary T. Webb) approached bro Allen[:] "here is water" said she "what hinders me from being baptized"; "If thou believest thou mayest" answered he, "I believe that Jesus is the Christ the Son of the Living

---

33. See Thomas, *Alexander Campbell and His New Version*, 37.

God," she replied he then straightway immersed her[.] Truly thought I this looks like the case of Philip and the eunuch.[34]

No amount of German scholarship could discourage a preacher like Allen from responding to the Ethiopian's question with Philip's response when the opportunity presented itself so neatly. It is precisely moments like this that have led scholars to characterize Disciples and other primitivists as beholden to an ahistorical reading of scripture. Richard T. Hughes and C. Leonard Allen, following Dwight Bozeman's work on the primitivist strain in Puritan thought, have gone so far as to apply Mircea Eliade's terms to suggest that restorationists such as Stone and Campbell operated within a framework of sacred versus profane time. Sacred time, as explained by Eliade, is "reversible," "indefinitely recoverable, indefinitely repeatable," "a sort of eternal mythical present that is periodically reintegrated by means of rites."[35] This "primordial" time is treated as a model for the present, one that can be repeated because it exists outside of history. By this logic, Allen and Mary Webb, trading lines from Acts, were repeating a timeless scene of confession and baptism.[36]

As has been discussed, though, Allen was conscious of the Bible's historical specificity. As Campbell instructed, he paid careful attention to the historical origins of the biblical texts and made an effort to think about practical details like the size of Noah's ark. Viewed as the sourcebook for early Christianity, the New Testament becomes a collection of historical documents, and the effort required to contextualize those documents, in order to interpret them correctly, becomes an act of historical imagination.

---

34. Notebook of John Allen Gano, University of Kentucky archives.

35. Mircea Eliade, *The Sacred and the Profane: The Nature of Religion*, trans. Willard R. Trask (New York: Harcourt Brace Jovanovich, 1987), 69–70. See also Richard T. Hughes and Leonard Allen, *Illusions of Innocence: Protestant Primitivism in America, 1630–1875* (Chicago: University of Chicago Press, 1988); Theodore Dwight Bozeman, *To Live Ancient Lives: The Primitivist Dimension in Puritanism* (Chapel Hill: University of North Carolina Press, 1988).

36. The equation of primitivist ecclesiology with the appeal to primordial, rather than historical, time as suggested by Hughes and Allen has become a scholarly commonplace. See, for example Monica Najar, *Evangelizing the South* (Oxford: Oxford University Press, 2008), 34–35; James Bratt, ed., *Antirevivalism in Antebellum America* (New Brunswick, NJ: Rutgers University Press, 2006), xv; and David Manning, "'That Is Best, Which Was First': Christian Primitivism and the Reformation Church of England, 1548–1722," *Reformation & Renaissance Review* 13, no. 2 (Nov. 2011): 153–93. Manning's is a nuanced study of primitivism in the English church which nevertheless tacitly assumes the relevance of the Eliadean primordium to primitivist thought.

Hughes and Allen linked Christian primitivism to an American impulse toward the recovery of an ideal era, an exemplary past outside of time. "Most Americans were not concerned to recover their recent past, or even an ancient past which was merely history, fully as corrupt and degenerate as the recent past from which they had sprung," they wrote. "But they were concerned to recover the primordial past that stood behind the historical past.[37] Hughes and Allen took pains to explain the difficulty of ascribing ahistorical impulses to a form of Christianity, which Eliade himself plainly labeled an historical religion inasmuch as it "affirms the historicity of the person of Christ."[38] They describe a point of historical fidelity at which Christians, while revering the Incarnation as an historical moment, come to fetishize a past which is something other than history and which may be relived rather than merely re-enacted. "When the normative history is swallowed up in myth to such an extent that the believer loses the clear distinction between his own time and the primal time, then that historic tradition has lost its historicity. At that point, the particular time that was merely normative now has become the eternally repeatable primordium within which the believer lives and moves and has his being apart from which life itself has no meaning or significance."[39]

Hughes and Allen suggest that Disciples, as exemplars of nineteenth-century Christian primitivism, reached such a point, finding a "sense of historylessness" to be the "heart of restoration thinking."[40] While in terms of idealizing the New Testament era there is something to this, what such approaches to primitivism miss is the radically historicized nature of restorationist readings of the Bible as the sourcebook for that "primordial" past. However Eliadean ideas of sacred and profane time may apply to other religious traditions, they obscure essential elements of nineteenth-century restorationism which a more text-based approach illuminates. For early Disciples, the Bible did not concern an exemplary past outside of time, but rather documented specific, historically and geographically locatable, and avowedly irrepeatable events. "The Bible is a book of facts," Campbell wrote, "not

---

37. Hughes and Allen, *Illusions of Innocence*, 2.
38. Hughes and Allen, 72.
39. Hughes and Allen, 5–6.
40. Hughes and Allen, 207.

of opinions, theories, abstract generalities, nor of verbal definitions."[41] A good Baconian, Campbell's definition of "facts" was nothing but historical, and he distinguished them from "truths" specifically by their location in time: "Fact means something done."[42] Most of the Bible, moreover—"exactly four-fifths" in Campbell's estimation—is taken up with the relation of facts. "History is therefore the plan pursued in both Testaments," Campbell argued.[43]

The Living Oracles' paratexts bear this out. The third and fourth parts of Campbell's appendix are a "Geographical Index" connecting New Testament events and personalities to the world map and a numbered timeline of the common sort attached to nineteenth-century bibles, mapping the events of the New Testament onto world history. They are not the work of a man committed to the idea of a New Testament primoridum outside of space and time.

Crucially, this commitment to the historicity of the biblical era, quite distinct from an appeal to a mythical primordium, is carried through in Campbell's sense of contemporary Christians' relationship to the early church. Simply put, for Campbell the biblical era is temporally and geographically distant, and therefore irreducibly distinct, from nineteenth-century America. In one of his prefaces to the epistles, for example, he railed against their traditional theological use by reminding the reader that "these letters were written nearly eighteen centuries ago." This fact means two important things for the reader. In terms of interpretation, "excepting the prophetic part of these writings, not a word or sentence in them, can be explained or understood, by all that has happened in the world, for eighteen hundred years." In terms of application, the contextual differences between his readers' time and that of the apostles cannot be collapsed: "As the Apostles did not write, with any of our questions before their minds, or with a reference to any of our systems, it is presumptuous in the extreme, to apply what they have said on other questions, to those which have originated since."[44] The New Testament should be the sole source of contemporary faith

---

41. Campbell, *The Christian System*, 18.
42. Campbell, 110.
43. Campbell, 18.
44. Campbell, ed., *The Sacred Writings of the Apostles and Evangelists of Jesus Christ* (1835), 26.

and practice, but its distance from our own time and place necessitates an effort in understanding it. Bible reading begins with history.

Campbell enumerated several authoritative sources from which historical context could be gleaned. First and foremost, like others, Campbell primarily emphasized scripture as its own interpreter: each text itself gives clues to its circumstances of production. The book of Acts, further, provides an historical overview of the period in which most of the letters were produced, intimating some of the same scenes: "This book is the grand link, which connects the previous histories with the epistles, and constitutes the key to the right interpretation of them; without which they would have been, in a great measure, unintelligible."[45] The Old Testament, further, contains prophecies—which Campbell, incidentally, considered a form of history—of New Testament events which can illuminate the historical documents.

Moreover, Campbell was in no way opposed to applying "extrinsic sources of information" to the Bible. His philological concerns on some level required it—the precise meanings of the words and phrases of the original Greek could be found only by analysis of their use in other contemporary sources. Table XI of Campbell's appendix, which explains idioms found in the New Testament according to "ancient usages, manners, and customs," is the clearest illustration of this use of extra-biblical sources to establish historical context.[46]

The most obvious aids to the reader which Campbell provided had to do with re-establishing the genres of the various New Testament texts in service of historicizing them. The Bible is composed of texts that fall into a wide range of genres—narrative, genealogy, first-person visionary account, poetry, letter, or often some combination of these. In the typical King James layout, however, norms of presentation and paratextual addition conspire to suppress these designations. The standard chapter and verse divisions of English bibles ultimately go back to the Vulgate edition produced by Sanctes Pagninus in 1527 and the 1551 Greek New Testament of Robert Stephens.[47] The editors of the Geneva Bible were the first to begin each verse on its own line, a layout that the King James translators adopted and which became standard

---

45. Campbell, 24.
46. Campbell, 25.
47. See Daniell, *The Bible in English*, 275.

in English bibles. In terms of genre, this might suit Psalms and Prov-
erbs as poetry and aphorism, but the overall effect is to eliminate the
sense that some of the biblical texts are doing different things than others; particularly when cross-references, chapter summaries, and guide
phrases are added, the Bible's multiple genres appear on the printed
page as a new, now immediately identifiable genre: "scripture." The
New Testament epistles look like the Bible, not like letters.

Campbell believed that when the paragraphs of a narrative or a letter were "chopped," "minced," and "crumbl[ed]" into verses (as John
Locke complained, in a passage cited by Campbell), the original sense of
the text was lost as every line became its own "independent aphorism."[48]
"The reader must recollect that no one sentence, in the argumentative
part of a letter, is to be explained as a proposition, theorem, proverb,
or maxim, detached from the drift and scope of the passage."[49] Allen
and other Disciples ministers made a habit of ridiculing the traditional
ministerial practice of preaching on a given verse or portion of a verse
of scripture: what Methodists referred to as "taking a text" they termed
"scrap preaching."[50]

Accordingly, Campbell eliminated the standard verse numberings
throughout *The Living Oracles*, forming the texts into paragraphs. In
the gospels, Campbell adopted the sense-oriented section breaks and
brief headings used by George Campbell, which he found appropriate
for works of history. Rejecting Doddridge's section breaks and headings
for Acts and Revelation, Campbell created his own for the former and
presented the latter in paragraphs, with Roman numerals giving the
standard chapter numbering.[51] Campbell stripped the epistles of chapter breaks and in-line verse numbers completely—such divisions made
no sense for letters, he argued. Throughout, Campbell included occasional verse and chapter numbers at the beginnings of paragraphs to
assist readers in finding their place with respect to conventional bibles.
In the first and second edition these are sparse. "To checker the margin
with a column of figures marking every verse in the common version,

---

48. Campbell, *MH* 6, no. 3 (1832): 274–75.
49. Campbell, ed., *The Sacred Writings of the Apostles and Evangelists of Jesus Christ*
(1835), 27.
50. See, for example, Thomas M. Allen in the *Christian Messenger* (Georgetown, KY) 4
(Dec. 1830): 185–87; reproduced in Jennings, 197–200.
51. Thomas, *Alexander Campbell and his New Version*, 27–28.

appeared no way profitable to the reader," Campbell wrote. "It rather perplexes the eye and distracts the attention of the reader, as well as dislocates the sense, and perpetuates what ought soon to be forgotten."[52] In response to reader complaints—he reports that they had been "much called for by many readers"—Campbell relented for the third edition, in which nearly every verse is numbered in the margin.[53] For the fourth, stereotyped edition, Campbell went back to more selective numbering.

With respect to genre, Campbell felt very strongly about titles, as well, because a title "sometimes expresses the *design* of the book," giving insight into the all-important intention of the author.[54] Although Campbell noted that "in most of the Greek copies" Acts is titled "The Acts or Transactions of the Apostles," this name conflicts with the contents of the book. "Acts of Apostles" is more proper, he wrote, since "only a few transactions of a few apostles are mentioned in it."[55] Campbell also insisted that the gospels be titled "testimonies"—"The Testimony of" rather than "The Gospel According to"—because they are works of eyewitness history rather than simple statements of belief. "All of these histories testify thousands of items, which, though subservient to their main design, are different from, and not the gospel of Jesus Christ, properly so called," Campbell wrote.[56]

Campbell's obsession with genre opens onto what he repeatedly emphasized as the most important requirement for coming into the understanding distance—obtaining knowledge of each author's purpose in writing each text: "No person can be said to fully understand *what* is written in it, unless he know [sic] *why* it is written."[57] Campbell wrote prefaces or "prefatory hints" for the gospels, Acts, each epistle through James, and Revelation; he quoted MacKnight's prefaces for the remaining letters. These editorial introductions are dominated by his concern to make each author's purposes plain to the reader. At a basic level, Campbell followed pretty much every Christian commentator before him in acknowledging the rule of faith as the primary purpose of the New Testament documents: their essential purpose was to witness

---

52. Campbell, ed., *The Sacred Writings* (1828), xii.
53. Campbell, ed., *The Sacred Writings* (1835), 49.
54. Campbell, *The Christian System*, 16.
55. Campbell, ed., *The Sacred Writings* (1835), 23.
56. Campbell, ed., *The Sacred Writings* (1828), 391.
57. Campbell, ed., *The Sacred Writings* (1835), 39.

to readers that "Jesus the Nazarene is the Son of God, the Saviour of men."[58] As indicated by his preference for "Testimony" over "Gospel," though, Campbell's radically historicized view of the New Testament documents obligated him to observe that each text was also an artifact of immediate, historically-situated purposes of a human author. The overall purpose of revelation—witnessing to Christ—might be unchanging, but these immediate purposes were discrete and contextual: "Now, it requires not a moment's reflection, to see that Paul had one design in writing to Timothy, another in writing to Philemon, and another in writing to the congregation in Rome."[59] These situational differences were particularly evident with regard to the epistles, but they applied in the same way to the gospels. Matthew wrote for "his countrymen, the Jews," and so he emphasized Jesus's Davidic lineage, while John, writing "at a great distance from Judea, ... would not think of troubling [his audience] with a roll of lineage about [Jesus's] pedigree."[60]

Campbell's historicized approach to the Bible led him to show the characters and authors of the New Testament to be historical, human presences. Understanding these presences was a required part of understanding their textual productions: "Now, as the design of a writer is his own guide in the selection and arrangement of his materials, arguments, and evidences; so is it the only infallible guide, when known, to the interpretation of what he has written."[61] As human beings, the apostles can have human motivations. Paul's goals in 1 Corinthians, for example, were "to support his own authority, dignity, and reputation; to vindicate himself from the aspersions and calumnies of the factious; and to diminish the credit and influence of those aspiring demagogues and leaders."[62] The authors can also be imagined to be limited in their knowledge—not of the Gospel, but of their historical circumstances. Paul, for example, wrote to the congregation at Rome "according to the best information he had respecting them, not having been himself at Rome."[63] Campbell posits that Matthew, wishing to recite the lineage of Christ to his Jewish audience, "would apply to the Registrar's office,

---

58. Campbell.
59. Campbell, 12.
60. Campbell, 15.
61. Campbell, 15.
62. Campbell, 35.
63. Campbell, 30.

for a copy of the roll of the lineage of the house of David, well attested; and from this, trace Jesus to David."[64]

This kind of historical reconstruction of the life of an evangelist is an act of imagination that is distinctly different than the imaginative conjuring of an ideal time outside of time—surely there are no registrars in Paradise. Nevertheless, while Campbell worked to reconstruct an historical moment in which the events of the New Testament took place and were recorded, he stopped short of rendering the actors involved as fully-realized human beings. These historians cannot concoct, they can only make choices about which truths to tell and emphasize. They did not shape their histories so much as arrange them. Campbell quotes MacKnight—himself a renowned professor of rhetoric—to emphasize that despite the necessity of communication strategies, when the New Testament authors write, "every thing is told naked and unadorned, just as it happened."[65]

This is the tension that has led historians to miss the historicizing impulse at the core of primitivist thought: for Campbell, the biblical texts had to both have a history and transcend it. Moreover, it was not just the evangelists and apostles whom Campbell believed transcended their historical situations. Just as the authors of the New Testament were human actors who both formed scripture according to their own lights and served as perfect conduits for revelation, Campbell believed that later scholars could make scripture understood by dint of their personal qualities. He wrote of the three translators whose work he incorporated into *The Living Oracles* as examples of those rare scholars, appearing "once or twice in a hundred years," "whose literary acquirements, whose genius, independence of mind, honesty, and candor, may fit them to be faithful and competent translators."[66] Campbell emphasized his debts to these scholars—"We stand on the shoulders of giants"—but could not avoid placing himself in their line: "Like the wren on the back of the eagle, we have as large a horizon as the eagle, which has carried us above the clouds."[67] Critics noticed this. "Mr. Campbell," Landis wrote, "is determined not to submit to the inconvenience of waiting, as other

---

64. Campbell, 14–15.
65. Campbell, 22.
66. Campbell, 6.
67. Campbell, 46.

authors are compelled to, till the tardy public utter forth their praises of his productions. He has acquired the art of self-praise, and extols himself, and his works still more."[68]

Campbell saw himself as an interested editor who took a heavy hand with the text, and yet offered readers unmediated access to it. What was timeless for Campbell, really, was as much a scholarly commitment as a religious one: the impulse of the Bible's various human handlers to provide readers a transparent understanding of whatever the Bible was imagined to be. Campbell understood the apostles' and evangelists' composition of the New Testament, Griesbach's collation of manuscripts, the translation work of George Campbell, Doddridge, and MacKnight, and his own editing of it as one historical thread. At each point the words might change, but the commitment to transparent understanding was eternal.

---

68. Landis, "Campbellism," 316.

FIVE

TRANSLATING TIME
THE NATURE AND FUNCTION
OF JOSEPH SMITH'S NARRATIVE CANON

KATHLEEN FLAKE

Luther nailed his complaints to the door and the church fathers countered with decrees of anathema. In such exchanges of creedal statement and dogmatic restatement, most of modern Christianity has formed and reformed itself. Joseph Smith, the founder of Mormonism, wrote stories, however. Not surprisingly, then, it is a literary critic and not a theologian who labels Smith "an authentic religious genius ... in the possession and expression of what could be called the religion-making imagination." Indeed, Harold Bloom credits Mormonism's very survival to "an immense power of the myth-making imagination."[1] Of course, myth in the sense used here refers not to fiction as the opposite of fact but to highly symbolic narratives that attempt to account for existence by providing a history of divine and human interaction.[2] This essay seeks to illuminate the relationship between Smith's mythmaking and the nature of Mormonism as a radical adaptation of traditional Christianity.

Analysis of Smith's writings is dominated by polemics between those within and those antagonistic to the Church of Jesus Christ of Latter-day Saints (LDS or Latter-day Saints), Smith's largest institutional

---

1. Harold Bloom, *The American Religion: The Emergence of the Post-Christian Nation* (New York: Simon and Schuster, 1992), 96–97.

2. Emphasizing as it does the "bond between man and what he considers sacred," my definition of myth takes its cue from Paul Ricoeur, *The Symbolism of Evil* (Boston: Beacon, 1967), 5. For an introduction to the question of veracity and myth, including biblical myth, that is as insightful as it is brief, see Michael Fishbane, *Biblical Myth and Rabbinic Mythmaking* (New York: Oxford University Press, 2003), 1–7.

legacy.[3] Reasons vary, no doubt, for academic aversion to studying Smith's texts. Most obviously, they are numerous, including nearly 800 pages of published revelations that comprise the LDS scriptural canon.[4] There is also Mark Twain's famous judgment that at least some of it is "chloroform in print."[5] Scholars themselves are famous, however, for thriving on what bores others. The more probable barrier to academic interest in Smith's writings is the purported otherworldliness of their production. Golden plates, seer stones, Egyptian mummies, and a who's who of biblical and nonbiblical angelic messengers have a decidedly chilling effect on scholars of American religion, except as a lens for psychological analysis.[6] The manner in which confessional function and mystical production merge in LDS canon is a further deterrent. The question of Smith's veracity as a prophet was, from the beginning, inseparable from his production of text.[7]

Whatever the cause, it remains the case that the academy tends to give Smith's writings short shrift, if not a wide berth, and to focus on Smith's personal history or thought world.[8] Even Bloom's effort "to

---

3. A comprehensive bibliography of both sides of the polemic, as well as independent scholarship on the varieties of Mormonism, is found in James B. Allen, Ronald W. Walker, and David J. Whittaker, *Studies in Mormon History, 1830–1997: An Indexed Bibliography* (Urbana: University of Illinois Press, 2000).

4. The LDS Church's canon consists of (1) the King James Version of the Bible as edited by Smith; (2) the Book of Mormon; (3) The Pearl of Great Price, a collection of Smith's revelations, including the Book of Abraham and an account of Smith's early revelatory experiences; and (4) the Book of Doctrine and Covenants, a compilation of Smith's revelations concerned primarily with the organization of the church. The Doctrine and Covenants is Smith's most discursive scripture. Even so, it too suggests the importance of historical narrative to Mormonism by introducing each revelation with a paragraph concerning its historical context, including description of relevant persons and events that induced the revelation on a specified date.

5. Mark Twain, *Roughing It* (Hartford, CT: American Publishing, 1872), 127: "The book [of Mormon] is a curiosity to me, it is such a pretentious affair, and yet so 'slow,' so sleepy, such an insipid mess of inspiration. It is chloroform in print."

6. First published in 1945, Fawn M. Brodie's *No Man Knows My History* remains the most popular psychobiography of Smith, as evidenced by Knopf's 1971 publication of an enlarged, second edition. For a more recent example of the genre, see Dan Vogel, *Joseph Smith: The Making of a Prophet* (Salt Lake City: Signature Books, 2004). For an analysis of the genre, see D. Michael Quinn, "Biographers and the Mormon 'Prophet Puzzle': 1974–2004," *Journal of Mormon History* 32, no. 2 (2006): 226–45.

7. See Terryl L. Givens, *By the Hand of Mormon: The American Scripture that Launched a New World Religion* (New York: Oxford, 2002), 84, 86–87.

8. To the extent that the academy, usually through its historians, has considered Smith's writings, its attention has been limited to the content of the Book of Mormon. See, e.g.,

bring us closer to the workings of religious imagination" relies largely on an analysis of Smith's personal charisma and the speculative concepts deducible from his narratives. For Bloom, "Joseph Smith, and his life, personality, and visions far transcended his talents at the composition of divine texts."[9] Given Smith's dramatic life and death, there is reason to be interested in the man himself. Smith was twenty-four years old when, in 1830, he published the Book of Mormon and formally organized his followers into a church. Fourteen years, many thousands of believers, multiple wives, three cities, two temples, and one presidential campaign later, Smith was murdered in Illinois. Likewise, his theological concepts, including as they did plural marriage, premortal existence, and deification, to name a few, differed enough from the Western Christian tradition to warrant attention. Ultimately, however, neither Smith's life nor his speculative thought is sufficient to explain the nature or continuing vitality of either the LDS Church or its critics—at least, that is the argument of this essay, which, presuming to begin where Bloom leaves off, looks to the mythos to explain the man, not vice versa.

By considering the narrative function of Smith's writings, I hope to show the extent to which Smith's reappropriation of the biblical story competed with traditional Christian theologies, offering his believing readers a particular-to-them sense of time and, consequently, a sense of what is real. My analysis begins, however, with the classic religious studies question: how may Smith's writings be adequately understood independent of the faith claim they make upon believers? My approach relies upon Ricoeur's hermeneutic of revelation, as well as his writings on time and narrative that provide a model for placing reason and revelation in conversation to "engender something like an understanding of faith."[10] Here, the "something like" is based on an analysis of Smith's

---

Nathan Hatch, *The Democratization of American Christianity* (New Haven, CT: Yale University Press, 1989); and Thomas O'Dea, *The Mormons* (Chicago: University of Chicago Press, 1968). The two exceptions to scholarship's exclusive focus on the Book of Mormon are Jan Shipps, *Mormonism: A New Religious Tradition* (Urbana: University of Illinois Press, 1986); and Philip L. Barlow, *Mormons and the Bible: The Place of the Latter-day Saints in American Religion* (New York: Oxford University Press, 1991) and are discussed below.

9. Bloom, *American Religion*, 82; see also 97, 104–108. For the most recent biography, see Richard Lyman Bushman, *Rough Stone Rolling* (New York: Knopf, 2005).

10. Paul Ricoeur, *Essays on Biblical Interpretation*, ed. Lewis S. Mudge (Philadelphia: Fortress, 1980), 73. My arguments throughout rely heavily on Ricoeur's work distinguishing

self-understanding as a translator and the relation of that self-under-standing to the texts he produces.

The second portion of the essay turns to the narrative content and style of these texts to demonstrate how they leverage the form, sub-stance, and authority of the biblical myth to subvert definitive aspects of traditional Christianity.[11] My hypothesis is that Smith's religion-mak-ing success is related to his having deployed the formal attributes of narrative to challenge the Christian tradition in ways not possible through discursive debate or speculative theology. As myths that seek to explain human existence, the definitive function of Smith's stories is "one of cosmicization; of giving meaning and shape to the world; of stating what is really real, self-founded."[12] As such, Smith's narrative elaboration on Christian scripture constituted a competing myth that, true to its genre, "recalibrated categories and redistributed privilege."[13] Specifically, I will attempt to show that Smith's biblically based narra-tives recalibrated traditional Christianity's theology of human creation, fall, and salvific potential, as it relates to the origin and end of evil. As such, Smith's new mythos overtly redistributed the privilege central to both Jewish and Christian biblical myth: the capacity to know God, as expressed most directly in Exodus 19 and John 17. To state these aspects of Smith's work discursively obscures the narrative forms in which they are communicated to and function among believing read-ers. Again, though necessitated at times by the analytical approach of the essay, reducing Smith's event-driven narratives to propositional statements is alien to the religious system he created. Thus I conclude

---

between philosophical and religious language. More specifically, I employ his concept that the revelatory capacity of religious narrative is not measured by its source but by its func-tion. Thus the question is not whether the author is inspired but, rather, does the text illuminate reality through the world it offers the reader and does it obtain a response in the lived experience of not merely an individual but a community of readers who find in the text a livable future. See, inter alia, Paul Ricoeur, "Philosophy and Religious Language," in *Fig-uring the Sacred: Religion, Narrative, and Imagination* (Minneapolis: Fortress, 1995), 35–47.

11. This will require me to deduce theology from narrative but only as a means to com-pare Latter-day Saint and traditional Christian thought. Otherwise, it would not be possible to compare the apples of Smith's stories with the oranges of traditional Christian philosophy.

12. W. Taylor Stevenson, "Myth and the Crisis of Historical Consciousness," in *Myth and the Crisis of Historical Consciousness*, ed. L. W. Gibbs and W. T. Stevenson (Missoula: University of Montana and Scholars Press, 1975), 5.

13. Bruce Lincoln, *Theorizing Myth: Narrative, Ideology, and Scholarship* (Chicago: University of Chicago Press, 1999), 216.

with a discussion of the function of Smith's narratives in creating a livable future for his believing readers.

As with other myths that have founded a sense of peoplehood, Smith's narrative history of human and divine interaction is ultimately oriented to a future time that serves as a basis for acting in the present. Like much American religion, however, Mormonism did not seek to transcend time but to capture the eternal in time or, in religious terms, to build Zion. Smith's narratives provide, in the story of Enoch, the model of the Latter-day Saint version of this endeavor and convey the deep differences between LDS and traditional Christian theological anthropologies. Hence, a few words about Zion, as a realizable future, will be in order.

Necessarily brief, these comments on Mormonism's sense of time—or, more specifically, its sense of a history oriented to a future aeon—illustrate the way in which Smith's narratives contribute to the capacity of the Latter-day Saints to constitute and reconstitute themselves and their church in the face of changing circumstances, including the recent international composition of its membership. Ultimately, I argue that Smith's narratives provide a world of meaning by which his believing readers understood and continue to understand themselves existentially in terms of a global future and not merely their American past.

TRANSLATING TIME

"Recourse to documents signals a dividing line between history and fiction," observed Ricoeur when considering the difference between stories granted the status of depicting past fact and those deemed the exclusive product of human imagination.[14] Joseph Smith's work clearly illustrates this elementary point in the extent to which he claims to translate from documentary sources, and his followers rely on these claims for their sense of the historicity of his work. It is just as clear, however, that Smith straddled this line and tested the already permeable boundaries between history and fiction, as well as their corollaries: translation and creation, reason and revelation.

The first and best known of Smith's publications was a narrative of epic scale and purportedly based on a record engraved on ancient

---

14. Paul Ricoeur, "Narrated Time," in *A Ricoeur Reader: Reflection and Imagination*, ed. Mario J. Valdés (Toronto: University of Toronto Press, 1991), 346.

metal plates. The record was translated by Smith, and the plates were then returned to the angel from whence they came. A nearly 600-page story of a people's "bond with the sacred," the Book of Mormon begins with an account of an Israelite family's flight from sixth-century BCE Jerusalem and subsequent establishment of a civilization in the Western Hemisphere.[15] The story climaxes in Christ's postresurrection appearance and organization of his church there. The story ends circa 400 CE with the destruction of the civilization through sin-induced warfare. Still the *sine qua non* of Smith's prophetic claims, more than 192 million copies of the Book of Mormon have been published in 112 languages since 1830.[16]

Smith published also an account of Abram's struggle against idolatry in Ur and his vision of the heavens that would make him Israel's patriarch and Pharaoh's astronomer. On its title page, the text is denominated "a Translation of some ancient Records ... writings of Abraham while he was in Egypt."[17] Thus, as with the Book of Mormon, the claim to a historical source was overt. In this case the documents resorted to were purchased by the church in 1835 from the estate of a European adventurer whose American heir brought four mummies and several papyri to Smith to see if he could, as rumor had it, translate hieroglyphs.[18] First published in 1842, the Book of Abraham is today included in the LDS Church's canon and given equal status to the Bible and the Book of Mormon.

Finally, and most important for this analysis, Smith revised the Bible itself, producing what is most commonly called the "Joseph Smith Translation of the Bible" (JST). Begun in the summer of 1830 and occupying Smith's time as political and economic exigencies allowed,

---

15. Ricoeur, *Symbolism of Evil*, 5.

16. See Tad Walch, "12 Things that I Learned about the Church that I Didn't Know before General Conference," at www.deseret.com/faith/2020/10/4/21500695. This figure is as of October 2020 and accounts only for the LDS Church's dissemination of the book. Figures from the Community of Christ are not available. In 2003, the University of Illinois published a reader's edition for classroom use. The first trade edition of the Book of Mormon was published in 2004 by Doubleday.

17. The Book of Abraham, in *The Pearl of Great Price* (Salt Lake City: The Church of Jesus Christ of Latter-day Saints, 1981), 29 (hereafter PGP).

18. A detailed account of the book's exotic history can be found in H. Donl Peterson, *The Story of the Book of Abraham: Mummies, Manuscripts and Mormonism* (Salt Lake City: Deseret Book Co., 1995).

the "new translation," as he called it, was never published in its entirety during his lifetime and was arguably incomplete at his death in 1844.[19] Smith's changes to the King James Version (KJV) were, however, numerous and ranged from simple grammatical modifications or modernization of archaic words to lengthy additions of new material. Approximately 3,400 verses in the KJV were affected, one-third of which were in the Old Testament and the remaining two-thirds in the New Testament. These changes were embedded directly into the text, not appended as marginalia.[20]

Primacy of narrativized event over theological idea is characteristic of all of Smith's writings but is most striking when read in the context of an otherwise familiar biblical plot. In the words of one most familiar with it, the JST is an unabashed "recitation of events purporting to be actual historical occurrences. The obvious impression ... is that the reader is being treated to a record of historic events lost from all other versions of the Bible."[21] JST Mark's version of the institution narrative is typical. Additions to the KJV are indicated here in italics: "This is my blood of the new testament, which is shed for many. *And as oft as ye do this ordinance, ye will remember me in this hour that I was with you and drank with you of this cup, even the last time in my ministry.* Verily

---

19. Whether or not Smith completed the project has been a matter of debate among his followers. Compare Robert J. Matthews, *"A Plainer Translation," Joseph Smith's Translation of the Bible: A History and Commentary* (Provo, UT: Brigham Young University Press, 1985), 207–14; and Richard P. Howard, *Restoration Scriptures: A Study of Their Textual Development* (Independence, MO: Herald Publishing House, 1995), 130–31. For a summary of the problem and its contemporary resolution, see Robert L. Millet, "Joseph Smith's Translation of the Bible: A Historical Overview," in *The Joseph Smith Translation: A Restoration of Plain and Precious Things*, ed. M. S. Nyman and R. L. Millet (Provo, UT: Brigham Young University Religious Studies Center, 1985), 22–49. Generally speaking, however, it is doubtful that Smith considered any of his works finished in the sense that he did not feel free to revisit them at a later date, including after publication. Smith explicitly rejected the notion of inerrancy. See, e.g., Book of Mormon, title page ("And now, if there are faults they are the mistakes of men; wherefore, condemn not the things of God").

20. Matthews (*Plainer Translation*, 253) summarizes these changes in three categories according to their effect: "restorative" of original biblical meaning or material, "inspired commentary," and "harmonization of doctrinal concepts" revealed to Smith. Barlow (*Mormons and the Bible*, 51–52) breaks these categories down further into six types, including the grammatical and commonsensical. For a detailed examination of Smith's approach to the KJV text, see K. P. Jackson and P. M. Jasinski, "The Process of Inspired Translation: Two Passages Translated Twice in the Joseph Smith Translation of the Bible," *Brigham Young University Studies* 42, no. 2 (2003): 35–64.

21. Matthews, *Plainer Translation*, 246.

I say unto you, *Of this ye shall bear record; for* I will no more drink of the fruit of the vine *with you,* until that day that I drink it new in the kingdom of God. *And now they were grieved and wept over him.*"[22] While the theological implications of Smith's changes are profound, they are stylistically subordinated to the narrative event. No attempt is made to elucidate "this hour" for the reader, much less explain the shift of traditional emphasis from the impending cross to the instant meal table or the implication that Jesus may yet drink with others. Smith's focus is on events to the exclusion of explanation, but the result is no less theologically significant to Christian tradition.

Because of concerns over the reliability of available manuscripts for the JST, only Smith's revisions to the first six chapters of Genesis were given canonical status by the Latter-day Saints prior to the late twentieth century. These six chapters, as well as an introductory chapter of entirely new material, were printed in church periodicals during Joseph Smith's lifetime. Beginning in 1851, after being included with other of his revelations in a compendium titled The Pearl of Great Price, JST Genesis was widely circulated among church members. In 1880, these same chapters were formally canonized as "the Book of Moses" and printed in copies of LDS scriptures. Thus, like the Book of Mormon's Israelite exodus to America, the JST's creation narrative has always informed the LDS ethos.[23]

In contrast to their canonical status within Mormonism, Smith's texts pose insurmountable problems for those who would verify his

---

22. Unless otherwise indicated, all quotations from the JST in this essay are taken from *Joseph Smith's "New Translation" of the Bible: A Complete Parallel Column Comparison of the Inspired Version of the Holy Scriptures and the King James Authorized Version* (Independence, MO: Herald Publishing House, 1970).

23. Matthews, *Plainer Translation*, 177–206. In 1867, the Community of Christ, then known as the Reorganized Church of Jesus Christ of Latter Day Saints, was the first to publish the JST. Initially, its use of the JST was a marker of its claim to be the legitimate (versus the Utah-based LDS Church) heir to Joseph Smith's legacy. Today, the position of each is reversed. In 1981, the more significant portions of the JST, not already published in The Pearl of Great Price, were published as notes to the LDS edition of the KJV, resulting in the canonization of the JST nearly a century and a half after its production. A comparison of the evolving positions of the Community of Christ and the LDS Church is found in Thomas E. Sherry, "Changing Attitudes toward Joseph Smith's Translation of the Bible," in *Plain and Precious Truths Restored*, ed. R. L. Millet and R. J. Matthews (Salt Lake City: Deseret Book Co., 1995), 187–212. For an account of the LDS Church's 1981 canonization of the JST, see Robert J. Matthews, "The New Publications of the Standard Works—1979, 1981," *Brigham Young University Studies* 22, no. 4 (1982): 287–424.

claims to have translated them from historical sources. The Book of Mormon purports to be written in "Reformed Egyptian," a language particular to its subject community of exiles and otherwise unknown. Moreover, the absence of its source document makes impossible or at least contextual any scientific verification of its historicity. Portions of the Book of Abraham papyri have been available since 1967, but the partial nature of their discovery only guarantees continuation of debate, especially since the discovered parts do not show a direct relation to Smith's translation. Moreover, the hieroglyphics included in Smith's text appear to be edited portions of the Egyptian Book of Breathings and bear interpretations unrelated to the original.[24] Thus, notwithstanding the retention of the subtitle "Translated from the papyrus, by Joseph Smith" in its canon, the LDS Church's explanation of the process by which the book was created is that "it was principally divine inspiration rather than his knowledge of languages that produced the English text of the Book of Abraham. His precise methodology remains unknown."[25] As for the JST, one need not look far for its source, nor be concerned with Smith's knowledge of ancient languages. It is true that, during a brief hiatus between internecine and external battles, Smith established a "school of the prophets" in the frontier town of Kirtland, Ohio, at which English and Hebrew grammar were studied; the latter because of the serendipitous proximity of Joshua Seixas, author of the 1833 *Manual Hebrew Grammar for the Use of Beginners*. Whatever mastery Smith achieved over his native tongue, the consensus is that his command of Hebrew was rudimentary. More to the point, his use of it has been deemed more imaginative than expert. "I simply do not think he cared to appear before the world as a meticulous Hebraist," concluded a modern scholar. Rather, Smith "used the Hebrew as he chose, as an artist, inside his frame of reference, in accordance with his taste, according to the effect he wanted to produce, as a foundation

24. For a description of the eleven fragments from the Lebolo papyri and their significance, see John A. Wilson, "A Summary Report," *Dialogue: A Journal of Mormon Thought* 3, no. 2 (1968): 68–85; and Klaus Baer, "The Breathing Permit of Hor: A Translation of the Apparent Source of the Book of Abraham," *Dialogue: A Journal of Mormon Thought* 3, no. 3 (1968): 109–33. For a more recent critical analysis of the text in light of the discovered papyri, see Stephen E. Thompson, "Egyptology and the Book of Abraham," *Dialogue: A Journal of Mormon Thought* 28, no. 1 (1995): 143–60.

25. *Encyclopedia of Mormonism* (New York: Macmillan, 1992), s.v. "Translation and Publication of The Book of Abraham" (by H. Donl Peterson).

for theological innovations."[26] It is unnecessary to speculate on Smith's linguistic capacities, however, because Smith's translation of the Bible is based on an 1828 edition of the KJV, printed by H. and E. Phinney of Cooperstown, New York. As a source document for Smith's translation, the Phinney edition was not only in Smith's native tongue, but already cured of many obsolete words, as well as archaic spellings and pronouns.[27] Nevertheless, as indicated above, the JST was titled and uniformly referred to by Smith as a "translation of the scriptures."[28] As such, the JST constitutes Smith's most obvious transgression of the common understanding of what it means to translate.

Though in 1815, one could be directed to "a place near Monmouth-street, where 'they translate old shoes into new ones,'" it is doubtful that one could properly "renovate, turn, or cut down ... or make new [Bibles] from the remains of (old ones)."[29] This was unthinkable at best, heresy at worst, and certainly not "translation." Because religious diversity made heresy an elusive concept in early nineteenth-century America, most of his contemporaries had to settle for labeling Smith a fraud. Sensitive as he was to these charges and no doubt knowing the difference between shoes and Bibles, Smith's stubbornly persistent use of "translation" to describe the process by which he created his texts invites analysis. Specifically, it invites consideration of what about the term Smith found pertinent to his experience, notwithstanding its obvious impertinences. Such an approach holds the possibility of getting past the tendency to polemics caused by taking Smith's claim to translate at face value and, as I hope to show, reveals an instructive tension in Smith's choice of the term. Staying in that tension and not seeking quick release in claims of mendacity or prophecy provides reason some access to Smith's faith.

Contemporaneous sources indicate that Smith made his more extensive changes to KJV Genesis by employing the same methods as

---

26. Louis C. Zucker, "Joseph Smith as a Student of Hebrew," *Dialogue: A Journal of Mormon Thought* 3, no. 2 (1968): 41–55, 53.

27. For details on the KJV edition used by Smith, see Kent P. Jackson, "Joseph Smith's Cooperstown Bible," *Brigham Young University Studies* 40, no. 1 (2001): 41–70.

28. For Smith's characterization of his task as a translation, see B. H. Roberts, *A Comprehensive History of the Church of Jesus Christ of Latter-day Saints*, 6 vols. (Salt Lake City: Deseret News Press, 1930), 1:238–39, 341. See also Doctrine and Covenants 73:4, 76:15, 90:13, and 124:89 (hereafter D&C).

29. *Oxford English Dictionary,* s.v. "translate."

when working from records purportedly written in ancient languages. Smith is quoted as saying: "After I got through translating the Book of Mormon, I took up the Bible to read with the Urim and Thummim. I read the first chapter of Genesis, and I saw the things as they were done, I turned over the next and the next, and the whole passed before me like a grand panorama; and so on chapter after chapter until I read the whole of it. I saw it all!"[30] A more authoritative account is provided by Smith himself in February 1832. "Upon my return from Amherst [Massachusetts] conference, I resumed the translation of the Scriptures ... While translating St. John's Gospel, myself and Elder Rigdon saw the following vision" of the resurrection of the dead.[31] Finally, in an 1843 funeral sermon, probably alluding to the account in Matthew 27:52 of graves opening at the death of Jesus, Smith spoke of "the visions that roll like an overflowing surge, before my mind." More specifically, he said, "I saw the graves open & the saints as they arose took each other by the hand ... while setting up."[32] Thus, although many emendations are editorial, the more radical of Smith's changes to the Bible were understood by him as a function of what he saw when

---

30. Joseph Smith, as quoted by Lorenzo Brown in "Sayings of Joseph, by Those Who Heard Him at Different Times," Joseph Smith Jr. Papers, Church History Library, The Church of Jesus Christ of Latter-day Saints, Salt Lake City. Brown's statement is based on his recollection in 1880 of a conversation that occurred in 1832. For questions concerning the reliability of this account, see Matthews, *Plainer Translation*, 25–26n12. Referred to in Exodus 28:30 and Leviticus 8:8 as an object placed in "the breastplate of judgment," *urim* and *thummim* are the transliterations of the Hebrew words for "light" and "perfection." For the only major study of the subject since 1824, see Cornelis Van Dam, *The Urim and Thummim: A Means of Revelation in Ancient Israel* (Winona Lake, IN: Eisenbrauns, 1997). Van Dam (*Urim and Thummim*, 232) rejects the traditional view that the urim and thummim was a type of lot oracle and argues that it was a single gem, "a miraculous authenticating light," that shone to verify divine revelation to the high priest. Joseph Smith described his apparatus as "two transparent stones set in the rim of a [silver] bow fastened to a breast plate" that came into his possession with the golden plates for the purpose of translating the Book of Mormon; see *Times and Seasons* 3, no. 9 (1842): 707. See also *Encyclopedia of Mormonism*, s.v. "Urim and Thummim" (by Paul Y. Hoskisson). For a discussion of the role of divining instruments in Smith's production of the Book of Mormon, see D. Michael Quinn, *Early Mormonism and the Magic World View* (Salt Lake City: Signature Books, 1998), 169–75. Later, Smith would say that, as he became more experienced at the process of translating, he no longer needed mechanical aids; see Matthews, *Plainer Translation*, 25, 40.

31. The specific verse in question was John 5:29. See Roberts, *History of the Church*, 1:245–52. See also D&C 76.

32. Joseph Smith, "Discourse" (Apr. 16, 1843), in *Words of Joseph Smith*, ed. Lyndon Cook and Andrew F. Ehat (Provo, UT: Grandin Book, 1991), 196, 198.

reading it. At least with respect to the JST, it appears that when he read he saw events, not words. What he saw, he verbalized to a scribe.[33]

One of Smith's Book of Mormon scribes provided, in his own failed attempt to translate, the occasion for the most direct description of Smith's method. "You have not understood," God told Oliver Cowdery through Smith: "you have supposed that I would give it unto you, when you took no thought save it was to ask me. But ... you must study it out in your mind; then you must ask me if it be right and ... you shall feel that it is right. But if it is not right you shall have no such feelings, but you shall have a stupor of thought that shall cause you to forget that thing which is wrong; therefore you cannot write that which is sacred save it be given you from me."[34] Cowdery appears to have thought he could engage in the "inspired translation" of the Book of Mormon by parroting God's reading. In contrast, as implied by the above statement, Smith believed it necessary to determine independently how to represent what he read or saw. The appropriate question to God by the prophet-translator was whether his interpretation was correct, not what God's interpretation was.

Arguably, then, "translate" expressed Smith's experience of "study[ing] it out in [his] mind" or his sense of agency in front of the text. Smith did not think of himself as God's stenographer. Rather, he was an interpreting reader, and God the confirming authority. He did not experience revelation "as dictated, as something whispered in someone's ear" and, thus, provides a useful illustration of Ricoeur's argument that revelation is not propositional but "pluralistic, polysemic, and at most analogical in form."[35] Of equal significance, however, is the manner in which Smith's description of revelation communicates a sense of being limited by a text. It was possible to not "be right" in one's reading. Smith experienced revelation as an interpretive response to the text: not freely associated from, but bound by the "world of the text"

---

33. For a description of the experience from the scribe's point of view, see Oliver Cowdery to W. W. Phelps, Sep. 7, 1834, in *The Improvement Era* 2, no. 3 (1899), and excerpted in "Joseph Smith—History: Extracts from the History of Joseph Smith, the Prophet," in PGP, 58n.

34. Oliver Cowdery, *Messenger and Advocate* (Kirtland, OH) 1, no. 1 (1834): 14, as quoted in D&C 9:7–9.

35. Paul Ricoeur, "Toward a Hermeneutic of the Idea of Revelation," in *Essays on Biblical Interpretation*, ed. Lewis S. Mudge (Philadelphia: Fortress, 1980), 74, 76.

in front of him, even if in an altered mental state or vision. In sum, Smith's use of "translate," for all its discursive weaknesses, conveyed his experience of creative agency before a text and, simultaneously, his sense of being bound by the text as an account of events or as history.[36] Taking the most obvious example, it can be said that, notwithstanding its English source, the JST asks to be understood as a translation, because it does not arise out of the infinite variations available to fiction but, rather, within the limits of an existing narrative of past events.

In Smith's usage, "translate" is best understood as a metaphor whose "clash between semantic fields" creates a third valence—"a pertinence within impertinence"—that illuminates Smith's method by contrasting the ways in which it was both like and not like translating.[37] His reading and writing of sacred text was like translating insofar as Smith was "study[ing] it out in [his] mind" in response to a source document. It is not like translating insofar as Smith made large additions to his sources and claimed for them the historicity of the original. In the contrast, another meaning arises that depends upon the recognition of the metaphor's incongruity, namely, Smith's claim of power as a prophet to rewrite the prophets. In other words, as with all metaphors, Smith's "translate" requires that one "continue to perceive the previous incompatibility through the new compatibility" of what Smith was signifying about both himself as prophet and his texts as scripture. For his believing readers, these contraries combine to express Smith's prophetic

36. For another explanation of Smith's approach to the Bible, see Barlow, *Mormons and the Bible*, 57–61; my emphasis, however, is on the extent to which Smith felt bound by the text, even as he changed it (see ibid., 61). Moreover, Barlow explains Smith's approach to the text largely in terms of contemporary practices that did not distinguish authors from editors, arguing that Smith used these conventions "creatively" and consistent with "prophetic writers of ancient times." My differences with this argument are slight and result primarily from my emphasis on those sections of the JST that are not merely editorial, but radical reformulations of the biblical narrative. I believe these additions are too extensive to be rationalized by nineteenth-century editorial conventions, especially given the Bible's near-fetishistic canonical status during this period. Finally, though I, too, consider ancient "bible writers" to be a useful analogy to Smith's production of new text, I do not ground the analogy in Smith's felt sense of "godly authority or insight" or "concern … with enlightening the world through revealed truth" (ibid., 60–61). These are the elements of Smith's own story which I argue are not necessary to and can obscure the nature and effect of his reformulation of the biblical narrative.

37. For a summary of his theories on the operation of metaphor and the excerpts used here, see Paul Ricoeur, "The Function of Fiction in Shaping Reality," in Valdés, *Ricoeur Reader*, 124–25.

authority to divine the truth about God's past acts within the narrative limits of ancient, prophetic history. For the academic reader, these contraries suggest an imagination both governed by text and productive of it, reconfiguring the past to suggest what could be, to even create the possible and the real.

Each of Smith's works is an elaboration on climactic moments in the Bible story. The main characters in the Book of Mormon are refugees from Palestine immediately prior to the Babylonian assault who ensure the continuation of Israel's covenant by taking it to the Western hemisphere. Escaping foreign captivity and domestic colonization by successive imperial reigns and creating a parallel story to the Jewish diaspora and Christian synthesis, the Book of Mormon peoples received the resurrected Christ and the fulfillment of God's promise to Abraham. This same promise is the centerpiece of Smith's Book of Abraham and becomes the occasion to provide an alternative account of human origins in creation, as well as of Israel's origins in the Abrahamic covenant. Most aggressively, in the first six chapters of JST Genesis, Smith wrests the entire Christian narrative from its traditional moorings, giving it a new beginning and eliding differences between old and new covenants. Among the more audacious changes is the addition of a precreation event into the Genesis narrative and a new "Genesis 1" that ascribes a specific purpose to creation. These changes suggest another metaphor for understanding Smith's "translations."

Today, the Bible itself is believed to be largely the product of periodic manipulation of foundational texts. "Redaction" has become the preferred term for an invasive revision of a source that seamlessly inserts new material in an authoritative text in order to meet new exigencies. Though only a gleam in the eye of the academy at the time Smith was writing and still a source of concern for literalist readers, redaction has become the regnant explanation for the construction of the Bible as having "experienced change, accretions, and reinterpretations as it was being transmitted through centuries."[38] Of the Tanach's redactors, it has been said that "what Israel took over was not slavishly copied; Israel

---

38. Douglas A. Knight, "Cosmogony and Order in the Hebrew Tradition," in *Cosmogony and Ethical Order: New Studies in Comparative Ethics*, ed. Robin W. Lovin and Frank E. Reynolds (Chicago: University of Chicago Press, 1985), 137.

transformed what she borrowed by baptizing it into her own faith."[39] Israel's "baptism" is commonly understood to have been performed by the sixth-century BCE priestly "P" who, inter alia, Judaized his people's Babylonian-informed understanding of human origins.[40] The next section of this essay analyzes the JST as an analogous "baptism" of Genesis via Christianity into Mormonism. For purposes of comparison, I rely upon Ricoeur's typology from *Symbolism of Evil* to identify not only the distinguishing features of P's redaction but also Christian theologizing upon it.[41] This allows analysis of Smith's adaptation of Genesis in light of definitively Christian readings of the same text, namely, doctrines of creation ex nihilo and original sin and shows the means by which Mormonism's alternative theological anthropology not only is grounded in scriptural authority but is also sustained by narrative devices.

In order to include, in a treatment of this limited page length, sufficient evidence from Smith's virtually unknown adaptation of Genesis, I assume the reader's general knowledge of the traditional biblical account and must generalize a Christian consensus regarding God's sovereignty, human fault, and the origins of sin. I recognize that differences of opinion on these doctrines define many of Christianity's distinctive denominations. For the purposes of this essay such differences may be treated as nuances in comparison to Smith's contrary conclusions to certain generalizations shared by Roman, Orthodox, and Protestant Christians, namely, that (1) the world was created from nothing and constituted an expression of God's absolute goodness; hence, (2) humans, as created beings, are ontologically unrelated to God and brought evil into being by their action.[42] The following section analyzes

---

39. Bernhard W. Anderson, *Creation versus Chaos* (New York: Association Press, 1967), 26.

40. There are, of course, two creation accounts in the first chapters of Genesis: P's priestly fifth-century version in chapter 1 and J's (or the Yahwist's) ninth-century account in chapter 2. Hermann Gunkel's 1895 assessment of them remains authoritative: "Genesis 1 is related to the poetic recensions [from the Babylonian Marduk myth] somewhat like P in general relates to the parallel traditions in J or E: on the whole a strongly Judaicized reworking, sober prose in place of ancient poetry, at the same time a higher view of God replacing an earlier naivete´, and yet also individual features that are very ancient" ("The Influence of Babylonian Mythology upon the Biblical Creation Story," in *Creation in the Old Testament*, ed. Bernhard W. Anderson [Philadelphia: Fortress, 1984], 48).

41. Ricoeur, *Symbolism of Evil*, 171–74.

42. My argument presumes that Smith's rejection of these precepts, without more, is sufficient to demonstrate Mormonism's radical diversion from traditional Christian theology, though certainly it may be argued otherwise. See, e.g., the arguments made by Stephen

Smith's redaction of Genesis as a subversion of these classic Christian propositions. The point of this analysis is, however, not to describe the subversion of meaning or the curious changes Smith makes in the Genesis story. Rather, Smith's version of the story is told to illuminate the mode of his subversion: the manner in which he deploys myth to challenge or, in Lincoln's terms, "recalibrate" the categories of thought and privileges inherent in the status quo of Christian theologizing on the divine-human relationship.[43] Subsequent sections consider the relation of Smith's narratives to Mormonism's viability as a livable alternative to the ethos of traditional Christianity.

JOSEPH SMITH'S NARRATIVE REBUTTAL
TO TRADITIONAL CHRISTIANITY

As conveniently categorized by Ricoeur in his comparisons of pagan and Jewish creation myths, three aspects of Genesis are central to P's monotheistic challenge to his pagan neighbors: Adam's ancestral role as the first human, his defection from God by eating the forbidden fruit, and the subordination of Eve and the serpent to Adam's story.[44] Together these elements of the Genesis story distinguish it as an anthropomorphic myth that is motivated, Ricoeur argues, by the need to give meaning to the universal human experience of evil while simultaneously upholding Israel's faith in an ethical or good God whose creation is good (not tragic, like that of the Greeks) and good ipso facto (not ordered from chaos, like that of the Babylonians).[45] The narrative

---

E. Robinson in Craig L. Blomberg and Stephen E. Robinson, *How Wide the Divide? A Mormon and an Evangelical in Conversation* (Downers Grove, IL: InterVarsity, 1997). But see also the decision of the Society of Christian Philosophers to boycott Brigham Young University and the society's related decision to establish guidelines for regional meetings, excluding "any institution professing to be Christian while at the same time subscribing to a doctrinal position directly contradicting the ecumenical creeds accepted by all branches of the Christian Church, Orthodox, Catholic, and Protestant" (Peggy Fletcher Stack, "Mormon Christian Dialogue?" www.beliefnet.com).

43. Lincoln, *Theorizing Myth*, 216n14.

44. Ricoeur, *Symbolism of Evil*, 232–78.

45. Too simply stated, the cosmologies of Israel's neighbors were characterized by gods who either struggled to create order out of chaos (the Babylonians) or disrupted order by tempting and blinding humans (the Greeks). For the former, evil is primordial and salvation from it comes through a "final victory of order over chaos" in creation. For the latter, humans have a tragic fate and their salvation "consists in a sort of aesthetic deliverance issuing from the tragic spectacle itself" Ricoeur, *Symbolism of Evil*, 172–75. Of course, elements of each these types may be found in the Bible. For example, KJV Revelation 12:7 refers to a

does not fully cooperate with P's argument for the absolute priority of good over evil, however. Both the snake, who appears with the offer of evil, and Eve, who responds to it, imply the existence of evil in creation and prior to human act. Thus, biblical scholarship has postulated that Eve and the snake are marginal figures in Adam's story, even residuals of pagan mythology. While the snake as a demon and Eve, its instrument, express the possibility of evil, they are not necessary to the story, merely adding "enigmatic depth" to the Israelite narrative of Adam's transgression.[46] Thus interpreted, these same three features of the Genesis account frame the traditional Christian doctrines of creation ex nihilo and original sin. Smith's narrative begins by enlarging the frame and, in doing so, makes ideological space for human participation in the divine nature.

In Smith's redaction of Genesis, people—as uncreated children of God—come first, and the world later. This reversal of events is made by adding to the established narrative an account of a precreation council comprised of spirit persons with form and agency, but not bodies of flesh. According to the JST, God called the council in order to present a plan for the governance of the yet-to-be-created earth, the site of the next progressive state of his gathered children. The positing of this event and its description of premortal existence inevitably contest traditional Christian theology. Imbedded as they are in a narrative, the theological principles at stake in the JST council must be inferred from its drama of a confrontation between God and Lucifer over how to obtain the successful return of earth's future inhabitants from their probationary state, as well as over who would be sent with the power to ensure that result. God had already offered a plan that would give primacy and "honor" to "my beloved Son, which was my beloved and chosen from the beginning." Lucifer, the Son of the Morning, begged to differ and presented himself as an alternative: "Behold I, send me, I will be thy Son, and I will redeem all mankind, that one soul shall

---

"war in heaven: Michael and his angels fought against the dragon; and the dragon fought and his angels." Similarly, the Book of Job depicts a kind of tragic spectacle precipitated by God's wager with Satan. What is distinctive about the Genesis creation narrative is, however, its abjuring such notions of evil—as either primeval chaos or tragic existence—in order to establish absolutely God's goodness notwithstanding the humanity's universal experience of the "not good."

46. Ricoeur, *Symbolism of Evil*, 233–35.

not be lost, and surely I will do it; wherefore, give me thine honor" (JST Gen. 3:2–3). Though other conversation is described in the council, these are actually the first words quoted from any character. First words are not a given; they are the chosen set point of a story's trajectory. These first words spoken in Smith's narrative stand in powerful contrast to the first words, both chronologically and literally, in traditional Christianity's cosmic history: "Let there be light," says God over a perfect creation, into which evil has yet to appear and, when it does, comes as a result of human action. These words communicate that God has power over evil because evil is subordinate to—or comes after and is foreign to—God's absolutely original and fundamentally good creation. In contrast, Smith's addition of the premortal council to the traditional Genesis narrative teaches that the option of evil existed, as did humans, primordially or prior to earthly creation.

The JST narrative implies three reasons for God's rejection of Lucifer's alternative. Most obviously, it constituted rebellion in its antagonism to God's plan and in its demand for "God's own power." There was also a third, more substantive problem, however. Lucifer's proposed means of ensuring that "not one soul would be lost" was meant to "[destroy] the agency of man." Since, in this cosmology, there is no existence without agency, Lucifer's plan would have made God's plan a nullity.[47] Thus, in Smith's cosmology evil as the possibility of defection from God is present from the beginning and prior to the world's creation. Of course, this means also that creation is not ex nihilo. As such, the myth recalibrates the created-uncreated dichotomy fundamental to the Christian tradition's definition of human unrelatedness to the divine. More will be said of this in a moment. For now, we return to the story.

Smith's recounting of the temptation of Eve and Adam in the garden is fairly traditional, but as a consequence of evil's role in the premortal council, the serpent's subtle nature and malicious intent is not a surprise to the reader. Or, to use Ricoeur's term, evil does not appear to

---

47. Smith would later elaborate discursively on these ideas first expressed narratively: "Man was also in the beginning with God. ... not created or made ... independent in that sphere in which God has placed it, to act for itself, as all intelligence also; otherwise there is no existence. Behold here is the agency of man, and here is the condemnation of man; because that which was from the beginning is plainly manifest unto them, and they receive not the light" (D&C 93:29–31).

"happen" to Eve and Adam. The serpent's invitation to rebellion is simply Lucifer 'pursuing his earlier, failed agenda. This point is impressed upon the reader by the fact that the JST story of the council is inserted into the traditional Genesis narrative immediately after the command to humans not to eat of the fruit and before the serpent makes his entrance. As such, the council story explains God's command and does so in the context of an additional instruction to Adam and Eve: "nevertheless thou mayest choose for thyself, for it is given unto thee; but, remember that I forbid it" (KJV Gen. 2:17). The narrative effect of this addition is to explain the serpent's existence in the garden and the KJV's characterization of it as "more subtle than any beast in the field which the Lord God had made" (KJV Gen. 3:1). The inference of this observation is made explicit in the JST: evil precedes creation. This requires Smith's narrative to also confront directly the problem of the existence of evil in an otherwise good creation.

Among the options he does not take are the alternatives to the Priestly redactor: a cosmogonic or tragic ethos. The JST does not portray earth's creation as the "final victory of order over chaos" after a cosmic battle among the gods. Rather, the JST maintains the Bible's distinctive provision of a primordial ancestor "whose condition is homogeneous with ours."[48] Adam, and in Smith's narrative one must also include Eve and the snake (as Lucifer), stood with the rest of future humanity, watched or participated in the debate and made their respective choices. As important, victory over evil is not final. Smith's god is not a Marduk who vanquished evil and, thereby, achieved order in the end (as creation). Smith's god is sovereign from the uncreated beginning: Lucifer is cast out of heaven summarily, as well as subject to God's adjudication of the parties to the fall. Moreover, notwithstanding its a priori existence, evil in the JST is not tragically "the very worldliness of the world ... the state of being in the world, the misfortune of existing."[49] God's creative act remains radically separate from evil that is now "cast down" and must find a way back into relation with these beings in order to disrupt God's good work. Thus, in the JST, the struggle between good and evil is both cosmological and

48. Ricoeur, *Symbolism of Evil*, 175.

49. Paul Ricoeur, "'Original Sin': A Story in Meaning," in *The Conflict of Interpretations*, ed. Don Ihde (Evanston, IL: Northwestern University Press, 1974), 273.

existential: it is, we shall see, considered constitutive of human agency. God's goodness and sovereignty is measured by the power to redeem human agents in extremis, not the power to create them ex nihilo.[50]

Smith's redaction of Genesis continues to emphasize that choice is manifest and freedom is—temporally at least—absolute. Therefore, the terms under which Adam and Eve occupy the garden differ in the JST. While they are commanded not to eat of the tree of the knowledge of good and evil, they are told also, in contrast to the KJV: "Nevertheless, thou mayest choose for thyself, for it is given unto thee; but remember that I forbid it" (JST Gen. 2:21). As with all narratives, this dialogue requires interpretation and at least two conclusions are possible. One is legalistic. If they "may" choose, then to choose is not disobedient, even when told not to choose. In the larger context of the operation of agency in Smith's cosmology, it is more likely that the "may" refers to a necessary condition of Adam and Eve's existence, not a license to do other than what they had been commanded. This view is supported by the fact that the story of the premortal council, with its emphasis on agency, is inserted in the narrative after God's instruction not to eat the fruit and, as indicated, prior to the serpent's offer of an alternative. Adam and Eve have a choice, but they have also been instructed in the right choice and given an example of the dangers of a wrong choice. Smith's Book of Abraham speaks more obliquely but to the same point and more broadly applied. There God says to the premortal assembly: "Whom shall I send? And one answered like unto the Son of Man. ... And another answered. ... And the Lord said: I will send the first. And the second was angry and kept not his first estate; and, at that day, many followed after him" (Abr. 3:27–28)

Not surprisingly, given its overt presence in the JST account of the garden, the nature of evil and its consequences is a large theme in Smith's account of the world's first family. Particular care is taken to reiterate Lucifer's motives to implement his own plan at the expense of God's. The reader is told that Lucifer, now the cast-down Satan, "sought

---

50. While in Mormon theology there is no existence without agency, the agency that operates in this world is conditioned by the gift of the atonement of Jesus Christ. The Book of Mormon, at 2 Nephi 2:26–27, provides: "because that they are redeemed from the fall they have become free forever, knowing good from evil; to act for themselves and not to be acted upon, save it be by the punishment of the law at the great and last day Wherefore, men are free according to the flesh; and all things are given them which are expedient."

also to beguile Eve, for he knew not the mind of God; wherefore he sought to destroy the world" (JST Gen. 3:7). Here, to Lucifer's grandiosity and rebellion is added the additional problem of ignorance, that is, he knows not "the mind of God." Thus, in the JST version of the garden, as at the council, Satan is displaying not only malice but also a fundamental misunderstanding of the way life works, when he prompts the serpent to argue, consistent with the KJV: "Ye shall not die ye shall be as gods, knowing good and evil" (JST Gen. 3:11). With the council narrative as background, the JST reader sees Satan's approach has not changed and neither has the substance of his offer: death masquerading as power. Evil is rebellion against God's plan and the embracing of its opposite: the voluntary or free adoption of an antiorder that seeks to destroy human freedom in order to obtain power as an end in itself. It is Lucifer, not the fallen Eve or Adam, who conveys the definition of sin and defines it in terms of rebellion as a lust for power obtained at the expense of agency and, thus, life itself. Stated as an abstract principle, it is obvious that this characterization of Satan and his goal are not original to the JST. As Ecclesiastes tells us, there is nothing new under the sun; particularly the religious sun. I do not dispute him. My point here is the manner in which this principle is historicized or realized for the reader by its conveyance through narrative and, more especially, the authorized biblical plot rather than a separate narrative. Many of Smith's subsequent additions to the KJV plot continue to elaborate by inference on this theology of evil. One more example must suffice: Smith's version of the contest between Cain and Abel. The JST Cain, the firstborn, is introduced to the readers as a disappointment to his parents' hopes that he will not "reject" the Lord, in contrast to his younger brother Abel, who "walked in holiness before the Lord." Cain's first words in the narrative are "Who is the Lord, that I should know him." Moreover, Cain's offering of the first fruits of his field is depicted as a response to Satan's command, not God's. When the Lord rejected the offering and accepted Abel's, Cain was "very wroth," notes the KJV, and the JST adds: "Now Satan knew this, and it pleased him" (JST Gen. 5:4, 8, and 11). The addition of the character of Satan to this story continues the theme of choice and agency. Indeed, it may be said that the character of Satan is a foil that offers his own and opposite bond in direct imitation of the sacred in each instance in which he appears to

Cain. After the KJV warning that "sin lieth at the door," the JST has the Lord say to Cain: "Satan desireth to have thee, and except thou shalt hearken unto my commandments, I will deliver thee up, and it shall be unto thee according to his desire" (KJV Gen. 4:7 and JST Gen. 5:9).

At this point in the story, Smith adds eight verses where the KJV makes do with one referencing Cain's killing of Abel. Smith's verses provide motive for the crime. Cain, we are told, "listened not any more to the voice of the Lord" and "loved Satan more than God." As a consequence, Satan invites Cain to enter into a secret covenant "that he would do according to his [Satan's] commands" and, in exchange, Satan promises "this day I will deliver thy brother Abel into thine hands." The reversal implicit in this contract is made explicit when Cain rejoices: "Truly I am Mahan, the master of this great secret, that I may murder and get gain … and he gloried in his wickedness." Later, he exults over the body of his brother: "I am free; surely the flocks of my brother falleth into my hands." The exiled Cain will later teach his Satanic covenant to his sons whose "works were abominations, and began to spread among all" (JST Gen. 5:11, 13–16, 18, and 38–39). But, always in Smith's narrative, individuals are free and capacitated to choose, as is evidenced by the women who resist their husbands' acceptance of Cain's antiorder. The secrets of Cain's order were not shared with the women in the family "because that Lamech [Cain's fifth generation descendant] had spoken the secret unto his wives, and they rebelled against him, and declared these things abroad, and had not compassion. Wherefore Lamech was despised, and cast out, and came not among the sons of men, lest he should die" (JST Gen. 5:40–41). Thus, for Smith, the potential for evil is coexistent with existence itself, but sin—the embracing of evil and antiorder—came into the world through Cain.

What, then, is Adam and Eve's contribution to this myth of the origin of evil in the world? The JST account of God's response to Adam and Eve's choice to eat the forbidden fruit is consistent in relevant detail to the KJV story. They are driven from the garden that brought forth its fruit spontaneously into a world that requires their labor to sustain them and the new life they will engender. At this point, however, the JST introduces sixteen verses to the KJV text. These verses emphasize that their exile was not only from ease and painlessness but also from God's presence. Now, instead of God calling upon them, they "called upon the name of the Lord and they heard the voice of the Lord, from the way toward the garden of Eden, speaking unto them. And he gave unto them commandments." Here is the next major turn away from the KJV in the JST narrative, resulting in an addition of 600 words to the text. Exile from God's presence does not put them out of reach of his voice. In Smith's account, Adam and Eve are taught by heavenly messengers to worship God, offer sacrifice, "repent, and call upon God in the name of the Son for evermore." They are further told "as thou hast fallen, thou mayest be redeemed, and all mankind, even as many as will" (JST Gen. 4:3–9).

Like the Book of Mormon, the JST places the knowledge of Christ and the offer of salvation prior to Jesus's birth. Explicitly, salvation is the plan from the beginning and atonement is God's anticipatory response to human defection. Hence, a BCE figure in the Book of Mormon will explain: "if Adam had not transgressed he would not have fallen, but he would have remained in the garden of Eden. And all things which were created must have remained in the same state in which they were after they were created; and they must have remained forever, and had no end. And they would have remained in a state of innocence, having no joy, for they knew no misery; doing no good, for they knew no sin. But behold, all things have been done in the wisdom of him who knoweth all things" (2 Ne. 2:26). What Adam and Eve originate for their progeny is not evil, but death: "by reason of transgression cometh the fall, which fall bringeth death" (JST Gen. 6:61). In the JST narrative, humans are by nature separate, not evil. "The Fall" is not a fall into evil, but into alienation. Adam and Eve's legacy is not to change human nature but, rather, to change the conditions under which that nature will be developed, that is, out of God's presence and in a world where "God gave unto man that he should act for himself. Wherefore, man could not act for himself save it should be that he was enticed by the one or the other," according to the Book of Mormon (2 Ne. 2:16).

Later in the JST Genesis narrative, God will mourn in vision to Enoch that the antediluvians have failed to "choose me their Father" (JST Gen. 7:40). This is the bond with the sacred described in the JST: humans with an uncorrupted but corruptible capacity to know good from evil, placed in an environment that requires them to choose between manifest options. The choice is one of affiliation, of whom to love in an environment that makes one free to choose. On the one hand, "the gospel began to be preached from the beginning, being declared by holy angels, sent forth from the presence of God; and by his own voice, and by the gift of the Holy Ghost. And thus all things were confirmed unto Adam by an holy ordinance; and the gospel preached; and a decree sent forth that it should be in the world until the end thereof" (JST Gen. 5:44–45). On the other hand, "Satan came among them [the children of Adam and Eve], saying I am also a son of God, and he commanded them, saying Believe it [the gospel] not. And they believed it not; and they loved Satan more than God. And men began from that time forth to be carnal, sensual and devilish" (JST Gen. 4:13). This is, using Ricoeur's terms, the occasion for the "servile will, of the bad choice that binds itself."[51] Or, as described in the Book of Mormon: "our first parents were cut off both temporally and spiritually from the presence of the Lord; and thus we see they became subjects to follow after their own will" (Alma 42:7).

Both literally and figuratively speaking, Smith's narrative presents a dramatic departure from the traditional Adamic myth whose "intention is to set up a *radical* origin of evil distinct from the more *primordial* origin of goodness of things."[52] Mormonism's evil is as uncreated and preexistent as is good. Both are always potential to the act, as choice, of the uncreated person. As the attendees to the counsel and, later, earth's inhabitants, humans must choose between the two plans and their personal fate is decided by their choice. Implicit in this personal struggle is the notion that the power is in these persons not only to discern but also to vanquish evil. This, too, is a central dynamic in Smith's challenge to traditional Christianity's theological anthropology. In Smith's completely original Genesis 1, Moses's experience of the divine at the burning bush is followed by an assertion of his newly realized identity against Satan, who comes demanding to be worshipped: "Who art thou? For behold, I am a son of God, in the similitude of his Only Begotten; and where is thy glory, that I should worship thee?" Moses then summarily dismisses him with the command "Get thee hence, Satan; deceive me not." Subject to Moses's superior power, Satan must

---

51. Ricoeur, *Symbolism of Evil*, 156.
52. Ricoeur, *Symbolism of Evil*, 233.

comply.[53] Thus, the agency and power of persons to effect their will, first manifested in the narrative of a heavenly council, characterizes earthly life as well.

The significance of human relatedness to God as *imago dei* and the extent of human access to divine power is made explicit in Moses's second theophany. After being taught of "worlds without number" and shown the earth and all its inhabitants, Moses asks "why these things are so." God answers: "this is my work and my glory—to bring to pass the immortality and eternal life of man" (Moses 1:30, 39). With this reply, Smith rejected 1,500 years of Christian theological anthropology by making God ontologically related to creation. God is both defined as Father and glorified as God by the capacity and purpose to engender the divine life in humans. To Smith, "Father God" is not only a metaphor for expressing divine love, but is definitive of God and indicative of human possibility, even human capacity to receive the divine nature.

Thus, while JST Genesis appears to share with non-Christian creation dramas "a mode of thought according to which order comes at the end and not at the beginning," Smith's order is not "the last act of a drama that concerns the generation of the gods."[54] Rather, human existence is part of a plan that does not have a beginning or an end. Existence is an ongoing process by which God engenders in human beings the quality of life that characterizes their divine Father. The ultimate purpose of this redemptive plan is to enable humans to engender life and, thereby, experience divine joy. Hence, Smith's version of Eve, exiled from Eden and taught by angels the message of redemption, rejoiced to Adam: "were it not for our transgression, we never should have had seed, and never should have known good and evil, and the joy of our redemption, and the eternal life which God giveth unto all the obedient" (JST Gen. 4:11). "Eternal life" is comprised of being partakers of the divine nature or in possessing the capacity to engender in others the life one has received via the plan. The Book of Mormon states the full extent of LDS optimism: "Adam fell that men might be; and men are, that they might have joy" (2 Ne. 2:25).

---

53. Moses 1:15–16, 22. The Herald House publication of the Joseph Smith Translation omits JST Genesis 1. It is included in the Latter-day Saint canon as "Moses 1" in the Book of Moses in PGP. The Book of Moses contains JST Genesis 1–6.

54. Ricoeur, *Symbolism of Evil*, 233, 177.

Nevertheless, "men" are in a serious predicament. While the JST does not permit the conclusion that, as a consequence of Adam's sin, the human race is *massa peccati*, it does impute to Adam and Eve the cause of all humanity's subjugation to death—cast out of God's presence and destined for physical dissolution. The JST's largest single addition to the KJV is an account of a people and, more particularly, their prophet Enoch, who overcame both alienation and dissolution and obtained for his posterity the promise of the same. In Smith's elaboration on the figure of Enoch, Smith orients his Adamic myth toward a future that informs his believing readers' sense of present meanings and possibilities. Enoch and his ideal city provide the type of Zion to which saints of the latter days are to aspire. For the instant analysis, it is equally important, however, that the promise of Zion is obtained by human petition, not divine fiat. This is the final example of Smith's baptism of traditional Christianity into his restorationist project. It is possibly an even greater affront to tradition: giving humans a role in the preservation of the divine plan and, in so doing, constituting a means of their progressing toward the divine life itself.

URZEIT GLICHT ENDZEIT

Stories begin with a view to their end, just as types must take their bearings from antitypes. Both of these truisms meet in the Adamic myth's orientation to a future that overcomes the breach occasioned by the fall and, for Christian readers, through one who will mediate a new covenant of salvation. Thus, unlike the Babylonian cosmogonic myth that was directed toward "cultural-ritual re-enactment" of a past event and the Greek tragic myth that explained the present "spectacle of Terror and Pity," the Adamic myth was most essentially eschatological: it was oriented to the "man to come."[55] This was for Christianity the "second-man," the offer of "so much more" in Jesus Christ. Intermediate types were offered by the biblical narrative, however: figures that represented the promise of overcoming the fall and of ideal fulfillment of human potential as *imago dei*. In the traditional narrative, Abraham is the first and most fully drawn of such figures.[56] In the character of Enoch, Smith found an earlier figure to suggest another measure of

---

55. Ricoeur, *Symbolism of Evil*, 260.
56. Ricoeur, *Symbolism of Evil*, 262.

human potential: theurgy, or the right to access heavenly powers and even to influence future events related to salvation.

After the JST describes the evolution of a godly order and rebellious antiorder among Adam and Eve's immediate progeny, the generations of the patriarchs are listed consistent with the KJV. While the KJV was able to tell Enoch's story in thirteen words—"And Enoch walked with God, and he was not; for God took him"—the JST required 4,600 (KJV Gen. 5:24). Smith's Enoch is the most representative of Mormonism's understanding of the divine-human relationship and its rejection of contemporary Christian anthropology. For the sake of brevity, two themes must suffice to make this point. First, in the JST, Enoch "built a city that was called the city of Holiness, even Zion."[57] The people were also called Zion "because they were of one heart and of one mind and dwelt in righteousness and there were no poor among them." In short, the story of Enoch tells of a community that experienced the end of evil. This is made clear in their overcoming the separation from God occasioned by the fall: "Enoch and all his people walked with God, and he dwelt in the midst of Zion." They triumphed over their enemies because Enoch "spake in the word of the Lord," and, when he did, humans and nature "were turned out of their course." Ultimately, not only Enoch, as implied in the KJV, but also his city were taken up to heaven without experiencing death.[58] Second, and most significant for the argument of this essay, Smith's narrative depicts an extended theophany in which Enoch is portrayed as obtaining guarantees of redemption from God in virtue of Enoch's God-given right to access heavenly power and exercise it in temporal affairs. This is the final example of the way in which Smith's mythos "recalibrates" categories of thought and privilege inherent in the status quo of Christian theologizing on the divine human relationship.[59]

The JST account of Enoch's theophany begins with God showing Enoch what will happen to the wicked among his grandson's (Noah's) generation. Their fate in this world and the afterlife not only causes

---

57. All quotations from the JST related to the Enoch narrative are from JST Genesis 7 and in the interest of space will not be individually referenced when quoted below, except where further elaboration is needed.

58. JST Gen. 7:27 ("Zion, in process of time, was taken up into heaven. And the Lord said unto Enoch: Behold mine abode forever").

59. Lincoln, *Theorizing Myth*, 216n14.

the heavens to "weep, and shed forth their tears as the rain upon the mountains" but also moves God to weep. This mystifies Enoch, who asks, "How is it thou canst weep, seeing thou are holy, and from all eternity to all eternity?" The reply emphasizes God's relationship to the earth's inhabitants. Notwithstanding his "commandment, that they should love one another; and that they should choose me their Father ... they are," God explains, "without affection, and they hate their own blood." After watching the devastation of the flood, Enoch's attitude changes. In contrast to his initial shock that the Lord would mourn such as these, he now "wept over his brethren, and said unto the heavens, I will refuse to be comforted." Enoch petitions God to promise that he will never again destroy the earth by flood. The JST provides: "the Lord could not withhold; and he covenanted with Enoch, and sware unto him an oath." The promise is the familiar one, though it contains an additional element. God not only swears that "he would stay the floods," but also that "he would call upon the children of Noah." This additional promise echoes Smith's character-ization of Adam and Eve after their fall: separated from God but not out of the range of his voice. According to the JST, "the gospel was preached [unto Adam and Eve after their expulsion]; and a decree sent forth that it should be in the world until the end thereof; and thus it was" (JST Gen. 5:45). In the JST, human cooperation is a neces-sary element in the performance of this decree. In Smith's cosmology, human communication with the divine is not only a necessary con-stant, but its message is that humans must assume responsibility for the execution of God's plan for human salvation. This is more plainly evidenced by Enoch's next request.

After witnessing in vision Noah's survival of the flood and the prom-ised continuation of his progeny, Enoch is next shown the death of the Messiah. Even more appalled by this turn of events, Enoch again "wept and cried unto the Lord," obtaining a second promise. His preface to the request is, however, an unusual one: "for inasmuch as thou art God, and I know thee, and thou has sworn unto me, and commanded me that I should ask in the name of thine Only Begotten; thou has made me, and given unto me a right to thy throne, and not of myself, but through thine own grace; wherefore I ask thee if thou wilt not come again on the earth?" This is probably the most dramatic example of the theurgic force of Smith's revisions to Genesis and reveals another dimension of Smith's rejection of the classic theological anthropology of Christianity. In the JST account, Enoch realized for himself and his people the hope of overcoming on earth the breach in the bond with the sacred through the establishment of Zion. In addition, by rights given to him by God, Enoch obtained from God the promise that he would continue to manifest himself to Enoch's posterity and, through them, minister salvation to the world.[60] Though Enoch is portrayed as having obtained this promise "not of myself, but through ... grace," it is no less the case that Smith's narrative contemplates that humans may influence the divine will. This is demonstrated in God's response to Enoch's assertion of right in conjunction with his petition that God not abandon Enoch's progeny, notwithstanding the death of the Messiah. God swears, "Even as I live, even so will I come in the last days ... to fulfil the oath which I have made unto you."

Thus, in the figure of Enoch, Smith found a figure of covenantal hope earlier than Abraham, linked that hope directly to the coming of a messiah, and directed its fulfillment to an end times conditioned on human agency to call down the powers of heaven. The JST's repetition of the covenant to Noah makes this more explicit. The KJV provides that the bow is a reminder of God's everlasting covenant with "every living creature" to never again destroy the earth by flood. In contrast, the JST Noah is told the bow is a sign of the covenant with Enoch "that, when men should keep all my commandments, Zion should again come on the earth" (JST Gen. 9:21–23; cf. KJV Gen. 9:16). Moreover, as with Enoch himself, those who would realize the promise of the covenant must contribute to its realization by obtaining heavenly powers on a temporal plane. They must "embrace the truth and look upward." When they do "then shall Zion look downward ... [and] shall come down out of heaven and possess the earth, and shall have place till the end come." These are the terms of "the everlasting

---

60. This is the clearest signal that, for Smith, Enoch represents an antecedent to the Abrahamic covenant that "I will establish my covenant between me and thee and thy seed after thee in their generations for an everlasting covenant, to be a God unto thee, and to thy seed after thee" (see Gen. 17 and 22:15–18). For extension of the Abrahamic covenant to the Christian movement, see, e.g., Luke 16:22–23 (the righteous to rest in the bosom of Abraham) and Galatians 3:8 and 29 (through Christ, the gentiles become the seed of Abraham and "heirs according to the promise"). For Smith's elaboration on this covenant, see Abr. 2.

covenant" that affects the reconstitution of the bond with the sacred and holds the key to the end of evil. Though this promise of a latter-day Zion that would receive Enoch's Zion, as well as partake of its theurgic powers, obtains from the past, as narrativized by Smith, it constitutes a sacred history that oriented the Latter-day Saints to a particular future. It provided an identity that carried them from New York to the Ohio frontier, through extermination orders in Missouri to exile from Illinois, and finally to the Rocky Mountains, building city after city in hope of Zion.[61]

Though occupied with an ancient figure, the Enoch narrative directs faithful readers of the JST to a future project: the return of Zion in fulfillment of God's promise to Enoch and, through Enoch, to all the posterity of Noah. In the "last days," there would be "great tribulations … but my people will I preserve," God promised. Specifically, "righteousness will I send down out of heaven, and truth will I send forth out of the earth, to bear testimony of mine Only Begotten" (JST Gen. 7:67, 69). To Latter-day Saints, this is nothing less than the heavenly messengers sent to Smith and the unearthing the Book of Mormon's "golden plates," which constituted a second witness of Christ by restoring "many plain and precious things" lost from the Bible (1 Ne. 13:28–29, 35, and 40). Smith's narratives weave Mormonism into biblical history, but not as an aspiration to "live ancient lives" so definitive of the Latter-day Saints' Puritan progenitors. Smith's followers did not believe their "commonwealth should subside into the routine of the communal covenant: a rhythm of declension and return with a basically static religious and social framework" modeled on a biblical past.[62] Rather, the Latter-day Saints aspired to become Enochs in their own right: walking and talking with God and exercising their own powers within a new Zion wherein God would make his millennial abode. In 1836, the Latter-day Saints dedicated their first temple with a song that included the lyric:

---

61. Shipps (*Mormonism*, 47, 53, and 57) was the first to recognize this "pattern of reappropriation" of the Bible story that fueled the LDS reenactment on the American frontier of ancient Israel's saga of gathering, exodus, and kingdom building. Relying largely on pioneer sources, she concluded that LDS reappropriation was, however, "an exterior story rather than an interior one."

62. Theodore Dwight Bozeman, *To Live Ancient Lives: The Primitivist Dimension in Puritanism* (Chapel Hill: University of North Carolina Press, 1988), 345, 349.

The latter day glory begins to come forth;
The visions and blessings of old are returning;
The angels are coming to visit the earth. ...
The knowledge and power of God are expanding.
The vail o'er the earth is beginning to burst.[63]

The Latter-day Saints understood themselves both as beneficiaries of God's grace and as God's agents for overcoming of the effects of the Fall. The full eschatology of Smith's Adamic myth is found in the promise made to Enoch, like the promise made to Abraham "that his people would have a salvific relation with God is an inexhaustible promise ... as such it opens up a history in which this promise can be repeated and reinterpreted over and over again."[64]

The building of Zion remains the "future project" of the LDS Church and is "intimately related to the ways in which it remembers itself."[65] The promise of Zion still orders the experience of Smith's faithful readers, providing them a beginning and an end between which they, as his readers—by means of their own heuristic powers of imagination—get their bearings to act. Their local ecclesiastical units are called "stakes," symbolic of the stakes that anchor the tent of Zion, and are collectively referred to as "the stakes of Zion." Thus, as with other myths that have founded a sense of peoplehood, Smith's narrative history of human and divine interaction was ultimately oriented to a future time that served as a basis for acting in the present. It provided a world of meaning by which his believing readers understood themselves existentially, including their future and not merely their past. Most fundamentally, Smith's writings give his believing readers a different sense of what was and what will be and, as a consequence, give significance to and a sense of what is real in the present. Just as the story of a realized messiah and the coming kingdom profoundly reoriented the Jews called "Christian," Smith's writings of the "fulness of times" provided a unique means by which the Latter-day Saints' alterity has been maintained, even as they integrated with contemporary society.

---

63. "The Spirit of God like a Fire Is Burning," in *Collection of Sacred Hymns, for the Church of the Latter Day Saints* (Kirtland, OH: F. G. Williams, 1835; repr., Independence, MO: Herald Heritage, 1973), hymn 90.

64. Ricoeur, "Creativity in Language," in Valdés, *Ricoeur Reader*, 472.

65. Ricoeur, "Creativity in Language," in Valdés, *Ricoeur Reader*, 472.

CONCLUSION

With respect to academic arguments over the New Testament's historicity, philosopher Mary Warnock has argued that the debates "show a failure to understand the full part that imagination plays not only in religion but in literature, history and in life itself, lived as it is through time, yet demanding a constant effort to make sense of time, to turn events into stories."[66] Analogously, it can be said that the nature and function of Smith's texts can best be understood not in terms of historical veracity but as a means to "make sense of time," specifically biblical time. Or, in terms of narrative theory, Smith's mythmaking may be best understood in terms of its capacity to make "human time," that combination of what is already (our past) with what is anticipated (our future) to comprise the reality out of which we act in the present.[67] Thus, by maintaining the narrative function of the Bible in his own writings, Smith made more than a claim to history. He gave his believing readers a sense of what was experientially real, not merely philosophically true. Wittgenstein's observation about Christianity is equally true of Mormonism. "Christianity is not," he said, "based on a historical truth; rather it offers us a (historical) narrative and says: now believe! But not, believe this narrative with the belief appropriate to historical narrative, rather ... make a quite different place in your life for it."[68] Attention to narrative function furthers Wittgenstein's point by positing that the believing reader's commitment is not partial. The reader does not make "a place" for the narrative but enters—takes his or her life experience—into the narrative as a world of possibility.

This is not to argue against the kind of verification fundamental to scientific history, though it does side with Warnock's observation that a positivist approach can miss the role of human imagination in not merely perceiving but also constructing reality. Rather, it is to argue for something besides the power of description at work in certain narratives, especially those that rise to the level of mythos and make a

---

66. Mary Warnock, "Religious Imagination," in *Religious Imagination*, ed. James P. Mackey (Edinburgh: Edinburgh University Press, 1986), 155–56.

67. Ricoeur, "Narrated Time," 354.

68. Ludwig Wittgenstein, *Culture and Value*, ed. G. H. von Wright with Heikki Nyman, trans. Peter Winch (Chicago: University of Chicago Press, 1980), 32e; quoted in Van A. Harvey, *The Historian and the Believer*, 2nd ed. (Chicago: University of Chicago Press, 1996), xxvii.

claim to religious authority. Smith's narratives do not display fact to be assented to but draw the reader into a malleable reality by means of the malleable plots that traditionally provided the basis for Jewish and Christian ethos and ethic. It can be said that Smith was translating time, not text. Specifically, he translated biblical time in service to, he said, an "ushering in of the dispensation of the fullness of times ... a whole and complete and perfect union, and welding together of dispensations, and keys, and powers ... from the days of Adam even to the present time" (D&C 128:18). Whatever his intention, the effect was to deploy the biblical text in a manner that radically subverted centuries of theologizing on who God is and how humans are to worship God.

Making room for a more poetic function at work between this reading-and-writing prophet and his confirming God allows that "truth," as Ricoeur has said, "no longer means verification, but manifestation. ... What shows itself is in each instance a proposed world, a world I may inhabit and wherein I can project my own most possibilities."[69] This is the power to which Bloom credited Mormonism's survival: not Smith's history making but his "myth-making imagination at work to sustain so astonishing an innovation."[70] It is the power to shape reality, not merely describe it. To the extent that self-consciousness can be ascribed to him, it is probably why Smith abjured theology for mythmaking. Regardless, scholars who would understand the relative longevity and appeal of his project, especially as it has transcended its American milieu, can ill afford to ignore the capacity of Smith's narratives to make sense of time.

---

69. Ricoeur, "Toward a Hermeneutic of the Idea of Revelation," 102.
70. Bloom, *American Religion*, 97.

SIX

THE GOLDEN BIBLE IN THE BIBLE'S GOLDEN AGE
THE BOOK OF MORMON
AND ANTEBELLUM PRINT CULTURE

PAUL GUTJAHR

In his masterful tome on the English Bible in the seventeenth century, historian Christopher Hill comments that he is "not entirely happy with the present fashion of attributing power to literature." Pointing out that not all books have an equal ability to influence human thought and behavior, Hill writes: "If any book in sixteenth- and seventeenth-century England had power, it was the Bible; but this was because men and women believed in its truth."[1] Hill's point is well taken. Although a vast amount of current scholarship has dedicated itself to exploring the "cultural work" certain texts have done in American society, such work is notoriously difficult to define with any historical accuracy, and the fact remains that certain texts have the ability to influence more than others.[2] Nowhere is the power of the written word greater than in the case of sacred texts. Books such as the Bible and the Koran have repeatedly moved their readers to actions as personal as self-mutilation and as corporate as the Crusades, not because they simply contain good ideas, but because their readers believe their words to be divinely inspired truth. If one is interested in the power of the written word, there is no better place to look than various forms of holy writ.

The rare ability to influence readers toward radical life change makes the Book of Mormon, one of America's first indigenous sacred

---

1. Christopher Hill, *The English Bible and the Seventeenth-Century Revolution* (New York: Penguin Books, 1993), 335.

2. Brook Thomas, *The New Historicism and Other Old-Fashioned Topics* (Princeton, NJ: Princeton University Press, 1991), 27–32.

texts, worthy of thoughtful and prolonged investigation.[3] In the years following its initial appearance in 1830, the Book of Mormon sold slowly, but gradually gathered momentum. Enjoying ever larger and more frequent press runs in its 190-plus-year history, by 2022, close to 200 million copies of the book have been distributed worldwide. This distribution figure is all the more important when it is considered in light of the religious historian Rodney Stark's argument that by the mid-twenty-first century Mormonism will grow into a religious tradition to rival the size and importance of Christianity, Islam, and Hinduism.[4] Whether Stark's projection proves to be correct or not, it is obvious by the virtue of the place Mormonism holds as the world's fastest growing religion that the book which gave the Church of Jesus Christ of the Latter-day Saints its popular name is one of the most important written texts ever to emerge in the United States.

Such importance, however, has not translated into a broad-based interest among scholars to understand either the book's composition or initial reception. Where the book is studied, it is largely examined by those with some connection to its religious tradition or by scholars of American religious history. Literary and cultural historians have paid this immense best-seller little heed.

This essay focuses on the Book of Mormon when it first appeared in 1830. Scholars who have commented on the initial appearance of the Book of Mormon most frequently tend toward social or theological critiques of the issues surrounding the volume, such as the charisma of its author or the religious fluidity and doctrinal chaos of the Second Great Awakening. Such lines of inquiry completely miss the fact that the Book of Mormon was, after all, a book which circulated within certain definable characteristics of early America's print milieu.[5] To un-

---

3. In keeping with the *Chicago Manual of Style* and LDS style guides, I do not italicize Book of Mormon.

4. Rodney Stark, "The Rise of a New World Faith," *Review of Religious Research* 26:1 (Sep. 1984): 18–27.

5. Examples of good scholarship historicizing the Book of Mormon in antebellum America include: Vogel in Brent Lee Metcalfe, ed., *New Approaches to the Book of Mormon: Explorations in Critical Methodology* (Salt Lake City: Signature Books, 1993), 21–52; Richard L. Bushman, "The Book of Mormon and the American Revolution," *Brigham Young University Studies* 17 (1976): 3–20.; Timothy L. Smith, "The Book of Mormon in a Biblical Culture," *Journal of Mormon History* 7 (1980): 3–22; Grant Underwood, "Book of Mormon Usage in Early LDS Theology," *Dialogue: A Journal of Mormon Thought* 17, no. 3 (Autumn

derstand the volume's initial physical and narrative forms, one must understand that the book appeared at a time when religiously-bent American readers were immersed in a print culture with two basic, overarching characteristics: the culture was saturated both with the Bible and an interest in historical writing. This essay argues that the the Book of Mormon's initial material design, narrative format, linguistic peculiarities, and marked preoccupation with American history can only be understood within the context of the volume's appearance in a print culture permeated on almost every level by the resonances of biblical and historical writing.

The Book of Mormon appeared in what many scholars of American religion consider the United States' most biblical age. From political discourse to the naming of towns, every aspect of American culture was saturated with biblicism.[6] The accessibility and prevalence of the text is perhaps most vividly seen in how the American Bible Society ceaselessly flooded the nation with millions of copies of the Bible and New Testament before the Civil War. From 1829 to 1831 alone, the society distributed over half a million copies of the scriptures in the first of four nineteenth-century "General Supplies," gargantuan efforts bent on providing a "bible for every (American] household."[7] Coupled with this biblical ubiquity was the emergence of countless Protestant religious revivals that formed the core of what American historians have come to call the Second Great Awakening. If any book touched the lives of Americans in the opening decades of the nineteenth century, it was the Bible.

1984): 35–74; Nathan O. Hatch, *The Democratization of American Christianity* (New Haven, CT: Yale University Press, 1989), 113–22; H. Michael Marquardt, *Early Nineteenth Century Events Reflected in the Book of Mormon* (Salt Lake City: Utah Lighthouse Ministry, 1979), 114–35; John L. Brooke, *The Refiner's Fire: The Making of Mormon Cosmology, 1644–1844* (New York: Cambridge University Press, 1994), 149–83; and, perhaps most interestingly, Rick Grunder, *Mormon Parallels* (Ithaca, NY: Rick Grunder Books, 1987). Joseph Smith Jr. has had many biographers. The information presented in this essay derives from: Donna Hill, *Joseph Smith: The First Mormon* (Garden City, NY: Doubleday and Co., 1977), 15–105; Fawn M. Brodie, *No Man Knows My History*, 2nd ed. Rev. (New York: Alfred A. Knopf, 1971), 1–82; and Richard L. Bushman, *Joseph Smith and the Beginnings of Mormonism* (Chicago: University of Illinois Press, 1984), 9–42.

6. Philip L. Barlow, *Mormons and the Bible: The Place of the Latter-day Saints in American Religion* (New York: Oxford University Press, 1991), 3–10.

7. *Annual Reports of the American Bible Society*, Vol. I. (New York: Daniel Fanshaw, 1838), 530–31.

Amid this golden age of the Bible in America stood Joseph Smith Jr. Smith was twenty-four years old when he finally convinced a skeptical Palmyra printer to undertake publishing the Book of Mormon. Having arrived in Palmyra, New York, in 1816 with his parents and eight siblings, the Smith family would lead the life of a poor farm family until a dishonest land agent took advantage of their desire to better their lot in 1825 and cheated them out of their farm. This reduced the Smiths to lead the even harder life of tenant farming. This chronic poverty and nomadic existence caused Joseph Smith Jr. to turn to treasure hunting and religious revivalism in the hope of bettering his life.[8] He had little luck with either. He could neither locate hidden treasures with seer stones or divining rods nor settle on joining a specific religious denomination.

It was in the midst of this continuing poverty and religious confusion that Smith experienced in 1820 at the age of fourteen what he would later call his "First Vision."[9] Seeking clarity in the midst of the "war of words" waged by the competing revivalist preachers, Smith retreated to some woods near his home to ask the Lord, "Who of all these parties are right; or, are they all wrong together?"[10] Here, he later recounted, two heavenly figures visited him telling him that the religious denominations preaching and leading revivals throughout his area "were all corrupt," and that he should not give his allegiance to any of them.[11] The figures told him to wait, and so Smith waited three years before another angelic figure visited him to begin the process of recovering gold plates which contained the record of an ancient people. In 1827, the Lord finally allowed Smith to obtain the plates—buried in the earth like other treasures he had sought—and begin translating them. Smith claimed he translated these plates into the text of the Book of Mormon.

When first published in March 1830, the Book of Mormon was nearly 600 pages long and defied easy description. The book was primarily concerned with the stories of two families. The narrative begins with

---

8. Marvin Hill, "The Rise of Mormonism," *New York History* 61 (1980): 411–30; Alan Taylor, "The Early Republic's Supernatural Economy: Treasure Seeking in the American Northeast, 1780–1830," *American Quarterly* 38 (Spring 1986): 6–34.

9. Jan Shipps, *Mormonism: The Story of a New Religious Tradition* (Urbana: University of Illinois Press, 1985), 25–39. There is some debate about the exact year of the First Vision.

10. Joseph Smith, *History of the Church of Jesus Christ of Latter-day Saints,* 7 vols., 2nd. ed. Rev. (Salt Lake City: Deseret Book Co., 1963), 1:4.

11. Smith, *History of the Church*, 1:6.

the story of Lehi. Fleeing Jerusalem in 600 BCE, Lehi travels by boat with his family to America. Later in the book, the narrative switches to tell the story of Jared's family who, after the failure of the Tower of Babel, also crosses the Atlantic Ocean and settles in America. These families and their descendants were all dedicated record keepers, and a portion of these records ultimately reach Joseph Smith Jr. in the form of the buried gold plates. One finds a clue to how antebellum readers first responded to the Book of Mormon in how its earliest critics quickly gave it the derogatory name the "Golden Bible." Diedrich Willers, a German Reformed Pastor of New York, offers the oldest contemporary description of Mormonism in a letter where he writes: "Because the plates from which the original was translated, according to the allegation, were of gold, in the region hereabouts this book is known by the title 'The Golden Book'"[12] Willers wrote this letter on Mormonism in the summer of 1830; soon the nickname "Golden Bible" was firmly affixed—at least by non-Mormons—to Smith's new book. The first major anti-Mormon publication testifies to this fact. E. D. Howe and Philastus Hurlbut's 200-page diatribe in 1834 against the fledgling religion drew attention to the work's principal point of attack by printing the words "The Golden Bible" on its title page in a type size which dwarfs every other line on the page.[13]

Smith was intimately involved in the Book of Mormon's production process, and he carefully signaled through every aspect of the volume that this was no ordinary book.[14] One sees this attention to detail in how he chose to have the volume bound. The Book of Mormon emerged right in the middle of the American Bible Society's first General Supply. The two most common editions of the Bible distributed by the Society during this two-year push were 1829 Minion and 1830 Non-Pariel imprints.[15] Smith's Book of Mormon was bound in such a way that it looked strikingly similar to these two American Bible Society editions. Roughly the same size, all three volumes were bound

---

12. D. Michael Quinn, trans. and ed., "The First Months of Mormonism: A Contemporary View by Rev. Diedrich Willers," *New York History* (July 1973): 326.

13. E. D. Howe, *Mormonism Unvailed* (Painesville, OH: Printed and Published by the Author, 1834), title page.

14. William Mulder and Russell A. Mortenson, eds., *Among the Mormons* (Lincoln: University of Nebraska Press, 1973), 42, 45–46.

15. Margaret Hills, *Production and Supply*, Essay #18, Part III (New York: American Bible Society Archives, 1964), 8.

in brown leather with twin gold bars impressed on the spine at regular intervals. The volumes also shared a black label imprinted with gold letters on the spine bearing the volume's name. In every respect, Smith made his book look strikingly like a Bible.

More than physical similarities between the Bible and the Book of Mormon attracted many Americans to Mormonism in the early 1830s. Early Mormon converts frequently speak of how they came to a faith in Smith's teachings by reading the Book of Mormon and the Bible side-by-side. One such convert, Eli Gilbert, wrote that upon receiving a copy of the Book of Mormon, he "examined the proof; the witnesses, and all other testimony, and compared it with that of the bible, (which book I verily thought I believed,) and found the two books mutually and reciprocally corroborate each other; and if l let go the book of Mormon, the bible might also go down by the same rule."[16] Luman Shurtliff, another early convert to Mormonism, agreed: "When through reading, my mother asked me what I thought of the Mormon book. I told her that I was satisfied that the Book of Mormon was not made by man and I did not believe any man living by his knowledge of the Bible could do it and have it harmonize and agree with prophets, revelations and teachings of Christ and the apostles as that book did."[17] Far from being contradictory, the Bible testified to the authenticity of the Book of Mormon and vice versa.

There are many reasons for early Mormon converts to make such a strong connection between the Bible and the Book of Mormon. One of the most striking, and overlooked, reasons is how the King James Version had been the American Protestant Bible version of choice for nearly 200 years. The absolute dominance of the King James Version in early American culture allowed its language and style to establish itself in a unique linguistic role. Because Elizabethan English was no longer the common idiom among antebellum Americans, Americans associated the style of language found in the King James Version with the sacred. Thus the King James Version not only contained holy words, but its massive presence and linguistic influence in American culture

---

16. *Messenger and Advocate* (Kirtland, OH), Oct. 1834, 10.

17. Luman Shurtliff, Autobiography, typescript, 22, L. Tom Perry Special Collections, Harold B. Lee Library, Brigham Young University, Provo, Utah.

fostered the impression that all holy words must sound like the language found on its pages.[18]

Joseph Smith had intentionally tried to emulate the biblical style of the King James in his volume. Far from attempting to make his book fit in with the contemporary idiom, Smith wanted his book to stand out and give the impression that it was holy scripture. While various translators of the Bible in English were beginning to take the "eth" endings off words in this period, Smith was putting them on.[19] Thus, when another early Mormon convert, Warren Foote, came across the Book of Mormon in 1833, he was overwhelmed by the similarities of the two books because they had such similar language. Having "read the Bible three times through by course," Foote was overwhelmed by the thematic and linguistic similarities between the two books.[20]

The Book of Mormon not only appeared in the midst of the American Bible Society's first General Supply, but also in the midst of the first great wave of American retranslation efforts centered on the English Bible. Whereas a single American had attempted an English Bible translation in the two centuries prior to 1820, no fewer than eight new American translations of the English Bible appeared between 1820 and 1840.[21] It is important to note the intensely textual nature of biblical scholarship at this time. Before the German Higher Criticism with its emphasis on historical and the extra-biblical sources had made serious inroads in American biblical scholarship, the Bible was treated as a largely self-contained, self-referential volume.[22] Difficult scripture pas-

---

18. Nowhere is a view that King James English is the most holy idiom better evinced than in the translation debates that raged in antebellum America over whether an English translation of a more contemporary hue should replace the King James Version of the scriptures. For examples of this battle over the language in the King James and that language's place in antebellum American culture, see "Revision of the English Bible," *The New Englander* XVII (1859): 159–60; "Does the Bible Need Re-Translating?" *The Church Review and Ecclesiastical Register* X (Apr. 1857): 20–25; "The New Testament, Translated from the Original Greek," *The British and Foreign Evangelical Review* 29 (July 1859): 588–93; and "Revision Movement," *The Southern Presbyterian Review* 10, no. 4 (Jan. 1858): 517–19.

19. Alexander Campbell, ed., *The Sacred Writings of the Apostles and Evangelists of Jesus Christ Commonly Styled the New Testament* (Buffaloe, VA: Alexander Campbell, 1826).

20. Warren Foote, "Autobiography," typescript, 2, Perry Special Collections.

21. Margaret Hills, *The English Bible in America: A Bibliography of Editions of the Bible & the New Testament Published in America 1777–1957* (New York: American Bible Society, 1962), 63–164.

22. James Turner, *Without God, Without Creed: The Origins of Unbelief in America* (Baltimore: Johns Hopkins Press, 1985), 143–50.

sages could be explained by other passages; there was no need to go outside the text. This made an accurate core text and a credible, understandable translation of that text absolutely essential. In the years leading up to the Civil War, both the Bible's core text and its translation became the sites of fierce debate as various constituencies argued for what they believed to be the best original manuscripts and best translations of those manuscripts.

In broad strokes, the debates over authentic biblical source material and accurate translation work fell into two primary camps: (1) those which strove to attain the best literal translation of the original manuscripts and (2) those which strove to give readers a Bible in a more contemporary idiom, including words that cleared up long-contested doctrinal debates such as baptism and eternal punishment.

The first camp found its denominational center in the Unitarians. More than any other single emerging American religious tradition, Unitarianism showed a marked interest in new English translations of the scriptures. Driving this interest was the desire to restore the scriptures to their "primitive integrity"—their most pure, original, and accurate form.[23] Unitarians believed centuries of Christianity had led Protestants to read the Bible in the theologically disfiguring context of creeds.

For Unitarians, the most blatant example of Christian creedal corruption came in the doctrine of the Trinity. Encapsulating the central problem with this doctrine, one Unitarian wrote "the word TRINITY is not to be found in the New Testament, and that it was invented by Tertullian, is a matter of little consequence; but that the doctrine itself should be nowhere stated in the New Testament, we conceive to be a matter of very great consequence."[24] The weight of tradition and church history meant nothing to Unitarians in the face of biblical evidence that showed the Christian belief in the Trinity was nothing more than a "modern doctrine" which had no precedent in ancient Christianity.[25]

One of the ways Unitarians chose to discredit Trinitarian doctrine involved attacking the accuracy of the biblical texts upon which the

---

23. George W. Burnap, *Popular Objections to Unitarian Christianity* (Boston: Wm. Crosby and H. P. Nichols, 1848), 56.

24. Thos. Starr King and Orville Dewey, *The New Discussion of the Trinity* (Boston: Walker, Wise, and Co, 1860), 51.

25. Andrews Norton, *A Statement of Reasons for Not Believing the Doctrines of Trinitarians,* 3rd ed. (Boston: American Unitarian Association, 1867), 40.

doctrine was based. Unitarians set out to prove that not only was there "no such word as Trinity in the Bible, from beginning to end," but that all verses even hinting at such a doctrine could not be found in the most ancient manuscripts of scripture.[26] Unitarians argued that verses such as 1 John 5:7, which reads, "For there are three that bear record in heaven, the Father, the Word, and the Holy Ghost; and these three are one," were "spurious" texts found in "no part of the original Epistle of John."[27] They argued that all verses showing an affinity to the doctrine of the Trinity were later additions to the most ancient biblical manuscripts.

The Unitarians could forcefully mount this kind of attack because of the unusually high degree of education they could bring to bear on the argument. A number of the early Unitarian Bible translators not only came from Harvard Divinity School, but held teaching positions there. Andrews Norton, John Gorham Palfrey, and George Noyes all produced English translations of at least portions of the Bible before the Civil War. They also all held, albeit at different times, the Dexter Professorship of Sacred Literature at Harvard. When they questioned the accuracy of the scriptural text, they backed up their claims with arguments stemming from their specialized theological and linguistic training. This high level of education, coupled with the conviction that the scriptures had been disfigured by the very scribes who had been responsible for their preservation and transmission, provided the foundation for a massive Unitarian effort to purge the Bible's text of all its impurities.

All three of these scholars based their translations on the critical Greek text of the German biblical scholar Johann Griesbach for his Bible's Greek version. This, in itself, was a significant statement. Griesbach's text was no ordinary version of the New Testament Greek. Griesbach had made it an object of his study to examine the oldest manuscripts of scripture he could find in the libraries of France, Germany, England, and the Netherlands.[28] His goal behind such extensive research was quite simple. He wanted to examine these manuscripts in order to provide a new compilation of the New Testament that would be more accurate than the "Received Text," the Greek text most

---

26. Burnap, *Popular Objections*, 52.

27. Burnap, *Popular Objections*, 53.

28. Delling qtd. in Bernard Orchard and Thomas R. W. Longstaff, *J. J. Griesbach: Synoptic and Text-Critical Studies 1776–1976* (New York: Cambridge University Press, 1978), 7.

commonly used in translating the New Testament prior to the end of the eighteenth century."[29]

Griesbach contributed much more than a new scholarly edition of the Greek text of the New Testament in 1774 and 1775. In order to put together what he claimed to be the most accurate and ancient New Testament text, Griesbach formulated a method whereby he could date the numerous manuscripts with which he worked so that he might give preference to their contents according to their age. The problem was that nearly all manuscripts could only be dated by approximate, non-empirical evidence. Believing that the manuscripts closer in date to Christ's life would contain fewer errors, Griesbach invented a system of dating and classifying different manuscripts based on a theory of textual "recension."[30] "Recensions" were basically different versions of the New Testament. Griesbach believed that by tracing the trends in textual variation, one could systematically determine which manuscripts were copied to make other manuscripts, eventually arriving at a determination about which manuscripts were the oldest and most reliable. Griesbach then produced a Greek text annotated in ways which allowed its reader to determine which sections of the text came from which recension family.

The second camp in American biblical translation found its earliest proponent in Alexander Campbell and the Disciples of Christ. Campbell was also interested in primitive integrity, but his translation work focused on capturing the original meaning of the text. Central to their concern was rectifying the age-old mistranslation of the word βαπτιζω, which the King James had not translated, but simply transliterated as "Baptism." Beginning with Alexander Campbell's 1826 translation of the New Testament, βαπτιζω would be translated "immerse," a change that would be followed in numerous new English Bible translations before the Civil War.

Neither a history in book publishing nor a background steeped in linguistic training led Alexander Campbell to offer a new version of the New Testament to Americans in the mid-1820s. Born in Ireland, Campbell arrived in the United States in 1809. Almost immediately

---

29. Oliver Everett, "Novum Testamentum Graece, ex recensione J. Jae. Griesbachii," *North American Review* 15 (1822): 460–86; John Gorham Palfrey "Griesbach's New Testament," *North American Review* 31 (1830): 267–75.

30. Everett, "Novum Testamentum Graece," 484.

he joined the first of two churches he would pastor in Pennsylvania. Tired of petty denominational squabbles, he did not affiliate with a denomination until 1813, when he became a Baptist having been convinced that immersion was the only proper way to baptize. In the years that followed, Campbell travelled throughout Ohio, Indiana, Virginia, Kentucky, and Tennessee preaching a gospel based on the tenets of the church found in the New Testament. His was a ministry centered on restoring the primitive Christian church of the first century CE by encouraging his adherents to look to the Bible and its depiction of early Christianity as the sole model of Christian living.[31]

To unloose the power of Christianity and unify its adherents, Campbell believed that the Bible must first be unfettered. Campbell preached that "each religious party had sought to secure the Bible within its own sectarian cell," thus trammeling the sacred volume with all manner of creeds, confessions, and church structures founded on human, not biblical, precedents.[32] Campbell condemned all practices which could not be validated by Apostolic example. To determine what was, in fact, validated by Apostolic example, one must go to the Bible.[33] Campbell would guide his ministry by the overarching rule "where the Scriptures speak, we speak; where the Scriptures are silent, we are silent."[34] As early as 1816, Campbell began to have problems with his fellow Baptists, some of whom did not share all his radical views of primitive church restoration. Friction grew between Campbell and the Baptist association with which he was connected until he eventually broke entirely with the Baptists in 1832 to form his own denomination in partnership with Barton Stone, a fellow restorationist. Calling their new denomination the "Christian Church"—later known as the "Disciples of Christ"—Campbell and Stone began a movement that would become the fastest growing denomination in antebellum America, numbering 22,000 in 1832 and growing to around 200,000 by 1860.[35]

---

31. Jesse R. Kellems, *Alexander Campbell and the Disciples* (New York: Richard R. Smith, 1930), 47–131.

32. Robertson Richardson, *Memoirs of Alexander Campbell*, 2 vols. (Philadelphia: J. B. Lippincott & Co., 1868), 2:40–41.

33. Alexander Campbell, *The Christian System*, 4th ed. (Cincinnati: H. S. Bosworth, 1866), 6.

34. Richardson, *Memoirs of Alexander Campbell*, 1:352.

35. Harry Stout, ed. *Dictionary of Christianity in America* (Downers Grove, IL: Inter-Varsity Press, 1990), 214.

Campbell centered his denomination around what he called "New Testamentism," a core belief in the absolute primacy of the New Testament's portrayal of primitive Christianity over any and all extra-biblical creeds or traditions.[36] This belief makes the publication of his own New Testament in 1826 more understandable. If the New Testament was the single most important source for determining what the Christian Church should look like, Campbell felt compelled to give the purest possible version of this blueprint to his followers. Campbell felt he could improve on the King James Version, which suffered inaccuracies because of its translators' theological biases, tendency toward interpretive compromise, and the reality that older, more reliable manuscripts had become available from which a better translation of the New Testament could be made.[37]

Like the Unitarians, Campbell turned to Griesbach to provide him with "the most nearly correct text in Christendom."[38] Then consulting the work of a number of other translators like George Campbell, James Macknight, Philip Doddridge, and Charles Thomson, Campbell sought to provide a Bible translation that most accurately reflected the original meaning of the New Testament writers.[39] For Campbell, this meant clarifying any ambiguous terms in English, or in Greek, which existed in the King James. One of the chief offenders when it came to ambiguity leading to doctrinal error was the word "baptism." Campbell thought the meaning of the word was clear. Βαπτιζω had meant immersion in the first century, and it should mean immersion now. With this clarity and confidence, he substituted the word "immersion" for nearly every Greek appearance of βαπτιζω[40]

As important as Campbell's translation was in terms of its commitment to a particular view of baptism, it would be terribly misleading

---

36. Alexander Campbell, ed., *The Christian Baptist* (Buffaloe, VA: Alexander Campbell, 1823–30), 1:94.

37. Alexander Campbell, ed., *The Sacred Writings of the Apostles and Evangelists of Jesus Christ Commonly styled the New Testament,* 2nd ed. (Bethany, VA: Alexander Campbell, 1828), vi; Cecil K. Thomas, *Alexander Campbell and His New Version* (St. Louis: Bethany Press, 1958), 171–72.

38. Campbell, *Christian Baptist*, 4:167.

39. Thomas, *Alexander Campbell*, 17–43.

40. *A Debate Between Rev. A. Campbell and Rev. N. L. Rice, on the Action, Subject, Design and Administrator of Christian Baptism, reported by Marcus T. C. Gould* (Lexington, KY: A. T. Skillman & Son, 1844), 67.

to characterize the book simply as an immersion translation. For Campbell, the quest for primitive integrity involved a translation's presentation. Following the lead of John Locke, Campbell chose to publish his New Testament with a minimum of intrusive chapter and verse markings.[41] The text was printed in a single column, and Campbell was most excited about his Bible editions which were clearly printed and thus could be easily read.[42] He also chose to place any apparatus at the volume's end rather than in the margins. Campbell's format changes sprang from his conviction that the Bible should be easy to read and understand. He strove to avoid "cutting up the sacred text into morsels," which Bible editors were so fond of doing with their verse markings and marginalia.[43] Such apparatus could kill the best attempts at trying to understand accurately the Bible's meaning by distracting readers from engaging the larger themes and arguments of the text. In both translation and formatting, Campbell's highest goal was to give his readers a text that most clearly presented the New Testament Christ and the New Testament Church.

While discussions of textual purity and primitive integrity racked the American Protestant world in the 1820s and 1830s, Smith offered his countrymen a sacred book which was able to strike at the core of such discussions. In claiming that his book was published from gold plates recently discovered in upstate New York, Smith was able to offer American Protestants much more than a mere revision of a corrupted biblical text; he gave them a new sacred text translated directly from original source material. All other purity claims paled in comparison.

Unlike the Bible, the Book of Mormon was not a message that had been passed down from one century to the next through mutilated and partial manuscripts. B. Pixley, a Baptist preacher and early critic of Mormonism, was angered by Smith's statements of biblical corruption and the need for a better text. He wrote in 1832: "The Gospels too, we are given by them [Mormons] to understand, are so mutilated and altered as to convey little of the instruction which they should convey Our present Bible is to be altered and restored to its primitive purity,

---

41. John Locke, *A Paraphrase and Notes on the Epistles of St. Paul to the Galatians, 1 and 2 Corinthians, Romans, Ephesians,* 2 vols., ed. Arthur W. Wainwright (Oxford: Clarendon Press, 1987).

42. Thomas, *Alexander Campbell,* 26–64.

43. Campbell, *The Sacred Writings* (1828), xxxvii.

by Smith, the present prophet of the Lord, and some books to be added of great importance, which have been lost."[44] The Book of Mormon stood as an answer to a mutilated Gospel record. It was a record that Smith had translated directly from the original plates used by writers and editors that predated all the available biblical manuscripts—and even many of the Bible's actual writers—by hundreds of years.[45]

Having worked from the same gold plates which the ancient authors had written upon gave Smith and his followers the ability to attribute an unprecedented and unrivaled degree of purity to the Book of Mormon. The Book of Mormon itself points to how the holy scriptures had been corrupted over time by declaring that "the most plain and precious parts of the Gospel of the Lamb" had been withheld by the corrupt scribes and clergy of the Catholic Church (BOM, 1830 ed., 31). Joseph Smith referred to the Book of Mormon as "the most correct of any book on earth."[46] The first Mormon newspaper, the *Evening and Morning Star*, printed excerpts of the Book of Mormon for its readers, and pointed to the book as presenting humankind with a restored and full gospel by proclaiming: "It will be seen by this that the most plain parts of the New Testament, have been taken from it by the Mother of Harlots while it was confined in that Church, —say, from the year AD 46 to 1400."[47]

The purity of the Book of Mormon was further underlined by the early Mormon newspaper editor and printer William W. Phelps, who stated: "The book of Mormon, as a revelation from God, possesses some advantage over the old scripture: it has not been tinctured by the wisdom of man, with here and there an Italic word to supply deficiencies."[48] Even though the King James Version had been released with no extended marginal commentary, it had always contained notes on alternative readings for various passages. Griesbach had reminded scholars of how plentiful alternate readings were in his own work by using a complicated system of brackets, parentheses, and typefaces to explain the alternate readings possible in his work. Joseph Smith did not have to use any such devices to account for scribal differences and

---

44. Mulder and Mortenson, *Among the Mormons*, 74.

45. Joel Johnson, Autobiography, typescript, 4, Perry Special Collections.

46. Smith, *History of the Church*, 4:461.

47. *Evening and Morning Star* (Independence, MO/Kirtland, OH, 1832–34), June 1832, 3.

48. *Evening and Morning Star*, Jan. 1833, 58.

inaccuracies. The Book of Mormon had come straight from the plates of Mormon. Although Mormons were encouraged to use the Book of Mormon alongside the Bible, the message was clear: the Book of Mormon superseded the Holy Bible because it was a purer word from God.

Smith reinforced the message of his book's purity in several ways. Principal among these was his choice to write his new revelation from God in the form of a history of an ancient people. In the Book of Mormon, Smith wove ancient and American history together to create a text which appealed to an American reading public who had a voracious appetite for all types of history books, and to American Protestants who were increasingly concerned with the growing debates over the historicity and reliability of the Bible.

Scholars have pointed out that beginning with the Revolution, Americans exhibited a striking interest in establishing their own history as one of the ways in which they could create their own national identity and distance themselves from their European pasts. Although it would be grossly misleading to say that they had wiped the slate clean in terms of their relationship to Europe, with the American Revolution the country had certainly turned a page. The problem that now had to be faced was what would be written on that page and by whom. The question was a daunting one. The country was expansive with a diverse and decentralized population. How could unity and a sense of national identity be brought to a young nation with a greater sense of colonial independence than interdependence? Early Americans found partial answers to these questions of national cohesion and identity in turning to the field of history.[49]

In the decades following the Revolution, United States citizens showed a profound interest in their country's history. The formation of the United States was a bold national experiment almost without precedent. Americans, once deeply proud of their connections with Europe, increasingly became concerned with the development of their own cultural and national identity. Aside from creating a new form of government, Americans wanted to create and define everything from

---

49. Bert James Lowenberg, *American History in American Thought: Christopher Columbus to Henry Adams* (New York: Simon and Schuster, 1972), 184–257; John Franklin Jameson, *The History of Historical Writing in America* (Boston: Houghton, Mifflin and Co., 1891), 80–121.

their own literature and language to their own art and architecture. Of course, they did not pursue these goals in a vacuum, they looked for models. Just as American Protestants looked to the primitive Christian church as the key example to be followed, the ancient civilizations of Greece and Rome provided the country with standards of republican and democratic virtue. As if the intervening European civilizations which separated them from the glories of Greece and Rome had corrupted the values they saw so necessary to the success of their national experiment, it was the return to these ancient regimes which captured the imagination of America between the Revolution and Civil War.[50]

Along with this interest in Greece and Rome, Americans pursued a greater knowledge of their own country's history as well. Beginning in the 1780s and growing in intensity in the decades that followed, Americans sought to record and teach their country's past by founding historical, genealogical and preservation societies, historical journals, historically biased school curriculums, and national holidays.[51] The publishing industry also worked to satisfy the public's interest in history. In the 1820s alone, "three out of every four of the most popular books were historical."[52]

Into this historically-minded culture and print milieu appeared the Book of Mormon, a book which proclaimed on its title page that it was "the Record of the People of Nephi" and a "Record of the People of Jared" (BOM, 1830 ed., title page). That the Book of Mormon advertised itself as a "record" was of critical importance. A "record" was not an invented tale, but, in the words of Noah Webster's recently published American dictionary, was an "authentic memorial," "a register; an authentic or official copy of any writing, or account of any facts and proceedings, entered in a book for preservation."[53] The words "authentic," "memorial," and "facts" are all worthy of note here. Smith's book was more than a long-winded parable of truth filled with prophecies, metaphysics, and moral advice; it was a book of authentic history.[54]

50. Harry R. Warfel, *Letters of Noah Webster* (New York: Library Publishers, 1953), 59–60.

51. George H. Callcott, *History in the United States 1800–1860: Its Practice and Purpose* (Baltimore: Johns Hopkins University Press, 1970), 25–53.

52. Callcott, *History*, 33.

53. Noah Webster, ed., *An American Dictionary of the English Language* (New York: S. Converse, 1828), s.v. "Record."

54. That Mormons were not immune to this interest in history and the authenticity

Smith had underlined the true nature of his book by placing it firmly within the genre of history writing. History was not fiction. Thus the Book of Mormon was true.

The historical, narrative quality of the book comes across in the noticeable lack of biblical apparatus included in the 1830 edition of the book. Whereas Smith was careful to invoke a biblical likeness in his book through its binding, content, and diction, he does little to copy biblical formatting such as chapter and verse divisions. What is striking about this choice is that the flow of the narrative is enhanced. There is a seamless quality to the 1830 edition of the Book of Mormon which accomplishes the very thing that John Locke and Alexander Campbell were after—namely, the entire message of the book is stressed as a continuous narrative rather than a segmented and disjointed collection of stories.

This seamless quality invokes the style of historical writing at the time. History was more than recorded philosophy and events, it was also a story intended to bring past events to life in the present. A concern with good storytelling was an earmark of antebellum history writing. Examples not only include Gibbons's immensely popular *Decline and Fall of the Roman Empire,* but the historical fiction of the first best-selling novelists of this period: Washington Irving, Sir Walter Scott, and James Fenimore Cooper. Other similarities in Smith's work and the histories written at the same time include the overwhelming emphasis on male characters in the story. In nearly 600 pages of text, one is able to count the number of female characters mentioned by name on a single hand (BOM, 1830 ed., 5, 15, 160, 278, 332). It is men and their armies, sons, and political intrigues which compose the stuff of history. Smith further mimics historical writing of the period by devoting huge sections of his narrative to describing military campaigns and tactics.

---

associated with historical records can be seen in the following excerpt from the autobiography of Warren Foote, an early convert to Mormonism: "I read the Bible a great deal and was very fond of reading histories. Some time about the month of Feb. 1830, my Father borrowed a Book of Mormon (which went by the name of Golden bible) which I read through. I, like my Father, believed it to be a true record" (2). The early Mormon newspaper, *Messenger and Advocate,* published out of Kirtland, Ohio, from October 1834 to September 1837, provides a vivid illustration of the Mormon interest in history. A regular series of historical articles appeared in this paper highlighting the civilizations of several ancient races including the Phoenicians, Egyptians, Assyrians, and Greeks, among others. *Messenger and Advocate* 3:5 (Feb. 1837) 455; 3:6 (Mar. 1837) 471; 3:7 (Apr. 1837) 493; 3:8 (May 1837) 504; 3:9 (June 1837) 536; and 3:10 (July 1837) 643.

Histories of the antebellum period are frequently characterized by a disproportionate amount of space being given to military maneuvers and the personalities behind them.[55]

Smith fuses his interest in history with his concern for showing the veracity of his text through an extensive use of time lines and genealogies in the Book of Mormon. The first time line found in the book comes with the volume's first major character, Nephi, who travels with his family to America after leaving Jerusalem in 600 BCE. Time is then counted until the coming of Christ to America, at which point a new time line begins. The reader is repeatedly told exactly when the story is taking place with frequent entries like "behold, it came to pass that fifty and five years had passed away," "five hundred and nine years from the time Lehi left Jerusalem," and "it came to pass in the thirty and first year" (BOM, 1830 ed., 123, 221, 468). Time and chronological placement are major themes of Smith's work.

When one considers that the Book of Mormon appeared in a religious culture pondering the authenticity and accuracy of the Bible, such a preoccupation with time lines becomes more clear. As biblical formats grew increasingly complex during this period, one of the most common features to grace the top of Bible pages is a date entry. These entries told the reader exactly when a certain event took place. For instance, Genesis, chapter one, states that the creation occurred in 4004 BCE, 1 Samuel, chapter 17, reveals that David slew Goliath in 1063 BCE, and Matthew, chapter 5, notes that Jesus preached the Sermon on the Mount in 31 CE. What Smith does in the Book of Mormon is internalize the time lines into his narrative. The Bible's text often only hints at the timing of its events, forcing commentators to approximate dates used in the marginal apparatus of Bibles. The problem is that these date entries were not sacred scripture, and thus especially open to debate. Such debates were gathering new force in the 1820s and 1830s with the rise of the science of geology and the discovery of fossils which could predate the date traditionally ascribed to Genesis by millions of years.[56] Smith sidesteps these problems by directly weaving a time line into his narrative, thus conflating his chronology directly into his sacred writ.

---

55. Callcott, *History*, 103.

56. Herbert Hovenkamp, *Science and Religion in America, 1800–1860* (Philadelphia: University of Pennsylvania Press, 1978), 119–45.

Smith further accents the authority given his book by using a complicated array of genealogies.[57] One of the ways genealogies are foregrounded in the Book of Mormon is to describe the relationship of the various scribes who helped compose the text. The chief editor of the work, Mormon, explains at one point that the plates upon which he worked were "handed down by the kings, from generation to generation, until the days of king Benjamin; and they were handed down from king Benjamin, from generation to generation, until they have fallen into my hands" (BOM, 1830 ed., 152). Smith is careful to record the genealogy of the plates so that each generation's scribe could be identified and the exact order of events could thus be carefully tracked. Unlike Griesbach, who built his theory of recension by tracing back the work of nameless scribes to find the oldest and most accurate manuscripts of scripture, Smith included the names of his work's scribes and gave his reader the impression that the entire work had a far more continuous flow than the Bible. Rather than a segmented narrative written by dozens of different authors over thousands of years, the Book of Mormon was written down by a few families of scribes whose relationships and work could easily be retraced.

The theme of genealogy also extends beyond the book to point to the religious authority of the book's author. In the book of Alma, one finds the following sermon of a character named Amulek:

> I am Amulek; I am the son of Giddonah, who was the son of Ishmael, who was a descendant of Aminadi: and it was the same Aminadi which interpreted the writing which was upon the wall of the temple, which was written by the finger of God .— And Aminadi was a descendant of Nephi, who was the son of Lehi, who came out of the land of Jerusalem, who was a descendant of Manasseh, who was the son of Joseph, which was sold into Egypt by the hands of his brethren (BOM, 1830 ed., 248).

---

57. An emerging interest in genealogy in this period is yet another reflection of the American appetite for history before the Civil War. John Farmer—the "Father of Genealogy in New England"—published the first study of American genealogy in 1829 entitled, *A Genealogical Register of the First Settlers of New England* (Lancaster, MA). The country's first genealogical society (the New England Historical Genealogical Society) began meeting in the early 1840s and officially formed itself into a society in 1846. For a discussion of the motivations of this society's founders, see William Jenks, "An Address to the Members of the England Historic-Genealogical Society," *New England Historical & Genealogical Register* 6, no. 3 (July 1852): 217–31.

Two interesting rhetorical strategies are at work in this passage. First, Amulek not only links himself back to his race's founding father, Nephi, but to the familiar biblical character of Joseph as well. This gives him credibility in a biblically literate pre-Civil War America where Joseph would be linked to the great patriarchs of the Jewish faith. Second, Joseph Smith would claim to be a direct descendant of this same Joseph, placing him in the same genealogical line as Amulek, Nephi, and Joseph. Such a lineage testifies to his credibility as a scribe and an interpreter of the sacred things of the Lord. The Book of Mormon, thus, helps to build its own credibility and the credibility of its prophet-author through the extensive use of genealogies.[58]

Examining the 1830 edition of the Book of Mormon as a book which circulated in the midst of an ever-expanding print culture allows one to understand better key elements of the volume's physical and narrative design, as well as its success among various nineteenth-century readers. The central issue for any sacred text is its credibility, and the Book of Mormon came across as trustworthy because of the way in which its text and packaging resonated within a complex register of material and intellectual motifs present in early nineteenth-century American print culture.

These print culture resonances included how the book's binding and use of Elizabethan English evoked the Bible, while its seamless formatting, preoccupation with male characters, and military campaigns evoked the historical writing of the period. This grounding in biblical and historical conventions of writing imbued the book with a certain credibility, which was further underlined by the extensive use of the biblical credentialing device of genealogies. All these components allowed the Book of Mormon to capitalize on key elements of an already extant print marketplace in ways which set the volume apart as a vitally important, and believable, new sacred text in antebellum America.

When the Book of Mormon first appeared, it did so as a book in the midst of a plethora of printed material debating the Bible's original meaning and original text. Much of the Book of Mormon's

---

58. There exists a profound link between author and book when one considers The Book of Mormon. Smith testified to the authenticity of his book, while at the same time it testified to his position as a new prophet through its scattered prophecies concerning the coming of one who would restore God's true gospel to a new chosen people. BOM, 1830 ed., 527, 545, 593.

attractiveness to its earliest readers was how it so boldly engaged these concerns with biblical purity and reliable, divine revelation by invoking the trustworthy genres of biblical and historical writing. Assassinated in 1844, Smith would not see the migration and growth of his church in the years to follow, yet he was able to witness the initial effectiveness of his book, which rewrote American history for its readers and offered them unparalleled claims of textual purity, authenticity, and trustworthiness.

SEVEN

JOSEPH SMITH'S USES OF PSEUDO-, INTRALINGUAL, AND INTERSEMIOTIC TRANSLATION IN THE CREATION OF THE MORMON CANON
THE BOOK OF MORMON, THE BIBLE, AND THE BOOK OF ABRAHAM[1]

ROBERTO A. VALDEÓN

INTRODUCTION

In recent years the Church of Jesus Christ of Latter- day Saints (also LDS Church), commonly referred to as the Mormon Church, has featured prominently on the front pages of newspapers and magazines. One of the contenders in the 2012 US presidential election was for the first time a member of the church. At the same time, a Mormon-inspired musical made its way into Broadway, received positive reviews from critics, and became a hit with audiences. But while quintessentially American in its origins, the appearance and spread of the LDS Church is related to a very unusual form of translation, which some scholars have pointed out as the perfect example of what they term pseudo-translation, including Toury, Hermans, and Vidal.[2] In a different text, in his discussion of the

1. I would like to express my gratitude to the Spanish Ministry of Education for funding my research at the University of Massachusetts Amherst during the period May 2011–June 2012, and to Edwin Gentzler for his invitation to join the UMass Translation Center. For the writing of this paper, I had the great privilege of discussing the topic with Mario De Pillis, Emeritus Professor of History at the University of Massachusetts and one of the world's leading specialists on US communal religions. He was the second non-Mormon to become the president of the Mormon History Association. He was also the cheerful host of many a dinner (including the hot meals of the freezing snowstorm week of October 2011), shared with Catholics, Quakers, Protestants, and agnostics. This paper is dedicated to him and his family.

2. Gideon Toury, *Descriptive Translation Studies and Beyond* (Amsterdam: Benjamins, 1995), 41, and "Enhancing Cultural Changes by Means of Fictitious Translations," in Eva Hung, ed., *Translation and Cultural Change: Studies in History, Norms and Image-Projection*

concept of equivalence, Hermans does not even refer to the Book of Mormon as a pseudo-translation but opts to present it as an example of a translation that has replaced the original.[3]

Toury defines pseudo-translations as "texts which have been presented as translations with no corresponding source texts in other languages ever having existed." He relates them to "genuine translation in terms of *cultural position*."[4] Santoyo points out that "pseudo-translations occupy a very special place in the history of literature. But it should not be forgotten that they also belong, in more ways than one, to the history of translation." He goes on to mention the Book of Mormon as an example of pseudo-translations, also called fictitious translations (a term first used by Popovič[5]). Santoyo places them alongside classic literary works such as *Don Quixote* and *Zadig* as well as more recent texts such as Borges's *Doctor Brodie's Report* and Chapman's *The Duchess's Diary*.[6]

However, the alleged translation of the Book of Mormon differs considerably from those of the literary works Santoyo mentions. The objective of literary pseudotranslations may be to attract a wider audience and the texts themselves may tell us about the characteristics of the target culture: "pseudo-translations often represent their pseudo-sources in an exaggerated manner."[7] In his classic *Descriptive Translation Studies and Beyond*, Toury mentions the case of the Book of Mormon but concentrates on a German literary text entitled *Papa Hamlet*. Toury concludes that the literary features of the latter were successful in situating it "in the niche allocated to it."[8]

More recently Toury has returned to the issue of pseudo-translations, using Popovič's term "fictitious translations," and referred in more detail

(Amsterdam: Benjamins, 2005), 3–17; Theo Hermans, *The Conference of the Tongues* (Manchester: St Jerome, 2007), 59; and María Carmen África Vidal Claramonte, *Traducción y asimetría* (Bern: Peter Lang, 2010), 17–18.

3. Hermas, *Conference*.

4. Toury, *Descriptive Translation Studies*, 40, 45.

5. Anton Popovič, *Dictionary for the Analysis of Literary Translation* (Edmonton: University of Alberta, 1976), 20.

6. Julio-César Santoyo Mediavilla, "Blank Spaces in the History of Translation," in Georges L. Bastin and Paul F. Bandia, eds., *Charting the Future of Translation History* (Ottawa: University of Ottawa Press, 2006), 21–22.

7. Popovič, *Dictionary*, 20; Toury, *Descriptive Translation Studies*, 45–46.

8. Toury, *Descriptive Translation Studies*, 47–52.

to the Book of Mormon. He connects the ultimate success of the LDS Church to the promotion of the text as a true religious book: "Moreover, the new Church developed not only due to a marked refusal to lift the veil connected with the *Book of Mormon*, but actually due to an ongoing struggle to *improve* the disguise and fortify it."[9] This point can be substantiated by comparing the first and subsequent editions of the book, which was first published in 1830 in Palmyra (New York State) under the title the Book of Mormon: An Account Written by the Hand of Mormon, Upon Plates Taken From the Plates of Nephi. The front page claimed that Joseph Smith Junior was its "author and proprietor." Ten years later, the front page of the third edition included some significant changes. The long title was reduced to the Book of Mormon, and Joseph Smith Jr. became simply the translator. The opening page also indicated that the third edition had been "carefully revised by the translator." All this points to the uniqueness of the Book of Mormon among pseudo-translations.

In this sense, it looked more "like a genuine religious book, which—according to previous traditions in the Anglo-American cultural space—had to be a translation."[10] It is not clear what the word "genuine" refers to in this context, though. In fact, the Book of Mormon is only one of the forms in which translation was to become instrumental in the creation of a Mormon canon. The book is now one of the four pillars of the LDS Church, the other three being (1) the King James Version of the Bible, also known as the Authorized Version (as we know, a translation itself), (2) the Doctrine and Covenants, and (3) the Pearl of Great Price. In one way or another the concept of translation permeates through all of them, although here, besides the Book of Mormon, we will focus on the last of these pillars, the Pearl of Great Price, which comprises other texts also *translated* by Smith.

RELIGIOUS TRANSLATION, A SHORT OVERVIEW: FROM CHRISTIANITY TO MORMONISM

Translation and the Bible

The mythical origin of the translation of the Book of Mormon differs considerably from the translation of the religious texts of other

---

9. Toury, "Enhancing Cultural Changes," 11–14.
10. Toury, "Enhancing Cultural Changes," 12.

faiths. However, the concept does allow us to speak of a historic parallelism with the emergence of other faiths. Bowen et al. mention that translation and interpreting have been fundamental in the spread of religions, albeit with different purposes. Even a non-proselytizing religion like Judaism relied on interpreters for centuries. Interpreters were used in courts and schools and some of their names are known to us, such as that of Hutzpit the Interpreter, who was tortured and executed by the Romans. Some interpreters even became rabbis.[11]

Translation also played a key role in the spread of Christianity, first in Europe with the translation of the Bible into Latin, commissioned in 383 CE by Pope Damascus I. The Vulgata was later considered a very ambiguous text because "depending upon the interpreter and critic, the first half of the Bible might recount events about Jews or presage ones about Christians," so new efforts were made to produce a new version from a more philological approach. This caused great controversies across Europe: Erasmus's retranslations into Latin were greeted with enthusiasm by some, but were heavily criticized by others.[12]

These controversies did not prevent Europeans from taking the Bible and their faith to other parts of the world. Interlinguistic and intercultural mediation was instrumental in spreading Christianity outside the old continent. Writing about European imperialism, Bhabha has used the expression "evangelical colonialism," and points out that, as European missionaries could not be trusted to do the job, "native catechists therefore had to be found, who brought with them their own cultural and political ambivalences and contradictions, often under great pressure from their families and communities."[13] Dutch Calvinist missionaries in Indonesia, Spanish Catholic friars in Peru, and English Anglican missionaries in India evangelized distant lands and translated Christian texts for non-European infidels.[14]

Religious translation has been at the very origin of Translation

---

11. Margareta Bowen, David Bowen, Francine C. Kaufmann, and Ingrid Kurz, "Interpreters and the Making of History," in Jean Delisle, and Judith Woodsworth, eds., *Translators through History* (Amsterdam: Benjamins and Unesco Publishing, 1995), 253.

12. Lu Ann Homza, *Religious Authority in the Spanish Renaissance* (Baltimore: Johns Hopkins University Press, 2000), 52–61, 81.

13. Homi K. Bhabha, *The Location of Culture* (London: Routledge, 1994), 49.

14. Webb Keane, *Christian Moderns: Freedom and the Fetish in the Mission Encounter* (Berkeley: University of California Press, 2007); Alan Durston, *Pastoral Quechua: The History of Christian Translation in Colonial Peru, 1550–1650* (Notre Dame, IN: Notre Dame

Studies as a contemporary academic discipline through the works of scholars such as Eugene Nida. From the 1960s onwards, Nida, an American (and Christian) academic and translator, has exerted an enormous influence on the field, especially after the introduction and discussion of the concepts of dynamic and formal equivalence.[15] In spite of Nida's pioneering efforts, the translation of the Bible has remained a particularly demanding task. Kirk writes that

> Bible translation has been a continuing effort of the Christian community. The pace was modest during the Middle Ages; it is estimated that portions had been translated into 35 languages by 1500. Translation accelerated rapidly during the Reformation period and afterwards, so that by 1800 parts of the Bible had been translated into 68 languages, and by 1900 into 522 languages.[16]

Today, according to the United Bible Societies, 400 translation projects are under way. As of 2020 the Bible has been translated into 704 languages, the New Testament into 1,551. This points to the difficulties posed by Bible translation two thousand years after it became "a major preoccupation" for Christianity.[17]

Shackle has mentioned some of the difficulties involved in the translation of sacred texts such as the Bible: "Fidelity versus freedom, the cultural contexts of originals and translations, the conditioned choices of formal as well as of linguistic reorganization."[18] These difficulties, which start at the lexical level, continue to attract the interest of specialists.[19] Moreiras connects these difficulties to the babelian notion of confusion originating in the book of Genesis:

University Press, 2007); and Norman Etherington, *Missions and Empire* (Oxford: Oxford University Press, 2005).

15. Eugene Nida, *Towards a Science of Translation* (Leiden: E. J. Brill 1964); Eugene Albert Nida and Charles Russell Taber, *The Theory and Practice of Translation* (Leiden: E. J. Brill, 1969).

16. Peter Kirk, "Holy Communicative?: Current Approaches to Bible Translation Worldwide," in Lynne Long, ed., *Translation and Religion: Holy Untranslatable?* (Clevedon: Multilingual Matters, 2005), 89.

17. Lynell Zogbo, "Bible, Jewish and Christian," in Mona Baker and Gabriela Saldanha, eds., *Routledge Encyclopedia of Translation Studies* (London: Routledge 2009), 21.

18. Cristopher Shackle, "From Gentlemen's Outfitters to Hyperbazaar: A Personal Approach to Translating the Sacred," in Long, *Translation and Religion*, 20.

19. Cf. Jason Thomas McKinney's discussion of the Pauline epistles in "Secret Agreements and Slight Adjustments: On Giorgio Agamben's Messianic Citations," *The Journal of Religion* 91, no. 4 (2011): 496–518; and George Aichele and Richard Walsh's discussion

God's war is a terrible act of paternal love. With his Babelic name, Confusion, God provides untranslatability. But, in doing so, he also gives the possibility of translation. The untranslatable, that is, the properly idiomatic that refuses to let itself be made common possession, is the necessary and perhaps sufficient condition for the task of the translator.[20]

The Book of Mormon may be a unique case in the history of religious translation: through it, the untranslatable as a condition for the task of the translator was resolved by divine revelation.

Mormonism: Mythical Origins and Translation

Writing about the missionary efforts of the Catholic Church in colonial Peru, Durston summarizes the problems encountered by the mendicant orders as they faced issues of intercultural and interlinguistic mediation in colonial Spanish America:

> Religious traditions of the dogmatic, revealed type tend to impose strict limits on the translation of canonical texts in order to guarantee the role of ritual specialists as well as the distinctive, sacral character of the texts themselves. Similar limitations apply at the level of religious terminology, such as terms for deities and institutions; translators often prefer to leave them untouched by introducing them as loan words instead of searching for a risky equivalent in the target language and culture. Religious translation programs usually involve a tension between the need to translate in order to fulfil missionary or pastoral mandates and the fear that translation will lead to corruption and betrayal, and such tensions have not been dealt with systematically in translation studies.[21]

For Joseph Smith, these tensions were solved on September 22, 1827, when the angel Moroni entrusted the founder of the church with some golden plates, which he was to translate into English.[22] Seemingly, Moroni had visited Smith for the first time on September

---

of the concepts of *metaphormosis* and *transfiguration* in the English versions of the New Testament in "Metamorphosis, Transfiguration, and the Body," *Biblical Interpretation* 19 (2011): 253–75.

20. Alberto Moreiras, "Pastiche Identity and Allegory of Allegory," in Amaryll Chanady, ed., *Latin American Identity and Construction of Difference* (Minneapolis: University of Minnesota Press, 1994), 229.

21. Durston, *Pastoral Quechua*, 11.

22. Mario S. De Pillis, "The Social Sources of Mormonism," *Church History* 37, no.1 (1968): 57.

21, 1823.[23] Some argue that Smith may have thought of translating an account of the history of Native Americans in 1826, after becoming acquainted with a theory that considered American Indians as descendants of the Israelites.[24] The appearance of the angel would be among the first of a series of revelations that were to change the history of American religions.

Before we deal with the concept of translation in the production of the Book of Mormon, it is also relevant to point out that Mormon scholars have mentioned a number of reasons for the eventual success of the church. For instance, Mormonism was linked to the frontier as a metaphor for the American expansion westwards.[25] De Pillis opposes this view considering that New York State, where the new religion had originated in the 1820s, was no longer a frontier (least of all Vermont, where Smith had lived). He also stresses that the initial members of the movement came from the American East and that their doctrines were clearly "eastern" in spirit, that is, influenced by religious Puritanism. Thus, De Pillis claims, Smith appealed to the minds of his "excited, credulous, practical, intellectual, socially conscious Yankee followers," who were keen to combine a desire for abundance and an interest in social well-being.[26]

In this sense, Mormonism epitomizes the communitarian efforts so characteristic of early American culture at a time when Europeans and their descendants put their religious (and non-religious) ideals to the service of social experiments. Taysom has explored some of the differences and similarities between two such groups, the Mormons and the Shakers (a variant of Quakerism, almost extinct at present, with only a few of its members living in Maine). One of the most notable differences is indeed the origin of Mormonism as a truly American religion. Whereas the Shakers, like most other religious minorities, had originated in Europe and moved to North America in their search for

---

23. Perry Benjamin Pierce, "The Origin of the 'Book of Mormon,'" *American Anthropologist*, Oct. 1899, 678.

24. G. St. John Scott, "A Conjectural Reading of the Book of Mormon," *Forum of Modern Language Studies*, 42, no. 4 (2006): 448.

25. Pierce, "Origin," 675.

26. De Pillis, "Social Sources of Mormonism," 51–53.

religious tolerance, the Mormons emerged as a true American movement, albeit Christian in its origin.[27]

Another important difference between these two movements is the origin of their sacred texts. Whereas the Shakers relied on the Bible, the Mormons complemented the Old and New Testaments with the translation of a mysterious document that was to become one of the pillars of the new faith. In fact, when we write about the use of translation in the creation of a Mormon canon, we can speak of, at least, three distinct types of transformations. First, the golden plates claim to record the origins of the Nephites (one of the Middle Eastern groups believed to have emigrated to the Americas), who were seeking the Promised Land. Smith allegedly translated these plates into English. After the completion of the Book of Mormon, Smith undertook the retranslation of the Bible following another revelation that compelled him to do so. This could be regarded as a case of intralingual translation as Smith was not familiar with Hebrew or Greek. Finally, Smith performed the intersemiotic translation of some Egyptian papyri that the new church had purchased in Ohio. This gave way to the Book of Abraham.

THE THREE TYPES OF TRANSLATION
IN THE CREATION OF A MORMON CANON

Pseudotranslation and the Book of Mormon

Smith's most influential work is, undoubtedly, the so-called translation of the golden plates whose author was claimed to have hidden in the hills of New York State. Many centuries later, his son, Moroni, appeared to Smith and asked him to prepare himself for an important task: the discovery and translation of some golden plates containing the history of the inhabitants of pre-Columbian America. Following Dahl, we can briefly summarize the content thus: the book tells us the travels of the Jaredites, the Nephites and the Lamanites from their original base in the Near East to the New World. The Jaredites were the first ones to arrive in modern-day United States but they became extinct as a result of internal strife. The other two groups followed in about 600 BCE just before the destruction of Jerusalem by king

---

27. Stephen C. Taysom, *Shakers, Mormons, and Religious Worlds. Conflicting Visions, Contested Boundaries* (Bloomington: Indiana University Press, 2011).

Nebuchadnezzar. These groups were more successful than the Jaredites: they settled down in the Americas and became wealthy. However, they could not help internal rivalries and, in the end, their civilization came to an end. Finally, Moroni, "the last of the Nephite scholars and priests," buried the records of his people to be found centuries later by Smith, after Moroni's revelations to America's first prophet.[28]

Smith had, thus, access to the mythical golden plates, which needed to be translated into English for the purposes of conversion. According to Smith, the story had been written in a language called reformed Egyptian. Although Smith belonged to a poor family and had no formal education, he was able to understand the orthography and meaning of this unfamiliar language thanks to the existence of an instrument called the "Urim and Thummin," which could help the interpretation of the original language.[29] Apparently, Smith did not start the translation work right after the discovery of the plates because he needed time to familiarize himself with the interpretation instruments: he eventually translated most of the plates between December 1827 and June 1829.[30]

Once Smith's work was completed, it needed publication to achieve its proselytistic goal. Towards the end of the nineteenth century, Pierce sarcastically wondered why Smith had not used the golden plates to secure financial and institutional support for the publication of the book: "There is a little printing office in Palmyra, but no angel can be invoked to subsidize the printer." The golden plates, Pierce continues, could not be used as a guarantee because once the translation process was completed, they had to be stored away from public eyes.[31] In this sense, the Book of Mormon goes far beyond Toury's discussion as a case of fictitious or pseudo-translation.[32] The whole process, from Moroni's first appearance in 1823 until the publication of the book in 1830, spans seven years, during which translation cemented not merely the mythical origin of the document but also its veracity. In the end, the

28. Curtis Dahl, "Mound-builders, Mormons, and William Cullen Bryant," *New England Quarterly*, 34, no. 2 (1961): 178–90.

29. W. D. Davies, "Reflections on the Mormon 'Canon,'" *Harvard Theological Review* 79, no. 1/3 (1986): 48.

30. Terryl L. Givens, *By the Hand of Mormon: The American Scripture That Launched a New World Religion* (Oxford: Oxford University Press, 2002), 27–28.

31. Pierce, "Origin," 681.

32. Toury, "Enhancing Cultural Changes."

translation or transcription work and its subsequent publication were supported by the donations of believers or patrons, such as Martin Harris, Joseph Knight, and Peter Whitmer.[33]

The mythical origin of the Book of Mormon was, as can be imagined, one of the main reasons why funding for the publication was difficult to obtain. The arguments against Smith's claims are too obvious to be discussed here. For this reason, Givens recalls, Smith's believers went to great lengths to authenticate Smith's text as a translation by consulting a "celebrated" professor, Charles Anthon, of Columbia University. Anthon's role in the story would give way to a controversy of its own. Leaving aside the polemical stories around the publication and authentication, several witness accounts make clear that the translation process involved a great deal of dictation. Large parts of the texts are based on the King James Version of Isaiah 2–14 and 48–54 and Matthew 5–7, among many others. This has been confirmed by textual evidence provided by other researchers. [34]

Irrespective of these issues, the epistemological comparison between the translation of an extant "original" religious text, such as the Bible, and the mythical translation of the Book of Mormon shows that the rationale behind them is not so dissimilar. Writing about the translation of the former, Jasper discusses the difficulties posed by certain Greek terms to be rendered into English: different choices entail a different understanding of the original concepts. He notes that the Bible "has always been a translated text, and, indeed, within its own pages there are already translations." He wonders "What is the Bible—the original Bible? In one sense there is no answer for it is all endless translation." Jasper underlines that some of the translators of the Bible have regarded their versions as the ultimate version in their own language. He quotes the case of William Tyndale, an English reformer who was one of the first translators of the Bible into English: "William Tyndale, too, believed his English text to be the very word of God." This view is not so distinct from Smith's own creation of the Book of Mormon, or even his adaptation of the Bible some years later. Both contain elements of faith, naïveté, ambition, and deceit, albeit to various degrees. [35]

---

33. De Pillis, "Social Sources of Mormonism," 57.

34. Givens, *By the Hand of Mormon*, 29–31.

35. David Jasper, "Settling Hoti's Business: The Impossible Necessity of Biblical Translation," in Long, *Translation and Religion*, 105–07, 109.

Smith's believers would eventually hail the text as a major achievement. This has continued until the present day as translation is regarded as part of the authentication process. Some authors even stress that there are reasons to believe the book is what it claims to be. Sperry, for instance, contends that the book is a translation because the text "is not English freely composed but is rather that type of English that would be produced by a translator who frequently follows the original too closely, the syntax of which is thus made plain in the English dress. In other words, I hold that the English of the Book of Mormon often betrays a too-literal adherence to an apparent Hebrew original."[36] That is, the book is authentic because it is a translation, and it is a translation because of its foreignizing elements.

In any case, the "translation" of the Book of Mormon and the subsequent disappearance of the original solved the issue of fidelity to the text. Being based on the mythical golden tables that, once the translation was produced, went missing does away with all the problems arising from text comparison and, above all, from the scrutiny of critical eyes. In that sense, the book is the very word of God inasmuch his translator and founder of the church, as well as his followers, do not harbour any doubts about its divine origin. As such, the text is an act of faith as is the translation process itself. There are no techniques, no translation mistakes, no unintelligible context.[37] It even solves the problems raised by revisionist groups of other religious texts.[38] Burke's analysis of gender-biased language would also be superfluous in the Book of Mormon: if the original is not available, there is no comparison to be made, no rewriting necessary. The translated version, at least into the first language, *is* the original.

The Book of Mormon was, thus, established as the canonical text of the new church, the one by which all standards were to be measured. Although the origin of the new religion does not differ much from other major Western faiths, including Judaism, Christianity, and Islam, which are based on divine revelations, Smith availed himself of three witnesses

---

36. Sidney B. Sperry, "The Book of Mormon as Translation English," *Journal Book of Mormon Studies*, 4, no. 1. (1995): 214.

37. Jonathan Gold, "Guardian of the Translated Dharma: Sakya Pandita on the Role of the Tibetan Scholar," in Long, *Translation and Religion*, 119–25.

38. Burke, "The Translation of the Hebrew Word 'ish in Genesis: A Brief Historical Comparison," in Long, *Translation and Religion*.

(Martin Harris, David Whitmer, and Oliver Cowdery) in order to counter possible allegations of fraud.[39] They came from New York State, Pennsylvania, and Vermont respectively, their origins clearly supporting the theory that Mormonism was basically an (US) Eastern religion.

In the long run, though, the lack of an original would contribute to accentuate the isolation of the church, as social issues came to the fore in the newly formed nation: as there was no original to support the choices made by Smith, there was no way to justify the policy banning blacks from the Mormon priesthood, informed by the words on the darker Lamanites. In fact, one of the main storylines of the book was the downfall of the Lamanites. In the first book of Nephi, they are blamed for "wars and rumors of wars" (1830 ed., 28). This would finally lead to the segregation of the Lamanites and the Nephites as Nephi feared the Lamanites might "come upon us and destroy us: for I knew their hatred towards me and my children, and they which were called my people" (1830 ed., 72). This led to the dissociation of the former from the foundation of the church. As the Lamanites became more warlike and incredulous, a change also operated in their skin:

> As it came to pass that I beheld that after they had dwindled in unbelief, they became a dark, and loathsome, and a filthy people, full of idleness and all manner of abominations (1830 ed., 28).

> And the skins of the Lamanites were dark, according to the mark which was set upon their fathers, which was a curse upon them because of their transgression and their rebellion against their brethren, which consisted of Nephi, Jacob, and Joseph, and Sam, which were just and holy men (1830 ed., 228).

This text, together with Smith's own translation of the Egyptian papyri, which we will comment on below, established the basis for the racist tones of the church and would later become an embarrassment for its leaders. The concept of darkness had a biblical origin, and Smith used it generously throughout his own text. Darkness was associated with abominable and filthy acts, opposed to the positive connotations of the word "light." Later on, in the second book of Nephi, Smith

---

39. Rodney Stark, *The Rise of Mormonism* (New York: Columbia University Press, 2005), 32; De Pillis, "Social Sources of Mormonism," 64.

insists on the color of the skin as indicative of the godly ways of the tribes that believed in Christ:

> And then shall they rejoice: for they shall know that it is a blessing unto them from the hand of God; and their scales of darkness shall begin to fall from their eyes; and many generations shall not pass away among them, save they shall be a white and delightsome people (1830 ed., 117).

The association between filthiness and skin darkness is repeated again in three of the books comprised in the Book of Mormon: Jacob, Alma, and Mormon. In the Book of Alma, Smith claims that the mark set upon them by God was passed on to those who "mingle his seed with those of the Lamanites," establishing the basis for racism and segregation (1830 ed., 128, 228–29, 528).

Some authors like Bushman, an emeritus professor of history at Columbia University, and a Mormon, believe that the complexity of this issue goes beyond the question of "simple racism." Bushman claims that references to skin colour went beyond "conventional American racism" as the book makes the Indians the ancestors of American civilization, so can it be claimed that the founder was a racist?[40] But Smith's words would eventually cause embarrassment to the church, as the manifest racism that had characterized the American society from time immemorial was banned and continues to be gradually and painfully being overcome. Whereas new legislation undermined the previous "separate but equal" doctrine, however unsuccessfully it was enforced, the LDS Church itself had a harder time in adapting to the new political situation: their canonical text was often critical of the darker tribes, which were indeed supposed to be the ancestors of Native Americans.[41] For Mormon believers, this may be a plausible explanation to justify Smith's words historically, but the controversy remained and it was obvious that it did little to improve the Mormon image in the mainstream of US society, where the church was regarded with great suspicion. The lack of an original text, which contributed to the establishment of the book as a true translation, posed an additional problem in the attempt to redress the controversial issue of racism since there was no way to

---

40. Richard Lyman Bushman, *Joseph Smith: Rough Stone Rolling* (New York: Alfred A. Knopf, 2005), 98.

41. Howard Zinn, *A People's History of the United States* (New York: Harper 2005), 449–50.

ascertain that Smith's alleged translation contained the information of an original. The solution, however, would still take some time to come.

Intralingual Translation of the Bible

The second type of translation that consolidated the canon of the movement can be referred to as "intralingual," even though Smith himself claimed that it was the consequence of another revelation that had prompted him to write a new version of the Bible. In fact, it is intralinguistic in that it involved the transformation of verbal signs of one language into other verbal signs of the same language.[42] Although Smith had been trained in the teachings of Christianity through the King James Version, Davies stresses that the founder of the LDS Church had doubts about this rendering of the holy book, which moved him to introduce changes in order to improve it for a contemporary American readership: "In June 1830, Joseph Smith had already reported that God had revealed to him that many things had been taken from the words that Moses himself had written, but some of these were to be recovered."[43] In the opinion of some researchers, this demonstrates his obsession with the ambiguity of language, which he had encountered in the Authorized Version of the Bible, a problem that he attempted to solve by revising and amplifying its content.[44]

Barlow notes that although this area of Mormon history is less known than the production of the Book of Mormon, it is an important part of the canon. Smith himself referred to it as "this branch of my calling."[45] The new translation, or revision process of the Bible, began in 1830.[46] Smith devoted much of his time to this task until the year 1833, although the revision did not stop until his death in 1844 and it was never finished.[47] Again the founder of the LDS Church used the term "translation" for the process he was engaged in, probably because, as with the transcription of the golden plates first and the interpretation of the Egyptian papyri later,

---

42. Roman Jakobson, "On Linguistic Aspects of Translation," in Lawrence Venuti, ed., *The Translation Studies Reader* (London: Routledge, 2000), 114.

43. Davies, "Reflections," 46.

44. Samuel Brown, "Joseph (Smith) in Egypt: Babel, Hieroglyphs, and the Pure Language of Eden," *Church History*, 78, no. 1 (2009): 31.

45. Philip L. Barlow, "Joseph Smith's Revision of the Bible: Fraudulent, Pathologic or Prophetic?" *Harvard Theological Review*, 83, no. 1 (1990): 46.

46. Davies, "Reflections," 47.

47. Barlow, "Joseph Smith's Revision," 47.

the concept of translation provided his work with the element of veracity and respectability he desired for his divine mission.

The rationale behind the "translation" of the Bible thus understood was to imprint Smith's text with his own beliefs of what the Old and New Testaments should be like. Marquardt underlines that it was "the belief of Joseph Smith that the gospel of Jesus Christ contained in the New Testament consisted of the same essential beliefs and ordinances since the beginning of humankind." For this reason, it was clear that the Christian precepts preceded the birth of Christ. This called for a revision of the Old Testament that contemplated the practice of the gospel before the arrival of Christ. Smith, let us remember once more, was not familiar with Hebrew or Greek, so he could have not turned to the source texts. Although his followers were aware of this weakness, it simply became irrelevant because "he got his corrections via revelation." Smith incorporated, for example, a series of additions to Genesis in which the Book of Mormon informed the Old Testament of the precepts of the New.[48] This is not a translation in the more essentialist sense of the word: Smith considered these additions the result of his divine visions to translate the Bible for a contemporary audience, as Marquardt notes.[49] In other cases, however, we could speak of intralingual translation in the sense that he attempted to clarify those passages of the King James Version that he judged too obscure for a nineteenth-century American believer.

Smith's revision of the Bible would eventually give way to another major problem within American society at large. As he read the Old Testament and became familiar with the lives of figures such as Solomon and David, he "apparently concluded that their polygamous marriages had brought society to an attainable of virtue and had therefore received divine sanction," thus creating what Keller calls "the ancient polygamy-fiction."[50] Fictitious translation was, again, another feature of his work. In the end, this translation-revision of the Bible would give way to the second major problem with American society: polygamy.

---

48. H. Michael Marquardt, *The Rise of Mormonism*, 1816–1844 (Longwood, FL: Xulon, 2005), 323, 326.

49. H. Michael Marquardt, *The Joseph Smith Revelations: Text and Commentary* (Salt Lake City: Signature Books, 1999), 183.

50. Francis Richardson Keller, *Fictions of U.S. History: A Theory and Four Illustrations* (Bloomington: Indiana University Press, 2002), 91.

Smith's revised version of the Bible first came out in 1867 and was published again in 1944. Both were published by a smaller organization within the Mormon movement, the Reorganized Church of Jesus Christ of Latter Day Saints, later known as the Community of Christ. However, the LDS Church continued to use the King James Version for official purposes. As Davies underlines, LDS members regarded Smith's new version as "inspired" but it was not completely assimilated with the exception of Matthew 23:39 and Matthew 24.[51] The existence of a more significant text, the Book of Mormon, and the social problems related to some of their customs and rituals later introduced by Smith, notably polygamy, may have relegated Smith's Bible to a secondary position within the movement.[52] The historic move from persecuted to executioner also affected the position of the church within mainstream society.[53]

In the end, the Mormon Church would accept other documents as part of their sacred texts, including the divine revelations made to their founder through the angel Moroni and his re-writing of the Bible. The "Inspired Version" or the "Joseph Smith Version" reflected the founder's preoccupations with the linguistic issues that characterized his "divine" call and that were an integral part of the search for a universal language deprived of the ambiguities he had found in the Authorized Version.[54] Thus, language and Smith's intralinguistic "translation" of the Bible eventually became part of the Mormon canon.

Intersemiotic Translation and the Egyptian Papyri

The third translation to play a key role in the Mormon movement, Smith's rendering into English of the Egyptian Papyri, is the type that Jakobson called "intersemiotic," that is, the transformation of a message shaped in one system of signs into a different system. It served as the basis for his Book of Abraham.

In 1835 Michael H. Chandler had excited the population of Kirtland, Ohio, with the exhibition of four Egyptian mummies as well as some papyri. Chandler is believed to have attempted to understand

---

51. Davies, "Reflections," 47.
52. Barlow, "Joseph Smith's Revision," 46–47.
53. Sally Denton, *American Massacre: The Tragedy at Mountain Meadows, September 1857* (New York: Alfred A. Knopf, 2003).
54. Brown, "Joseph (Smith) in Egypt," 31.

the meaning of these documents by contacting American researchers, but at the time the key to read hieroglyphics was not known yet. It seems that Chandler contacted Smith because he had heard of Smith's skills to translate a language called reformed Egyptian.[55] The church would eventually purchase the papyri for $2,400, and Smith, together with W. W. Phelps and Oliver Cowdery, attempted to decipher their meaning. They concluded that the papyri were the missing link with Abraham and Joseph. The translational process began after the creation of a system that could allow them to interpret the symbols. At the time the work of the French researcher Jean François Champollion into the meaning of Egyptian hieroglyphics was not known, so there was no way to ascertain whether Smith's translation was accurate.[56] The work carried out by Smith and his scribes produced three manuscripts that, once again, are the product of Smith's dictation. As Marquardt claims, the founder could not possibly decipher it so the most likely explanation is that

> The symbols inspired him with ideas. The text produced was represented by Joseph Smith as an inspired revelatory interpretation (translation). The saints knew Joseph Smith had no knowledge of Egyptian and that the contexts of the papyrus would have to be revealed by God.[57]

Smith's work was published in Nauvoo, Illinois, in 1842. Two decades later the papyri were reported to have been destroyed in a fire in Chicago. In 1880 the Book of Abraham would be published as part of the Pearl of Great Price and, thus, became part of the Mormon canon.

However, the history does not end here. The papyri were legendary documents, but their existence also seemed to support Smith's claims that he may have had a "divine" gift for translating. Thus, the translation of the Egyptian documents could not only serve to support Smith's linguistic abilities and his translation of the Book of Mormon, it could also give him credit as the founder of the LDS Church. The publication of the translation of the papyri, and the fact that these documents existed, clearly situated Smith in what Toury calls "the niche allocated to it," that is, in the minds of those that had been attracted to the new

---

55. H. Donl Peterson, *The Story of the Book of Abraham: Mummies, Manuscripts, and Mormonism* (Springville, UT: CFI, 2008), 2–3; Brown, "Joseph (Smith) in Egypt," 26.

56. Marquardt, *Rise of Mormonism*, 389; Peterson, *Story of the Book of Abraham*, 38–39.

57. Marquardt, *Rise of Mormonism*, 395.

religion.[58] In fact, the author left abundant notes and drawings that attested to this translational effort. For his followers, Smith did not only have a divine mission, he was also gifted as a translator.

Quite unexpectedly, the Egyptian papyri Smith and his colleagues had translated in the previous century were discovered in 1966 in New York's Metropolitan Museum of Art. This opened the possibility to compare the original documents with the translation accepted as official by the LDS Church. It marked a sharp contrast with the origins of the Book of Mormon, whose *hidden* mythical source texts did not allow any comparisons with the target text. For the first time it was possible to determine the accuracy of the translation as well as Smith's abilities as a translator. In 2012, Robert Ritner, from the Oriental Institute of the University of Chicago, published the first complete English translation of the so-called Joseph Smith papyri. Ritner provided not only his own version, based on the contemporary knowledge of Egyptian hieroglyphic writing, but also extracts from previous versions, allowing readers to draw comparisons between Smith's text and his own. Ritner, as one would expect, provides a clear criticism of Smith's skills as a translator.[59]

As the original documents appeared and were translated afresh, we move into a new terrain. Here we are not dealing with a case of fictitious translation but rather with erroneous translation. Smith did not have the knowledge to provide an accurate version of the content of the papyri, although he did have the original documents. However, the argument goes beyond whether Smith's translation was accurate or erroneous. The existence of an extant original document is complemented with the survival of Smith's work on the text and that of his collaborators, which gave way to what has been called his theology of language. Researchers have had access to the so-called Kirtland Egyptian papers philological exercises (abbreviated as KEP) and to a notebook called "Grammar and alphabet of the Egyptian language." Of course, these documents have no connections with any Egyptian language whatsoever, but the controversy of their erroneous or fictitious nature has "deflected attention from their meaning as religious documents per se." Smith's efforts are indicative of his obsession with language, with bringing light to ambiguity

---

58. Toury, *Descriptive Translation Studies*, 52.

59. Robert K. Ritner, *The Joseph Smith Egyptian Papyri: A Complete Edition* (Salt Lake City: Signature Books, 2012).

and darkness.[60] Once again, the translation of the papyri would become problematic for the church because of Smith's reiteration of the concept of darkness to typify the fall of man.

Israel A. Smith, the founder's grandson, later pointed out that "he merely translated on the basis of his own learning and study. He referred to it as a 'purported' record."[61] His descendant, who became a president of the Reorganized Church of Jesus Christ of Latter-Day Saints, also added that there was no indication to believe that his ancestor supported the content or teachings of the papyri. We may wonder, why is this important? Smith's Book of Abraham, together with the associations between the fall of man and dark skin in the Book of Mormon, has become the basis for the critique of Mormon racism (which Barlow euphemistically calls "the vestiges of Mormon racism").[62] The Book of Abraham is not part of the Community of Christ canon, although this group accounts for a small percentage of the Mormon movement (around a quarter of a million members as opposed to over fourteen million LDS members). The claim that Smith did not support the contents of the translation may have been useful within the official discourse of the church, but the issue continued to be regarded an intrinsic element of the Mormon canon and, therefore, problematic. The solution would have to wait until the twentieth century.

CONCLUDING DISCUSSION

Religion and language have always depended on each other to create and sustain economic, social and national identities. During the Reformation and Counter-Reformation periods the translation of the Bible into European languages promoted the expansion of modern nations such as Denmark and Holland.[63] In the early modern period, the established churches of colonial powers translated the Bible and other religious texts into local languages. For example, the Catholic Church

---

60. Brown, "Joseph (Smith) in Egypt," 28, 30, 32.

61. Peterson, *Story of the Book of Abraham*, 196.

62. Philip L. Barlow, "Before Mormonism: Joseph Smith's Use of the Bible, 1820–1829," *Journal of the American Academy of Religion*, 57, no. 4. (1989): 765.

63. Tore Kristiansen, "Danish," and Roland Willemyns, "Dutch," in Ana Deumert and Wim Vandenbussche, eds., *Germanic Standardization: Past to Present* (Amsterdam: Benjamins, 2003), 80, 98.

commissioned the translation of the catechism into Quechua, Aymara, and Nahuatl, among other pre-Columbian languages.

In the United States, English may have already established itself as the lingua franca of the peoples who had emigrated to the emerging nation, but the concept of translation into English was to prove instrumental in the development of the new religion's canon. In a way the origin of the church seems to respond to Bourdieu's concern when, following Spinoza, one wonders, "How can you understand the sacred texts, those of the prophets, of the Bible, if you don't know who wrote them, when they wrote them, how they wrote them."[64] To the members of the church, some of these questions have a clear and incontrovertible answer.

However, other Americans would need to come to terms with a community that had accepted Smith's "translations" at face value. Moore stresses that non-Mormons needed to realize that, when dealing with LDS members, it was not so important what was true, but what people thought was true, or had chosen to believe to be true.[65] In this sense, Barlow believes that the founder was part of a society that believed in the literality of the Bible. Unlike many of his contemporaries, Joseph Smith was not satisfied with the Bible, so he recreated the scriptures to complement his search for a Promised Land: "he produced more scripture, scripture which echoed biblical themes, reinforced biblical authority, interpreted biblical passages, was built with biblical language, shared biblical content, corrected biblical errors."[66] By resorting to the concept of translation, he was lending authority to the new Christian faith he was creating. He also introduced himself as part of the biblical prophecy. It did not matter that, as researchers from various fields were to prove in the future, his texts were characterized by numerous mistakes or inventions concerning the native peoples of America, whose story he claimed to have written. It did not matter that his interpretation of the Egyptian papyri, whose glyphs he attempted to decipher, was erroneous. The papyri confirmed his search

---

64. Pierre Bordieu, "The Political Field, the Social Science Field, and the Journalistic Field," in Rodney Benson and Erik Neveu, eds., *Bourdieu and the Journalistic Field* (Cambridge: Polity, 2005), 32.

65. R. Lawrence Moore, *Religious Outsiders and the Making of Americans* (New York: Oxford University Press, 1986), 27.

66. Barlow, "Before Mormonism," 741.

for a Promised Land, and this confirmation could only be disseminated through his purported translation.

The many uses of "translation" in the writing of the Book of Mormon were, thus, a key to the creation of the Mormon canon. At the same time, translation links and separates Joseph Smith and his followers from other Christian denominations. While the book may be embedded within the Judeo-Christian traditions of the Old and New Testaments, Mormons accepted that the text could be traced back to many centuries before the birth of Christ.[67] It was also believed that the storyline was set in a continent that could not have been mentioned in the Old and New Testaments. The new faith, though, was believed to be Christian in spirit.[68] To most of the Anglophone world of the nineteenth century, the Bible was the King James Version, whose language had contributed not only to the religiousness of the country but also to shape the oratory of its politicians. However, probably out of a feeling of dissatisfaction with both, Smith suggested that for the Bible to be accepted as the base of its church, it had to be translated correctly because "ignorant translators, careless transcribers, or designing and corrupt priests have committed many errors."[69]

Translation, thus, contributed to the gradual acceptance of the church within the new nation, as it had contributed to the normalization of European languages and the promotion of national identities during the Reformation and Counter-Reformation, not only of the major languages and cultures, but also of minority and smaller languages such as Welsh, Danish, and Dutch.[70] Translation had been at the base of religious and national identity formation. Within the new American society, it continued to be so: the effect of the text would have been different, had Smith claimed that it came from plates written in English rather than reformed Egyptian.[71] In fact, the reworking of the Bible was not unique to Smith. In the fifty years prior to the

---

67. Davies, "Reflections," 44–46.

68. Stephen J. Stein, "America's Bibles: Canon, Commentary, and Community," *Church History*, 64, no. 2, (1995): 172.

69. Davies, "Reflections," 46.

70. Alex Jones, "The Nineteenth-Century Media and Welsh Identity," in Laurel Brake, Bill Bell, and David Finkelstein, eds., *Nineteenth-century Media and the Construction of Identities* (London: Palgrave, 2000), 311; Kristiansen, "Danish," and Willemyns, "Dutch," in Deumert and Vandenbussche, *Germanic Standardization*, 80, 98.

71. Toury, "Enhancing Cultural Changes," 11.

publication of the Book of Mormon there had been some revisions of the King James Version, although these had been based on translations from the Hebrew or Greek manuscripts.[72] However, both moves seem to point to a contemporary dissatisfaction with, at least, part of the wording of the authorized English version.

Smith's version of the Bible was indeed unique in that he did not rely on the original manuscripts, but rather on divine revelations. The members of the new church, though, relegated the text to a secondary position. There might be different reasons for this, as the Smith version contradicted the Book of Mormon at times. Additionally, the text was owned by Smith's wife, a member of the Community of Christ branch, which would eventually publish the text. It would take a few decades for the LDS Church to come to terms with Smith's text, and accepted it as an "inspired version" of the Bible. But the ontological use of the concept of translation to sustain his efforts in the creation of the new church is telling of the role of translation in the normalization of social and religious groups to become part of mainstream society.

Thus, the combination of divine revelations and cultural translation produced a narrative that, while providing an alternative to conventional religions, relied on its own metadiscourse in its aim for conversion and wider acceptance within American society, which could partly explain the reason why Mormonism keeps attracting followers a century and a half after its foundation.[73] In fact, the use of divine authentication was not new. Durston has argued that divine intervention was at the base of the religious discourse in colonial Peru. In the Andes translation of sacred texts into the languages of the colonized had been guaranteed through the divine mediation of the church. Durston mentions the difference between endogenous translation, where the emphasis lies on the target text, and exogenous translation, "where the translators are members of the source culture and seek to introduce their own texts and textual traditions into a foreign language and culture."[74]

There are, though, obvious differences between the Catholic Church in Peru and the LDS Church in the United States. For one thing, the

---

72. Barlow, "Joseph Smith's Revision," 50–51.

73. Douglas Robinson, *Who Translates? Translator Subjectivity Beyond Reason* (Albany: State University of New York, 2001), 55.

74. Durston, *Pastoral Quechua*, 12, 24.

former was already an established church whereas the latter was striving for acceptance. Besides, the Catholic Church used translations that could be contrasted with "original" texts, whereas Smith claimed that his translations were based on divine revelations. But, ultimately, the origins and existence of a source text do not produce any significant differences between the LDS Church and other Christian denominations: the faith of their members depends on what is purported as sacred translated texts.

Translation was also a useful instrument in the establishment of a hierarchy within the church itself. In fact, in a conference held to decide on authority within the movement, Joseph Smith was defined as "seer, a translator, a prophet, and apostle of Jesus Christ."[75] The fact that his position as a translator comes second, before his role as a prophet and as an apostle, is highly indicative of the importance attached to translation as constituent of authority, only superseded by his function as the recipient of revelations within the church. As Vidal Claramonte points out, the Book of Mormon was an example of the perfect translation in terms of equivalence not because of the skills of the translator but because of the intervention of an external authority.[76]

In contemporary American society this is further supported by the acceptance of the church in the country's political, social and economic life. The 2008 and 2012 candidacies of Mitt Romney to the presidency of the United States clearly epitomizes this move towards conventional life. Mormonism has come a long way as a trustworthy minority religious group, as more of its members get elected to occupy positions as honest politicians. At the same time, as they joined the ranks of corporate America, the communitarian spirit of the past has gradually disappeared.

The final acceptance of the movement within American mainstream society has needed readjustments on both parts. One of the most interesting changes is once again related to issues of translation. As we have seen, Smith's translations of the golden plates and of the Egyptian papyri included clear racist elements. The embarrassment these caused to the church was aggravated by the missionary success of the LDS Church in areas such as Latin America and Africa. In his writings,

75. Bushman, *Rough Stone Rolling*, 121.
76. Vidal Claramonte, *Traducción y asimetría*, 16.

Smith spoke of people with darker skin as loathsome, filthy, and idle. If his book was a faithful translation of the golden plates, then we could speak of a racist religion, even if it was claimed that Smith did not support these views.

As the situation of the black population evolved within the U.S., and attitudes and laws began to change, the movement needed to address the use of racism, even if it had been dismissed as non-existent.[77] Finally, the problem was solved as it had been initiated: via a revelation. In 1978 Spencer W. Kimball, the president of the LDS Church at the time, announced that he had had a direct revelation from God stating that black men could be admitted to priesthood. In a column published by the influential *The New York Times,* Mario De Pillis recalled the reasons for the Mormon reluctance to change: "The tradition of the church has resisted change because of two fundamental scriptures—also revealed to Smith: the Book of Mormon and the Pearl of Great Price."[78] Thus Smith's "accurate translations" contributed to the racist practices that would later characterize the church. The lack of a source text that might prove him wrong could only be counteracted through the same medium: a divine revelation. From here, translation could reclaim its terrain.

In fact, translation has continued to thrive as part of the proselytizing efforts of the LDS Church worldwide.[79] As priests, Mormons

77. John A. Tvedtnes, "The Charge of 'Racism' in the Book of Mormon," *FARMS Review* 15, no. 2 (2003). Authors close to the Mormon movement argue that Smith was not a racist and the references to the color of the skin of the Lamanites are not informed by racism. Tvedtnes, for instance, claims that racism is not present in "the truth of the history of the Book of Mormon any more than it could influence the truth of the biblical account, which frequently disapproves of the people of Israel marrying foreigners" (184). Tvedtnes, a Mormon, published the quoted paper in *The FARMS Review,* a journal of Brigham Young University's Neal A. Maxwell Institute. This discourse is, as can be expected, common among Mormon scholars.

78. Mario S. De Pillis, "Mormons Get Revelations Often but Not Like This," *New York Times,* June 11, 1978.

79. Until 2011, the LDS Church had recognized the role of translation through two separate actions. On the one hand, the institution provides official translations of essential documents. On the other, it had a web page entitled "Welcome to Mormon Translation," a Wikipedia-style portal that allowed its members to contribute to the ongoing process of translating and disseminating Mormon (non-core) documents. The presentation of the page explicitly referred to translation as "The Problem": "the LDS Church actively translates a lot of basic documents into a wide variety of languages, its efforts are limited to those books, manuals and other materials considered crucial to the functioning of the Church and its members. Novels, poetry, history and even many doctrinal works are usually not translated by the Church. As a result, members that do not speak English simply don't have access

need languages for their missionary work abroad (Romney, for instance, was a two-year missionary in France). Apart from a knowledge of local languages, translation remains a part of the conversion efforts of the LDS Church because their canonical texts need to be translated into other languages. De Pillis believes that the translation of the Book of Mormon and other texts into other languages make, in fact, a better doctrine by any standards, as they are not burdened by the old-fashioned language of the King James Bible that Smith had used as the example for his "translations," even if he claimed that he was trying to improve on it.[80]

Another significant feature of the first translations of the Book of Mormon into other languages is the fact that the names of the translators were acknowledged. Take, for example, the French version, published in 1852. The title page explicitly mentioned that it had been "traduit de l'anglais par John Taylor et Curtis E. Bolton," whereas the Spanish text came out in 1886 translated by Meliton G. Trejo and James Z. Stewart. Later, foreign editions of the book would have to be officially sanctioned by the church, which has a strict control of their content. Thus, one of the problems of Bible translation, namely the choice between literal or formal correspondence on the one hand, and the functional or dynamic equivalence on the other, is solved.[81] The whole process is supervised by the church, carried out by members of the church, published by the church and distributed by the church, even if translators themselves have to deal with the nitty-gritty of the translation process. There is only one official translation, which can be modified at the church's own discretion, no doubt via divine revelations.

At present, the movement has what they call the ten prevalent languages: Chinese, English, French, German, Italian, Japanese, Korean, Portuguese, Russian, and Spanish.[82] Most materials are authored in English and translated into the other languages. The web page of the LDS

---

to thousands of valuable and helpful books." (www.mormontranslation.com). The church provided a solution through the site. It had projects in ten languages. Interestingly, these projects were carried out via automatic translation, which was later revised by registered readers. The portal was available until 2011 when it was abandoned altogether.

80. Personal communication, 2012.

81. Richard L. Rohrbaugh, "Foreignizing Translation," in Deitmer Neufeld, ed., *The Social Sciences and Biblical Translation* (Houston: Society of Biblical Literature, 2008), 12.

82. See www.lds.org/church/news/language-pages-provide-church-materials-in-more-than-100-languages?lang=eng. Consulted June 2, 2021.

Church also gives prominence to translation: it currently offers materials in over 100 languages, and the LDS Church has a strict control over the translation process. According to Point 21.1.8 of *Handbook 2 of the Selected Church Policies*: "When a sacred text is translated into another language ... there are substantial risks that this process may introduce doctrinal errors ... To guard against these risks, the First Presidency and Council of the Twelve give close personal supervision to the translation of the scriptures from English into other languages."[83] As the church now regulates the translation process, which has greatly evolved from the early days, when the name of individual translators into Spanish and French was acknowledged, the names of current collective translators are not available anymore. Translation, which was at the very base of the birth of the movement, does continue to play a key role in the spreading of the church, but today only Joseph Smith has the honor of being recognized as a translator, even before a prophet.

---

83. See www.abn.churchofjesuschrist.org/study/ensign/1993/04/news-of-the-church/modern-language-editions-of-the-book-of-mormon-discouraged?lang=eng.Consulted June 2, 2021.

EIGHT

NARRATIVE REVOLUTIONS
IN NAT TURNER AND JOSEPH SMITH

LAURA THIEMANN SCALES

The early 1830s were banner years for preachers and prophets in America. Circuit riders and evangelists fanned out over the whole of the settled US, and church membership increased exponentially under the influence of itinerant clergy. An explosion of religious periodicals allowed newly formed and reinvigorated denominations to reach thousands of potential converts; by 1830, there were 605 different religious journals, and the American Bible Society was producing more than a million Bibles a year.[1] The age saw a rise in a variety of eccentric religious activities, including speaking in tongues, divinely inspired "shaking" and dancing, spirit-possession, and faith healing. Numerous self-proclaimed prophets emerged, including William Miller, founder of the Adventists; "Count de Leon" Bernhard Müller, who claimed to be the Messiah; Robert Matthews, the prophet Matthias; Elijah Pierson, the prophet Elijah; and John Humphrey Noyes, founder of the Oneida community. And two particularly charismatic and divisive prophets emerged on the national scene: in April 1830, Joseph Smith, claiming to have miraculously discovered and translated the Book of Mormon, founded the Church of Jesus Christ of Latter-day Saints; and in August 1831, the slave Nat Turner, citing visions from God, organized a bloody slave revolt, killing dozens of local families and setting off panicked reactions throughout the South.[2]

---

1. Nathan O. Hatch, *The Democratization of American Christianity* (New Haven, CT: Yale University Press, 1989), 142, 141.

2. For more on this period, see Louis P. Masur, *1831: Year of Eclipse* (New York: Hill and Wang, 2001), which gives a broad view of that year's cultural significance. See also Daniel Walker Howe, *What Hath God Wrought: The Transformation of America, 1815–1848*

Turner and Smith both sought to gain direct access to the transcendent, and, through their own extraordinary testimony, to bring the voice of the divine bodily to earth. As mediators for the divine, these visionaries pushed at the conventional boundaries of scripture and of prophecy, claiming immediate access to voices thought distant, and taking on biblical roles thought long dead. Outsiders to mainstream culture, both received direct prophecies from God, and both ultimately produced written testimonies that were as unusual in their narrative technique as in their wide influence. These narratives—*The Confessions of Nat Turner* (1831) and the *Doctrine and Covenants of the Church of the Latter-day Saints* (1835)—create powerful and influential personas out of Nat Turner and Joseph Smith while deliberately obscuring their roles as authors of their own works. Both Turner and Smith, I will argue, strategically blur the narrative categories they inhabit. Their astonishing narratives help us to reconfigure our understanding of the Second Great Awakening and its impact—both theological and narratological. Though the pairing is an unlikely one, bringing together Turner and Smith reveals the ways that the Second Great Awakening crosses racial and regional boundaries and creates a new public understanding of prophecy. Turner and Smith both employed a type of mediated voice that challenged fundamental assumptions about individuality, subjectivity, and narrative authority. Nat Turner, by casting himself as a new Messiah and creating powerful testimony out of ventriloquized narrative, and Joseph Smith, by creating a theology that understands all humans as potential prophets—and as potential gods—participate in a fundamental revision of the meaning of prophetic voice in America.

Prophecy is necessarily bound up with narration; by definition, a prophet must pronounce his or her message to a wider audience. But what does it mean to possess such earthly authority yet speak in the voice of another? Through their prophecies, each appears to speak from a position of narrative weakness: Nat Turner, enslaved and imprisoned, can speak only through an amanuensis with his own ambitions, while Joseph Smith begins as God's amanuensis and translator, speaking in

---

(Oxford: Oxford University Press, 2007); Jon Meacham, *American Lion: Andrew Jackson in the White House* (New York: Random House, 2007); and David Reynolds, *America, Empire of Liberty: A New History of the United States* (London: Allen Lane, 2009).

God's first-person voice and seemingly possessing no original voice of his own. Paradoxically, each becomes an authoritative narrator and—even more radically—in the process of narrating, actually becomes divine. *The Confessions of Nat Turner* and the prophecies Joseph Smith published as the *Doctrine and Covenants* destabilize the standard narrative categories of author, narrator, and character. In the models of prophecy that develop out of the Second Great Awakening, the first-person narrator is no longer an individual actor in control of his or her identity, and the third-person narrator is no longer an authority in sole control of the story. Humans talk back to and share control with the divine, blending together first- and third-person speech and blurring the boundaries of narrative personas. Neither mere passive conduits nor fully self-possessed, these prophets call into question the meaning and value of liberal personhood, which idealizes the person that is sharply delimited, inviolate, and self-owning, and create instead a new model of multiple, mediated personhood.

Although their major prophetic revelations took place within the same year, historians and critics rarely consider Joseph Smith and Nat Turner in the same sphere.[3] Smith is usually placed in the context of upstate New York revivalism and occult mysticism, while Turner is classified with his fellow slave rebels and with those influenced by Southern evangelical Protestantism. Smith had almost certainly heard of Turner, but they were not direct influences on one another. Of course, the differences among the political, social, and cultural milieus of a poor white Northerner and an enslaved black Southerner are great. Yet the commonalities in their stories—and the strange mode of prophetic voicing that they share—lead me to suggest that we see Smith and Turner not just as sharing a general prophetic vocabulary, but also as revealing a historically specific mode of narration that crosses their local geographies and cultures, one that would become influential well beyond their peculiar religious and political spheres. The millenarian, evangelical religious culture of the early nineteenth century that placed

---

3. To my knowledge, Richard H. Brodhead, "Prophets in America ca. 1830: Emerson, Nat Turner, Joseph Smith," *Journal of Mormon History* 29 (Spring 2003): 51–53, is the only other critical work to date which brings together Joseph Smith and Nat Turner. This article provides a valuable survey of the prophetic landscape in America around 1830, as well as a comprehensive comparison of what Brodhead calls the "uncanny" similarities in the careers of Turner and Smith.

direct contact with the divine at the center of its practices and that emphasized the narrative consequences of that contact—the redefinition
of scriptural authorship and the reassignment of narrative authority—
shaped both self-proclaimed prophets.[4] While the transformations of
the first Great Awakening were primarily about who (traditional ministers, evangelical preachers, lay exhorters, women, African Americans,
Native Americans, the poor) could receive and transmit the divine
word, the prophets of the Second Great Awakening focused on the
authority to narrate God's word, to author scripture—to intermingle
one's own human authority with divine language.[5]

Richard Brodhead notes that Smith and Turner share "an obsessional
concentration on the divine word in its mediated, printed form."[6] For
Turner, that conflict was rooted partly in racial authority. For Smith,
that tension was rooted partly in class authority. For both men, a radical
claim to scriptural authority, the power to author or narrate scripture,
was at the heart of their work.[7] Both narratives demonstrate an intense

---

4. While Smith and Turner both sampled from a variety of Christian denominations,
both were directly influenced by the Methodists. Turner's first owners, Benjamin and Elizabeth Turner, were Methodists who had a chapel for traveling ministers on their property and
brought Turner to services. J. Gordon Melton, *A Will to Choose: The Origins of African American Methodism* (Plymouth, UK: Rowan and Littlefield, 2007), 145. Smith's wife Emma was
a Methodist, and he tried to join the church in 1828, though he was rejected because of
his affiliations with "necromancy" and folk magic. Linda King Newell and Valeen Tippetts
Avery, *Mormon Enigma: Emma Hale Smith* (Urbana: University of Illinois Press, 1994), 25.

5. The period was marked by the explosion of revivalism and the rise or popularization
of many religious movements, including Methodists and Baptists in the South, Transcendentalists and Unitarians in New England, and Spiritualists, Millerites and Shakers in New
York. While the first thirty years of the nineteenth century saw an increase in revival activity,
the exact boundaries of the Second Great Awakening are contested, and many dispute even
the identification of this era as a coherent movement. Jon Butler, for instance, argues for an
earlier and more gradual start to the revival culture of the nineteenth century, identifying
strains of revivalism as early as the Revolution. Jon Butler, *Awash in a Sea of Faith: Christianizing the American People* (Cambridge, MA: Harvard University Press, 1990), 221. The
particular parameters of the movement are less important to my argument than a general
sense of the emerging redefinition of the relationship between the human and the divine in
the nineteenth century.

6. Richard H. Brodhead, "Millennium, Prophecy and the Energies of Social Transfor-
mation: The Case of Nat Turner," in *Imagining the End: Visions of Apocalypse from the Ancient
Middle East to Modern America*, ed. Abbas Amanat and Magnus Bernhardsson (London: I.
B. Tauris, 2002), 47.

7. Randolph Ferguson Scully in "'I Came Here Before You Did and I Shall Not Go
Away': Race, Gender, and Evangelical Community on the Eve of the Nat Turner Rebellion,"
Journal of the Early Republic 27 (Winter 2007): 661–84, characterizes Turner's rebellion as
"profoundly shaped by the shared religious world crafted by black and white evangelicals,

interest in the apparatus of prophecy, calling upon readers to imagine the complicated steps of interpretation, translation, and transcription that transform divine language into human form. Both prophets add a complicating layer of narration to the already mediated status of voice in their narratives through their use of amanuenses. Both mix narrative genres, combining biblical style with modes ranging from gothic fiction to the personal journal. And both produce first-person narratives that strangely obscure personhood, leaving the reader asking, "who speaks?" Turner and Smith participate in a revolution against narrative conventions, resisting the practices that place them in subordinate positions, that classify them as characters rather than narrators, as ventriloquists' dummies rather than authors, as passive human vessels rather than the voice of the divine. In the years surrounding the Second Great Awakening, prophecy began to be redefined as a means not just of gaining access to the divine, but of gaining divinity itself—a mediumship that reinvents as multiple, rather than destroying, subjectivity.

The prophets of the Second Great Awakening, to be sure, did not represent the first such manifestations of divine spirit in human form. Anxieties and doubts about the status of the self-possessed individual had been building for decades. Indeed, Turner and Smith provide a new prophetic alternative to the models of mediated voice circulating in the US since the eighteenth century. In conceptions of spiritual possession that emerge from the first Great Awakening in the 1730s and 1740s via lay enthusiasts and ministers like Jonathan Edwards and George Whitefield, the Holy Spirit fully occupies the body and usurps the voice of the mystic, the preacher, or the convert.[8] This model of passive mediumship anticipates the later

---

and particularly by the tensions between black and white men over the source, nature, and implications of religious authority" (676). Richard Lyman Bushman in the introduction to *The Papers of Joseph Smith* describes Smith's sensitivity to his lower-class status: "He came from a social class that bore the onus of contempt almost as a way of life. Poor tenant farmers like the Smiths were looked down upon as shiftless and crude. The ridicule that followed his stories of revelation could only have magnified his unease and led him to compensate with abrasive behavior and brave flourishes." Bushman, "Joseph Smith's Place in History," *The Papers of Joseph Smith* (Salt Lake City: Deseret Book Co., 1989), 6.

8. Much of the religious expansion of the Second Great Awakening was institutional in nature, manifested in the flowering of new denominations and the growth of old ones; in fact, the number of Christian denominations doubled and the number of ministers increased twentyfold. Yet, as Nathan Hatch has persuasively argued, this is also a time when laypeople

challenge to notions of self-possession, but, in its time, renders the divine as incompatible with the human, thereby maintaining the separation between the human self and the divine other. Leigh Eric Schmidt describes how converts in the eighteenth century often focused on hearing the Holy Spirit rather than speaking in the divine voice, thus establishing the limits of human power before the spirit: "The acquiescence of listeners opened up a way of imagining how God acted upon them; their yielding made clear the lines of divine power and human submission."[9] So too, Jonathan Edwards, in his *Treatise on Religious Affections* (1746), emphasizes the limited nature of human spiritual power; despite the spectacle of some conversions, Edwards "carefully explains that this new spiritual 'principle' does not confer on the convert new 'faculties' ... but rather supplies a new motive and new orientation" for religious expression.[10] Even those who did appear to claim radical new faculties for themselves did so in a way that finally magnified God's power rather than their own. Nancy Ruttenburg outlines how the itinerant preacher George Whitefield engaged in "publicly staged imitations of Christ, as when he warned his auditors that they should meet him on the last day, and exhorted them, 'Behold my hands and feet! Look, look into my wounded side, and see a heart flaming with love'"—an act of ventriloquism that anticipates prophets like Smith and Turner. Whitefield's version of impersonation, however, carefully negates his own personhood and denies his own presence; Christ's presence and Christ's words literally take over his self and his voice, and it is only the "denial of authorship—of one's words, of one's self, of one's self-presentation" that allows his audacious imitation. In the face of criticism that he was asserting his own messianic identity, Whitefield repeatedly emphasizes that he would "never claim as my own what is Thy sole propriety!"—that is, God's voice or Christ's body—and Ruttenburg describes Whitefield as the mere "fleshy apparatus" through which

---

begin to gain more power over church hierarchy, and when even religious leaders work against conventional authority structures. Hatch, *Democratization of American Christianity*, 4.

9. Leigh Eric Schmidt, *Hearing Things: Religion, Illusion, and the American Enlightenment* (Cambridge, MA: Harvard University Press, 2000), 56.

10. Joanna Brooks, *American Lazarus: Religion and the Rise of African-American and Native American Literatures* (Oxford: Oxford University Press, 2003), 39.

God can speak.[11] This passive, selfless status, one which emphasizes God's ultimate ownership of the authority to narrate spiritual affairs, is precisely what Smith and Turner, among other prophets of the era, move beyond.

Charles Brockden Brown's novel *Wieland* (1798) gives a terrifying vision of religious mediation and imagines the failure to maintain the boundaries of the self against both divine and human others.[12] For Brown, an unknowable God might cause one to murder one's own family; one can so little know the difference between one's own delusions and God's true voice that a confidence-man's voice can mimic the Holy Spirit's. The key question in *Wieland* is "Who is the author?," and the answer—a frightening one in the early republic—is "We can't know."[13] Inviting the same question, Turner and Smith radically depart from Brown's vision by developing modes of prophecy that merge as joint authors, rather than set into opposition, the human and the divine.[14] The inability to identify the author, the narrator, or the character had become, in both a theological and literary sense, the cultural norm by the 1830s, and Smith and Turner emblematize a narrative form that embraces, rather than fears, that ambiguity. The popular reception of these two self-proclaimed prophets reflects worries about the instability of the individual—and the public's susceptibility to egotists and madmen who claim to speak for God. But Smith and Turner themselves, their many followers, and the other prophets of this era abandon the fundamentally liberal anxiety about the boundaries of personhood. Both reveal this new prophetic personhood through narrative technologies—the use of scriptural style, the use of an amanuensis to imply high rank (rather than illiteracy or lack of authorial agency), the blur-

---

11. Nancy Ruttenburg, *Democratic Personality: Popular Voice and the Trial of American Authorship* (Stanford, CA: Stanford University Press, 1998), 94, 96, 97.

12. For more on voice and selfhood in *Wieland*, see especially Jay Fliegelman, introduction, *Wieland* by Charles Brockden Brown (1991); Nancy Ruttenburg, *Democratic Personality: Popular Voice and the Trial of American Authorship* (1998); and Eric A. Wolfe, "Ventriloquizing Nation: Voice, Identity, and Radical Democracy in Charles Brockden Brown's *Wieland*," *American Literature* 78 (2006): 431–57.

13. Ruttenburg, *Democratic Personality*, 217.

14. In many ways the popular depiction of Turner in the press after his rebellion—as well as in "The Confessions" itself—draws on the gothic precedent that *Wieland* sets, portraying him as a frightening religious fanatic whose delusions are as threatening to the nation literally as Theodore Wieland's are figuratively.

ring of first- and third-person narration—that underlines this merger of human and divine. The moments in their narratives where they appear most self-possessed are simultaneously the moments when they most fully embody the divine other.[15]

This toppling of narrative hierarchies corresponds with and perhaps even emanates from the overturning of more literal earthly hierarchies. Early nineteenth-century prophets emphatically model themselves after biblical prophets, rather than contemporaries or recent predecessors. Rechristening himself Matthias, for example, Robert Matthews declared himself to be an 1800-year-old Jewish prophet in line with Christ. Elijah Pierson, calling himself "Elijah the Tishbite," attempted, in his first act as a prophet, to raise his wife from the dead.[16] Smith conversed with—and included himself in the ranks of—Moses, Elijah, and Ezekiel. Turner declared that the voice he heard was no less than "[t]he Spirit that spoke to the prophets in former days."[17] Just as ancient prophets' allegiance to Yahweh over imperial rulers made them unique champions of justice and individual rights, nineteenth-century prophets looked to vanquish the authority of established hierarchies—both of church and of state—to posit a radically new cosmological order.[18] Nat Turner's and John Brown's violent uprisings, terrible testaments

---

15. In this argument I am both indebted to and departing from the work of Russ Castronovo in *Necro Citizenship* and Ruttenburg in *Democratic Personality*. Castronovo argues that the occult in the nineteenth century "mystifies hierarchical social structures by turning to the spiritual," thus threatening political engagement. I hope to recover, instead, the ways in which mediums and prophets entangle and reverse, rather than obscure, social and political hierarchies. Ruttenburg analyzes the "pre-liberal history of American democracy" and argues for the emergence of "an authoritative, public voice unconnected to rational debate in a Habermasian public sphere." My argument focuses on a similarly non-liberal public voice, but Ruttenburg tends to emphasize the "inarticulate and uncontainable" nature of that voice, where I underscore the new interpretive capabilities that emerge when prophets give up liberal self-containment. Russ Castronovo, *Necro Citizenship: Death, Eroticism, and the Public Sphere in the Nineteenth Century United States* (Durham, NC: Duke University Press, 2001); Ruttenburg, *Democratic Personality*.

16. Paul E. Johnson and Sean Wilentz, *The Kingdom of Matthias* (New York: Oxford University Press, 1994), 90, 38.

17. Thomas R. Gray, "The Confessions of Nat Turner," rpt. in Henry Irving Tragle, comp., *The Southampton Slave Revolt of 1831: A Compilation of Source Material* (Amherst: University of Massachusetts Press, 1971), 309

18. On ancient prophets' commitment to anti-imperialist justice, see Paul D. Hanson, "The Origin and Nature of Prophetic Political Engagement in Ancient Israel," in Neal Riemer, Paul D. Hanson, and Cornel West, eds., *Let Justice Roll: Prophetic Challenges in Religion, Politics, and Society* (Lanham, MD.: Rowman & Littlefield, 1996).

against the institution of slavery, provide obvious examples of how divine authority might, at least momentarily, supersede both the authority of the law and the bounds of accepted moral code. Fittingly, the religious ferment of this era initiated many mid-century social reform movements, including such millennial endeavors as perfectionism, utopianism, abolition, women's rights, and temperance.[19]

Yet nineteenth-century prophets did not just replicate the model laid out by their ancient counterparts; they also negotiated narrative power. As James Darsey describes it in his study of the prophetic tradition in America, the ancient prophet has little control over his own voice: "the prophet, properly understood, speaks for another. The prophets of the Old Testament were spokesmen for Yahweh. They were called to deliver a message that was not their own, often against their will. ... Prophecy is in a significant respect a performance from script."[20] In this view, which corresponds in many ways to eighteenth-century models, prophecy requires speech that emanates from a body, but that is not *of* that body. Indeed, to view a prophet as actively involved in the production of prophecy would seem to undermine the legitimacy of the entire prophetic project, to dismiss the divine voice as wholly invented. Accounts of prophecies like Smith's, which are largely written in the first person—but in *God's* voice, not Smith's—seem to bear out this model.[21] Yet the audacious prophets of the Second Great Awakening do not conform to this sense of passivity, nor does the era more generally, with its emphasis on charismatic leadership and personal revelation. Susan Juster delineates a more instructive model, which defines prophecy in the late eighteenth-century Anglo-American context, according to three stages: the hearing, the interpreting, and the delivering

---

19. For more on the religious origins of reform movements, see Robert Abzug, *Cosmos Crumbling: American Reform and the Religious Imagination* (Oxford: Oxford University Press, 1994); Susan Curtis, *A Consuming Faith: The Social Gospel and Modern American Culture* (Baltimore: Johns Hopkins University Press, 1991); Timothy Smith, *Revivalism and Social Reform: American Protestantism on the Eve of the Civil War* (Baltimore: Johns Hopkins University Press, 1980); John Stauffer and Steven Mintz, eds., *The Problem of Evil: Slavery, Freedom, and the Ambiguities of American Reform* (Amherst: University of Massachusetts Press, 2007).

20. James Darsey, *The Prophetic Tradition and Radical Rhetoric in America* (New York: New York University Press, 1997), 16.

21. On Joseph Smith, see, for example, Richard Lyman Bushman, "The 'Little, Narrow Prison' of Language: The Rhetoric of Revelation," in *Believing History: Latter-day Saint Essays*, ed. Richard Bushman, Reid L. Neilson, and Jed Woodworth (New York: Columbia University Press, 2004).

of God's message. The key middle step—interpretation—distinguishes a prophet from a mere passive medium. For Juster, prophets "had to be skilled decoders of arcane symbolism, capable of discerning subtle shades of meaning in the apocalyptic texts that might mean the difference between life and death in the here-and-now."[22] Unlike many of their immediate spiritual forebears, who tended to abrogate their own selfhood, Turner and Smith spoke in their own voices and claimed their own independent authority. Nat Turner never heard anything like a direct order to kill, but he read and interpreted vague signs and symbols—an eclipse, a vision of blood on leaves—as divinely vivid messages about how and when to plan his revolt. Because he could read God's language, Smith decoded the mysterious hieroglyphs on the golden plates that would become the Book of Mormon.

THE DE-AUTHORIZATION OF SCRIPTURE

When narrative omniscience and divine omniscience became contested in the early nineteenth century, one began to lose a sense of a single authority from whom power and knowledge flows. The narratological and theological questions that arose came together in biblical studies. As higher criticism filtered over from Germany to the United States in the first decades of the nineteenth century, biblical scholars began to rethink scriptural authority, deemphasizing God's role as "author" of the Bible, and placing new weight instead on historicity, cultural context, manuscript sources, and other issues affecting the Bible's human authorship.[23] Under historical criticism, scripture becomes infused with human voices and subject to the same array of influences

---

22. Susan Juster, *Doomsayers: Anglo-American Prophecy in the Age of Revolution* (Philadelphia: University of Pennsylvania Press, 2003), 32–33, 43.

23. Historical criticism is particularly significant in its American incarnation because it was key to the rise of liberal Protestantism and the broad movement away from Puritan orthodoxy that swept across the social classes and crossed sectarian boundaries. For more on higher criticism, see Jerry Wayne Brown, *The Rise of Biblical Criticism in America, 1800–1870: The New England Scholars* (Middletown, CT: Wesleyan University Press, 1969); Hans Frei, *The Eclipse of Biblical Narrative: A Study in Eighteenth and Nineteenth Century Hermeneutics* (New Haven, CT: Yale University Press, 1974); Robert Grant with David Tracy, *A Short History of the Interpretation of the Bible* (Philadelphia: Fortress Press, 1984); Richard A. Grusin, *Transcendentalist Hermeneutics: Institutional Authority and the Higher Criticism of the Bible* (Durham, NC: Duke University Press, 1991); Barbara Packer, "Origin and Authority: Emerson and the Higher Criticism" in *Reconstructing American Literary History*, ed. Sacvan Bercovitch (Cambridge, MA: Harvard University Press, 1986).

and authorities as a literary text; as Unitarian minister William Ellery Channing put it, "the Bible is a book written for men, in the language of men, and … its meaning is to be sought in the same manner as that of other books."[24] Scripture *becomes* literature.

This renegotiation of spiritual authority garnered diverse responses, even among liberal religious thinkers. Channing's 1819 "Baltimore Sermon," which sets out the principles of Unitarianism, grapples with the complex questions of mediumship that the new biblical criticism raises: how to interpret divine voice as mediated through various narrators; how to understand God's newly immediate presence in human lives. In rejecting the Trinity, Channing's sermon rejects what it views as a passive mediumship that holds humans to be mere vessels for divine agency—and consequently, any notion of intersubjectivity between the divine and the human. To imagine that a body—even Christ's—could contain more than one consciousness is, for Channing, to concede the Calvinist "doctrine of irresistible Divine influence on the human mind."[25] To Channing, the doctrine of the Trinity, which held that "Jesus Christ, instead of being one mind … consists of two souls, two minds; the one divine, the other human; the one weak, the other almighty; the one ignorant, the other omniscient" constitutes "an enormous tax on human credulity" and an affront to "the universal language of men," which is "framed on the idea, that one person is one person, is one mind, and one soul."[26] Facing the problem of passive mediumship, Channing concludes that no subject, not even Christ, could transcend the post-Enlightenment "universal language" of unified personality and self-ownership. Channing reveals the challenge that prophetic mediumship—by positing consciousness as multiple—presents to both orthodox Christianity, which depends on God's complete omniscience, and to liberal Christianity, which depends on human self-possession.

Yet many fellow anti-orthodox Protestants solved the Calvinist problem of spiritual passivity differently. Unlike Channing, the evangelist Charles Grandison Finney (a familiar fixture in the "burned-over district" of Joseph Smith's youth) believes it to be the absolute obligation

---

24. William Ellery Channing, *Unitarian Christianity: A Discourse on Some of the Distinguishing Opinions of Unitarians, delivered at Baltimore, May 5, 1819* (1819), 20.

25. Brown, *Rise of Biblical Criticism*, 64, 67.

26. Channing, *Unitarian Christianity*, 42–43.

of the sinner to accept the Spirit bodily, to "be filled with the Spirit." In his 1834 *Lectures on Revivals of Religion*, he describes God's presence as altering one's spirit and one's behavior: "there is such a thing as being so deeply imbued with the Spirit of God, that you must and will act so as to appear strange and eccentric. … If you have much of the spirit of God, it is not unlikely you will be thought deranged, by many."[27] This is the kind of mediumship that Channing could not imagine, one that preserves human subjectivity yet allows it to be imbued with and transformed by another consciousness. From the perspective of liberal self-possession, this new kind of spiritual selfhood can be imagined only as deranged, disordered, and disrupted.

Many others voiced Finney's exhortation to "be filled with the spirit," and it was heeded by more. In the South, where Baptist and Methodist revivalists targeted slave and free converts alike, the evangelical focus on conversion through dramatic personal experience of God made this mode of religious practice especially attractive to African Americans, since it allowed the integration of key African religious traditions with Christian doctrine, and emphasis on personal "revelations of the Holy Spirit" corresponded closely to the practice of spirit-possession that was common to African religions.[28] In addition, personal revelation instituted, if only informally, a new Christian tradition of "continuous revelation," the belief that revelation continues to happen in the present, rather than being relegated to prophets of the past, another crucial

---

27. Charles Grandison Finney, *Lectures on Revivals of Religion* (New York: Leavitt Lord & Co., 1835), 115.

28. There was a great increase in the number of conversions, both black and white, at the end of the eighteenth and beginning of the nineteenth centuries. For instance, one estimate of Baptist church membership holds that the number of African-American Baptists increased from 18,000 in 1793 to 40,000 in 1813, and that African Americans accounted for about one-quarter of Methodists in America in 1790, just six years after the church was formally organized. Barry Hankins, *The Second Great Awakening and the Transcendentalists* (Westport, CT: Greenwood Press, 2004), 67. Baptists and Methodists taught "revolutionary equality" in their early years, frequently inciting fears of slave uprisings among the white community, although both retreated from this rhetoric of equality in the antebellum era. Mechal Sobel, *Trabelin' On: The Slave Journey to the Afro-Baptist Faith* (Princeton, NJ: Princeton University Press, 1979), 159. For more on how Nat Turner merges Christianity with African religious traditions, see Makungu M. Akinyela, "Battling the Serpent: Nat Turner, Africanized Christianity, and a Black Ethos," *Journal of Black Studies* 33, no. 3 (Jan. 2003): 255–80. See also Donald G. Mathews, *Slavery and Methodism: A Chapter in American Morality, 1780–1845* (Princeton, NJ: Princeton University Press, 1965).

element of African religious practices.[29] The possibility of continuous revelation—with its implication that scripture might be written even now—is essential to understanding the brand of prophecy that arose out of the Second Great Awakening.

The Shakers, who settled in New England at the end of the eighteenth century and won many converts at the start of the nineteenth century, provide an even more explicit example of continuous revelation. Shaker faith is based in part around rituals of individual spirit-possession and glossolalia in which personal experience supersedes the authority of minister, church, and doctrine. Even scripture had no precedence over personal revelation: for their first few decades, Shakers actually forbade writing down their doctrine so as not to diminish direct communication with God, insofar as scripture was too mediated a format. In 1808, Shakers radically extended these teachings when a new set of doctrines proclaimed prophetic founder Ann Lee to be a new embodiment of Christ.[30] An ordinary person—and a woman no less—became not only prophetic but divine, an actual embodiment of God; prophecy transforms the believer into a transcendent being in her own right. Ann Lee's divinization provides a powerful metaphor for the transformation that happens in all believers when the "gift of the Spirit" descends upon them. The experience of the divine is wholly active, compelling one's body into ecstatic movement, one's voice into unfamiliar language, and one's entire spirit into something approaching God. It is this model of divinization—evident in so many religious practices of the time, and influential for so many later writers, from Walt Whitman to Harriet Beecher Stowe—that both Turner and Smith apply to their own cases of prophecy.

As scripture acquires a more complex narratology, the biblical model of mediumship shifts, thus changing the relationship between the voices of author and narrator, or between God and prophet. The reader or interpreter now becomes the active figure in divining meaning; rather than approaching scripture passively, as pronouncement, the reader must apply his or her own knowledge and authority to

---

29. John Thornton, *Africa and Africans in the Making of the Atlantic World, 1400–1800* (Cambridge: Cambridge University Press, 1992), 270–71.

30. Clarke Garrett, *Spirit Possession and Popular Religion: From the Camisards to the Shakers* (Baltimore: Johns Hopkins University Press, 1987), 195–96, 149, 213, 237.

interpret the narrative. Of course, redefining the relationship between reader and Bible also redefines the relationship between worshiper and God. When scriptural authority becomes more diffuse, the connection between the human and divine need no longer be mediated through scripture or through priestly interpretation. If the voice of God is no longer tied exclusively to scripture—to the revelation of past events—God seems to leap into the present.

This collapse of temporal categories (scripture is made in the here and now; prophets tread the plantations of Virginia and the backwoods of New York) coincides with a collapse of narrative categories and diegetic levels. Both Nat Turner's *Confessions* and Joseph Smith's *Doctrine and Covenants* seem to establish a stable tripartite narrative form: an extradiegetic frame narrative (Thomas Gray's preface to Turner's *Confessions*; the Testimony of the Twelve Apostles that opens *Doctrine and Covenants*), the first-person voice of a self-proclaimed prophet (Nat Turner; Smith and other prophets), and the voice of God as contained by that prophet. But those narrative "containers" are leaky, and the status of personhood becomes murky at each layer, not just for the prophet, but for the narrator and God as well. Nat Turner and Joseph Smith become by turn character, narrator, author, reader; by turn, human and divine. Narrative upheavals beget spiritual and political ones.

THE RISKS OF PROPHETEERING

The historical facts of Nat Turner's uprising are straightforward: on August 21, 1831, Turner and a group of about fifty fellow slaves mounted an attack on white households in Southampton County, Virginia, and killed nearly 60 people before the local militia confronted them. All of the insurgents were eventually killed or captured, and nearly all the captured were put to death, including Turner himself.

Although the facts of Turner's rebellion are clear, the written account of this story, *The Confessions of Nat Turner*, creates narrative problems that have long confounded critics.[31] *The Confessions* was written not by

---

31. For previous readings of authorship trouble in Nat Turner's "Confessions," see especially David F. Almendinger Jr., "The Construction of *The Confessions of Nat Turner*," in *Nat Turner: A Slave Rebellion in History and Memory*, ed. Kenneth S. Greenberg (Oxford: Oxford University Press, 2003); Richard H. Brodhead, "Millennium, Prophecy and the Energies of Social Transformation," 219–20; M. Cooper Harris, "Where is the Voice Coming From? Rhetoric, Religion, and Violence in The Confessions of Nat Turner," *Soundings: An*

Nat Turner himself but by Thomas Gray, a slave owner and lawyer, who interviewed Turner in jail before his trial and execution. Gray contends that *The Confessions* are Turner's own words, which he merely copied down. Yet it is clear that the text is some amalgamation of Nat Turner and Thomas Gray, that Gray has inflected the narrative with a voice that panders to the white audience. Moreover, Turner's narrative of the uprising also serves as a legal confession, since it was read in lieu of testimony at his trial and used as evidence against him in sentencing him to death. In their published form, Turner's words come embedded in materials including Gray's preface, legal attestations by the court, a transcript of the judge's sentence, and lists of those killed and those accused. Nat Turner's own voice is thus highly mediated, appearing to lack agency to the extent that "Turner's text at first glance remains locked within the prisonhouse of slavery."[32]

If the literary assessment of *The Confessions* places Turner in a passive position, so too does the dominant historical assessment of his role as a self-proclaimed prophet, which imagines him as madly possessed. Contemporaneous newspaper reports latched on to his status as a religious leader as a sign both of his insidiousness and of his potential delusion. The *Constitutional Whig* described him as "a preacher and prophet … stimulated by fanatical revenge, and perhaps misled by some hallucination of his imagined spirit of prophecy." The *Richmond Enquirer* wrote: "Nat, the ringleader, who calls himself General, pretends to be a Baptist preacher—a great enthusiast—declares to his comrades that he is commissioned by Jesus Christ, and proceeds under his inspired directions." In his conclusion to *The Confessions*, Gray contended: "He is a complete fanatic, or plays his part most admirably."[33] Labeling Turner as hallucinatory, fanatical, warped, "enthusiastic," and egocentric, these accounts strip him of rationality and subjectivity, and recall Finney's forewarning that those who possess the spirit would be considered "eccentric" and "deranged." To understand Turner as a prophet, acting on God's behalf and not merely his own, is to understand that only

---

Interdisciplinary Journal 89 (Spring 2006): 135–79; and Eric J. Sundquist, *To Wake the Nations: Race in the Making of American Literature* (Cambridge, MA: Belknap Press of Harvard University Press, 1993).

32. Sundquist, *To Wake a Nation*, 45.

33. Gray, *Confessions*, 53, 45, 317.

prophetic logic can supply an adequate understanding of his goals and of his status as a subject.[34]

Present-day critics generally place the Southampton insurrection in the context of other religiously motivated slave uprisings or conspiracies such as those led by Denmark Vesey and Gabriel Prosser, or in the context of the rise of African American Protestant Christianity in the early nineteenth century.[35] Yet examining Turner in the broader prophetic context of the Second Great Awakening or applying the example of Ann Lee to Nat Turner's case enables us to see why whites might have been so afraid of Nat's prophetic claims: just as her divinization produces transcendence in all Shakers, his rebellion suddenly turns all slaves into potential prophets.

It is peculiar enough to read a first-person narrative, supposedly a documentation of that person's speech, which is inflected (or perhaps infected) with another person's voice. It is more peculiar that there are two coexisting first persons, two "I's," in *The Confession*. Even as Turner's words at times reveal Gray's bias, Turner maintains his own powerful hold over the narration; this is not by any means a simple case of ventriloquism, but a narrative with multiple priorities and a shifting sense of power.[36] The narrative begins and ends with Gray himself as

---

34. Despite their attempts to cast his motives as mere delusions, the white establishment took his prophetic status quite seriously; in the aftermath of his rebellion, many Southern states passed laws prohibiting blacks from holding independent religious meetings to prevent similar religiously inspired uprisings. The Virginia legislature drafted legislation in 1831 that allowed blacks to attend religious assemblies only when organized by slave owners and prohibited even white-run meetings if they were held at night. Gray, *Confessions*, 455. That Turner claimed such religious authority for himself clearly raised both fear and anger in the white mainstream, and they converted his claim of prophecy into a kind of egotistic madness—a single-minded delusion—in attempting to sap his prophetic mediumship of its power.

35. See Scot French, *The Rebellious Slave: Nat Turner in American Memory* (Boston: Houghton Mifflin, 2004); and Stephen B. Oates, *The Fires of Jubilee: Nat Turner's Fierce Rebellion* (New York: Harper & Row, 1975). For a broader view of slave revolts in the United States, see Eugene Genovese, *From Rebellion to Revolution: Afro-American Slave Revolts in the Making of the Modern World* (Baton Rouge: Louisiana State University Press, 1979). Michael P. Johnson's recent study has uncovered evidence that Vesey's conspiracy may have been fabricated by white slaveholders. See Johnson, "Denmark Vesey and his Co-Conspirators," *The William and Mary Quarterly* 58, no. 4 (Oct. 2001): 915–76.

36. Sundquist acknowledges this complicated nexus of power when he uses Orlando Patterson's theory of the parasitic master-slave relationship to describe the relationship between Turner and Gray—this is not merely narrative oppression, but a peculiar interdependence in which Gray might be a kind of parasite on Turner who is mediated through Turner's consciousness.

the "I," switching in the middle to Turner's first-person voice. Gray also interrupts a handful of times with parenthetical remarks and questions for Turner to answer. But without the benefit of quotation marks or explanation to separate Turner's voice from that of Gray, the narrative can seem as if it is spoken by a single, double-voiced narrator. As Turner's narrative ends, for example, other than the start of a new paragraph there are no indications, through punctuation, page break, or textual commentary, that we are switching narrators: two sentences beginning with "I" simply follow upon one another, and the reader inevitably lags for a moment in logic:

> I am here loaded with chains, and willing to suffer the fate that awaits me.

> I here proceeded to make some inquiries of him, after assuring him of the certain death that awaited him.[37]

The parallel structure of the two sentences, the echoing of "I," "here," and "fate that awaits" / "death that awaited," creates a strange identification between the two speakers, a momentary blurring that is made even more curious by the way that Gray's chilling confirmation of Turner's impending death—"assuring him of the certain death that awaited him"—is turned into a comfortable, "assuring" echo of Turner's own voice.

Undeniable as the issues of earthly control at stake are here, we should read the narrative struggle as a literary one. Both Gray and Turner invent distinctive literary voices that draw on previous genre conventions. Gray's preface, for instance, is full of overwrought language that seems to come straight from a gothic novel: "It will thus appear, that whilst every thing on the surface of society wore a calm and peaceful aspect; whilst not one note of preparation was heard to warn the devoted inhabitants of woe and death, a gloomy fanatic was revolving in the recesses of his own dark, bewildered, and overwrought mind, schemes of indiscriminate massacre to the whites. ... No cry for mercy penetrated their flinty bosoms. ... Men, women and children, from hoary age to helpless infancy were involved in the same cruel fate."[38]

With broad brush strokes, Gray makes Turner into a "gloomy fanatic"

---

37. Gray, *Confessions*, 316.
38. Gray, *Confessions*, 304.

"still bearing the stains of the blood of helpless innocence about him," a gothic villain who lives in his own tortured mind. This overwrought tone reveals his lingering presence in the account of the rebellion; we unmistakably hear Gray's voice break in, for example, in the cry of "Vain hope!" which appears in the middle of Turner's ostensible narration.[39] Yet Gray's ultimate literary goal in sensationalizing the tale is not to demonize Turner as a subject but to create a vivid, familiar, marketable literary character. In this imaginative creation, Turner both literally (as a slave) and figuratively (as a novelistic character) becomes profitable for Gray, a failed planter who desperately needed to pay off his debts. Gray obtained a copyright for *The Confessions* on the day before Turner's execution, gaining legal ownership of Turner's voice, testimony that sold between 40,000 and 50,000 copies. Converting the insurrection into romantic tragedy enables Gray to turn a tidy profit from his prophet.

Seemingly denied subjectivity, Turner, I contend, inhabits the text as his own being. This is, in many ways, a bildungsroman, a narrative of Turner forming an imagination, inventing a creative ability for himself to counteract both Gray's gothic mystification of his identity and the passive model of prophecy that would convert him into a mere "enthusiast." Turner appears in *The Confessions* essentially as a character named "Nat"—a first-person voice rather than a literal historical actor. He is never called by his full name except in the title, and even legally he is tried as "Nat *alias* Nat Turner." This "Nat" is not the historical Nat Turner, but his literary incarnation, both a narrator and a character invented by the twin authors of Turner and Gray. Given the narration's odd form—the sense that one ventriloquizes the other—it is then useful to look at the relationship between Turner and Gray in terms of Turner's mediumship. The relationship between Turner and Gray, in other words, is implicated in the same kind of narrative knot that exists between Turner and God. Turner uses both his divine mediumship and his narrative mediumship to resist and threaten the specter of white authority that tries to possess him. Relegated to the position of literary character, Turner stages a rebellion of sorts within the narrative to claim joint ownership of the narration with Gray, just as he seems to transcend his role as medium and claim divinity alongside God.

---

39. Gray, *Confessions*, 311, 317.

From the start, Turner's status as a prophet emerges from multiple authorities. It is not God but his community that originally invents him as a prophet by interpreting the text of his speech and his body. His special abilities—his memory of events before his birth, his ability to read without being taught—lead those around him to declare that he "surely would be a prophet," just as his parents interpret his birthmarks as signs that he "was intended for some great purpose." Likewise, Turner's special abilities are not, at first, connected to any unusual communication with divine voices, but to his imagination, which, he says, was "restless, inquisitive, and observant of every thing that was passing. ... I would find many things that the fertility of my own imagination had depicted to me before; all my time, not devoted to my master's service, was spent either in prayer, or in making experiments in casting different things in moulds made of earth."[40] His own imagination, and that of his community, takes the place of revelation; human voices supplant, for the moment, the divine voice. Fittingly, Turner's childish activity mimics God's own original act of molding Adam out of earth. Turner seems to be creating his own scripture of sorts here, and casting himself as the prophetic hero.

When Turner, as an adult, finally does hear directly from God, his first revelation actually emerges out of his own imagination: "I was struck with that particular passage which says: 'Seek ye the kingdom of Heaven and all things shall be added unto you.' I reflected much on this passage, and prayed daily for light on this subject—As I was praying one day at my plough, the spirit spoke to me, saying 'Seek ye the kingdom of Heaven and all things shall be added unto you.'"[41] Rather than overwhelming him with a voice of power, the Holy Spirit imitates Turner, repeating the passage that he has already been pondering. This approach to prophecy plays on and tangles the experience of mediation, allowing the prophet to choose his own scripture, pronounce it, and interpret it himself; the Spirit's voice then mimics the prophet's, reversing the expected chain of command.

Thus, prophecy for Turner is about the interpretation of heavenly voices and signs, that crucial second step beyond hearing God's word, in Juster's definition. God speaks to him through visions of "white spirits

---

40. Gray, *Confessions*, 306–07.
41. Gray, *Confessions*, 307–08.

and black spirits engaged in battle," drops of blood that appear on the corn, strange lights in the sky. Turner becomes a reader of God's earthly text, submitting it to his own acts of imagination, decoding God's language: "I found on the leaves in the woods hieroglyphic characters, and numbers, with the forms of men in different attitudes, portrayed in blood, and representing the figures I had seen before in the heavens. And now the Holy Ghost had revealed itself, to me, and made plain the miracles it had shown me. ... And by signs in the heavens that it would make known to me when I should commence the great work." In that translation of God's text, he himself becomes translated from slave to prophet, from human to divine. Turner finds that "from the first steps of righteousness until the last, was I made perfect; and the Holy Ghost was with me;" he becomes Christlike, cleared of sin and coexistent with the Holy Spirit. And as befits a new Christ, he performs a miracle: "About this time I told these things to a white man, on whom it had a wonderful effect—and he ceased from his wickedness, and was attacked immediately with a cutaneous eruption, and blood oozed from the pores of his skin, and after praying and fasting nine days, he was healed."[42] Here Turner's miraculous power derives not from a laying on of hands, but from the telling of his story; the tale alone causes the white man's conversion. Turner's very voice—what Gray would most like to control—miraculously transforms both body and soul of a white man, thereby reversing both earthly and heavenly hierarchies.

Just as the character Turner achieves the height of his spiritual power, the narrator Turner reaches a climax of testimonial power. Though the narrative begins as a straightforward personal history— starting at childhood and progressing in a linear fashion— it reads like scripture once it turns to his career as a prophet; his messianic role is now to interpret the signs that "the great day of judgment was at hand." Despite Gray's somewhat frantic interruptions with questions, Turner's scriptural language strives to transcend the various narrative frameworks that have meant to contain his authoritative narration. Indeed, Turner's voice is so confident that he becomes a virtual ventriloquist to Gray's dummy, or, perhaps, the god to Gray's medium. Gray's prefatory and concluding remarks appear weak and derivative in comparison,

---

42. Gray, *Confessions*, 309.

barely containing the force of Turner's testimony. In response to Turner's prophecy that "the time was fast approaching when the first should be last and the last should be first," Gray asks, "Do you not find yourself mistaken now?"—applying earthly logic in the face of the rebels' capture and Turner's own impending execution, and attempting to show the absurdity of his prophecy. But Turner's reply upends Gray's logic entirely. "Was not Christ crucified," he replies—for Christ's life, too, seemed to contemporaneous observers to have ended in an utter failure of prophecy, only to reveal itself, for his believers, as utterly revolutionary.[43] Turner's prophecy (whether we take it as "really" divinely inspired or not) invents him as a Christ-figure, rather than as a slave. Recasting his execution as a crucifixion, Turner transcends his role as mere character, undermining the power dynamic that would keep Gray as sole controlling narrator.

At this moment of narrative crisis, Gray does appear to wrest control back from Turner; the narrative returns to a straightforward linear recounting of the killings, where Gray's influence, his attempt to portray Turner as a delusional murderer, become more telling. Finally, Gray takes over the first person entirely and returns to the gothicized outrage of his preface. David F. Almendinger, Jr. has shown that the account of the killings (given in Turner's first-person voice) that begins immediately after Turner's messianic claim, and that bears the plainest marks of Gray's influence, was drawn in part from materials that Gray gathered well before he interviewed Turner.[44] This documentary evidence proves what the narrative shifts in tone already made abundantly clear: Gray did not merely transcribe Turner's words. By speaking in the first person to a particular audience—white Southerners fearful of slave rebellion and familiar with the tropes of popular literature—Gray becomes trapped in a limited point of view that Turner, in contrast, transcends. Turner speaks through Gray and past Gray's audience to a scriptural audience beyond the confines of their particular local

---

43. Gray, *Confessions*, 309–10.

44. While Gray appears to have gathered some information about Turner's prophetic activities, including his reading of hieroglyphics and his baptism of the white man, before he interviewed Turner the bulk of the account of Turner's upbringing and his status as a prophet—those sections which I read as the most crucial sites of narrative rebellion for Turner—seem to have been original and "rendered ... faithfully." Almendinger, *Construction*, 33, 37, 38.

readership. This prophet casts his story as a new scripture. And the testimony that Nat Turner and his fellow rebels give through their deeds—the sudden act of killing—is powerful not because they speak for God, but because their act is itself godlike and creative in its terrible mystery, its sense that to speak the truth of slavery, one must transcend language, not just quote God. Gray encloses the event in conventional literary language to try to domesticate the terror, but ultimately, Nat Turner transcends his role as passive medium and performs a testimony of pure action, a kind of direct revelation.

Turner's narrative relationship with Gray exhibits many of the textual complications that we see applied to scripture in this era. It can be difficult to locate the source of narrative power; the status of narrator and character become confused; historical fact and myth blur together. The complex relationship among this double narrator, God, and the layers of earthly authorities mimics the narrative form at work in the cultural understanding of religion at the time. Turner ultimately achieves a narrative marriage with God, creating a narrative prophecy that allows both intersubjectivity and individuality on the part of both the human and the divine. Turner and Gray, the prophet and the profiteer, have no chance of achieving the same.

Nat Turner embodies a prophetic narrative selfhood that speaks to a scriptural audience outside of time and place, as opposed to Gray's localized, particularized white readership. What Turner does not achieve—what no slave can achieve—is self-ownership, sovereignty. Despite appearing to transcend physical bondage (Turner comes and goes from the condition of enslavement seemingly at will, leaving society to become a hermit, then returning willingly into slavery after receiving his prophecy) the prophet never achieves full liberal personhood. As Saidiya Hartman describes it, even an emancipated slave possessed only "the abased and encumbered individuality of the emancipated" in a system in which "Liberty, property, and whiteness were deeply enmeshed." Yet Turner questions whether liberal personhood and the "the resplendent, plenipotent, indivisible, and steely singularity that it proffers" ought to be the goal for a slave and a black man.[45] Instead, Turner embraces multiplicity and mediated voice, elusive and

---

45. Saidiya Hartman, *Scenes of Subjection: Terror, Slavery, and Self-Making in Nineteenth-Century America* (Oxford: Oxford University Press, 1997), 6, 122.

allusive versions of self. Indeed, to Hartman's question of "whether the appellation 'human' can be borne equally by all," Turner answers with a resounding "no." By declaring himself both "the property of Benj. Turner" and "a prophet" in his first paragraph, Turner seems to reject the category "human," rejecting the "Manichean identities" of either "man" or "chattel" imposed upon him by Gray and by white society, and embodies instead a divine, prophetic personhood.[46] If Turner's blackness denies him entry into the ordinary categories of selfhood and citizenship, it also allows him to opt out of those categories entirely. Prophetic personhood provides an alternative to liberal individuality and interrogates the very value of individuality.

PROPHECY BEYOND POSSESSION

The place of liberal personhood becomes equally problematic for Joseph Smith, who founded Mormonism in the year before Turner's rebellion and who mirrors Nat Turner's role as self-proclaimed, self-fashioning prophet. Although their social positions are quite different, Smith, like Turner, approaches prophecy from the social margins (as a poor white adolescent in rural New York) and rejects liberal individuality just as resolutely. Smith, however, has much greater power over his own act of narration and can establish a mode of prophecy even farther-reaching and more audacious than Turner's. Turner's rebellion incited whites to fear that all slaves might become prophets in Turner's image (and inspired the subsequent crackdowns to prevent any more such prophecy). Smith's new religion promises all humans that they are already divine. Those technologies of prophecy that underline the power differential between Turner and Smith—the amanuensis, the double "I" speaker, the interruption of narrative frame—are the same technologies that Smith embraces as central to his prophetic style and, indeed, to the cosmology of his new religion. Both prophets reject a definition of personhood as bounded, self-owning, and delimited. Where Turner dangerously implies his own divinity through scriptural style and comparisons to Christ, Joseph Smith declares his divinity outright.

Smith's first visions appeared in the 1820s, at the height of revivalism in the "burned-over" district of western New York; his first direct

---

46. Gray, *Confessions*, 306; Hartman, *Scenes of Subjection*, 6.

contact with God was explicitly inspired by the religious ferment of the time. In 1843, Smith described his first vision this way:

> There was a reformation among the different religious denominations in the neighborhood where I lived, and I became serious, and was desirous to know what Church to join. While thinking of this matter, I opened the Testament promiscuously on these words, in James, "Ask of the Lord who giveth to all men liberally and upbraideth not." I just determined I'd ask him. I immediately went out into the woods where my father had a clearing, and went to the stump where I had stuck my axe when I had quit work, and I kneeled down, and prayed, saying, "O Lord, what Church shall I join." He replied, "don't join any of them, they are all corrupt."[47]

Smith, who grew up in poverty, experienced the revivals of the burned-over district not through any one of the religious denominations, but through a whole range: his wife was a Methodist; his mother a peripatetic sampler of affiliations; his grandfather a Universalist who warned against adhering to any creed[48] It is no surprise, given Smith's unorthodox, anti-establishment exposure to religion, that his first contact with God involves personal interpretation of scripture followed by direct conversation. (Smith's God sounds quite a bit like Smith's grandfather—human and divine agency combined, indeed.)

The 1839 *History* gives a different account of his first vision that reinforces the future prophet's autonomous stance in the face of the divine. Smith describes first being paralyzed by an evil force, and then being rescued by God:

> I kneeled down and began to offer up the desires of my heart to God. I had scarcely done so, when immediately I was seized upon by some power which entirely overcame me and had such astonishing influence over me as to bind my tongue so that I could not speak. ... But exerting all my powers to call upon God ... I found myself delivered from the enemy which held me bound. No sooner did I get possession of myself so as to be able to speak, than I asked the personages who stood above me in the light, which of the sects was right.[49]

---

47. Dean C. Jessee, ed., *The Papers of Joseph Smith, Volume 1: Autobiographical and Historical Writings* (Salt Lake City: Deseret Book Co., 1989), 444.

48. John L. Brooke, *The Refiner's Fire: The Making of Mormon Cosmology, 1644–1844* (Cambridge: Cambridge University Press, 1994), 60.

49. Jessee, *Papers*, 1:272–73.

Passivity and voicelessness, that which we might expect from a prophet or a man possessed, are expressly the realm of "the enemy" in this account. When God steps in, Smith regains his own voice rather than channeling God's, acquiring "possession of *myself*" rather than experiencing possession by the Holy Spirit (emphasis added). Similarly, in an account of possession by the early LDS church member Newel Knight, when he is possessed by the devil, he acts with no control over his body: "His visage and limbs distorted and twisted in every shape and appearance possible to imagine; and finally he was caught off the floor of the apartment and tossed about most fearfully." But "possession" by God is entirely different; according to Smith, Knight said: "I now began to feel a most pleasing sensation resting upon me, and immediately the visions of heaven were opened to my view. I ... remained for some time enwrapt in contemplation."[50] The presence of the Holy Spirit makes Knight seem more himself. God's presence opens Knight's mind to new, otherworldly knowledge, which he can contemplate freely with his own self-awareness.

Smith's declaration that he has "possession of myself" might seem like a refusal of the mediated state and a retreat to individualism. Still, we ought to think of Mormon prophets' "self-possession" as an acknowledgement of their own divine nature: the prophet possesses himself spiritually. For Joseph Smith, and for Mormon theology more generally, prophecy is a fulfillment of the divinity already extant within the prophet. In creating a cosmology that envisions humans as coextensive with God—as literally capable of divinity—Smith moves even more radically away from the idea that prophecy is a passive channeling of God's voice. As in the evangelical traditions of the Second Great Awakening, prophecy, or the direct reception and interpretation of the Holy Spirit, is the essential experience of all believers. Mormon theology implies that all humans are constantly in a potential state of mediumship, that we contain and consist of God, and that through faith one might achieve divine knowledge. In Smith's vision of the afterlife, humans "partake" of God in the same way that Christ does: "As the Son partakes of the fullness of the Father through the Spirit, so the saints are, by the same Spirit, to be partakers of the same fullness, to

---

50. Jessee, *Papers*, 1:305–06.

enjoy the same glory; for as the Father and Son are one, so, in like manner, the saints are to be one in them" (D&C 5:3). In its blurring of the
lines between human and divine, the ultimate promise of Mormonism
lies in the human ability to achieve godhood.

The web of narrative authorities concatenating Smith's writings is
even more complex than that in Turner's *Confessions*. Very little of the
material attributed to him and written in first person did Smith actually inscribe himself; instead, he relied on a battery of amanuenses
and ghostwriters for his journal, his letters, and the *History*.[51] Just as
for Turner, it is often entirely unclear how direct a role Smith played
in composing these "personal" texts, and whatever his involvement,
it is certain that in his first-person narratives we find many voices
intertwined. Far from being covert, this method of writing became
essential to the Mormon understanding of prophecy. Smith himself
openly acknowledged that "his philosophy of journal-keeping ... observed that greatness requires that a man 'must not dwell upon small
things, though he may enjoy them,' which he explained to mean that
a prophet cannot be his own scribe."[52] Just as God uses a prophet to
speak to humans, somehow it is unbefitting for a prophet to write his
own prophecies; a certain level of mediation is *required*. Any prophetic
pronouncement, then, embeds at least three layers of narration: God,
prophet, and writer.

On his way to becoming a prophet with a team of scribes, Joseph
Smith began as something of a scribe himself, translating the Book of
Mormon from a set of golden plates that he found hidden in a hill. Like
the creative work that Smith's own scribes perform, this translation entails the use of a seer stone, or the Urim and Thummim, which provides
him the knowledge needed for translation.[53] In the act of translation

---

51. For example, "Of the 1,587 manuscript pages comprising the Smith journal, 31
contain holograph writing, where he is known to have put his own thoughts on the paper.
Another 250 were evidently dictated to scribes. The remaining pages were primarily the
work of four men: William Clayton, James Mulholland, Willard Richards, and George W.
Robinson." Dean C. Jessee, *The Papers of Joseph Smith, Volume 2: Journal, 1832–1842* (Salt
Lake City: Deseret Book Co., 1992), xxiii.

52. Jessee, *Papers*, 2:xxii.

53. Urim and Thummim, Hebrew for "revelation and truth" or "lights and perfec-
tions," refers to objects used to reveal God's will. A seer stone is a more general term for a
stone used in divining or in obtaining supernatural knowledge. Smith's family, and Smith
himself as a boy, were involved in various schemes to find lost objects, divine mines, salt

itself, Smith does not even need to look at the plates but places the stone "in his hat, and discovered that time, place, and distance were annihilated; that all intervening obstacles were removed, and that he possessed one of the attributes of the Deity, an All-seeing Eye."[54] Far from becoming God's mere amanuensis, Smith has actually gained a divine attribute, taken on transcendence, in a scene recalling Emerson's "transparent eye-ball."[55] Insofar as the act of translation transforms the translator as well as the text, in performing this task, Smith finds himself translated into celestial substance. Yet despite Smith's continued prominence as prophet and head of the church, the Church of Latter-day Saints was no mere cult of personality. The *Doctrine and Covenants of the Church of the Latter-day Saints*, which contains Smith's prophecies, actually contains nearly as many prophecies from other people as from Smith himself, including many joint prophecies. That a "joint prophecy" could even exist underscores the idiosyncrasy of the Mormon model of prophecy. Just as translation transcends rewriting, Mormon prophecy surpasses passive, individuated mediation, and becomes instead a fulfillment of human potential. The prophet cannot exist merely as himself; he needs an apparatus of multiple voices to produce divine authorship. As soon as the prophet approaches divinity himself, his voice splinters. Possessive individualism is incompatible with prophecy.

This jointed structure of prophecy varies from the norm, as do the formal patterns in the written prophecies. As in Nat Turner's *Confessions*, we find a blurring of pronouns in the prophecies, so that it is not always immediately clear who is talking. God is, of course, a good guess much of the time ("Behold I am God, and give heed unto my word, which is quick and powerful"), but other times it seems to be the prophet speaking ("The works, and the designs, and the purposes of God cannot be frustrated"), or the spirit of another person ("And the Lord said unto me: John, what desirest thou? … And I said until him: Lord, give unto me power over death"), or a third-person narrator

---

deposits, and buried treasure using such seer stones—common practice in the rural United States at this time (Brooke 30). The dual terminology reveals something of the strange mix of influences on Smith's development of Mormon religious practices.

54. Purple, qtd. in Brooke, *Refiner's Fire*, 152.

55. Ralph Waldo Emerson, "Nature," *Emerson's Prose and Poetry*, ed. Joel Porte and Saundra Morris (New York: W. W. Norton, 2001), 29.

("The rise of the Church of Christ in these last days … [w]hich commandments were given to Joseph Smith") (D&C 6:2; 3:1; 7:1–2; 20:1–2). Even within a given section, shifts in vocal register or in addressee are common, thus confusing roles and muddying narrative authority. Smith and Sidney Rigdon, who share a prophecy given on February 16, 1832, for example, seem at various points the characters, authors, and narrators of the passage. In the preface to the prophecy they are characters, described and quoted by a third-person narrator; as the prophecy begins and God speaks, they seem to narrate a description of God: "Great is his wisdom, marvelous are his ways;" then God speaks directly in first person; and finally, without transition, Smith and Ridgon speak up in first person themselves: "We, Joseph Smith, Jr. and Sidney Rigdon, being in the Spirit on the sixteenth of February, in the year of our Lord one thousand eight hundred and thirty-two, by the power of the Spirit our eyes were opened, and our understandings were enlightened. …" (D&C 76:2, 11–12). Scripture often has a slippery narrative voice, but this multiplicity is unusual in its seemingly untroubled shifting of authority. God is no longer the sole controlling voice in prophecy, no longer the sole author of scripture.

This moment also foregrounds the shift that the prophecies often make between timeless pronouncement of divine truth and temporal specificity—names and dates that anchor the prophecy to a particular person, time and place seem to break into divine authority, reminding us that this is not just a universal scripture, but something emerging from a particular group of historical actors. Even in the midst of grand statements, the God of these prophecies often feels the need to supervise the mundane affairs of his prophets and of the church—giving specific instructions about which people should and should not hold which church office; chastising particular people for running their households poorly and praising others for their righteous ways. At one point God tells them not to trust Oliver Cowdery, the second priest of the church, to carry money on the journey to Missouri; at another point God gives specific dimensions for new buildings in Kirtland, Ohio, and suggests which members ought to have their houses built first (D&C 94). Smith's God involves himself in the most everyday concerns of his chosen people. The quotidian narrative of the early years of the church—how Smith lost the original manuscript of the

Book of Mormon, the jealousies and infighting between leaders, the moves from New York to Ohio and beyond—becomes intertwined with the official scriptural narrative of emerging Mormon doctrine. The text becomes a strange hybrid of competing styles, competing stories, and competing voices.

In the process, the prophecies develop a sense of God as an author, a writer struggling to revise and elucidate his own work to make it clearer to humanity. In one prophecy, *Doctrine & Covenants* 19, Christ acts as rhetorician, giving an authoritative proclamation, then stopping to parse his own language and rescind much of the power of his own statement. He begins by reminding us of his divinity and promising eternal damnation, including "weeping, wailing and gnashing of teeth, yea, to those who are found on my left hand." But he then retreats, explaining that when he says "eternal punishment," he does not actually mean punishment for eternity: "For, behold, the mystery of godliness, how great is it! For, behold, I am endless, and the punishment which is given from my hand is endless punishment, for Endless is my name. Wherefore—Eternal punishment is God's punishment. Endless punishment is God's punishment" (D&C 19:10–12). Eternal punishment suddenly no longer means that you will be punished eternally, but merely that the Eternal One will punish you. It is a rather confounding moment, in which Christ redefines his own words with contorted logic to soften the threat of damnation, undoing Calvinism in a moment of wordplay.

We have in these cases what Terryl Givens calls "dialogic revelation," revelation that happens not in the standard biblical narrative—unidirectional, hierarchical, and with high stakes for nations, leaders, and chosen peoples—but through an interplay of voices that brings God much closer to individual humans.[56] God does not simply pronounce, but reasons out his logic with humanity. In one prophecy epitomizing this new relationship, God actually offers himself up as a man: "And now come, saith the Lord, by the Spirit, unto the elders of his church, and let us reason together, that ye may understand; let us reason even as a man reasoneth with one another face to face" (D&C 50:10–11). In this image, the prophecy alludes to two well-known biblical passages: first, God's encounter with Moses on Mount Sinai, where he would not

---

56. Terryl L. Givens, *By the Hand of Mormon: The American Scripture That Launched a New World Religion* (Oxford: Oxford University Press, 2002), 219–35.

allow Moses to see him in his full glory, saying, "Thou canst not see my face: for there shall no man see me, and live;" and second, Paul's explanation, recalling that scene in Exodus, that on earth, "we see as through a glass, darkly; but then face to face" (Exod. 33:20, 1 Cor. 13:12). Joseph Smith's prophecy brings that most elusive of encounters—the egalitarian meeting of divinity and humanity—into the here and now.

That figurative drawing together of human and divine eventually becomes literal in Mormon doctrine. Ultimately, Smith's anti-authoritarian mode of prophetic narration leads to a doctrinal understanding of human subjectivity as coexistent with, not dependent on, God's own subjectivity. These doctrines took a decade to be fully articulated, though their essential qualities were present in Smith's prophecies from the start. Unlike most other Christian faiths, Mormon theology does not hold that humans were created by God, or that God created the world *ex nihilo*. Instead, Mormonism teaches that the human spirit is itself eternal—that like God, the soul has no express beginning or end, but that "human spirits had coexisted with God as a primal intelligence for eternity, rather than being created from nothing at a biblical beginning" (Brooke 201). Although this concept does not imply that humans are equal with God, it does create a fundamental and radical distinction between the Mormon belief system and that of other Christian sects. The human soul is not automatically depraved, sinful, or weak: "the human spirit has the foundation of its existence within itself."[57] Upending the hierarchy of divine and human, then, Smith's cosmology imagines that in the afterlife, all mortals have the potential to become gods, "equal in power, and in might, and in dominion" (D&C 76:94). While the supremacy of God remains constant, all humans have the capacity to dwell with God and to possess all God's knowledge. In fact, Smith makes one even more radical leap toward resemblance between God and humans, claiming that God was once human: "God himself was once as we are now, and is an exalted man, and sits enthroned in yonder heavens! That is the great secret....He was once a man like us; yea, that God himself, the Father of us all, dwelt on an earth, the same as Jesus Christ Himself did."[58] The progression from human to divine is

---

57. Sterling M. McMurrin, *The Theological Foundations of the Mormon Religion* (Salt Lake City: University of Utah Press, 1965), 4–5.

58. Joseph Smith, *History of the Church of Jesus Christ of Latter-day Saints*, 7 vols., 2nd. ed. Rev. (Salt Lake City: Deseret Book Co., 1963), 6:305.

one that God has followed as well. This teaching (which is controversial among the Latter-day Saints today) represents a logical, if extreme, endpoint to Smith's understanding of prophecy, and his elevation of human agency in the face of the divine.

The audacity of Joseph Smith's doctrine of divinization, even in comparison to Nat Turner's daring prophecy, reflects, in part, the differences in their earthly positions. Smith began in poverty but went on to become a powerful leader at the top of his own earthly hierarchy, a status that directed his prophesying, much as Turner's status as condemned slave informed his narrative insurrection. The doctrine of divinization that Joseph Smith developed through his prophecies in the 1830s represents a new means of imagining the relationship between the divine and the human, one that extends the shifts already made in the Second Great Awakening. If humans already exist as eternal, and if we might potentially gain divine knowledge even while on earth, then prophecy becomes an entirely different technology: a sign, and a fulfillment, of the mediumship we already embody.

The strange prophecies of Nat Turner and Joseph Smith take to its logical extreme a strain of American personhood—the self as divine, the self as multiple—that would become familiar in the writings of Emerson, Fuller, and Whitman as well as in popular modes like spiritualism. Turner and Smith show how these nonliberal forms of personhood pervade US culture from the fringes, and present a revolutionary, heretical, sometimes violent challenge to self-possession as we typically understand it. They also demonstrate how conceptions of scriptural and spiritual narrative voice become vital to questions of literary form, and help to shape emerging understandings of narrative authority in the Second Great Awakening. The prophetic style that positively values the amanuensis and the medium, that deliberately confuses narrative personhood, and that reverses ordinary social and narrative hierarchies would later become influential for novelists like Harriet Beecher Stowe, who herself claimed to have received *Uncle Tom's Cabin* in a kind of prophetic vision, and whose novel *Dred* is both based on Nat Turner's rebellion and saturated with Second Great Awakening religious discourse and narrative style. These prophetic forms would thus become part of a larger nineteenth-century cultural movement that emphasized flattened hierarchies between the spiritual and the human. And

235

well outside their particular cultural moment, Nat Turner and Joseph Smith reveal the ways that narratology and cultural criticism profitably inform one another. Both men strategically revise the formal grammars of prophecy to enact revolutions in the world—and beyond it.

NINE

DEMAGOGUES OR MYSTAGOGUES?
GENDER AND THE LANGUAGE OF PROPHECY IN
THE AGE OF DEMOCRATIC REVOLUTIONS

SUSAN JUSTER

On May 19, 1780, all of New England was plunged into darkness. At mid-morning, the sky turned an eerie yellow. Within an hour, it had become so dark that people had to dine by candlelight. In the afternoon, the clouds took on a "higher and more brassy color" with occasional flashes that resembled the Northern Lights.[1] We now know that the "Dark Day" of 1780 was caused by the common New England practice of burning fields to clear the brush more effectively and provide a fertile coating of ashes, but to men and women living amid the dislocations of revolution, the event had supernatural meaning. For some, it heralded the imminent appearance of Christ in the Second Coming; for others less certain of their ability to read celestial signs with such precision, it was at least a warning that "these are the latter days."[2] The millennial expectations unleashed by the Dark Day can be traced in numerous pamphlets, newspaper articles, and almanacs, and have been read by historians as evidence of the pervasiveness of millennial thinking in revolutionary America among all classes of people, from learned divines to ordinary farmers. Far from being the preserve of a small number of biblical scholars and theologians, prophetic exegesis was a vernacular genre in eighteenth-century British America, a way of interpreting past, present, and future events according to the narratives of biblical history. A people as literate and well versed in

---

1. *Boston Gazette*, May 22 and 29, 1780.
2. "A Farmer in the State of Massachusetts-Bay," *Some Remarks on the Great and Unusual Darkness that appeared on Friday, May 19, 1780* (Danvers, MA, 1780), 6.

millennial lore as the New England Puritans could scarcely avoid interpreting the Dark Day of May 1780 as a prophetic "sign of the times."

Thanks to the labors of intellectual historians like Ruth Bloch, James Davidson, and Nathan Hatch, we have a fairly good grasp of the extent and depth of millennial thinking (or, at least, of publications devoted to millennial themes) in North America during and after the revolutionary crisis. We know that, contrary to the situation in Great Britain, millennialism was a constant theme in religious literature from the early seventeenth through the eighteenth century; rather than spiking at specific moments in response to public crises, millennial expectations proved remarkably enduring through the ebb and flow of colonial politics. We know that, beginning with the Seven Years' War and escalating through the imperial crisis of the 1760s and 1770s, this tradition of millennial exegesis was increasingly politicized, though still consensual: the allegorical symbols of the prophetic scriptures (the four beasts, the seven vials, for example) came to represent concrete political figures and events, while sacred and human history were conflated in the eschatological drama of the Book of Revelation. We know that North American writers tended to favor a postmillennial (gradual progress) over a premillennial (cataclysmic collapse) interpretation of the Bible, even though the distinction between these two hermeneutic modes was less stark in the 1770s and 1780s than it would become a century later. Once independence was gained and Americans turned their attention from waging war to forming new governments, the political edge of millennial discourse was blunted and apocalyptic thinking declined. A kind of popular secular optimism, shorn of political urgency and latitudinarian in impulse, reigned as Americans looked benignly toward the future. Moments of doubt and despair certainly intruded on the national consciousness as Americans weathered the periodic economic and political crises of the 1780s and the partisan battles of the 1790s, but overall the prophetic scriptures were understood to herald the eventual triumph of the United States as the leader of the "free" and the Christian world, which were assumed to be one and the same thing.[3]

---

3. This paragraph is drawn from the following studies: Ruth Bloch, *Visionary Republic: Millennial Themes in American Thought, 1756–1800* (New York: Cambridge University Press, 1985); Nathan O. Hatch, *The Sacred Cause of Liberty* (New Haven, CT: Yale University

So subsumed into nationalist republican ideology was the millennial scenario in the revolutionary era that historians have tended to take for granted the intermingling of religious and political languages into a seamless discursive web in American culture, a web that stretches from John Winthrop to Franklin Graham. Snared in this web were a multitude of competing biblical images of America (Canaan or Egypt?) and a multiplicity of voices, from nativist Indian prophets to visionary women to millenarian slaves. Disentangling these images and voices takes some doing, given the investment Americans have had—then and now—in the myth of our exceptional past and our privileged future, a sense of entitlement to prosperity and power that stems from our very identity as a chosen people. But the millennial promise has never meant the same thing to all Americans.

The revolutionary crisis was a particularly fertile moment for millennial aspirations that could not be easily reconciled under the capacious umbrella of "Christian republicanism."[4] For a slave facing a lifetime of servitude and the hardening of racial attitudes in the late eighteenth century, the Millennium meant, literally, freedom. For nativist Indians, facing communal dislocation and the collapse of traditional folkways, the Millennium meant a war of red against white and the rebirth of ancient traditions out of the ashes of European civilization.[5] For the "black regiment," the legion of Congregational clergy who served the Continental Army in support of the rebellion, the Millennium meant national independence and the rejection of European cultural and political arrogance.[6] One man's heaven was another's hell: the

Press, 1977); James West Davidson, *The Logic of Millennial Thought in Eighteenth-Century America* (New Haven, CT: Yale University Press, 1977); Jon Butler, *Awash in a Sea of Faith: Christianizing the American People* (Cambridge, MA: Harvard University Press, 1990).

4. The phrase is Mark Noll's. See his "The American Revolution and Protestant Evangelicalism," *Journal of Interdisciplinary History* 23 (1993): 615–38.

5. For millenarian slaves, see Wilson Jeremiah Moses, *Black Messiahs and Uncle Toms: Social and Literary Manipulations of a Religious Myth* (University Park, PA: Pennsylvania State University Press, 1982); Albert Raboteau, *Slave Religion: The "Invisible Institution" in the Antebellum South* (New York: Oxford University Press, 1980). For Indian prophets, see Gregory Evans Dowd, *A Spirited Resistance: The North American Indian Struggle for Unity, 1745–1815* (Baltimore, MD: Johns Hopkins University Press, 1992); Anthony F. C. Wallace, *Death and the Rebirth of the Seneca* (New York: Knopf, 1969).

6. For accounts of the "black regiment," see Harry S. Stout, *The New England Soul: Preaching and Religious Culture in Colonial New England* (New York: Oxford University Press, 1986); and Donald Weber, *Rhetoric and History in Revolutionary New England* (New York: Oxford University Press, 1988).

slave-owning patriarchs who ruled the new republic and introduced their bondspeople to the promises of Christianity were horrified when the enslaved turned the Bible against them and preached the destruction of all whites, as Nat Turner did in 1831.

For all its internal contradictions and apocalyptic potential, the millennial strand in revolutionary political culture did not (until 1860, at least) divide white Americans into lasting political or intellectual enemies. When viewed from abroad, revolutionary millennialism looks remarkably *un*revolutionary. There were, outside native America, few inspired individuals preaching imminent death and destruction, no crowds of agitated citizens gathering en masse for the Apocalypse. Rather, millennial exegesis was primarily the preserve of writers—ministers and theologians, as well as literate lay people—not charismatic prophets.

The contrast with Europe in the same time period is striking. If we look at the British political landscape in the 1790s, we see a parade of arresting public figures who proclaimed themselves to be prophets of God. From Richard Brothers, whose intemperate calls for the overthrow of the British monarchy landed him in an insane asylum in 1795, to Joanna Southcott, whose "mystical pregnancy" in 1814 captivated the London reading public, the history of millennialism in Britain at the turn of the eighteenth century is dominated by inspired prophets and their popular followings. Learned publications on the finer points of biblical exegesis poured out of London's presses from the 1780s to the 1810s, to be sure, but this flood of printed matter was animated by the presence of living prophets who embodied the allegorical figures of the biblical texts in their very personas. While churchmen were busily speculating on the meaning of the mysterious "woman clothed with the sun" who appears in the twelfth chapter of Revelation, a host of female prophets were laying claim to that identity—Southcott, Mother Buchan, Dorothy Gott, Sarah Flaxmer, all proclaimed themselves the "Woman of Revelation" come to redeem a fallen nation. Southcott's followers numbered in the tens of thousands, testimony to the enormous popular interest in millenarianism that swept Britain in these years of political repression and continental war.[7] In France, Catherine

---

7. W. H. Oliver, *Prophets and Millennialists: The Uses of Biblical Prophecy in England from the 1790s to the 1840s* (London: Oxford University Press, 1978); J. F. C. Harrison, *The Second Coming: Popular Millenarianism 1780–1850* (London: Routledge and Kegan Paul,

Theot declared herself to be the "New Eve" who was sent to deliver the world from the transgressions of the first Eve; her compatriot Suzette Labrouse boldly announced that the regeneration of the world would occur when she was miraculously elevated to heaven.[8]

Such charismatic figures are rare in the annals of eighteenth-century North American millenarianism. There were occasional sightings of the Messiah, as when one Nat Smith "proceeded to assume & declare himself to be the Most High God and wore a cap with the word GOD inscribed on its front," but few were taken seriously.[9] The best-known prophet of the revolutionary era, Jemima Wilkinson, or the "Publick Universal Friend," attracted a small following in her native New England but was largely unknown outside the region. Forsaking public acclaim after a brief but unsuccessful preaching tour, she retreated with a handful of followers in 1790 to western New York, where she established a community she called "New Jerusalem" and lived out the remainder of her life in relative obscurity. Not surprisingly, her prophetic career left few traces in the millennial projects of the post-revolutionary era.[10] Dozens of local millenarian sects did spring up in the fertile soil of rural New England in the 1770s and 1780s, as Stephen Marini notes, but these tended to be short-lived religious communities that were unable to translate the inchoate anxieties and hopes of their impoverished followers into a national movement for millennial change. Out of these localized sects grew the Shakers (United Society of Believers in Christ's Second Appearing) and the Freewill Baptists, two of the most successful evangelical movements of the early nineteenth century, but in the process of institutional

1979); on Southcott, see James K. Hopkins, *A Woman to Deliver Her People: Joanna Southcott and English Millenarianism in an Era of Revolution* (Austin: University of Texas Press, 1982).

8. Clarke Garrett, *Respectable Folly: Millenarians and the French Revolution in France and England* (Baltimore: Johns Hopkins University Press, 1975).

9. Ezra Stiles, *Extracts from the Itineraries*, 418; quoted in Catherine A. Brekus, *Strangers and Pilgrims: Female Preaching in America, 1740–1845* (Chapel Hill: University of North Carolina Press, 1998), 85.

10. For accounts of Wilkinson's career, see Brekus, *Strangers and Pilgrims*, chap. 2; Susan Juster, "'Neither Male nor Female': Jemima Wilkinson and the Politics of Gender in Revolutionary America," in Robert Blair St. George, ed., *Possible Pasts: Becoming Colonial in Early America* (Ithaca, NY: Cornell University Press, 2000), 357–79; Paul B. Moyer, *The Public Universal Friend: Jemima Wilkinson and Religious Enthusiasm in Revolutionary America* (Ithaca, NY: Cornell University Press, 2015).

consolidation the charismatic powers of the sects' founders were diffused and ultimately transformed into theological abstractions.[11]

The clearest example of the fate of would-be prophets in revolutionary America is that of Ann Lee: proclaiming herself to be either the Second Coming of Christ in female form or the "Woman of Revelation" (depending on which sources one credits), Lee's status as a charismatic figure was uncertain and unstable. She published nothing in her own lifetime, so the Shaker community had to rely largely on memory and oral testimony about Lee's spiritual gifts until the society authorized a retrospective biography of its founder in 1816. Whatever her original aspirations may have been, it is clear that in the years following her death in 1782, her role as a prophet was deliberately suppressed by the Shaker leadership. Successive editions of *Testimonies of the Life and Character of Mother Ann Lee* downplayed Lee's charismatic powers (the gifts of healing, speaking in tongues, communing with the spirits of the dead) and emphasized instead her nurturing role as "Mother Ann." In the process, Lee's status as a female godhead was transposed into a theological principle of dual divinity. Not Lee herself but the principle of "female divinity" became the cornerstone of Shaker theology and practice as the sect entered the nineteenth century.[12] Here again, there was scant room for an inspired prophet (especially a female one) in the American millenarian tradition.

In the absence of a charismatic figure to galvanize public emotion, millennial expectations remained fairly subdued, if immanent, in revolutionary America. When inspired messengers did come forward, reaction could be swift and violent: no one knew better than the Delaware, whose villages were turned upside down in the 1760s by the nativist preachings of Neolin, how quickly the embers of millenarian despair could be ignited into a full-blown conflagration by the presence of a real prophet. But with so many mainstream religious figures and periodicals eager to satisfy the public desire for eschatological narratives in their sermons and treatises, millenarian fever could be safely

---

11. Stephen Marini, *Radical Sects in Revolutionary America* (Cambridge, MA: Harvard University Press, 1982).

12. See Jean Humez's introduction to *Mother's First-Born Daughters: Early Shaker Writings on Women and Religion* (Bloomington: Indiana University Press, 1993), for a discussion of how the character of Lee became transformed into the theological principle of "Holy Mother Wisdom."

contained in the world of print rather than being transformed into action. The sheer *printedness* of so much millennial speculation in the 1780s and 1790s stripped apocalyptic predictions of much of their urgency and violence; Americans could read about the coming battle with the Anti-Christ and the establishment of the Millennium without having to act on their fears or hopes, secure in the knowledge that others were being vigilant on their behalf. A kind of vicarious millenarianism thus lulled white Americans into the posture of complacent expectancy that has characterized the mainstream religious mood in this country ever since. Somehow, sometime, the Millennium will come; and when it does, Americans as a nation and a people feel relatively confident that they will be among the Elect at the end of time.[13]

We can see this dynamic at work in the transformation of one of the most recognizable biblical figures, the "Woman of Revelation," into an allegory of American exceptionalism during the revolutionary era. While there were few American candidates for this mysterious character, in contrast to the European prophetic scene, the figure of the "Woman" appears with some frequency in millennial tracts—but not in reference to a flesh-and-blood female prophet. Rather, it is America itself that assumes this persona. David Austin's 1794 compendium of millennial texts offers a stirring image of America as the Woman of Revelation. "See, on the wings of a bounteous providence, how she is wafted across the Atlantic, and settled in these peaceful American abode!" Victorious over the "Protestant Dragon," who "vomited forth for the destruction of the woman in the American wilderness" a "flood of troops, armies, and fleets," the Woman succeeds in fulfilling the scriptural prophecy by giving birth to the "Man-child"—the new republic.

Behold the regnum montis, the kingdom of the mountains, begun on the Fourth of July, 1776, when the *birth* of the MAN-CHILD—the hero of civil

---

13. As Lawrence Sweet observed in 1979, "Watching, waiting, and working for the millennium" is "America's favorite pastime." Quoted in Paul Boyer, *When Time Shall Be No More: Prophecy Belief in Modern American Culture* (Cambridge, MA: Harvard University Press, 1992), 12. Most Americans watch and wait, even while a vigorous subculture of prophecy devotees actively works to prepare for the Millennium. Boyer describes the culture of prophecy belief in contemporary America as a series of concentric circles, with an energetic core of true believers, a larger circle of nominal believers whose knowledge of biblical eschatology is hazy but who nevertheless believe that the Millennium will come some day, and an even larger circle of secularists who disdain the doomsayers of the evangelical fringe but are shaped by that very culture in ways they scarcely recognize (12–13).

and religious liberty took place in these United States ... Follow him, in his strides across the Atlantic!—See him, with his spear already in heart of the beast!—See tyranny, civil and ecclesiastical, bleeding at every pore![14]

Bombastic and patriotic, Austin's prose is typical of the kind of brisk, ready-to-hand millennial rhetoric that historians associate with the first, most optimistic phase of the American Revolution.

Women served the visionary republic, then, more as literary tropes than as flesh-and-blood participants. Invoked to represent the vulnerability of the American revolutionary experiment, the figure of the "Woman of Revelation" served a number of rhetorical and political purposes for these millennial writers. It added the emotional power of outraged femininity to the patriot cause and allowed revolutionaries to portray the English crown (the Beast) as a sexual as well as a political predator. It drove home the message of secular political addresses that the soul of America was imperiled as much by its own effeminacy as by the brutal overtures of the British "dragon," and urged Americans to transform herself from the fragile woman of the wilderness to the sturdy "Man-child" she gives birth to. The dramatic plot of Revelation is telescoped in the American renditions of the millennial script, as America is portrayed as both the Woman and the Man-child, the former representing her colonial vulnerability and the latter her newfound strength as an independent nation. Politically, the rhetorical coupling of America with the Woman of Revelation accomplished the same ends as the secular impulse to portray Liberty as female; redefined as allegory, woman's political usefulness could be safely contained in the realm of myth rather than action.[15] Readers found such allegorical maneuverings very reassuring.

*

14. David Austin, *The Millennium* (Elizabethtown, NJ, 1794), 393–94, 413. For other examples of this metaphorical association of America with the Woman of Revelation, see Samuel Sherwood, *Church's Flight into the Wilderness* (New York, 1776); William Foster, *True Fortitude Delineated* (Philadelphia, 1776), 17; [Wheeler Case], *Poems, Occasioned by Several Circumstances ... in the Present Grand Contest of America for Liberty* (New Haven, CT, 1778), 21.

15. On the use of female allegory in the early republic, see John Higham, "Indian Princesses and Roman Goddesses: The First Female Symbols of America," *Proceedings of the American Antiquarian Society* 100 (1990): 45–79; Jan Lewis, "'Of Every Age Sex and Condition': The Representation of Women in the Constitution," *Journal of the Early Republic* 15 (1995): 359–88. As Lynn Hunt and Joan Landes have shown in the context of the French Revolution, the iconic presence of women in the symbols of revolution was a graphic reminder of their marginality in the political culture of the new republic; Hunt, *Politics,*

To grasp the place of millennialism, then, in revolutionary America, we have to understand the politics of reading and myth-making. American prophetic writers were engaged as much in an extended critique of the culture of print itself as in scriptural exegesis. In this, they have much to tell scholars who see the revolutionary era as a pivotal moment in the history of print culture, a moment when the acts of reading and writing became politicized to an unprecedented degree and the new nation itself was constructed along textual lines.[16] Print was the medium of prophecy in the late eighteenth century, a fact of which prophets themselves were keenly aware as they sought to claim the privileges of authorship and instill the responsibilities of readership in their audience. For all their nationalist pride, American prophets were in fact following the lead of British millennialists, who elevated the art of textual prophecy to new heights during the last decades of the century. Differences of culture and politics notwithstanding, American and British millennialists shared a common conceptual vocabulary and hermeneutic position in the revolutionary era—one that locates them firmly within the orbit of the democratic public sphere as it was first described over forty years ago by the political theorist Jürgen Habermas.

The democratic or bourgeois public sphere that supposedly came into being in the reading rooms, coffeehouses, lyceums, and salons of eighteenth-century Europe and America was characterized above all by the qualities of transparency, universality, rationality, and negation of the self. Habermas contrasted the privatized authority of monarchical states, where sovereignty is maintained by "secrecy" and the suppression of ideas, to the impersonal rule of law in democratic societies, where the common good is promoted through public disclosure and the free circulation of opinions.[17] The ethos of publicity

---

Culture and Class in the French Revolution (Berkeley: University of California Press, 1984), 113–19; Landes, *Women and the Public Sphere in the Age of the French Revolution* (Ithaca, NY: Cornell University Press, 1988), 83.

16. Jay Fliegelman, *Declaring Independence: Jefferson, Natural Language, and the Culture of Performance* (Stanford, CA: Stanford University Press, 1993); Michael Warner, *Letters of the Republic: Publication and the Public Sphere in Eighteenth-Century America* (Cambridge, MA: Harvard University Press, 1990).

17. Jürgen Habermas, *The Structural Transformation of the Public Sphere: An Inquiry into a Category of Bourgeois Society*, Thomas Burger, trans. (1962; Cambridge, MA: Harvard University Press, 1989). As Habermas notes, the specific form of the "public" in Britain was "the bourgeois reading public of the eighteenth century. This public remained rooted in the world

that Habermas identified as the guiding principle of bourgeois civic life demanded widespread literacy and the establishment of a "republic of letters," where printed texts—shorn of the personalized traits of their authors—circulated widely among anonymous individuals who collectively imagined themselves part of a community of "unknown and *in principle unknowable* others," in Michael Warner's words.[18]

The ideal public man was thus one who rose above the entanglements of family and community to engage other men in the disinterested pursuit of universal principles through the medium of print. That such a vision of enlightened citizenship was encoded male in the gendered discourse of republican theory is now clear, thanks to the work of political theorists Joan Landes and Carole Pateman. The public sphere as it emerged in Britain and France in the eighteenth century was constructed via a series of ideological oppositions that associated the virtues of bourgeois civic life with manliness and the vices of aristocratic society with effeminacy.[19] To be manly was to be open and sincere, to use language to elucidate rather than obscure truths, to create a society where abstract reason and impartial appeals to scientific knowledge determined right from wrong. To be effeminate was to conceal and equivocate, to use artifice to deceive, to rely on superstition and primitive attachments to override the public good.

In such a semiotic universe, the world of religion was gendered female. Religious enthusiasm in general was derided by enlightened thinkers as a remnant of medieval superstition and fanaticism. Religious fanatics, like women, like the common people, were ruled more by their passions than their reason. If, in the republican critique, monarchies governed by the illicit powers of mystification and concealment, with the full duplicity of their deluded and ignorant subjects, the same was true of populist preachers who used verbal trickery to gull their credulous followers. Enthusiasts were depicted as "vulgar Mystagogues" who seduced their ignorant followers into error by their "*glib,*

---

of letter even as it assumed political functions" (85). For a study of the discursive traditions that shaped the public sphere in eighteenth-century America, see David Shields, *Civil Tongues and Polite Letters in British America* (Chapel Hill: University of North Carolina Press, 1997).

18. Warner, *Letters of the Republic*, 40.

19. Landes, *Women and the Public Sphere*; Pateman, *The Sexual Contract* (Stanford, CA: Stanford University Press, 1988); and Pateman, *The Disorder of Women: Democracy, Feminism, and Political Theory* (Stanford, CA: Stanford University Press, 1989).

deceitful Tongue[s]," their "cloudy, intricate, and Mysterious manner of writing."[20] The charge of "mystagoguery" has a certain irony, considering the general charge of democratic leveling that conservative churchmen often directed against dissenters who insisted that anyone with an inner call, regardless of special knowledge or formal training, could preach to the faithful. The powerful oratory of a John Wesley or a George Whitefield, both of whom were famed for reducing their audiences—men and women alike—to tears, was often decried as a form of demagoguery. Like radical democrats, evangelists in the Whitefieldian mode used simple but emotionally powerful words and images to elicit feelings of anger, disgust, and resentment against Satan's emissaries on earth (usually the standing clergy).

But whether described as demagogues or mystagogues, religious enthusiasts were condemned for using the unchecked power of language to lead true Christians (especially weak women) astray. In the essay *False Prophets*, the British author Henry Drummond castigated these enthusiasts for violating the ethos of publicity that was so essential to the maintenance of the public sphere. "They have come in secretly; they did not begin by proclaiming their doctrines publicly in the open streets, in the places of greatest concourse," he complained. Unlike "true preachers," who "proclaim from house-tops, in the market-places, in the great assembles, and concourse of the people," false prophets *"creep into houses, and lead captive silly women laden with sins, led away with divers lusts."* In these secret spaces, false prophets speak the degraded language of courtiers. "This false teaching they effect by *babbling*; that is, by waging a war of words, quibbling upon terms and expressions, instead of rightly dividing, dissecting the word of truth, so as to leave it open, and its very entrails exposed to the view of all."[21] Drummond's tirade, characteristic of many written after the prophetic frenzy of the early 1800s, concisely summarized the anti-republican tendencies of radical religion. Even though he himself was

---

20. For "vulgar Mystagogues," see Stafford Cleveland's description of Jemima Wilkinson in *The History and Directory of Yates County* (Penn Yann, NY, 1873), 1:38; and the satirical poem on the Methodists, *Fanatical Conversion; or, Methodism Displayed* (London, 1779), vii. Methodists and Moravians were considered two of the worst offenders of the art of "mystagoguery," according to Anglican churchmen; see George Lavington, *The Moravians Compared and Detected* (London, 1755), ix, xiii.

21. Henry Drummond, *False Prophets* (London, 1834), 4, 6.

no democrat, he recognized in the form and language of enthusiastic religion a serious threat to the conventions of reasoned public discourse that kept a free society from collapsing into anarchy.

These, then, were the oppositions that structured the discourse of politics in the "age of revolution": reason versus mysticism, plain speaking versus "glib tongues," transparency versus concealment, enlightenment versus ignorance, manliness versus effeminacy. These were also the oppositions structuring the discourse of prophecy. Were prophets conservatives who reached backward to an archaic form of authority, to the "mystery" of monarchies with their secret societies and closed systems of knowledge, or democrats who shrewdly used the print culture of the new bourgeois public sphere to proclaim a message of spiritual equality? Did they speak in the arcane language of Old Testament patriarchs or in the modern tones of enlightened republicanism? Were they, to use the terminology of the day, demagogues, who manipulated the vulgar and uninformed by a glib appropriation of the language and symbols of democratic politics, or mystagogues, who seduced the weak and credulous through the exploitation of primitive religious passions?

The answer depended largely on the gender of the prophet. Male and female prophets assumed different audiences for their texts, positioned themselves differently as divine oracles, and expounded radically different models of reading. Prophets and prophetesses, in other words, enacted different versions of spiritual "citizenship" that turned many conventional assumptions about the relationship between language and authority on their head. By making the act of interpretation itself a principal object of study, prophets and their followers contributed to broader political discussions about the rights of subjects to know and interpret the laws that bound them. The same question that animated prophetic discourse—who has access to truth?—was at the heart of the political controversies of the late eighteenth century in both Britain and America. These debates pitted reason against inspiration, literacy against experience, knowledge against secrecy, and—often—men against women. Male prophets tried to find an uneasy middle ground between secular politics and the mysteries of faith. Female prophets, by contrast, rejected wholeheartedly the linguistic and epistemological precepts of enlightened republicanism while insisting that they, too, spoke for the common people.

*

The ultimate symbol of democratic politics was, of course, Thomas Paine, whose writings introduced a new literary style to hundreds of thousands of readers. Paine's objective was to open up public life to all men by breaking down the linguistic barriers (the "bewitching bonds ... of enticing eloquence," as one democrat put it) of class and custom.[22] In England, Paine's direct counterpart in the world of religious prophecy, a "republican prophet" if such a thing could be said to exist, was James Bicheno, whose measured writings in the 1790s and early 1800s injected a degree of gentility and rationality into prophetic discourse. An enthusiastic supporter of both the American and the French Revolutions, and of political reform at home, Bicheno was a consistent spokesman for the expansion of knowledge and learning throughout the European continent. Disclaiming any direct access to divine revelation ("I am no prophet," he declared),[23] he sought to provide a commonsense "translation" of the prophetic scriptures for his readers. "I make no pretensions to any extraordinary qualifications for the interpretation of Prophecy," he insisted; "If I have any true light, and be not deceived by the illusions of fancy, it is derived from the source which is open to all."[24] Through the use of natural reason, the "mazes of these wonderful visions may be treated with precision" and their predictions enlisted in the service of democratic reform.[25] The bulk of his writings consisted of simple translations of the arcane symbolism of the prophecies into concrete historical and contemporary referents.

Bicheno was as disdainful of his more mystical counterparts as his republican allies, and he tried to distance himself from both the "dreams" of Joanna Southcott and the "visions" of Richard Brothers.[26] Yet he shared more with Brothers, in particular, than either man would perhaps have wished to admit. On most counts, Richard Brothers—certifiable lunatic and political *cause célèbre* of the 1790s—inhabited a world far removed from that of republican politics. Brothers's intemperate calls

---

22. "Declaration of the Belfast Volunteers," rpt. in the Philadelphia periodical, *The American Museum* 10 (Sept. 1791): 153.

23. James Bicheno, *The Fulfillment of Prophecy Farther Illustrated by the Signs of the Times* (London, 1817), preface.

24. Bicheno, *Fulfillment of Prophecy*, vi.

25. James Bicheno, *The Signs of the Times; or, The Overthrow of Papal Tyranny in France, the Prelude of Destruction to Popery and Despotism; but of Peace to Mankind* (London, 1793), n.p.

26. Bicheno, *Fulfillment of Prophecy*, 6.

for a political revolution that would place him at the head of a reconstituted Hebrew nation as king and high priest inspired little confidence in republican circles, and his rabid hatred of the commercial classes made him an unreliable ally for those middling groups who favored a reformist agenda. Yet he drew unabashedly on the Painite tradition of plain speaking in disseminating his prophetic visions to the public. In the preface to his principal text, *A Revealed Knowledge of the Prophecies and Times*, Brothers spoke frankly of his status as the chosen one. "[W]hen I began to write, I believed it necessary to adopt the same language as the Scripture does, regularly imitating it in the words—ye, thee, and thou; but God spoke to me in a vision of the night, and said—'Write in the same manner as I always speak to you, write as other men do, write accordingly to the Custom of the Country you live in; you will then be better attended to, and what you write will be more easily understood.'"[27] In blunt, simple language, Brothers's writings—like those of Bicheno—laid out a prophetic key to current events that any reader could understand. Promising to "remove the Covering of secrecy" that had hitherto prevented his fellow citizens from understanding the prophetic scriptures, Brothers's pamphlets constituted a catalogue of names, dates, places, and events that are unusually specific by the standards of the genre.[28] The "loud and unusual Thunder" heard in January 1791 was none other than "the voice of the Angel" of Revelation proclaiming destruction upon the city of London; the French Revolution was a direct fulfillment of the Book of Daniel.[29]

Such frank language represented the triumph of reason over priestcraft for his many admirers. Whereas "the *priests* have, as it best suited their interests, opinions or inclinations, introduced a set of dogmas and abstruse, metaphysical mysteries, which the people have been wont to imagine *too sacred* for their inquiry," argued John Crease, Brothers wrote "in all the familiarity of conversation—as one man to another."[30] His testimony was, in William Sales's view, a "plain and honest language, void of equivocation," not the "FLATTERY and FALSEHOOD" of priests

---

27. Richard Brothers, *A Revealed Knowledge of the Prophecies and Times*, Book the Second (London, 1794), iii.

28. Brothers, *Revealed Knowledge*, Book the First, 53.

29. Brothers, *Revealed Knowledge*, Book the First, 41; Book the Second, 7.

30. J. Crease, *Prophecies Fulfilling; or, The Dawn of the Perfect Day* (London, 1795), 29, 16.

and magistrates.[31] Critics, not unsurprisingly, ridiculed the prosaic quality of Brothers' "celestial compositions." "When the final sentence of destruction against London is sealed," sneered Henry Spencer, "then the following words will appear in the Heavens, written in gigantic characters: 'IT IS DONE.' How sublimely simple the expression! how tremendously laconic! 'It is all over, my boys! you are done up.'"[32]

Even more than their British counterparts, American male prophets articulated a radical political agenda to the dissemination of plain prophetic truths throughout the reading public. Benjamin Gale, for whom "the whole tenor of Divine Revelations appears to originate from one general contest and struggle between *rulers*, for an undue extension of power, and the *ruled*, in order to maintain their *natural* and *constitutional rights*," understood this eternal political struggle of liberty against power in linguistic terms as well, as a battle between allegorical and literal readings of the divine scriptures. "There has long been a strange disposition among men to convert some of the most plain and simple doctrines of revelation into *allegory*, *metaphor* and *mystery* ... and from this source, the doctrines of revelation are often rendered *dark*, *intricate*, *mysterious* and *unintelligible*, to the great *joy* and *sport* of *infidels*." False prophets, like tyrannical rulers, use "*unintelligible jargon*" to lead the common people astray.[33] Another ardent republican prophet, William Scales, styled himself an American Jesus, of lowly origins and simple understanding. Disdaining the "flowery elevated stile" of the learned world, he urged his readers to "read this piece with candour ... without quibbling, carping, or wrestling reason and scripture," for those who "are not pleased with plain language are in a state of spiritual death." Scales's pamphlet endorsed the revolutionary ideal of universal enlightenment: "I know indeed the arts of your spiritual task masters; they will, with their beguiling words ... endeavor to keep you in ignorance. But let me beseech you to see for yourselves; don't give up your understandings to other men."[34]

---

31. William Sales, *Truth or No Truth; or, A Discourse on Prophets* (London, 1795), 3.

32. Henry Spencer, *A Vindication of the Prophecies of Mr. Brothers and the Scripture Expositions of Mr. Halhed* (London, 1795), 28–29.

33. Benjamin Gale, *A Brief Essay; or, An Attempt to Prove from the Prophetick Writings of the Old and New Testament, what Period of Prophecy the Church of God is now under* (New Haven, CT, 1788), 23, 56.

34. William Scales, *The Confusion of Babel Discovered: or, An Answer to Jeremy Belknap's Discourse upon the Lawfulness of War* (America, 1780), v–vi.

The best example of this fusion of republican and millennial language can be found in the writings of David Austin, perhaps the closest thing America had to a charismatic prophet in the topsy-turvy decade of the 1790s. Recovering from a near fatal bout with scarlet fever in 1796, Austin—then a well-respected Presbyterian preacher in Elizabethtown, New Jersey—heard the voice of God calling him to the prophetic office. "I beheld the blessed Jesus as our elder brother," he recounted in his journal. "Here I seemed to stand, stripped of myself, and of all self-dependence, looking faintly at the blood which seemed to have issued from the Saviour's side." In this vision, he was directed to read the third chapter of Zechariah, which "sent faintness into my soul and weakness into my bones ... So powerful was the impression of that chapter upon my mind ... that it dropped me to the floor, and produced the self-abasement of which the journal hath spoken. The character and standing of *Joshua* was presented as my *own*."[35] What did it mean for Austin to take on the role of Joshua to the American people? As he describes his prophetic "office," his responsibilities were largely those of a republican publicist rather than a charismatic seer: he initiated a project to collect and publish the sermons of various evangelical clergymen (the first four volumes of *The American Preacher*) in order to disseminate Christian literature more widely throughout the country; he founded a magazine, *The Christian Herald, or the Union Magazine*, which became the leading periodical of millennial thought in the early 1800s; and he circulated a proposal for a national "concert of prayer" in which Americans in their individual homes and communities would pray as one at a designated hour—a perfect expression of the anonymous public sphere. Austin's claim to prophetic status thus rested on his efforts to circulate national texts and to create an imagined community of Christians via collective reading and prayer.[36]

---

35. David Austin, *The Voice of God to the People of the United States, by a Messenger of Peace* (Elizabethtown, NJ, 1796), 36, 49. For two contemporary descriptions of Austin's prophetic career, see William Sprague, *Annals of the American Pulpit* (New York: R. Carter and Bros., 1859–69), 2:195–206.

36. See Benedict Anderson, *Imagined Communities: Reflections on the Origin and Spread of Nationalism* (London: Verso, 1983), for a discussion of the role of print in forging a sense of national identity. The "concert of prayer" is described by Timothy Hall in his study of eighteenth-century itinerancy as an expression of the new community brought into being by the spread of commerce and print culture; Hall, *Contested Boundaries: Itinerancy and the Reshaping of the Colonial American Religious World* (Durham, NC: Duke University Press, 1994).

No more stirring rendition of the "visionary republic" as a Habermasian public sphere can be found than in Samuel Hopkins's learned *Treatise on the Millennium*, which was published three years before David Austin had his near encounter with death. In Hopkins's vision of the Millennium, learning and print combine to create a universally enlightened society. "Those things which now appear intricate and unintelligible, will then appear plain and easy. Then public teachers will be eminently burning and shining lights ... And the conversation of friends and neighbors, when they meet, will be full of instruction and they will assist each other in their inquiries after the truth, and in pursuit of knowledge." Everyone will have "sufficient leisure to pursue and acquire learning of every kind that will be beneficial to themselves and to society." Universal brotherhood will be facilitated by the creation of a single, universal language: "In the Millennium, all will probably speak *one language* ... And that language will be taught in all schools, and used in public writings, and books shall be printed; and in a few years will become the common language, understood and spoken by all." The withering away of national and linguistic differences will have the happy effect of "render[ing] books very cheap, and easy to be obtained by all." In time, this "universality of language will tend to cement the world of mankind so as to make them *one* in a higher degree."[37] Thomas Paine could not have said it better.

If the emphasis on plain language was particularly pronounced among American male prophets, it was also more closely tied to a robust tradition of oral address that persisted in America well into the nineteenth century. The "Prophet Nathan" spoke for many American writers when he issued a simple plea to his readers: "Will you suffer me, as a friend, to converse with you (if not personally, yet with my pen), about your *difficulties?*" The art of conversation, however encoded in print, was still the paramount ideal of communication in revolutionary and post-revolutionary America, and writers strove to simulate spoken conventions as closely as possible in their written texts.[38] Simon Hough addressed his audience through a series of imagined dialogues between himself and a "hireling" minister, enlisting both their moral and

---

37. Samuel Hopkins, *A Treatise on the Millennium* (Boston, 1793), 59, 75–77.

38. On the "elocutionary revolution" of the eighteenth century, see Fliegelman, *Declaring Independence*.

political sympathies on behalf of liberty of conscience.[39] David Austin published numerous pamphlets in the form of epistolary exchanges, which enabled him to carry on conversation with real and imagined correspondents over the finer points of prophetic interpretation.

In contrast, British writers in the tradition of Brothers and Bicheno were much more self-consciously immersed in the expanding world of print culture, which formed not only the medium but the message of their republican brand of prophecy. As much as the simple language of Brothers's writings, his reliance on new modes of dissemination ("the *penny-post!*" marveled Henry Spencer)[40] angered his many detractors. Circulating first among the highest echelons of state power and spiraling outward to the very margins of British political culture, Brothers's texts were intended for the same public then being courted by the London Corresponding Society and other radical organizations. As scribe to the Lord, Brothers translated the oral tradition of revealed Christianity into print in the same way that the corresponding societies translated an inchoate popular radicalism into literature form. Such a creative appropriation of republican print culture was not unique to the lunatic fringe of British prophecy. Indeed, one could say that late eighteenth-century prophecy was itself the product of an expanded print culture; William Reid, for one, blamed the spread of both infidelity and religious heresy on the widespread availability of cheap print. "We have seen the principles of Infidelity transferred from *books* to men; from *dead* characters to *living* subjects," and the result was a flood of blasphemous literature. "Prophecies ... teem from the British press, some of them in weekly numbers, till government, perfectly aware of these inflammatory means, prudently transferred the prince of prophets [Brothers] to a mad-house."[41] James Bicheno penned an extensive paean to the liberating effects of the print revolution in his final pamphlet, which appeared in 1817. He chose as his main text the tenth chapter of Revelation, in which an angel descends to earth holding a "little book open in his hand." For Bicheno, the book the angel held

---

39. Simon Hough, *The Sign of the Present Time; or, A Short Treatise Setting Forth What Particular Prophecies are Now Fulfilling in the Author's Judgment* (Stockbridge, MA, 1799).

40. Spencer, *Vindication of the Prophecies*, 19.

41. William H. Reid, *The Rise and Dissolution of the Infidel Societies in this Metropolis* (London, 1800), iv–v, 2.

represented the *"invention of printing,"* making this "one of the most sublime visions in all the Apocalypse."[42]

No wonder, then, that so many male prophetic writers in England and America embraced the idea of revolution with such enthusiasm. Their vision of the Millennium corresponded so closely with the vision of republican liberty espoused by political radicals that we can speak of a shared sensibility uniting men across the political and religious spectrum regardless of denomination. Deists and evangelicals made common cause to defend the emerging public sphere against its numerous enemies, political and spiritual, who would reduce the republic of letters to the Tower of Babel. William Scales, in his millenarian manifesto *The Confusion of Babel Discovered,* turned the tricks of these false prophets against themselves, and in the process offers us a wonderfully wicked counter-image to contrast to the millennial hopes of Samuel Hopkins. "I know that I have as good a right to form words as others; especially when the words I form are expressive of the tricks of the deceivers," he argued cleverly. "The word bamboozlement I formed from the verb to bamboozle, which means to deceive a man out of common sense by much fair speeches, by much insinuation, much sophistical argumentation and pretensions of friendship ... By the word cajolement, I mean the fair, the beguiling, the enchanting speeches and conventions of false teachers."[43] Not a universal language but a confusion of tongues was the fruit of false teachers.

*

This anti-republican vision was not a mere abstraction or a clever play on words, but was embodied in the practices and beliefs of female prophets. While less visible as public personages than their European counterparts, female prophets and their sects did serve the new American republic in another way: as negative images of the idealized public sphere that male prophets and male republicans were busily erecting in the aftermath of revolution. David Hudson accused Jemima Wilkinson of fleeing into the wilderness of upstate New York in order to isolate her deluded followers from the virtues of enlightened society. "To emigrate with her followers into an entire wilderness, where, as she

---

42. Bicheno, *Fulfillment of Prophecy,* 64, 69.
43. Scales, *Confusion of Babel Discovered,* vii–viii.

supposed, they would remain for a long time without the means of ordinary instruction, and in a great measure cut off from a constant intercourse with an enlightened community," he argued, "seemed more likely to perpetuate her dominion."[44] But it was Ann Lee, in particular, who was the prime target of patriot writers seeking to discredit the anti-republican world of female mystagoguery. Lee's fault (according to her numerous critics) was that she was, first of all, not American but British and hence of suspect political affiliation; and, second, that she instituted a very authoritarian mode of spiritual leadership by her claims to special charismatic powers. "To be a body of more than two thousand people, having no will of their own, but governed by a few Europeans conquering their adherents into the most unreserved subjection, argues some infatuating power; some deep, very deep design at bottom," warned Amos Taylor. "The Mother, it is said, obeys God through Christ; European elders obey her; American laborers obey them."[45] Another apostate, Reuben Rathbun, explained that he was freed from Mother Ann's dominion only when he took up the Bible and read it for himself. "I was astonished with myself that ever I imbibed such absurd ideas; but the reason was, I never searched the scriptures to see if these things were so, but believed and received everything I heard without giving myself liberty to doubt the truth of it." Because the Shaker Elders forbade their followers from reading any books, Rathbun charged, the Believers were "vicious in their natures and ungovernable."[46]

Critics reserved their sharpest attacks for the distinctive Shaker mode of worship, however, in which chaos and impropriety prevailed. "When they meet together for their worship," another apostate wrote, "some will be singing, each one his own tune; some without words, in an Indian tone, some sing jigg tunes, some tunes of their own making, in an unknown mutter, which they call new tongues ... till the different tunes, groaning, jumping, dancing, drumming, laughing, talking, and fluttering, shouting, and hissing makes a perfect bedlam; this they

---

44. David Hudson, *History of Jemima Wilkinson, A Preacheress of the Eighteenth Century; Containing an Authentic Narrative of Her Life and Character, and of the Rise, Progress, and Conclusions of Her Ministry* (Geneva, NY, 1821), 50.

45. Amos Taylor, *A Narrative of the Strange Principles, Conduct, and Character of the People Known by the Name of Shakers* (Worcester, MA, 1782), 3–5.

46. Reuben Rathbun, *Reasons Offered for Leaving the Shakers* (Pittsfield, MA, 1800), 16, 24.

call the worship of God."[47] Shaker worship thus presented itself as the perfect antithesis of Hopkins's well-ordered Millennium—despotic, singular, and unintelligible. It is not surprising that Lee and her closest disciples were briefly imprisoned for treason in 1780, and that charges of loyalism continued to dog the sect throughout its early years.

In retrospect, it is easy to see why these female-headed millenarian sects were accused of harboring anti-republican sentiments. After all, as Ruth Bloch argues, in many respects the ideas and practices of the Shakers and the Universal Friends were diametrically opposed to those of the American revolutionary movement. Both sects rejected history and reason, even (in the case of Lee) the Bible itself, as guides to the future in favor of the word of inspired prophets who claimed to be reincarnations of Christ. Both rejected traditional family and gender roles, although here the androgynous persona of Jemima Wilkinson and the Shaker conception of the dual-gendered godhead complicates any straightforward association of these two sects with antipatriarchal goals. Most damning of all, both groups portrayed themselves as "otherworldly," owing allegiance to no state but to the kingdom of God.[48]

Yet it seems to me that this characterization of female millenarianism as apolitical and authoritarian is only a partial truth. The point is not that male prophets had fully made the transition to the Enlightenment, with its elevation of reason as the supreme human virtue and the denigration of intuition, superstition, and blind faith, while women prophets remained somehow caught in an older, pre-political moment. Rather, we need to question the assumption that mysticism was an archaic hermeneutic practice, unsuited to democratic political discourse. Female prophets enacted a very different version of the "visionary republic" in their sectarian movements, one that located spiritual and political authority not in the masculine rule of reason but in the feminine realm of mystical power. In so doing, they provide historians with an alternative model of democratic politics that may, in the long run, have been more appealing to a certain sector of American women (those, for instance, who would find in Spiritualism a powerful means of combating social and political ills by the mid-nineteenth century.)

---

47. Valentine Rathbun, *An Account of the Matter, Form, and Manner of a New and Strange Religion Taught and Propagated by a Number of EUROPEANS...* (Providence, RI, 1781), 11–12.
48. Bloch, *Visionary Republic*, 90.

We can see this by examining more closely the value of literacy, surely the democratic virtue *par excellence,* in the writings and practices of male and female millenarians.

Most prophets, male and female, spoke proudly of their humble beginnings and rudimentary literary achievements, distancing themselves from the world of learned discourse even while they made effective use of the possibilities offered by the expansion of print culture. Illiteracy could be a badge of spiritual superiority for charismatic seers who spurned the world of men and human knowledge. But illiteracy had a different meaning for millenarian men and women. Simon Hough, a fiery lay millennialist from western Massachusetts, published several tirades against those "wavering, college learnt merchants of the gospel" who were leading good Christians down the path to spiritual death. The learned clergy tell men they cannot understand the prophetic scriptures because they are illiterate: "because men cannot go to college, and by human learning, obtain this spirit of discernment, and for fear of losing their lucrative employment, [the clergy] teach the world that they cannot be understood." Acknowledging the impossibility of understanding the Book of Revelation without the "dictates of the same spirit which dictated the penning of it," that is, without an internal spiritual guide, Hough insisted that this "spirit of discernment" could be obtained by human learning. All that is needed is for men to read the Bible for themselves. "O my brethren of the laity," he pleaded, "take heed to yourselves, put no trust in man, but read your Bibles."[49] The virtue of illiteracy, in other words, does not reside in forsaking the Bible in favor of direct inspiration but rather in rejecting the tutelage of learned men who pretend to have special knowledge of divine laws. The act of reading is, for male prophets, the supreme act of self-enlightenment, that which frees ordinary men from the dead hand of tradition and the sophistry of "hireling" ministers. "*Blessed is he that READETH,*" Benjamin Gale proclaimed.[50]

The "illiteracy" of female sectarian movements was of a very different order. Here, American and British prophetesses diverged on one crucial point: in the United States, women like Wilkinson and Lee

49. Simon Hough, *An Alarm to the World: Dedicated to All Ranks of Men* (Stockbridge, MA, 1792), 8–9, 23.
50. Gale, *Brief Essay,* 54.

rejected the presuppositions of print culture altogether in reaching for a spiritual power beyond the written word, while in England women like Joanna Southcott and Sarah Flaxmer cleverly exploited the technologies of print to proclaim a *new* Word, one rooted more in the medieval and Renaissance traditions of mystical writing than in the linguistic conventions of a Habermasian public sphere.[51] For American female sectarians, reading—divine texts or even the words of the founder—was discouraged and at times actively suppressed; the emphasis in these movements was on oral communication, on spiritual conversations between individuals who could see and touch one another. Those who were divinely inspired had special verbal powers (Ann Lee, though unable to read, was said to be able to speak fluently as many as seventy-two languages) that both set them apart from ordinary believers and allowed them to translate the spirit's message to their audiences.[52] The ability to "speak in tongues" became a hallmark of Shaker worship after Lee's death, a form of supernatural communication that was understood to supersede more conventional modes of access to God's word, including the Bible. For the Shakers, all printed texts were false representations of the true "word" of God, which could be known only in the hearts of believers. Lee herself became a kind of "living Bible" to her followers ("I am Ann the Word," she declared), and she called her disciples "my epistles, read and known of all men."[53] Refusing for years to contaminate the society's tenets and practices by committing them to print, Lee initiated a crusade in 1782–83 against formal learning that ultimately led to book burning.[54] Only in 1808, more than half a century after the founding of

51. For a discussion of the "baroque" tradition of visionary writing and its reformulation in the seventeenth century, see Michel de Certeau, *The Mystic Fable*, Vol. 1: *The Sixteenth and Seventeenth Centuries*, Michael B. Smith, trans. (Chicago: University of Chicago Press, 1992).

52. Hannah Adams, *An Alphabetical Compendium of the Various Sects which have Appeared in the World from the beginning of the Christian Era to the present Day* (Boston, 1784), lviii; and Rathbun, *Account of the Matter*, 6.

53. *Testimonies of the Life, Character, Revelations and Doctrines of Our Ever Blessed Mother Ann Lee* (Hancock, MA, 1816), 26. In similar fashion, the millenarian movement headed by Mother Buchan in England substituted the "living book of life, which is the love of God displaying itself through the body of a saint" for the "dead letter" of the Bible; James Purves, *Eight Letters Between the People Called Buchanites and a Teacher near Edinburgh* (Edinburgh, 1785), 49. Mother Buchan herself was also described as a "living bible"; *Satan's Delusions: A Poem on the Buchanites* (London, 1784), 9.

54. Clarke Garrett, *Spirit Possession and Popular Religion from the Camisards to the Shakers* (Baltimore: Johns Hopkins University Press, 1987), 198.

the society in England, did the Shakers agree to issue a public statement of their faith. As the preface of this work stated, "[I]n all this time of sixty years, the testimony [of the saints] hath been verbal ... without any written creed or form of government relating to themselves." Even now, the Shakers insisted, "we are far from expecting, or even wishing any of our writings to supersede the necessity of a living testimony ... for the letter killeth, *but the spirit giveth life*."[55] In like manner, Jemima Wilkinson in her one published work condemned all who are "begotten out of the letter" as unclean scribes and Pharisees, and promised to redeem America in the same manner as Jesus redeemed the Apostles: by the spirit rather than by the "book."[56]

This wholesale rejection of books and reading in favor of immediate inspiration set the Shakers and the Universal Friends apart from their male sectarian counterparts. However much they scorned college-educated ministers, no male millenarian ever extended this critique of book-learning to the Bible itself. In an age when women generally had much lower literacy rates than men, and in which debates over the benefits of female education still took place under the shadow of a long-standing association of learned women with sexual and moral deviance, it makes sense that some female millenarians would offer a vision of the "New Jerusalem" in which literacy was irrelevant and even harmful.[57]

The alternative was to redefine literacy itself, to use the advantages of print culture to undermine the very presuppositions on which that culture supposedly rested. This was the path that British female millenarians pursued, with vigor and creativity. Ann Lee's closest British counterpart—the woman who embodied anti-republican license and linguistic impropriety at its most pernicious—was Joanna Southcott. Southcott is perhaps most distinguished among her British and American counterparts by her sheer prolixity. The author of sixty-five pamphlets (and

55. *The Testimony of Christ's Second Appearing, Containing a General Statement of All Things Pertaining to the Faith and Practice of the Church of God in this Latter-Day* (Lebanon, OH, 1808), 12.

56. [Jemima Wilkinson], *Some Considerations, Propounded to the several Sorts and Sects of PROFESSORS of this Age ... by a Universal Friend of Mankind* (Providence, RI, 1779), 42, 44.

57. For debates over the wisdom of educating women, see Linda K. Kerber, *Women of the Republic: Intellect and Ideology in Revolutionary America* (Chapel Hill: University of North Carolina Press, 1980), chap. 7; and Mary Kelley, *Learning to Stand and Speak: Women, Education, and Public Life in America's Republic* (Chapel Hill: University of North Carolina Press, 2006).

thousands of pages of unpublished manuscripts), Southcott constituted a one-woman cottage industry in the world of British publishing from the time her first tract appeared in 1801 until her death in 1814. A conservative estimate puts the number of copies of her writings published between 1801 and 1816 at 108,000—a figure below that of Thomas Paine's *Rights of Man* but well above most other religious and political literature.[58] Her output was not only prodigious but also represented an extended reflection on the act of reading itself that placed texts and their relationship to readers at the very heart of her prophetic mission.

The contemporary and historical verdicts on Joanna Southcott converge on one score: her writings are tedious, circuitous, and maddeningly opaque. Written half in verse and half in prose, her "communications" are a crazy quilt of voices (first, second, and third person), images, and phrases that manage to be repetitive and obscure at the same time. These "rhapsodies of ignorance, vulgarity, indecency, and impiety" represented to the literary and ecclesiastical establishment not the true language of the "Spirit" (who "always speaks in good grammar and good sense") but a "farrago of nonsense."[59] Even those scholars who accord the Southcottian movement some measure of intellectual respectability find Southcott's writings, and her peculiar relationship to the world of print culture in general, an enigma. Clearly, as J. F. C. Harrison notes, the fact that her prophecies circulated largely in print had "momentous consequences" for the success of the movement and for broader questions of popular literacy in an age of restricted educational opportunities. The available evidence suggests that access to her printed works was remarkably broad, and the laborious work of copying, recopying, and indexing Southcott's manuscripts that her followers undertook in her lifetime and beyond constituted "a form of pseudo-learning" for the mostly poor farmers and artisans who made up the backbone of the movement.[60]

But precisely how Southcott's writings were read by her followers is a question of considerable more complexity. For woven into the very substance of her prophecies was a highly systematic if idiosyncratic

---

58. J. Hopkins, *Woman to Deliver Her People*, 84.

59. *A Letter to T.P. Foley* (London, 1813), 36–38, 43, 45.

60. Harrison, *Second Coming*, 88, 229. James Hopkins documents widespread ownership, or at least possession, of Southcott's pamphlets among her followers; in one congregation, for instance, the 123 believers possessed more than 1,400 copies of her work — an average of twelve per member. Hopkins, *Woman to Deliver Her People*, 115–16.

discourse on the practice of reading that demands closer attention. The image of the Bible as a "sealed" book whose contents can only be understood by those who have access to the prophetess's words was the dominant motif in Southcott's writings. The Bible, Southcott told her readers, was composed of "types" and "shadows," parables whose meaning could never be discerned by human reason or scholarly investigation. The "substance" of these shadows was revealed in Southcott's communications, and in the events these writings predicted would come to pass. Rather than urging men and women to read the scriptures in light of their natural reason, as male prophets from Brothers to Austin had done, Southcott insisted that the scriptures were and must remain a "mystery." Her deliberate obscurantism infuriated men like Robert Hann, for whom her writings were an "opium" that led readers to "prostitute their judgment, and give themselves up as willing sacrifices to delusion and imposture."[61]

Such charges of female mystagoguery had a long provenance in the history of Anglo-American dissent, but in the case of Joanna Southcott the accusations seems more than justified. Her communications were intended to confuse and unsettle—to "stumble," in her words—those who read them.[62] If believers could not arrive at spiritual truth through the usual means of enlightened reading, how, then, were they to be saved? Given the Southcottians' insistence that only those who had read Joanna's writings were worthy of being "sealed" for all time, an alternative practice of reading had to be devised, one that would retain the mysterious quality of the sacred texts while allowing believers some access to the divine truths contained therein. Southcott devised multiple strategies for this purpose, most prominently the age-old method of "promiscuous" reading—the random selection of passages without any order or sequence. As generations of Christians had done before her, she read the Bible by randomly opening the book and reading the first passage that appeared.[63] As David Hall has described, such a mode

61. R. Hann, *A Letter to the Right Reverend the Lord Bishop of London concerning the Heresy and Imposture of Joanna Southcott* (London, 1810), 13, 7.

62. Joanna Southcott, *A Dispute between the Woman and the Powers of Darkness* (London, 1802), 4; and the communication of July 12, 1802, in the Notebook of Divine Communications and Letters (item 327), Joanna Southcott Collection, Harry Ransom Center, University of Texas, Austin.

63. See, for example, Joanna Southcott, *Prophecies: A Warning to the World, from the*

of reading was commonplace in the early modern world of reformed Protestantism, where "intensive" reading—the rereading of certain texts, "not once or twice, but '100 and 100 times'"—was still practiced. In advocating the intensive and promiscuous reading of scripture, however, Southcott violated another central tenet of the reformed Protestant tradition—the belief that, in Hall's words, "the meaning of the Bible was self-evident. It was a book that made its message felt without there being any mediation—no intermediaries, no gloss, no message that called for interpretation. In the root sense of the word, the Bible was *immediately* available."[64] In Southcott's world, sacred texts (scripture and her own writings) were always and complexly mediated.

Her use of highly metaphorical forms of argumentation (the vocabulary of types, shadows, parables, dreams, visions) placed her squarely in the mystical tradition of early modern dissent, yet she also invented new methods for confounding her readers that relied heavily on manipulating the technologies of print. One of the most effective, and most provocative, was her practice of deliberately scrambling texts. She admitted in her reply to a critic, Louis Mayer, that she had reprinted his accusations not as a single block of text but broken into pieces, dispersed throughout some fifty pages of print, in order to impress upon her readers the idiosyncratic placement of truth in the scriptures.[65] On another occasion, at the Spirit's express command, Southmost ordered that the explanation of certain parables be published separately; a parable of the adulterous nation introduced by Rev. Thomas Foley (in *What Manner of Communication Are These?*) was explained in William Sharp's tract, *Sharp Answer to the World*, while Sharp's parables were explained in Foley's pamphlet. The Spirit explained: "I now tell thee, these two books that I ordered to be printed in this manner, that you could not understand one without going to the other ... perfectly so, I tell thee, stand the Scriptures of Truth!"[66]

Sealed Prophecies of Joanna Southcott (London, 1803), 53; and Southcott, *Explanation of the Parables Published in 1804* (London, 1806), 51.

64. David D. Hall, *Worlds of Wonder, Days of Judgment: Popular Religious Belief in Early New England* (1989; Cambridge, MA: Harvard University Press, 1990), 42, 26–27.

65. Southcott, *Explanation of Parable*, 55.

66. Rev. T.P. Foley, *What Manner of Communications Are These?* (London, 1804); William Sharp, *Sharp Answer to the World* (London, 1806); Joanna Southcott, *On Parables* (London, 1806), 59.

Southcott thus offered a very archaic, and very authoritarian, understanding of literacy to the British public. Her method confounds all the tenets of a Habermasian print culture: that language is transparent, that it is impersonal—that the relationship of signs to signifiers is not secured by the personal attributes or resources of any individual or social group but by the universal recognition of "rational" correspondences—and that knowledge is equally distributed throughout the population and not the special preserve of any one person or class. Whereas republican prophets like James Bicheno believed that the language of scripture was readily accessible to people across the social and political spectrum without specialized training, Southcott insisted that only true believers could understand the Word of God, and then only after it had been channeled through the interpretive faculties of an inspired prophet.[67]

How "democratic" is such an approach to language? The labels "radical" and "conservative" are not particularly helpful in trying to understand Southcottian prophecy in the context of the political struggles of the age of revolution. On the one hand, her mission was extremely autocratic. She was clearly jealous of her prophetic standing and refused to acknowledge any rivals or alternative routes to salvation save through her own writings. She was equally firm in her rejection of political radicalism, arguing that the only revolution needed or possible was a spiritual one. Above all, she resurrected an archaic form of Old Testament prophecy in which authority is rooted in the charismatic appeal of a single individual rather than in the collective worship of believers.[68] On the other hand, Southcott portrayed herself as the defender of the underprivileged classes—women (especially single women) and the poor, and offered them a vision of redemption through the agency of a "poor illiterate woman."[69] She, like the Methodist clergy she so

---

67. In this, she departed from the linguistic practices of female Methodist preachers, who — like male prophets — adopted an "ethos of simplicity" in their spoken and written performances that affirmed Methodism's theological message of universal redemption; Christine L. Krueger, *The Reader's Repentance: Women Preachers, Women Writers, and Nineteenth-Century Social Discourse* (Chicago: University of Chicago Press, 1992).

68. For a persuasive account of the authoritarian and coercive nature of charismatic religious figures, see Jon Butler, *Awash in a Sea of Faith.*

69. Anna Clark provides a good reading of the "feminist" implications of Southcott's theology in "The Sexual Crisis and Popular Religion in London, 1770–1820," *International Labor and Working Class History* 34 (1988), 56–69; see also Clark, *The Struggle for*

bitterly resented, was scornful of "learning" and "civilized" society, and preached the standard anti-clerical message of the day: that ministers are nothing but "hirelings" and hypocrites who know less about true Christianity than their humble followers. In a strange way, it may also be that her peculiar brand of obscurantist language was a mark of rebellion. After all, women who tried to adopt the prevailing discourses of political radicalism (such as appeals to reason and the "universal" rights of mankind) were not particularly successful in articulating a feminist vision of the polity in the 1790s.[70] Her retrieval of the archaic language of prophecy may, in the end, have constituted a far more effective challenge to democratic politics than the reasoned discourses of Mary Wollstonecraft or Hannah More.

A "mystical republic" thus offered powerful support to women whose inferior mental capacities and cultural "illiteracy" did not entitle them to civic or political standing.[71] What would become of the female millenarian tradition represented by Ann Lee and Joanna Southcott after the political storms of the revolutionary era had subsided? Ironically, it was republican prophets who found themselves pushed to the margins of Anglo-American political culture after 1815 rather than the mystagogues they scorned.

*

The flowering of millenarian sects in antebellum America (from the Millerites to the Mormons) represented a defiant resurgence of the mystical strand of eighteenth-century millennialism. Republican prophecy

---

the Breeches: Gender and the Making of the British Working Class (Berkeley: University of California Press, 1995), 107–11.

70. The fate of Mary Wollstonecraft's writings is a good case in point; for her reception in the United States, see Kerber, *Women of the Republic*, 222–31.

71. We can find evidence of a similar repudiation of enlightenment practices in the worship of African-American slaves and their descendants well into the nineteenth century. Though the desire for literacy was an important stimulus to conversion for African-American slaves in the late eighteenth century, who rightly saw in evangelical Protestantism an opportunity to capture the power of the written word for themselves, direct inspiration remained the paramount source of spiritual authority among Christianized slaves. As Albert Raboteau notes, slaves "valued the experience of God's power as the norm of Christian truth rather than the Bible"; *African-American Religion: Interpretive Essays in History and Culture*, Timothy E. Fulop and Albert J. Raboteau, eds. (New York: Routledge, 1997), 97. For an overview of the place of literacy in slave Christianity, see Sylvia R. Frey and Betty Wood, *Come Shouting to Zion: African American Protestantism in the American South and British Caribbean to 1830* (Chapel Hill: University of North Carolina Press, 1998).

did not so much disappear as become absorbed into a potent populist brew. Paul Boyer argues that the fusion of democratic and millenarian beliefs reached its zenith in the Millerite movement of the 1840s. "Just as the Jacksonians claimed that any (white male) citizen could perform the duties of government, so the Millerites insisted that untutored believers could unravel the apocalyptic mysteries. Millerism heralded the full democratization of prophetic belief in the United States," he argues.[72] If Millerism represents the apogee of the republican tradition of biblical exegesis, in which Every Man could read and interpret the prophetic passages for himself,[73] it was eclipsed in importance by the stunning success of Joseph Smith and the Mormons. Drawing on the diverse intellectual resonances ranging from medieval hermeticism to eighteenth-century mesmerism and Swedenborgianism, Smith's fantastic tale of buried treasure and "lost" scriptures written in ancient hieroglyphics reached an audience eager to recapture the power of the mystical word from a disenchanted world.[74] Other prophets would follow his lead, some (like the Prophet Matthias) for their own aggrandizement and some (like Matthias's most famous convert, the ex-slave Isabella Van Wagenen, who would become the abolitionist Sojourner Truth) out of genuine concern for spiritual renewal.[75] In England, the dramatic and well-publicized death of Joanna Southcott in 1814 from what she believed to be a "mystical pregnancy" dealt a serious blow to the millennial hopes of thousands of English men and women, but despite the ridicule heaped on her believers by churchmen and journalists, would-be successors to her prophetic mantle carried her message to a new generation of British millenarians. Well into the 1830s and 1840s, new prophets like John Wroe and "Zion" Ward claimed to be Southcott's true "heir," the Manchild she had promised to produce in her dying days.[76]

---

72. Boyer, *When Time Shall Be No More*, 85.

73. David L. Rowe, "Millerites: A Shadow Portrait," in *The Disappointed: Millerism and Millenarianism in the Nineteenth Century*, Ronald Numbers and Jonathan M. Butler, eds. (1987; Knoxville: University of Tennessee Press, 1993), 1–16.

74. John L. Brooke, *The Refiner's Fire: The Making of Mormon Cosmology, 1644–1844* (New York: Cambridge University Press, 1996).

75. Paul Johnson and Sean Wilentz, *The Kingdom of Matthias: A Story of Sex and Salvation in 19th-Century America* (New York: Oxford University Press, 1994); Nell Irvin Painter, *Sojourner Truth: A Life, A Symbol* (New York: W.W. Norton, 1996).

76. On Southcott's pregnancy and death, see Susan Juster, "Mystical Pregnancy and Holy Bleeding: Visionary Experience in Early Modern Britain and America," *William and Mary Quarterly* 3d Ser., 57 (Apr. 2000): 249–88.

The mystical tradition of millennial interpretation was thus carried into a new age by a "radical underworld" of prophets and visionaries, to paraphrase Iain McCalman, despite the best efforts of republican prophets and political radicals alike in the waning decades of the eighteenth century.[77] And there it would remain, for better or worse, to vex historians to the present day.

---

77. Iain McCalman, *Radical Underworld: Prophets, Revolutionaries, and Pornographers in London, 1795–1840* (Oxford: Oxford University Press, 1993).

TEN

THE BOOK OF MORMON
AS AMERINDIAN APOCALYPSE

JARED HICKMAN

Author's note: With the exception of one clarifying footnote, number 55, in response to an interpretative question raised in print by a reader, this essay has been substantively left as it originally appeared in 2014. The development of my views on the topic will subsequently appear in a planned book, The Romance of The Book of Mormon.

In October 1830, just months after he published the Book of Mormon in Palmyra, New York, new prophet Joseph Smith commanded Parley P. Pratt and others to light out for Indian Territory to share the new scripture.[1] The reason they felt compelled to undertake this task, despite the youthful fragility of their movement and the physical dangers and legal difficulties that stood in their way: early Mormons considered the Book of Mormon to be a "the record of [Amerindians'] forefathers," a group of Israelites led by the patriarch Lehi, who fled Jerusalem around 600 BCE before the Babylonian invasion.[2] According to the narrative, shortly after Lehi's American landing, two of his sons, Laman and Lemuel, are cursed by God with "a skin of blackness" in order to separate them and their progeny from their righteous and "fair" brother Nephi and his record-keeping descendants, the narrators of the Book of Mormon (2 Ne. 5:21; Alma 3:8). These dark-skinned "Lamanites" were understood by early Mormons to be the progenitors

---

1. Terryl L. Givens and Matthew J. Grow, *Parley P. Pratt: The Apostle Paul of Mormonism* (New York: Oxford University Press, 2011), 44–48.

2. Parley P. Pratt, *The Autobiography of Parley Parker Pratt* (Salt Lake City: Deseret Book Co., 1972), 51, 54–55; Joseph Smith Jr., The Book of Mormon: Another Testament of Jesus Christ (Salt Lake City: Church of Jesus Christ of Latter-Day Saints, 1981), cited hereafter by book, chapter, and verse within the text.

of the Native peoples of the Americas. On the basis of this foundational opposition, the Book of Mormon becomes, on multiple levels, a racial[3] apocalypse, albeit a contrarian one. Not only in the immediate temporal frame of the narrative do the dark Lamanites extinguish the fair Nephites in a thousand-year war, in the narrative's prophetically extended temporal frame, which encompasses the nineteenth-century moment of its readers, the resurgence of the Lamanites' Amerindian descendants in pre-Civil War America, by more bloodshed if necessary, is imagined. In an almost perfect inversion of (post-) Puritan racial theology, the Book of Mormon prophesies that Indian Israel, rather than the interloping Euro-American gentiles, will erect a New Jerusalem on the American continent.[4] In an era when the prevailing providentialist paradigm in the United States at best fostered a tragic image of "the vanishing Indian," it is perhaps no surprise that early readers of the Book of Mormon, whether they converted to Mormonism or not, located its theological interest not in its explicit Christian-doctrinal statements, which seemed derivative, but rather in the novel racial eschatology implicit in its narrative premises.[5] For those who did convert, like Pratt, the Book of Mormon inspired a "Mormon version of

3. Although Joseph Smith, "before his death, had begun replacing the skin- color references with terms that clearly referred instead to spiritual quality ["white" to "pure," for instance]" and never referred to the Nephite–Lamanite division in explicitly racial terms, it is clear that most early readers apprehended "Lamanite" as an ethnoracial category that corresponded to contemporary nonwhite, specifically Amerindian, peoples. Armand L. Mauss, *All Abraham's Children: Changing Mormon Conceptions of Race and Lineage* (Urbana: University of Illinois Press, 2003), 116–19; see Douglas Campbell, "'White' or 'Pure': Five Vignettes." *Dialogue: A Journal of Mormon Thought* 29, no. 4 (Winter 1996): 119–35, for details of textual history: witness the on-the-spot 1830 response of an outsider, German Reformed pastor Diedrich Willers, "The First Months of Mormonism: A Contemporary View by Rev. Diedrich Willers," trans. and ed. D. Michael Quinn. *New York History* 54, no. 2 (1973): 317–33, and the considered 1887 response of an insider, David Whitmer, who referred to the Nephites as a "white race." See Whitmer, *An Address to All Believers in Christ. By a Witness to the Divine Authenticity of the Book of Mormon* (Richmond, MO; the author, 1887), 12.

4. Compare Elizabeth Fenton, "Open Canons: Sacred History and American History in the Book of Mormon," reprinted in the present compilation.

5. "[From *The Exeter News-Letter*] The Book of Mormon," *New-Hampshire Patriot*, Sep. 19, 1831; Richard Lyman Bushman, *Joseph Smith: Rough Stone Rolling* (New York: Knopf, 2005), 94–99; Terryl L. Givens, *By the Hand of Mormon: The American Scripture that Launched a New World Religion* (New York: Oxford University Press. 2002), 89–116; Terryl L. Givens, *The Book of Mormon: A Very Short Introduction* (New York: Oxford University Press 2009), 69–74; and Dan Vogel, *Indian Origins and the Book of Mormon* (Salt Lake City: Signature Books, 1986).

Manifest Destiny" that posed more than an imaginary threat to the US state.[6] In response to Book of Mormon prophecies, early Mormons continually relocated on the advancing western frontier near "the borders of the Lamanites"—from Far West, Missouri, to Nauvoo, Illinois, to Salt Lake City, Utah—in the hopes of forming a Mormon–Lamanite alliance that would hasten the building of the New Jerusalem.[7] The Book of Mormon thus keyed the formation of an alternative chosen people—Mormons and Indians—whose millennial triumph, from the perspective of many Euro-Christians, amounted to the foreclosure of the nation's providential expansion. In fact, (Book of) Mormon millenarianism dovetailed with contemporaneous Amerindian spiritualities so productively that Gregory Smoak[8] goes so far as to say that the Book of Mormon has "forever linked" Mormonism with American Indian prophetic movements.

The first evidence for Smoak's historical judgment is Pratt's account of his brief ministry among a group of Lenni Lenape, or Delaware Indians, west of the Missouri River. The Delaware were pioneers of the eighteenth-century "nativist great awakening" that galvanized eastern tribes between the French and Indian and 1812 wars.[9] This context, Lori Taylor reminds us, is perhaps as important for the Book of Mormon as the Second Great Awakening: the Book of Mormon "came forth" not just in the "burnt-over district" of upstate New York amid revivalist talk of sin and salvation but in "Iroquois country" where nativist leaders like Red Jacket still voiced their alternative conception of the continental past and future.[10] The Delaware prophet Neolin was one of the first to articulate a vision of what might be called Amerindian apocalypse, which, at its core, promised the triumphant Native

---

6. Mauss, *All Abraham's Children*, 55; see also Jared Farmer, *On Zion's Mount: Mormons, Indians, and the American Landscape* (Cambridge: Harvard University Press 2008), 57–58.

7. Ronald Walker, "Toward a Reconstruction of Mormon and Indian Relations, 1847–77," *Brigham Young University Studies* 29, no. 4 (1989): 23–42, and Walker, "Seeking the 'Remnant': The Native American during the Joseph Smith Period," *Journal of Mormon History* 19, no. 1 (1993): 1–33.

8. Gregory E. Smoak, *Ghost Dances and Identity: Prophetic Religion and American Indian Ethnogenesis in the Nineteenth Century* (Berkeley: University of California Press, 2006), 71–73.

9. Gregory Evans Dowd, *A Spirited Resistance: The North American Indian Struggle for Unity, 1745–1815* (Baltimore: Johns Hopkins University Press 1992), 29–46.

10. Lori Elaine Taylor, "Telling Stories about Mormons and Indians," PhD diss. (State University of New York at Buffalo, 2000), 307–08, 342–44.

repossession of the continent by way of refusing Euro-Christian and restoring and reinventing Native lifeways. The Delaware leader with whom Pratt parleyed in January 1831 was William Anderson, or Kikthawenund, an aged chief who had lived the successes and failures of the nativist movement firsthand. The son of a Swedish father and Delaware mother, Kikthawenund had presided over multiple phases of the Delaware diaspora—from their original homelands around the Delaware River Valley to Ohio and Indiana (where the town of Anderson is named after him) and, finally, to Indian Territory in what is today Kansas, where he and his people had recently arrived when Pratt encountered them. Although Kikthawenund and the Delaware council elected not to join Tecumseh's pan-Indian confederacy around the time of the War of 1812, this decision should not be taken as evidence that Kikthawenund had abandoned nativist spirituality but rather, perhaps, that he and many other Delawares had already suffered so much for the cause. A Moravian missionary who proselytized among the Delawares on Indiana's White River during the first decade of the nineteenth century characterized Kikthawenund not only as "not inclined ... to Christianity" but as actively involved in "mak[ing] his people averse to it."[11] The man Pratt met twenty years later—despite the crushing defeat of Tecumseh's alliance and his own people's repeated dislocations in the interim—seems not at all to have relented in his nativist convictions. By Pratt's account, Kikthawenund was "at first unwilling to call his council ... as he had ever been opposed to the introduction of missionaries among his tribe."[12] What reportedly changed this die-hard nativist's mind was the fact that these missionaries were not peddling the Bible but a different book of scripture that purportedly spoke directly of and to him and his people. Dismissal of the Bible had been central to the nativist rejection of Euro-Christianity. As Gregory Dowd has shown, a standing argument of many nativists against Euro-Christian missionaries was that the Bible applied only to Europeans insofar as God had not seen fit to give the book to

---

11. Lawrence Henry Gipson, ed., *The Moravian Indian Mission on White River: Diaries and Letters, May 5, 1799, to November 12, 1806* (Indianapolis: Indiana Historical Bureau, 1938), 608; see also John P. Bowes, *Exiles and Pioneers: Eastern Indians in the Trans-Mississippi West* (New York: Cambridge University Press 2007), 40–41.

12. Pratt, *Autobiography*, 53–57.

Amerindians or Africans.[13] According to Pratt, once Kikthawenund began "to understand the nature of the Book [of Mormon] ... he ... became suddenly interested," eventually embracing "'the good news ... concerning the Book of our forefathers; it makes us glad in here'— placing his hand on his heart." The preaching of this alternative gospel reportedly caused such a stir among the Delaware that it "stirred up the jealousy and envy of the Indian agents and sectarian missionaries to that degree that we were soon ordered out of the Indian country as disturbers of the peace."[14]

Although one must certainly make allowances for Mormon propagandizing and Delaware politicking, it seems clear from this episode that the Book of Mormon answered (to) long-standing questions about the adequacy of the Bible in relation to the sacred-historical meaning of the Americas and their peoples. The fact that these did not clearly come up for description in established sources "widened already existing cracks in the canon" of traditional knowledge into "frightening crevasses," stripping even the Bible of some of its "aura of completeness," Anthony Grafton states.[15] As a possible asymptote of the Bible's universal claim, America has produced both the most strident extensions and the boldest super-sessions of biblical authority—the literalist hermeneutics of American evangelicalism and the new revelations of prophetic movements like nativism and Mormonism. One sees both kinds of grappling with biblical limitation at the limits of the nation in the case at hand. Pratt and Kikthawenund's synergy alarmed federal agents and sectarian missionaries alike, because it threatened an apocalyptic eclipse of the dominant apocalyptic narrative not only envisioned but being enacted in the pre-1860 United States. In that narrative, eventually sloganized as "Manifest Destiny," God had revealed Euro-Americans' warrant to colonize a promised land at the expense of Native and African Americans.[16] This apocalyptic narrative

13. Gregory Evans Dowd, *A Spirited Resistance: The North American Indian Struggle for Unity, 1745–1815* (Baltimore: Johns Hopkins University Press, 1992), 30.

14. Pratt, *Autobiography*, 53–57.

15. Anthony Grafton, *New World, Ancient Texts: The Power of Tradition and the Shock of Discovery* (Cambridge: Harvard University Press, 1992), 197–256; see also David N. Livingstone, *Adam's Ancestors: Race, Religion, and the Politics of Human Origins* (Baltimore: Johns Hopkins University Press 2008), 1–51.

16. Nicholas Guyatt, *Providence and the Invention of the United States, 1607–1876* (New York: Cambridge University Press, 2007), 173–258.

of white supremacy was enabled by a particular conjuncture of biblicism and racism. As Mark Noll has masterfully shown, "The problem with race and the Bible [in the pre-Civil War US] was far more profound than the interpretation of any one text … [It was] a problem brought about by the intuitive character of the reigning American hermeneutic," which enabled "commonsense reading of the Bible" and common-sense racism to reinforce each other.[17] A vicious circle developed: pre-1860 American readers predisposed by their sociocultural location to racism were authorized under the reigning hermeneutic to read that racism into a text that had been elevated to the status of literal word of God, thereby making their racism appear to originate from a source not only other but higher than themselves.

White domination acquired the sheen of incontestable divine decree. The Book of Mormon severs this vicious circle by simultaneously negating the authority deposited by literalist hermeneuts in "the Bible alone" and diametrically opposing another vision of racial apocalypse. Its form (indeed, its sheer facticity) and its content pointed up the—in multiple senses—partiality of biblicist nationalism at a moment when biblicist nationalism's practical and theoretical force seemed most comprehensive. In early 1831, as Jackson's Indian removal policy was squelching nativism east of the Mississippi, we find the Book of Mormon seemingly offering some measure of spiritual reinvigoration to a world-weary nativist like Kikthawenund.

Almost since its publication, then, the Book of Mormon has furnished a "fertile symbolic ground" for affirmations of Amerindian cultural and spiritual identity, anthropologist Thomas Murphy notes.[18] To reel off a few examples: Mormons were variously involved in each of the upsurges of the nineteenth-century Ghost Dance—perhaps the locus classicus of Amerindian apocalypse, leading Smoak to characterize "Ghost Dancing [as] a religious conversation between native peoples and … Mormons, concerning both peoples' identity and destiny."[19]

---

17. Mark A. Noll, *America's God: From Jonathan Edwards to Abraham Lincoln* (New York: Oxford University Press, 2002), 418; see also Noll, "The Image of the United States as a Biblical Nation, 1776–1885," in *The Bible in America: Essays in Cultural History*, ed. Nathan O. Hatch and Mark A. Noll, (New York: Oxford University Press, 1982), 39–58.

18. Thomas W. Murphy, "From Racist Stereotype to Ethnic Identity: Instrumental Uses of Mormon Racial Doctrine," *Ethnohistory* 46, no. 3 (1999): 455.

19. Smoak, *Ghost Dances and Identity*, 75–80, 124–26, 166–71.

South of the border, the Mexican Mormon convert Margarito Bautista Valencia produced a massive work of amateur scholarship in 1935 that grafted modern Mexican history onto the Book of Mormon history in a flurry of triumphalist nationalism. His confidence in the Book of Mormon's vision of Amerindian apocalypse prompted him to challenge the authority of white Mormon leaders in Utah over the Mexican saints, which galvanized like-minded Mexican Mormons (around a third of the total membership) in a separatist movement called the Third Convention.[20] More recently, Navajo Mormon leader George P. Lee was excommunicated for similarly citing the Book of Mormon as prooftext that the primary architects of the American New Jerusalem were to be the Amerindian descendants of Jacob, not the Euro-American gentiles.[21] Some contemporary Mayan Mormons interpret the *Popol Vuh* as a sacred Lamanite record that should be read alongside the Book of Mormon.[22] The Mormon topos of the Book of Mormon as an "unpaid debt" of Euro-American gentiles to Indian Israel implicitly identifies the Book of Mormon as an Amerindian cultural legacy, leading Lacee Harris, a Mormon of Northern Ute and Paiute ancestry, candidly to query: "When people tell me that my traditions develop from the Book of Mormon, I ask, 'Then why do I have to give up those traditions to be a Mormon?'"[23] These instances disclose the Book of Mormon's persistent agency in a complex process whereby "reculturation"[24]— the rendering of Amerindian culture in the entirely foreign terms of Judeo-Christian sacred history—leads to transculturation—the novel affordance of a "Lamanite subjectivity"[25] that empowers Native peoples—which, in turn, opens on the possibility of an ethnoculturation that (re)valorizes the very cultural particularities elided by the initial

20. Thomas W. Murphy, "Fifty Years of United Order in Mexico." *Sunstone* 20, no. 3 (1997): 69; Murphy, "'Stronger than Ever': Remnants of the Third Convention." *Journal of Latter-Day Saint History* 10 (1998): 1–12; and Murphy, "Other Mormon Histories: Lamanite Subjectivity in Mexico," *Journal of Mormon History* 26, no. 2 (2000): 179–214.

21. "The Lee Letters." *Sunstone* 13, no. 4 (August 1989): 50–55.

22. Thomas W. Murphy, "Reinventing Mormonism: Guatemala as Harbinger of the Future," *Dialogue: A Journal of Mormon Thought* 29, no. 1 (Spring 1996): 177–92; Murphy, "Other Mormon Histories."

23. Lacee A. Harris, "To Be Native American—and Mormon," *Dialogue: A Journal of Mormon Thought* 18, no. 4 (Winter 1985): 151.

24. Hilary E. Wyss, *Writing Indians: Literacy, Christianity, and Native Community in Early America* (Amherst: University of Massachusetts Press. 2000), 53.

25. Murphy, "Other Mormon Histories."

reculturation: the Book of Mormon collapses into *Popol Vuh*. The Book of Mormon's ready instrumentality in this process, I argue, makes it other than Euro-Christian.

No doubt the question arises as to how such a reading of the Book of Mormon can be squared with the fact that the text's most devoted readership—members of the LDS (Latter-day Saints) Church—has a deplorable record of theological racism. It can be argued that the Book of Mormon produces a dualism of "Indian-as-brother" and "Indian-as-other," as Jared Farmer has put it.[26] And amid the difficulties of actual intercultural encounter between Euro-American Mormons and Indians, it is undeniable that most Euro-American Mormons predictably disidentified with Indians in the terms "ordinary white racism."[27] Hence, although, as Armand rightly maintains, "the great majority of the white converts" to Mormonism "took very seriously the portrayal of the Indians in the Book of Mormon as Lamanites—that is, as literal Israelites ... destined to recover the spiritual and cultural greatness of God's chosen people,"[28] it is also clear that many Euro-American Mormons regarded contemporary Indians as the dark savages the white Nephite narrators often represented their ancestors to be—lost souls once in need of white Nephite paternalism and now in need of white Euro-American "Gentiles ... [to] be like unto a father to them" (2 Ne. 10:18). Furthermore, early Euro-American Mormon leaders occasionally downplayed the more radical implications of the Book of Mormon as a strategy of self-preservation. When the fledgling Mormon movement brought its largely northern constituency to the frontier slave state of Missouri in the mid-1830s, charges of fomenting insurrection among the Indians and harboring fugitive slaves were almost immediately leveled, and some Mormons overzealously deflected those charges in order to secure a place in the sacred circle of whiteness.[29] Consequently, at best Mormonism developed an "ambivalent theology of the Lamanite," allowing white Mormons to "practice a flexible 'politics of the Indian'" that more often than not has bent

---

26. Farmer, *On Zion's Mount*, 61; see also 57, 81, and 366–67.

27. Mauss, *All Abraham's Children*, 64.

28. Mauss, *All Abraham's Children*, 42, 63, 68.

29. Craig R. Prentiss, "'Loathsome unto Thy People': The Latter-Day Saints and Racial Categorization," in *Religion and the Creation of Ethnicity: An Introduction*, ed. by Craig R. Prentiss (New York: New York University Press, 2003), 130.

toward the status quo.[30] In recent years, any potential the Book of Mormon might have to foster a Lamanite liberation theology has been further undermined by the glaring incompatibility of DNA research on Amerindian peoples with the Book of Mormon claims. Mormon literalists have found themselves forced to shrink the speculative geography of the Book of Mormon to such a narrow extent as to raise the question of whether there is any meaningful relation, genealogical or otherwise, between ancient Lamanites and contemporary Amerindians.[31] Thus, the book whose primary source of interest was once as a history of Indians is now read in some quarters as having little to say about or to Amerindian people in particular.

The perhaps perverse stance of this essay is that, beyond these vicissitudes of interpretation, the Book of Mormon's formal logic and not just its eschatological content has made and will continue to make its theology of Native and/or nonwhite liberation irrepressible. As early as 1844, the mixed Native and African American writer-activist Robert Benjamin Lewis, "true father of Afrocentrism's wilder theories,"[32] seamlessly incorporated the Book of Mormon into a polemic vaunting

---

30. Keith Parry, "Joseph Smith and the Clash of Sacred Cultures," *Dialogue: A Journal of Mormon Thought* 18, no. 4 (Winter 1985): 74.

31. For the widely publicized controversy (John W. Kennedy, "Mormon Scholar under Fire: Anthropologist Says Latter-Day Saints' Teaching about Native Americans Wrong," *Christianity Today* 47, no. 3 [2003]: 24–25; "Mormons and Genetics: The Heretic: A Mormon Mentions the Unmentionable," *Economist* 365 [2002], no. 8303: 29) regarding biological evidence against Israelite emigration to the Americas, see Thomas W. Murphy, "Lamanite Genesis, Genealogy, and Genetics," in *American Apocrypha: Essays on the Book of Mormon*, ed. Dan Vogel and Brent Lee Metcalfe (Salt Lake City: Signature Books, 2002), 47–77; Simon G. Southerton, *Losing a Lost Tribe: Native Americans, DNA, and the Mormon Church* (Salt Lake City: Signature Books, 2004); Thomas W. Murphy and Simon Southerton, "Genetic Research a 'Galileo Event' for Mormons," *Anthropology News* 44, no. 2 (2003): 20; and Kevin L. Barney's 2003 response, "A Brief Review of Murphy and Southerton's 'Galileo Event,'" at www.fairmormon.org. Mormon apologists have rallied to John Sorenson's "limited geography" model of the Book of Mormon, which has been taken to suggest that the peoples described in the text were such a small and localized portion of ancient America's inhabitants that one should perhaps not expect to find an obvious genetic imprint in contemporary Native peoples, a position reflected in recent public stances taken by the LDS Church. John L. Sorenson, *An Ancient American Setting for the Book of Mormon* (Salt Lake City and Provo: Deseret Book and FARMS, 1996); Peggy Fletcher Stack, "Single Word Change in Book of Mormon Speaks Volumes," *Salt Lake Tribune*, Nov. 8, 2007; "Book of Mormon and DNA Studies," 2014, at www.lds.org/topics/book-of-mormon-and-dna-studies.

32. Stephen Howe, *Afrocentrism: Mythical Pasts and Imagined Homes* (New York: Verso 1998), 38.

the past and future greatness of the darker races.[33] Andress V. Lewis (no relation, apparently), a member of the "committee of coloured gentlemen" that published Lewis's *Light and Truth* in Boston, was the brother of Walker Lewis, one of the first African American converts to Mormonism and an abolitionist who, along with the likes of David Walker and William Cooper Nell, was a charter member of the Massachusetts General Colored Association.[34] Randall Moon notes the strikingly similar uses to which the Pequot Methodist minister William Apess put Indian-Israelite theory in the same time and place Smith was publishing and disseminating the Book of Mormon.[35] Such historical connections, sketchy though they are, further suggest a potential nonwhite attraction to the Book of Mormon from the time of its publication. As recently as 2000, the self-proclaimed Eritrean prophet Embaye Melekin (not a member of the LDS Church), authored an exhaustive commentary on the Book of Mormon that, in the wake of DNA's problematization of the Indians-as-Israelites theory, reinterprets the LDS scripture as an account of the migration of a group of Israelites not to the Americas but to the east coast of Africa. The readerly transformation Melekin undergoes as he plods straight through the Book of Mormon in many ways exemplifies the argument I will offer here. Melekin, initially self-identified as light-skinned and exclusively "Eritrean," begins by aligning himself with the white Nephite narrators over and against the black Lamanites—here coded as black sub-Saharan "Africans." But he ends by hailing the text's eschatological elevation of the Lamanites, which in his scheme signifies the eventual apotheosis of black Africa, to which he finally understands himself proudly to

---

33. R[obert] B[enjamin] Lewis, *Light and Truth: Collected from the Bible and Ancient and Modern History, Containing the Universal History of the Colored and the Indian Race, from the Creation of the World to the Present Time* (Boston: A Committee of Colored Gentlemen 1844), 34; on Lewis, see also Mia Bay, *The White Image in the Black Mind: African-American Ideas about White People, 1830–1925* (New York: Oxford University Press 2000), 44–46; and John Ernest, *Liberation Historiography: African American Writers and the Challenge of History, 1794–1861* (Chapel Hill: University of North Carolina Press, 2004), 101–13.

34. Connell O'Donovan, "The Mormon Priesthood Ban and Elder Q. Walker Lewis: 'An Example for His More Whiter Brethren to Follow,'" *John Whitmer Historical Association Journal* 26 (2006): 47–99. On the affinities of the Book of Mormon and Walker's 1929 *Appeal*, see Bushman, *Rough Stone Rolling*, 99.

35. Randall Moon, "William Apess and Writing White," *Studies in American Indian Literature* 5, no. 4 (1993), 53n1.

belong.[36] Despite the blunting of its radical edge over nearly two centuries by its primarily Euro-American Mormon interpreters, and even in the absence of its historical function as an explanation of Indian origins, the Book of Mormon text itself seems consistently to inspire a radical racialized apocalypticism.

A READING OF THE BOOK OF MORMON
AS METACRITIQUE OF THEOLOGICAL RACISM

The Book of Mormon seems to mythologize "the Jacksonian view of Indians common to most Americans in 1830"[37]:

> And [the Lord] caused the cursing to come upon [Laman and Lemuel], yea, even a sore cursing, because of their iniquity ... wherefore, as they were white, and exceeding fair and delightsome, that they might not be enticing unto my [their brother Nephi, the narrator's] people, the Lord God did cause a skin of blackness to come upon them And because of this cursing which was upon them, they did become an idle people, full of mischief and subtlety, and did seek in the wilderness for beasts of prey. (2 Ne. 5:21–24)

My burden is necessarily to show how this patent racism is somehow undone by the very text in which it is articulated. My claim is not only that the Book of Mormon ultimately does undo its rac(ial)ist orthodoxy but that it undertakes this undoing in such a way as to provide a meta-critique of theological racism, that is, a critique of theological racism by way of a critique of available critiques of theological racism. The Book of Mormon escorts the reader through several levels of insufficient critique of its foundational racism in order to arrive at a rather audacious insight in antebellum America's biblicist culture: racism is of such an order as to require nothing less than new ways of reading scripture and, indeed, new scripture altogether—fresh revelation from God himself.

Level 1: Troubling Racial Categories

The first level on which the Book of Mormon might seem to undo its racist dichotomy of righteous white Nephite and wicked black

---

36. Embaye Melekin, *Manifestations Mysteries Revealed: An Account of Bible Truth and the Book of Mormon Prophecies* (North York, ON: Embaye Melekin, 2000).

37. Bushman, *Rough Stone Rolling*, 98.

Lamanite is by partially unsettling the cut-and-dried contours and contents of these categories. On a macro level, the prolific, crabbed narrative of the Book of Mormon might seem to mitigate its foundational racist dichotomy by generating demographic doubles. Near the end of the narrative, the Book of Mormon effectively upstages the central story of Lehi's descendants by including the brief account of an earlier migration of Old World peoples to the Americas—the Jaredites, survivors of the destruction of the Tower of Babel (Ether). The highly compressed story of their 2,000-year tragic downfall is editorially interposed in the Book of Mormon right before the final annihilation of the Nephites as an epitome that underlines the moral of the main narrative. But insofar as it provides an additional case study of New World declension in which racial curses do not figure, it arguably relativizes the Manichean drama of white Nephites versus black Lamanites. The text further complicates rac(ial)ist considerations by having this temporally prior demographic double—the Jaredites—meet up, centuries later, with a demographic double contemporaneous with the Lehite lineage (Lamanites and Nephites), yet another group of emigrants, who left Jerusalem around the same time as Lehi and his family, led by Mulek, the son of Zedekiah, king of Judah (Omni 1:13–22). The last Jaredite, Coriantumr, is taken in by these Mulekites, whom the Nephites subsequently discover in the course of their flight from the Lamanites. If the Jaredites are constructed as ominous foreshadowers of the Nephites, then the Mulekites are their benighted doppelgangers—unlike Lehi and his family, they failed to bring Israelite sacred writings with them and so exist in a pitiful state of civilization without a coherent language or religion. But although spiritually and culturally superior to the Mulekites, the Nephites are numerically inferior—and vulnerable refugees, to boot—and so are absorbed by the Mulekites in their "land of Zarahemla," which remains the Nephite home base for the rest of the narrative. The significance of this demographic shift is registered in the narrative structure itself, for the absorption of Nephites by Mulekites marks the transition from the spiritually focused "small plates" of Nephi to the more secular "large plates" of the Book of Mormon, which present the abridged history of Nephite–Lamanite relations as filtered through the retrospective viewpoint of the book's eponymous editor. It might be argued that this conspicuous narrative

seam where the Book of Mormon braids together its multiple beginnings—Jaredites, Nephites, and Mulekites—implicitly interrogates
the nature and authority of origins: Amid the sheer proliferation and
interpenetration of founding "-ites" traced above, who are the "Nephites" now? What does "Nephite" mean? Or look like? At the same
time, the relative seamlessness with which the Nephites merge into the
numerically dominant Mulekites and the Mulekites assume the name
of the spiritually and culturally advanced Nephites (the label *Mulekite*
immediately drops from the text) suggests that any otherness of the
Mulekites pales by comparison to that of the Lamanites, whose attacks
drove the Nephites into the bosom of the Mulekites in the first place.
The alternative geneses represented by the Jaredites and Mulekites—
the former so much earlier in time as to be available only as foreboding
precedent and the latter so readily enfolded into the Nephite story as
to appear as a counterfactual blip, implying, in effect, the identity of
Mulekites with Nephites—ultimately do not decenter or defuse the
racialized Nephite/Lamanite agon.

The same might be said of subsequent demographic changes around
which the text explicitly retheorizes its racial categories. At times, the
text seems to destabilize Lamaniteness by proliferating and emphasizing signs other than "the skin of blackness." The Nephite prophet Alma
notes that a dissenting group of wicked Nephites led by one Amlici
"distinguished [themselves] from the Nephites" by marking themselves
"with red in their foreheads after the manner of the Lamanites"(Alma
3:4). So have the "Amlicites," as they are inevitably called, (also) become "Lamanites," with whom they indeed join forces against the
Nephites? (Alma 2:24) This multiplication of "Lamanite" "marks"—
red-painted foreheads, shorn heads, wicked traditions—that are readily
transferable as skin color is *not* seems to open the door to a religiocultural rather than ethnoracial definition of "Lamanite" (Alma 43:13).
But these redefinitions have inescapable limits that can be overcome
only by somewhat dubious logic chopping.[38]

---

38. Many readers of the Book of Mormon sense that the narrative's overt racism on
some level unravels amid its textual complexity but locate that unraveling too readily.
Mormon apologist John Tvedtnes posits a distinction between a "curse" that consisted in
separation from righteous tradition and a "mark"—"the skin of blackness"—that enforced
that curse (Tvedtnes, "The Charge of 'Racism' in the Book of Mormon," *FARMS Review*
15, no. 2 [2003]: 183–97). But this does little to resolve what Fenton calls "the vexed racial

Although Alma raises the possibility of the white "Lamanite," that is, an alternatively "marked" but nonetheless phenotypically white practitioner of wicked traditions "after the manner of the Lamanites," it is supremely telling that the racial corollary—a black "Nephite," that is, a practitioner of righteous "Nephite" traditions who simply happens to be nonwhite—proves an unthinkable proposition. The book of Alma details the evangelizing mission of the sons of the Nephite king, Mosiah, to Lamanite lands, which results in the conversion of the Lamanite king and many of his subjects. By Alma's standard, because these people had ceased "to believe in the tradition of the Lamanites, but believed those records which were brought out of the land of Jerusalem," they were "no more called Lamanites" (Alma 3:11; 23:16–17). But it seems they can't be called "Nephites" either—they are known as the "Anti-Nephi-Lehies" or the "Ammonites" (after one of the Nephite missionaries who baptized them) (Alma 56:57, 57:6). That is, they cannot be called "Nephites" until they become phenotypically white. Conversion allows these Lamanites to "open a correspondence with [the Nephites]," and the consequences seem to be more than

politics" of the Book of Mormon insofar as it suggests God's willingness to work with antiblack racism in order to maintain the purity of tradition (Elizabeth Fenton, "Open Canons"). Tvedtnes cites moments in the text when the Lamanites and Nephites trade moral places as evidence that "external differences such as skin color ... do not necessarily signify spiritual states," but the narrative's supposedly salutary sense of race's malleability always skews in a particular direction: the primary exemplum of how racial difference is "temporary" in the Book of Mormon is the whitening of Lamanite converts. Tvedtnes's downplaying gloss on the Book of Mormon's references to Lamanite whitening illustrates the limitations of his approach: "Whether this change occurred through intermarriage or some other unknown process, the event for the Nephites was apparently unique and unprecedented. Within the context of Nephite society and culture, this exceptional event would no doubt have been viewed as a sign from God that such distinctions were irrelevant for those numbered with Christ." That Tvedtnes himself is reading from "within the context of Nephite society and culture," as it were, is evinced by the fact that, logically speaking, the evidence that racial "distinctions were irrelevant" within the body of Christ would not be that the Lamanites turned white to look like Nephites but that the Lamanites retained their black skins. Non-Mormon scholars in the academy have occasionally fallen into similar difficulties in their attempts to read the Book of Mormon as more than a proof-text of garden-variety nineteenth-century racism. Fenton, following Craig Prentiss, "Loathsome unto Thy People," 128–29, emphasizes that "the Lamanites' story begins, but does not end, with racial delineation, and the 'skin of blackness' that covers them may be removed or transferred elsewhere" ("Open Canons"). My point is that although the narrative does hold out for the black Lamanites a pathway to rightness, which may seem to relativize the initial racial distinction, the fact that that pathway also seems to run to or through whiteness shows how the narrative actually reinforces racial distinction with a vengeance.

religio-cultural. We are told that "the curse of God did no more follow them" (Alma 23:18). If at this point it is at all ambiguous what this signifies, it is made crystal clear after a subsequent wave of Lamanite conversion: "Those Lamanites who had united with the Nephites were numbered among the Nephites; And their curse was taken from them, and their skin became white like unto the Nephites; And their young men and their daughters became exceedingly fair, and they were numbered among the Nephites, and were called Nephites" (3 Ne. 2:12–16). In the Book of Mormon history and reception history, spiritual enlightenment is ever haunted by the promise of racial *enwhitenment*. Lamanite righteousness seems teleologically bound to take the form of phenotypical whiteness. There is no such thing as a black Nephite, at least, not for long. By the same token, despite the fact that the initial articulation of the Lamanite curse promises that "the seed of him that mixeth with [the Lamanites'] seed" (consider the many Nephite dissenting groups like the Amlicites) "shall be cursed even with the same cursing," Nephite wickedness never explicitly and dramatically manifests as phenotypical blackness (2 Ne. 5:23). We never get an analogous pronouncement for any Nephites that "the curse of God did fall upon them." On this point, it seems significant that the prophet Jacob's jeremiad against the Nephites—in view of comparative Lamanite righteousness at the time—culminates not in "unless ye shall repent of your sins," your skins will be blacker than theirs, but rather, "their skins shall be whiter than yours" (Jacob 3:8).

As a last line of defense against charges of the Book of Mormon's racism, some liberal Mormon commentators turn to the 200-year period of social harmony that follows Jesus' visitation of the Americas in order to suggest the narrative's eventual eclipse of racial matters.[39] During this period there were reportedly not "any manner of -ites," and black and white peoples presumably intermarried insofar as they "were in one, the children of Christ and heirs to the kingdom of God" (4 Ne. 1:17). But, by the narrative's own lights, such universalism would have had a particular racial expression: the necessary outcome of this millennial mingling would be a wholesale whitening of those people sufficiently righteous to have survived the apocalyptic destruction attendant upon

---

39. See Eugene England, "'Lamanites' and the Spirit of the Lord," *Dialogue: A Journal of Mormon Thought* 18, no. 4 (Winter 1985): 25–32.

Christ's Old World crucifixion. When this utopian social order subsequently begins to break down, the old racial labels resurface, and the text initially wants to distinguish this revival of the categories as religiocultural rather than ethnoracial. It explicitly contrasts the "new" "Lamanites'" "hate" of "the children of God" with the "old" "Lamanites'" hate of "the children of Nephi from the beginning," tracing their identity to "revolt from the church" rather than racial difference (4 Ne. 1:20, 37–39). But if, as the narrative implies, by the end of the two hundred years of mass righteousness the people were phenotypically white(r), then what does it mean that a mere 200 years later, at the close of the narrative, we are left only with the surviving "Lamanites," who are implicitly nonwhite insofar as they are understood to be the principal ancestors of modern Amerindians? The eponymous Mormon emphasizes the religiocultural identity of Nephites and Lamanites at the end—they engage in the same morally depraved practices—and reasserts their difference in racial terms. He eulogizes the Nephites as his "fair ones," and he prophesies that the descendants of the Lamanite survivors "shall become a dark, filthy, and a loathsome people, beyond the description of that which ever hath been amongst us" (Morm. 4:10–12; 6:16–20; 5:15). While this may imply the Lamanites were white(r) at this time, at least by comparison to their modern Amerindian descendants, Lamanites seem ever destined to be "back in black." The Nephites, whether safely within or hopelessly beyond a state of grace, remain "fair ones," whereas the Lamanites become white when they attain grace but relapse into blackness when they lose it.

Regardless of virtue, the curse of a "skin of blackness" never quite seems to lift from its original targets, the Lamanites, and to descend on the Nephites. From beginning to end, racial difference trumps moral equivalence. The deck is perhaps stacked in a text whose white Nephite narrators repeatedly symbolize the state of grace through the color white: the fruit of the tree of life in Lehi's allegory of salvation is "white, to exceed all the whiteness I had ever seen"; and sanctification is frequently figured as having one's "garments washed white in the blood of the Lamb" (1 Ne. 8:11; Alma 5:21; 13:11). Physical and spiritual "darkness" robustly reinforce rather than neatly sift out from each other. The Book of Mormon thus performs the failure of a critique of racism whose main focus is to highlight the instability of rac(ial)ist categories. Instead, it demonstrates the perdurance of those categories even when their contents and contexts seem to change.

Level 2: Nephite Self-De(con)struction

The Book of Mormon plays out and shows the limitations of another form of antiracist critique, which might be described, following George Fredrickson, as romantic-racialist resignation before the eschatological elevation of the Other.[40] The Book of Mormon is painfully framed by the awareness—first prophetic and finally firsthand—of the divinely appointed destruction of the white Nephites at the hands of the dark Lamanites. Nephi sees the end of his American promised land before he even arrives: "And it came to pass that I beheld, and saw the people of the seed of my brethren [the Lamanites] that they had overcome my seed [the Nephites]; and they went forth in multitudes upon the face of the land" (1 Ne. 12:20). The Nephites always already know that they are not to rise to the ranks of world-historical peoples. This foreknowledge of their inevitable end shapes the narrative in profound ways. Nephite anticipation of self-destruction engages the narrative in self-deconstruction. For example, just after announcing the extinction of his people, the final Nephite narrator, Moroni, beseeches readers to see beyond the "imperfections" in the record he is about to deposit, thereby linking civilizational and narrative failure (Morm. 8:7–12). The Nephite narrators know that, in the end, they are a negative example: "Condemn me not because of mine imperfection," Moroni pleads, "neither my father [Mormon], because of his imperfection, neither them who have written before him; but rather give thanks unto God that he hath made manifest unto you our imperfections, that ye may learn to be more wise than we have been" (Morm. 9:31). To some extent, the Nephite narrators beat the ideology critic to the punch by writing without triumphalist illusions, drawing attention to and apologizing for potential aporias in their narrative.[41]

Even more strikingly, this tragic Nephite eschatology envisions not only Nephite extinction but Lamanite exaltation. In a kind of zero-sum

40. George M. Fredrickson, *The Black Image in the White Mind: The Debate on Afro-American Character and Destiny, 1817–1914* (Middletown, CT: Wesleyan University Press, [1971] 1987).

41. Compare Grant Hardy, *Understanding the Book of Mormon: A Reader's Guide* (New York: Oxford University Press, 2010), 9–10.

game, the ancient ignominy of the Nephites is made inversely proportional to the future glory of the descendants of the Lamanites—modern Amerindians. It is as though the (self-) critique of Nephite civilization cannot be complete without the ironic twist that the narrative's bugbear becomes the bearer of its best hopes. Knowing that their people will be extinguished, knowing that their record will be lost, the Nephite prophets address themselves to the descendants of their Lamanite "brethren" (Moro. 10:1–5). Nephite prophethood comes in some sense to be defined by a felt sense of stewardship for the posterity of one's mortal enemies. The early prophet Enos goes so far as to bind God in the following covenant: "If it should so be, that my people, the Nephites, should fall into transgression, and by any means be destroyed, and the Lamanites should not be destroyed, that the Lord God would preserve a record of his holy arm, that it might be brought forth at some future day unto the Lamanites, that, perhaps, they might be brought unto salvation" (Enos 1:14; compare Jarom 1:2). One hears two contradictory strains in Enos's prayer and in much of the white Nephite narrators' self-effacement. On the one hand, there is a disarming concession of any claim of providential superiority to the Lamanites in view of the foreseen course of sacred history. The Book of Mormon is history written not by the victors but the vanquished, and the Nephite narrators are not sore losers—they do not blame the referee in the sky but rather their own failures. Even while locked in the final battle to the death with the Lamanites, the Book of Mormon's eponymous editor (also a Nephite general) directly addresses their descendants, impressing on them their identity as "people of the first covenant" and wishing them the blessings of that relation (Morm. 7:10). On the title page, Mormon defines the primary audience and purpose of his book in terms of Amerindian destiny rather than Judeo-Christian testimony. As he puts it, the book is first "written to the Lamanites, who are a remnant of the house of Israel" and then "also to Jew and Gentile" (title page; compare Jarom 1:2). In this scheme, New World Israel—the Amerindians who descend from the Lamanites—trumps both gentile Euro-America and Old World Israel. Mormon establishes the book's primary intention as "show[ing] unto the remnant of the House of Israel [the Lamanite-descended Amerindians] what great things the Lord hath done for their fathers; and that they may know the covenants of the Lord, that they are not cast off forever" (title page). Only second-arily is the book aimed at "the convincing of the Jew and the Gentile that JESUS is the CHRIST, the ETERNAL GOD, manifesting himself unto all nations" (title page). Although contemporary Mormon interpreta-tion has tended to reverse these priorities, in Mormon's estimation, the scripture's preeminent function is to rehabilitate Lamanite race pride at a historical nadir, rather than to spread the good news of the Christian Gospel to white Americans. Hence, although white Nephites carve out the Book of Mormon narrative, it is a Lamanite book in relief.

On the other hand, there is something suspiciously sanctimonious about the Nephites' good sportsmanship, a pride smuggled in with all that humility. One might hear in Enos's plea for the preservation of the Nephite record not only selfless Christian love for one's enemies but a perpetuation of the text's foundational racial hierarchy. Yes, in view of Nephite extinction, the success of the white Nephite narrative is inex-tricably bound with the providential ascendancy of the Lamanites. But the flip side is that that providential ascendancy is to be mediated by the white Nephite narrative itself. Enos and the other white Nephite narrators imagine that when their record finally comes to light in the nineteenth century, the descendants of the Lamanites will still need to be "brought unto salvation," and they make their long-lost record the primary agent of that salvation. Hence, although reduced to "voices from the dust," the Nephite narrators—through the recovery of the Book of Mormon—remain in the position of telling the descendants of the Lamanites who they really are and how they should be (2 Ne. 3:19; 33:13; Morm. 8:23; Moro. 10:27). In sum, although the white Neph-ite narrators, like many nineteenth-century romantic racialists, accept being upstaged by the dark Other, they reserve for themselves the in-dispensable function of stage-managing the eschatological drama. For all its self-critique, the eschatology proffered by the white Nephite nar-rators preserves, in somewhat softer form, white Nephite superiority and centrality.

Level 3: Apocalypse in the Text/Apocalypse of the Text

The Book of Mormon's apocalypse is even more profound than the extraordinary reversal the white Nephite narrators countenance. In the end, not only the semantic critique of racial categories but the eschatological critique of the racial status quo is compromised by its site of enunciation—the white Nephite narrative. Ultimately, the Book of Mormon shows how the apocalypse announced in and by the text—the exaltation of the descendants of the Lamanites—entails the apocalypse of that very text—the cancellation of the white Nephite narrative. This is the fulfillment of its self-deconstructive tendency. By various means, the Book of Mormon invites us to confront the fact that "as the putative authors of the record in question, the Nephites were free to characterize their [Lamanite] antagonists as they wished."[42] It suggests that in order to dismantle the kind of theological racism the text features, what must be challenged is the very authority of the narrative that elaborates the framework in the first place. It is the narrative credibility of white supremacism, however allegedly scriptural its warrant, that must be called into question. Other pre-Civil War texts attuned to the insidiousness of race perform a similar operation. Both *Benito Cereno* and *Dred*, Peter Coviello and Gail Smith have respectively shown, engineer implosive narrative structures that dramatically reveal to the sentimental reader, inured to "racial knowingness," the utter inadequacy of his or her rac(ial)ist common sense: Herman Melville by conning us into identifying with a racist omniscient narrator over and against the hapless Captain Delano, thus perhaps catching us in Delano's selfsame blindness to the slaves' control of the ship; and Harriet Beecher Stowe by lulling us into a plantation romance only to jolt us with the recognition that a slave rebellion has been seething beneath the serene surface of the first half of the novel.[43] The Book of Mormon's version of this trick is much more threatening. Insofar as the Book of Mormon purports to be scripture, its self-deconstruction draws attention to that which the literalist hermeneuts of biblicist America were keen to ignore—the contingent human conditions of scripture writing and scripture reading, in other words, precisely the conditions from which might conceivably arise spurious notions of theological racism.

For many antebellum Americans, certainly those most likely to run across the Book of Mormon, the Bible was not subject to history;

---

42. Mauss, *All Abraham's Children*, 116.

43. Peter Coviello, "The American in Charity: 'Benito Cereno' and Gothic Anti-Sentimentality," *Studies in American Fiction* 30, no. 2 (2002): 155–80; Gail K. Smith, "Reading with the Other: Hermeneutics and the Politics of Difference in Stowe's *Dred*," *American Literature* 69, no. 2 (1997): 289–313.

rather, as the literal word of God, history was subject to it. This effect arose in part by virtue of the ur-canonical status the text had attained over centuries of reverence. The Book of Mormon could not possibly replicate such conditions of reception—the timelessness attached to the Bible simply as a result of its long-standing authority was inherently unavailable to the upstart text. But another source of the effect of biblical timelessness that the Book of Mormon could mime in an attempt to arrogate authority to itself was the distinctive narrative style of large portions of the Hebrew Bible. Meir Sternberg has argued that the Hebrew Bible's remarkably consistent style of narration, particularly across the historical books—a serene third-person omniscient narration beneath which any ripple of authorial presence subsides, creating an overwhelming reality effect—presupposes what he calls an "inspirational model" of author- and readership. The imperturbable knowingness of the biblical narrative—which simultaneously effaces the author and empowers the author to report God's thoughts—could only arise in a particular religiocultural context in which it was an "institutional fact" that a supreme divine being could speak through human beings. Following Sternberg, one could say the Hebrew Bible, by virtue of being produced by and for literalist readers, on a formal level presupposes and so produces literalist readers, which of course it continues to do. The seductive authoritativeness of the biblical voice, which can seem to come from nowhere, lends itself to the ongoing reception of the text in many quarters as the word of God. The reader with ears to hear might indeed hear something like divine omniscience in the Hebrew Bible's carefully crafted narratorial omniscience.[44]

Significantly, the Book of Mormon provides a conspicuous and self-conscious antithesis—or antidote—to this biblical timelessness. It presents multiple first-person narrators and editors who assiduously trace the provenance of their work.[45] In the opening book of Nephi, not only are readers manhandled at every turn by his aggressive first-person narration, they are given an account of how Nephi obtained the ore from which he made the very plates upon which his

---

44. Meir Sternberg, *The Poetics of Biblical Narrative: Ideological Literature and the Drama of Reading* (Bloomington: Indiana University Press, 1985), esp. 58–128.

45. Fenton, "Open Canons"; Givens, *Very Short Introduction*, 7–12, 34–35; Hardy, *Understanding*, xi–28.

words are inscribed. The effect is overwhelming: We are constantly reminded not only that we are reading Nephi's words but that these words were painstakingly engraved on "plates which I have made with mine own hands" (1 Ne. :17; 19:1–7; 2 Ne. 5:28–33). Throughout, the text eagerly authenticates itself by impressing on the reader the enduring materiality of a record literally handed down from one writer to the next: "Now I, Chemish, write what few things I write, in the same book with my brother; for behold, I saw the last which he wrote, that he wrote it with his own hand; and he wrote it in the day that he delivered them unto me" (Omni 1:9). The Book of Mormon thus works through rather than around or away from what David Holland has called the problem of "revelatory particularity."[46] The higher criticism's revelation of the intractable cultural and historical particularity of the Bible necessitated a reorientation toward revealed religion. Deists took it as occasion to abandon revealed for natural religion, asking how and why a universal God would confine Himself entirely to a single book of scripture from a single region of the world. Evangelicals went the opposite way and exceptionalized the Bible as the singular repository of God's literal word, the one-and-only-take-it-or-leave-it revelation. Both solutions evaded rather than confronted the problem of revelatory particularity, which demanded a full-blown theory and history of inspiration, of how and in what measure the divine has been and can be communicated through human language and action. The Book of Mormon goes some way in this direction by featuring admittedly imperfect individuals with exotic names claiming, in the first person, divine knowledge and then soliciting the reader's assessment of those claims. In so doing, the Book of Mormon "replicates the process of canon formation," as Terryl Givens has put it.[47]

It is a testament to the stagnant polemicism of the Book of Mormon studies that Givens, one of the text's foremost critics, can take the Book of Mormon's manifest preoccupation with (its own) historicity merely as occasion to restage the historicity debate rather than as an opportunity to think with the text's sophisticated inquiry into the production of

46. David Holland, *Sacred Borders: Continuing Revelation and Canonical Restraint in Early America* (New York: Oxford University Press 2011), 53–54, 147–48; Robert N. Hullinger, *Joseph Smith's Response to Skepticism* (Salt Lake City: Signature Books 1992), 154–65.

47. Terryl L. Givens, *The Viper on the Hearth: Mormons, Myths, and the Construction of Heresy* (New York: Oxford University Press, 1997), 83.

canonical authority. He leverages the text's self-authenticating gestures toward a characterization of the Book of Mormon as "authoritative discourse" (loosely appropriating Bakhtin). He seems to take this to mean that the Book of Mormon insists on being read in its own terms, which, in his hands, becomes tantamount to saying that the Book of Mormon must either be maximally true or abjectly false—either ancient scripture with universal claim or modern fraud deserving of universal dismissal, which keeps us trapped in the hermeneutical dualism that has stunted the Book of Mormon criticism.[48] The irony, of course, is that precisely the formal features—artless first-person narratives, methodical charting of its provenance, and incessant reminders of its materiality—through which the narrative wants to claim an unassailable objectivity on par with or even superior to the Bible can only highlight its overwrought subjectivity. By drawing attention to rather than away from the human medium of scripture, the Book of Mormon makes literalist hermeneutics in its particular case and in general a more difficult proposition. Put another way, the Book of Mormon is "Mormon's book," as Grant Hardy has suggested in his fine recent narratological analysis, in a way that, say, the first book of Samuel is not Samuel's book and, as such, cannot as readily slide into identity with "the word of God."[49] A certain friction is generated by the narrative's frank embeddedness in particular viewpoints and memory practices. Any theological authority accorded to the content is intimately bound up with the identity of the author-narrator. Who is saying what is said is made to matter, and this has significant implications for the text's racial politics.

Take Nephi, the narrator of the racial curse of his brothers, Laman and Lemuel, and, by definition, the text's prototypical white Nephite. He represents himself as righteously "desirous" to "see, and hear, and know" for himself all that has been revealed to the Israelite prophetic tradition and more (1 Ne. 10:17; 2:16). But his will to knowledge is inseparable from a will to power, a sense of calling to be a "ruler and a teacher over [his] [older] brethren," Laman and Lemuel (1 Ne. 2:22). Even as Nephi seems to observe his father's authority as prophet and father (1 Ne. 1:16; 16:20–27), he insistently characterizes his own narrative in negative terms as addressing not the "things of my father" but

48. Givens, *Very Short Introduction*, 123–25.
49. Hardy, *Understanding*, 9–10, 14–16.

the "things of God," his real Father, as it were (1 Ne. 6:3). It is made clear that although Nephi makes his "record in the language of [his] father," his record is "[made] with [his] own hand ... [and] according to [his] knowledge," gained by direct revelation from God (1 Ne. 1:3). He unabashedly filters his historical chronicle through that which is "expedient to [him]," "speak[ing] somewhat of the things of [his] father, and also of [his] brethren" only insofar as they contribute to "[his] account" of "[his] reign and ministry" (1 Ne. 10:1; compare 1 Ne. 1:16–17; 10:15).

The sheer "me" factor of Nephi's first-person narrative might be seen as enacting within the Book of Mormon itself something analogous to the higher criticism's reduction of scripture to cultural text, which brings the text's rac(ial)ism into a new light.[50] It becomes ever clearer that Nephi writes to a particular people, namely, *"my* people" (2 Ne. 33:1–4). Hence, one has every right to be skeptical when, in the course of celebrating his rise to sacred kingship over his prosperous people, he relates that he cursed his brethren with "a skin of blackness," callously punctuating the account of his brothers' divine misfortune with the comment that "we"—a first-person plural that now emphatically excludes his brothers and their descendants—"lived after the manner of happiness" (2 Ne. 5:27). The fact that many white Mormon readers haven't been so skeptical (in fact, Nephi is often lionized in contemporary Mormonism) has less to do with the Book of Mormon itself than with their own susceptibility to identifying with the narrative power that comes with whiteness and with the ironic adaptation to the Book of Mormon of a literalist hermeneutic that understands its duty to scripture to consist largely in taking the text at face value. The frankly limited scope of not only the two books of Nephi but the additional books designated as the "small plates" (the first six books of the Book of Mormon, each narrated in the first person and ostensibly unabridged by the eponymous editor, Mormon) in the name of privileging "spiritual" things instead becomes a measure of the profane imperatives of ethnocentrism. Hence, it is fitting that the vaunted small plates eventually peter out into something like pure ideology. The series of minor writers in the final short books of Jarom and Omni evince little to no prophetic intent. Rather than writing according to

50. Jonathan Sheehan, *The Enlightenment Bible: Translation, Scholarship, Culture* (Princeton, NJ: Princeton University Press, 2005).

the "commandments of the Lord," these admittedly "wicked" fighting men write only "according to the commandment of [their] father[s] … that our genealogy might be kept" (Jarom 1:1; Omni 1:2–3, 9). They write only to prop up Nephite cultural identity.[51] Hence, the Book of Mormon's replication of the process of canon formation does not simply function as a critique of the existing canon and justification of its own inclusion therein; it draws our attention to the partiality of any process of canon formation, including its own. Bushman is much closer than Givens to the mark when he deems the Book of Mormon "almost postmodern" in its concern with the conditions of its own production.[52] The Book of Mormon's metatextual navel gazing profoundly *destabilizes* its self-canonizing narrative, opening it to ethical critique from without and within. One could say the Book of Mormon precociously illustrates, against itself, the truism of 1990s culture warriors on the Left: canonization presupposes the victimization of an Other. The American scripture thus comes into view as an ethnocentric document, the governing cultural myth of the Nephite people.

The Book of Mormon's canon busting thus fully turns back on itself. Beneath the aporia preemptively acknowledged by the white Nephite narrators—the instructive "imperfections" in the record of a failed people—are a set of deeper, archival aporia that fundamentally challenge the narrative's authority. Beyond the white Nephite narrative's self-deconstruction lie the traces of something like a "Lamanite view of Book of Mormon history."[53] It is as though the Book of Mormon's obsession with provenance is so extreme as to dictate even the threatening disclosure of alternative versions of its own story. For instance, it is revealed that the Lamanites at least intermittently kept their own record, which prompted some nineteenth-century Mormon hermeneuts to speculate that Lamanites may have retained copies of the Book of Mormon record even after Moroni buried the gold plates (Mosiah 24:6).[54]

---

51. Compare Noel B. Reynolds, "The Political Dimension in Nephi's Small Plates," *Brigham Young University Studies* 27, no. 4 (1987): 15–37.

52. Bushman, *Rough Stone Rolling*, 87.

53. Richard Lyman Bushman, "The Lamanite View of *Book of Mormon* History," in *Believing History: Latter-Day Saint Essays*, ed. Reid L. Neilson and Jed Woodworth (New York: Columbia University Press, 2004), 79–92.

54. See George Reynolds, *The Story of the Book of Mormon,* 3rd ed. (Chicago: Henry C. Etten., 1888), 82–83.

When Lamanite voices *are* heard in the Book of Mormon, they offer a coherent and convincing counterreading of Book of Mormon history. In an epistle to a Nephite military leader, the Lamanite Ammoron[55] writes back—a rare Lamanite primary document, as it were:

55. In a response to the original publication of this essay, Joseph Spencer has argued that I have "drastically misrepresent[ed] the text" by ascribing a "Lamanite" identity to Ammoron, who Spencer asserts is "not a dark-skinned Lamanite but a light-skinned Nephite who has (through his brother [Amalickiah] usurped the Lamanite government" ("The Self-Critical Book of Mormon: Notes on an Emergent Literary Approach," *Journal of Book of Mormon Studies* 24, no. 1 [2015]: 191–92). While I appreciate Spencer's complication of the question of Ammoron's racial identity, I would counter that the "racially problematic status of Ammoron" is perhaps even deeper than Spencer has suggested. The character Ammoron explicitly identifies in two ways—as "a proud Lamanite" and "a descendant of Zoram, whom your fathers pressed out of Jerusalem" (Alma 54:23). Put simply, Ammoron suggests the long-brewing existence of a distinct "Zoramite" identity divergent from a "Nephite" identity and convergent upon a "Lamanite" identity. When afforded the privilege of direct discourse, Ammoron exposes what the Nephite narrative has worked hard to massage away—namely, that Zoram, the servant of the text's foundational villain, Laban, was physically "seize[d]" by Nephi and then arguably coerced into taking an "oath" to join Lehi's king group (4:30–37). Until Ammoron's outburst, the text has largely force-fitted Zoram into the "Nephite" category—for instance, depicting him as being blessed by father Lehi as "a true friend" to Nephi (2 Ne. 1:30). But traces of difference and even tension nonetheless remain. Lehi blesses Zoram as "servant of Laban," a reminder of Zoram's origination from a situation antagonistic to Nephi's; Nephi, in the course of his narration of the racializing separation of his people from Laman and Lemuel, speaks of "tak[ing]" Zoram with him in a way that arguably recalls or even reenacts Zoram's initial coercion; and Jacob registers that "Zoramites" empirically existed as a distinct kin group in a way that, say, "Samites" didn't (even as he then heuristically subsumes them as "Nephites") (Jacob 1:13). Most notably, after Jacob's demographic redefinition, the next time we hear of "Zoramites" in the Book of Mormon, the term refers to a group of people who have "separated themselves from the Nephites" (Alma 30:59). Although the text derives this people's name from their "leader" and not the original Zoram (Alma 30:59, 31:1; cf. Alma 16:5–8), one is of course invited to read this character in relation to the original—as implicitly a literal descendant of the original Zoram or as a namesake of the man who was so tensely joined with Nephi in the first place. In any case, "Zoram" comes into view as a fitting sign under which to imagine a group of people uneasily set in the "Nephite" camp. Despite—or, rather, because of—the consequent missionary campaign of Alma and the sons of Mosiah to these Zoramites, a critical mass of them "began to mix with the Lamanites" and eventually "became Lamanites" (Alma 35:10–11, 43:4). Hence, it is possible that Ammoron, "proud Lamanite" and "descendant of Zoram," was more than the opportunistic white Nephite appropriator of Lamanite culture and usurper of Lamanite governance that Spencer makes him out to be. In fact, the language the Nephite narrative uses to vent its fear regarding the instability of Zoramite identity is the mirror image of that deployed to imply the whitening of the Lamanites: whereas the righteous subset of Lamanites known as the Anti-Nephi-Lehies "open a correspondence" with the Nephites and, as a result, "the curse of God did no more follow them" (Alma 23:18; 24:8), one implication of which is that their skin whitened (3 Ne. 2:14–15); the Zoramites "enter into a correspondence with the Lamanites" (Alma 31:4), and their "mix[ing] with" and "bec[o]m[ing]" Lamanites arguably implies a darkening of their skin—in other words, that the curse of God now began

> Behold, your fathers did wrong their brethren, insomuch that they did rob them of their right to the government when it rightly belonged to them. ... If ye will lay down your arms, and subject yourselves to be governed by those to whom the government doth rightly belong, then will I cause that my people shall lay down their weapons and shall be at war no more. ... [Otherwise] we will wage a war which shall be eternal, either to the subjecting the Nephites to our authority or to their eternal extinction. And as concerning that God whom ye say we have rejected, behold, we know not such a being; neither do ye; but if it so be that there is such a being, we know not but that he hath made us as well as you. And if it so be that there is a devil and hell, behold will he not send you there to dwell with my brother whom ye have murdered, whom ye have hinted that he hath gone to such a place? (Alma 54:17–18, 20, 21–24; compare Mosiah 10:12)

Ammoron's rhetorical questions powerfully interrogate Nephite self-righteousness. They more than suggest a sophisticated Lamanite worldview that Nephite accusations of savagery would deny. Most importantly, this relativizing perspective suggests that the Nephites are not simply pure vessels of sacred truth but purveyors of the "traditions of their fathers," hamstrung by "custom" no less than the Lamanites to whom the Nephite narrative typically attaches these derogatory terms (Alma 9:16–17; 17:9,15, 20, 25; 47:17, 23). In sum, the Book of Mormon suggests it is not its own "whole story"; it "formally resists completion," as Elizabeth Fenton has put it in her ground-breaking recent Americanist literary treatment of the text.[56]

This apocalypse of the white Nephite narrative—the revelation of its rac(ial)ist partiality—is the ultimate implication of the Book of Mormon's distinctive racial apocalypse—which has the descendants of the black Lamanites rather than the white Nephites building the New Jerusalem on the American continent. The Book of Mormon's spiritual message of Lamanite liberation, I want to argue, depends for its full impact on engendering skepticism toward the white Nephite narrative. Put another way, the text's radical eschatological content is best

---

to follow them, as it were. (These are the only instances in the Book of Mormon in which the phrase "open" or "enter" "a correspondence" is used, which tightens the correlation.) In sum, Ammoron may have been culturally and even racially "Lamanite" in ways that justify my identification of him as such. In any case, as Spencer himself acknowledges, any ambiguity in the Ammoron example "in no way vitiates ... the larger thesis" (190).

56. Fenton, "Open Canons."

articulated not by what—for all their tragic self-effacement—the white Nephite narrators do say but what they conspicuously *do not* or rather *cannot* say. Along these lines, it is of the greatest significance that the full utterance of Lamanite liberation theology awaits nothing less than the apocalyptic intervention of the very voice of God in the text: it is the resurrected Christ himself, during his visit to ancient America, who offers the most thorough exposition of what I have called Amerindian apocalypse. Two passages—among those most quoted in early Mormon discourse, according to Grant Underwood's careful survey—are especially significant, detailing as they do the future relationship between the gentiles, identified with the white Euro-Americans to whom the Book of Mormon would eventually be revealed, and "the remnant of Jacob," identified with the Amerindian descendants of the surviving Lamanites, in the making of an American millennium:[57]

> If they [the white American gentiles] will repent and hearken unto my words … I will establish my church among them, and they shall come in unto the covenant and be numbered among this the remnant of Jacob [the American Indians], unto whom I have given this land [the American continent] for their inheritance. And they shall assist my people, the remnant of Jacob, and also as many of the house of Israel as shall come, that they may build a city, which shall be called the New Jerusalem. (3 Ne. 21:22–23)

This extraordinary passage, endowed with special authority as an utterance of Jesus, upends all of the common racist assumptions of antebellum white America. In Jesus' millennial scheme, it is not the Indian "remnant of Jacob" that must repent, but rather the white American gentiles. It is not the Indians who will be gathered into the benevolent fold of white Christian America, but rather repentant white Americans who will be gathered into the American house of Israel, privileged to be "numbered among the remnant of Jacob," a striking reversal of the trope of black Lamanites being privileged to be "numbered among" righteous white Nephites. America is suddenly no longer the promised land of white Christians, but rather the "land of [Indian] inheritance." And, finally, it is not the Indians who will secondarily "assist" white Christians in the building of the millennial kingdom, but

---

57. Grant Underwood, *The Millenarian World of Early Mormonism* (Urbana: University of Illinois Press, 1993), 78.

rather gathered white Christians who will be privileged to "assist" the Indians in establishing the New Jerusalem. According to Book of Mormon eschatology, then, the means to creating Zion was not through a white Christian utopia, but rather "a powerfully and divinely reinstated Indian nation."[58]

And if the white American gentiles did not repent "after the blessing which they shall receive, after they have scattered my people," the Amerindian "remnant of Jacob,"

> Then shall ye, who are a remnant of the house of Jacob ... be among them ... as a young lion among the flocks of sheep, who, if he goeth through both treadeth down and teareth in pieces, and none can deliver ... For I will make my people with whom the Father hath covenanted, yea, I will make thy horn iron, and I will make thy hoofs brass. And shalt beat in pieces many people. (3 Ne. 20:15–16, 19)

In this searing prophecy, Amerindian peoples become "invincible weapons of divine indignation," a force that will reverse the effects of white American gentile imperialism, reclaiming for Indian Israel what the Book of Mormon reveals is rightly hers.[59] Implicit in this apocalyptic vision is the definition of white gentile repentance as acknowledging and abiding by Native sovereignty. White American salvation depends upon being adopted into the Amerindian "remnant of Jacob." Book of Mormon eschatology thus prescribed for white Euro-Americans an ethnoracial conversion into Amerindians, the exact mirror image of the white Nephite—and, often, white Mormon—fantasy of converted Lamanites becoming "fair and delightsome." It is hard to imagine a vision more profoundly disruptive of US state ideology than the Book of Mormon's Indianized millennium.

By giving Christ himself the most thorough exposition of Amerindian apocalypse, the Book of Mormon makes a vital distinction between the voice of God and the voices of the Nephite narrators who claim inspiration from God. Implicit in this arrangement is the question of how capable the Nephite narrators are of faithfully transmitting

---

58. Michael Jensen, "'As a Lion among Beasts': Squaring Mormon Views of the Indian with Those of Nineteenth-Century White America," in *Archive of Restoration Culture: Summer Fellows' Papers, 1997–1999*, ed. Richard Lyman Bushman (Provo, UT: Joseph Fielding Smith Institute for Latter-day Saint History, 2000), 179.

59. Jensen, "As a Lion among Beasts," 181.

the message of Lamanite liberation. In fact, Christ makes the question explicit in what is certainly the most remarkable of what I have called the text's archival aporia. Just after having laid out his sweeping vision of Amerindian apocalypse, Jesus is brought—at his request—the Nephite records for his perusal. He immediately queries Nephi, a namesake of the original, regarding the prophecy of his "servant, Samuel, the Lamanite" regarding the resurrection of the saints, no mention of which he finds upon the Nephite plates.[60] His tone is rebuking: "How be it that ye have not written this thing," he pointedly asks, and "Nephi remembered that this thing had not been written," even though, he acknowledges, "all" the words of Samuel had been "fulfilled" (3 Ne. 23:9–13). Laid bare here is a reluctance on the part of the Nephite prophets to include in their narrative something they themselves recognize as true prophecy, because, at least in part it seems, it came from a Lamanite. The text's editorial process is brought into view, and it is at least suggested that the values governing that process may have as much to do with ethnic pride as divine inspiration.

The literal voice of God in the text singles out for distinction precisely the voice the Nephite narrative does *not*, at least not willingly, include—the prophetic voice of the Lamanite. It is only this voice that can properly convey the full significance of Amerindian apocalypse— Christ may give it its most thorough exposition but its most complete expression comes from Samuel. Christ may sound the Amerindian apocalypse, but Samuel provides us with a tangible sense of its sound, as it were—the echoes with which such a transformed world

---

60. Grant Adamson, in "Thomas Paine and the Prophecy of Samuel the Lamanite," paper presented at Faith and Knowledge Conference, Wesley Theological Seminary, Washington, DC, Feb. 22, 2013, has noted that another impetus for this extraordinary passage might be a claim made by Thomas Paine in a late-life "examination" of New Testament prophecies that was eventually made part 3 of *The Age of Reason*, a text with which the Smith family had a history (Bushman, *Rough Stone Rolling*, 25). Paine had targeted the mention of the resurrection of the saints in Matthew 27 as a fabrication since it was not prophesied elsewhere in scripture. Samuel's prophecy in the Book of Mormon thus might be read as an answer to Paine's promise of belief if such a prophecy could be supplied. Adamson's reading only makes Samuel's prophecy weightier, and so the fact that the Book of Mormon does not include any description of the resurrection of the saints only underscores my question: Why does the narrative so extravagantly deny itself something that would otherwise serve its purposes? The narrative's explicitly flagged and nonetheless persistent failure to report fully a prophecy that enjoyed reported fulfillment, explicit divine endorsement, and special critical utility in the Book of Mormon's moment of publication becomes another measure of the Nephite narrative's partiality.

would reverberate. It is significant that Samuel is always identified as "the Lamanite" rather than, say, an "Ammonite." He is depicted as an interloper in rather than a resident of Zarahemla (Hel. 13:2), which distinguishes him from the sons of Mosiah's Lamanite converts, who lived under Nephite protection in Zarahemla and "became" Nephite— and white (Alma 53:10). Samuel, by contrast, comes from and returns to "his own country … and his own people" (Hel. 16:7). His bracing otherness is immediately manifest in his incorrigible refusal and pointed inversion of Nephite paternalism. Samuel proclaims that if the Nephites "have been a chosen people of the Lord" in the past, then that time has passed, the Lord having passed his favor on to the Lamanites (Hel. 15:3). It is clear that the Lamanite prophet cedes nothing to the Nephites as his supposed spiritual superiors. If the white Nephites had long interpreted the black Lamanites in instrumental terms as a providential "scourge" meant to "chasten" them towards humility, then the Lamanite Samuel turns the tables to interpret the Nephites as mere instruments in the hands of the Lord to restore the Lamanites to their rightful place: "Salvation hath come unto [the Lamanites] through the preaching of the Nephites; and for this intent hath the Lord prolonged their [the Nephites'] days" (1 Ne. 2:24; Hel. 15:4). Once given the chance at salvation extended to the Nephites so many times over so many centuries, Samuel proclaims, the Lamanites demonstrate a unique "steadfastness" entirely foreign to the Nephites (Hel. 15:10; compare Alma 24:19; 26:32–33; Hel. 6:1, 4). Indeed, if the "more part" of the Lamanites are now "in the path of their duty, and … walk circumspectly before God," then the "more part" of the Nephites now do not believe the words of prophets like Samuel (Hel. 15:5; 16:6). In the end, Samuel prophesies, the Lord will "prolong" the Lamanites' "days" as an end rather than means—"because of their firmness when they are once enlightened" (Hel. 15:10). But Samuel goes even farther, imbuing the noble Lamanite character itself rather than "the preaching of the Nephites" with saving power, venturing that "*even if* [the Lamanites] should dwindle in unbelief, the Lord shall prolong their days" (Hel. 15:11, my emphasis). Needless to say, the Nephites did not warrant such a promise. Instead of a white Nephite missionary weepily deigning to make his benighted black brethren aware of the eternal fate that awaits them unless they abandon "the traditions of their fathers," the spectacle Samuel presents is of an enlightened dark prophet bluntly advising, in vivid and violent language, his fair Nephite brethren that "four hundred years pass not away save the sword of justice falleth upon this people" (Hel. 15:4; 13:5; compare Mosiah 28:3).

Ultimately, Samuel goes so far as to reverse the curse. But in so doing he does not merely transvalue white and black; he eliminates racial difference as symptom or sign of divine accursedness. More precisely, he suggests that the reason the Nephites will fall is precisely because of their facile equation of divine approval with outward appearances like skin color. Perhaps the most fundamental presupposition of the Nephite narrative is what Mormons sometimes call the "pride cycle": God blesses the righteous with material prosperity, leading them to forget God and become wicked, leading God to chasten them with misfortune, leading them to humble themselves before God and return to righteousness, thereby initiating the sequence again. Interestingly, this metanarrative is most succinctly laid out in one of Mormon's editorial intrusions in the chapter just before Samuel's sermon appears (Hel. 12). This arrangement recalls the initial pronouncement of the curse of the Lamanites with "a skin of blackness" in the context of Nephi's narration of his industrious people's material achievements—crops and livestock flourish, buildings and temples are constructed, plates and swords are forged. That passage assembles outward signs—whiteness and settler prosperity, on the one hand, blackness and nomadic poverty, on the other—into a sturdy evaluative edifice: How do you know if God favors you? If you are white and rich. The Nephite narrative's moral equation of righteousness and prosperity and its racial hierarchy are twinned expressions of a literalist confidence in the self-evident meaning of the world—you can tell good people from bad people based on how much stuff they have or what they look like. One *can* take things at face value. Hence, Samuel's chiastic double curse of the Nephites—"ye are cursed because of your riches, and also are your riches cursed because ye have set your hearts upon them"—functions as a critique not merely of materialism but of the literalist logic that also underwrites the narrative's simplistic dichotomy of white-prosperous-good/black-impoverished-bad. Samuel is concerned not with the alleged signs of divine accursedness but the substance of moral failure. If the Nephites are cursed, Samuel suggests, it is because they have cursed themselves by believing in racial curses, by complacently trusting in whiteness and other superficial qualities as reliable indices of the providential direction of things. Like many Native and African American prophets of the nineteenth century, Samuel thus undermines a crass providentialism of victors that aligns financial might and the racially white with divine right, eclipsing the Nephite narrative's most basic assumptions in the process. The inclusion of Samuel's voice in the Book of Mormon represents not only an aporia but an apocalypse within and of the text that completes the internal—and thus divinely approved, as it were—case for reading the Nephite narrative with a hermeneutics of suspicion. Paradoxically, the Book of Mormon is a scripture whose successful inculcation—at least so far as its eschatology is concerned—demands that we *not* read it as "scripture" insofar as that honorific presupposes a naive literalist cession of transcendental authority to the narrative voice. It systematically disables the very hermeneutic that enabled so many antebellum Americans to find confirmation of common-sense racism in the unquestionably sure voice of the Bible. It challenges not only the Bible's monopoly on authority but the notion that any single text—however high and holy its claims and tones—including itself, might warrant the type of all-in, nonnegotiable investment made by the literalist reader.

Instead of a literalist fetishization of one—or, with its addition, two—holy books, and the concomitant elevation of the bearers of those books, the Book of Mormon points us to an expanding library of holy books produced by God's children in every corner of the world:[61]

> Thou fool, that shall say: A Bible, we have got a Bible, and we need no more Bible. ... Know ye not there are more nations than one?
>
> Know ye not that I, the Lord your God, have created all men, and that I remember those who are upon the isles of the sea. ... For I command all men, both in the east, and in the west, and in the north, and in the south, and in the islands of the sea, that they shall write words which I speak unto them; for out of the books which shall be written I will judge the world, every man according to their works, according to that which is written. (2 Ne. 29:6–7, 11)

The Book of Mormon's Amerindian apocalypse not only undoes the white supremacist apocalypse of many Euro-American biblicists; it

---

61. Compare Fenton, "Open Canons."

opens onto a globalist apocalypse whose standard of judgment is truly ecumenical. One should expect to find holy books and covenant peoples everywhere. It is the achievement of this mindset that signals "the dispensation of the fulness of times." Sacred history cannot simply be switched to the autopilot mode of extending Euro-Christian empire; instead, it requires that empire's dismantling. The Book of Mormon thus indexes, providentially or not, a theological, cultural, and literary sea change beyond biblical Christianity driven by the disorienting cultural encounters of Atlantic modernity. It embodies the cosmic scandal of "Americanity."[62]

---

62. Anibal Quijano and Immanuel Wallerstein, "Americanity as a Concept, or the Americas in the Modern World-System," *International Social Science Journal* 134 (1992): 549–57.

CONTRIBUTORS

Catherine Brekus is Charles Warren Professor of the History of Religion in America at Harvard Divinity School. Her recent books include *Sarah Osborn's World: The Rise of Evangelicalism in Early America* and a companion volume, *Sarah Osborn's Collected Writings*. Her essay first appeared in *The Journal of Religion* 92, no. 4 (2012): 482–97.

William L. Davis received his PhD from UCLA and is the author of *Visions in a Seer Stone: Joseph Smith and the Making of the Book of Mormon* (2020). He thanks Colby Townsend and Gary James Bergera for their assistance and the opportunity to revise and update this essay, which first appeared in *Dialogue: A Journal of Mormon Thought* 49, no. 4 (Winter 2016): 1–58. The essay has also benefitted from Edward J. Varno and Betty McMahon of the Ontario County Historical Society, David Rodes, Sam Watters, Rick Grunder, H. Michael Marquardt, Connell O'Donovan, Brent Metcalfe, Dale R. Broadhurst, Michael Austin, and the anonymous reviewers for *Dialogue*.

Elizabeth Fenton is Professor of English at the University of Vermont. She is the author of *Religious Liberties: Anti-Catholicism and Liberal Democracy in Nineteenth-Century US Literature and Culture* (2011) and *Old Canaan in a New World: Native Americans and the Lost Tribes of Israel* (2020). She is also co-editor, with Jared Hickman, of *Americanist Approaches to* The Book of Mormon (2019). She presented an early version of her essay at the 2012 Society of Nineteenth-Century Americanists convention in Berkeley, California, and is grateful for the feedback she received there. She also thanks Robert S. Levine, Molly Robey, Val Rohy, and Sarah Sillin for commenting on drafts of the essay. Her essay first appeared in *The Journal of Nineteenth-Century Americanists* 1, no. 2 (2013): 339–61.

Kathleen Flake is Richard L. Bushman Professor of Mormon Studies at the University of Virginia. Appointed to the Religious Studies faculty, she teaches courses in American religious history and the interaction of American religion and law. She is the author of *The Politics of Religious Identity*. She has published in several scholarly journals and is on the editorial board of *Religion and American Culture: A Journal of Interpretation* and the *Mormon Studies Review*. A portion of her essay was presented in 2003 to the Yale Conference on "God, Humanity, and Revelation: Perspectives from Mormon Philosophy and History." She is grateful to Stephen Marini for his helpful comments as conference respondent and to many others who have contributed more informally to the essay's evolution. She also thanks the Vanderbilt University Divinity School for a teaching leave in support of this project. Her essay first appeared in *The Journal of Religion* 87, no. 4 (Oct. 2007): 497–527.

Paul Gutjahr is Ruth N. Halls Professor of English at Indiana University. Along with numerous articles and book chapters, he is the author of *An American Bible: A History of the Good Book in the United States, 1777–1880* (1999), *Charles Hodge: Guardian of American Orthodoxy* (2011), and *The Book of Mormon: A Biography* (2012). He has also edited two major anthologies: one on "American Popular Literature of the Nineteenth-Century" and the other on "American Bestsellers in the Nineteenth Century." He is the sole editor for the *Oxford Handbook of the Bible in America* (2017). His essay first appeared in *American Transcendental Quarterly* 12, no. 4 (1998): 275–93.

Jared Hickman is Associate Professor of English at John Hopkins University. He is the author of *Black Prometheus: Race and Radicalism in the Age of Atlantic Slavery* (2016) and the co-editor of *Americanist Approaches to* The Book of Mormon (2019) and *Abolitionist Places* (Routledge, 2013). His essay first appeared in *American Literature* 86, no. 3 (2014): 429–61, and later in *To Be Learned Is Good: Essays on Faith and Scholarship in Honor of Richard Lyman Bushman* (2018), *Timelines of American Literature* (2019), and *Producing Ancient Scripture: Joseph Smith's Translation Projects in the Development of Mormon Christianity* (2020). He is currently completing a book entitled "The Romance of The Book of Mormon."

Susan Juster is the Rhys Isaac Collegiate Professor of History at the University of Michigan and a John Simon Guggenheim Memorial Foundation Fellow. She is the author of *Doomsayers: Anglo-American Prophecy in the Age of Revolution* and the coeditor of *Empires of God: Religious Encounters in the Early Modern Atlantic.* Her essay first appeared in *The American Historical Review* 104, no. 5 (Dec. 1999): 1560–81.

Seth Perry is Associate Professor of Religion in America at Princeton University. His first book, *Bible Culture and Authority in the Early United States* (2018), explores the performative, rhetorical, and material aspects of bible-based authority in early-national America. His work has appeared in *Church History, Early American Studies,* the *Journal of the American Academy of Religion,* the *Journal of Scholarly Publishing,* the *William and Mary Quarterly,* the *Chronicle of Higher Education, Sightings,* and the *LA Review of Books.* His second book project is a biography of Lorenzo Dow, the early-national period's most famous itinerant preacher. He thanks the editors and anonymous readers at *Church History,* where his essay first appeared, for their helpful comments; Catherine Brekus, Clark Gilpin, and Richard Rosengarten for reading an early version of the essay; and B. M. Pietsch for reading a late one. His essay first appeared in *Church History* 85, no. 4 (Dec. 2016): 762–83.

Laura Thieman Scales is Associate Professor of English at Stonehill College (Easton, Massachusetts). Her work focuses on nineteenth-century American religious practices and narrative voice. Her essay first appeared in *American Literary History* 24, no. 2 (Summer 2012): 205–33.

Roberto A. Valdeón is honorary professor at South China Business College (Guangzhou, China), full professor in English Studies and Translation at the University of Oviedo (Spain), and member of the Academia Europaea. He is the author of about 200 publications, including contributions to journals such as *Language and Intercultural Communication, Across Languages and Cultures, Meta, Intercultural Pragmatics, Terminology, The Translator, Journal of Pragmatics, Target, Babel, International Journal of Applied Linguistics, Philological Quarterly, Journalism, Journalism Studies* and *Translating and Interpreting Studies.* He is Editor-in-Chief of *Perspectives Studies in Translation*

Theory and Practice and General Editor of the Benjamins Translation Library. He is the author of *Translation and the Spanish Empire in the Americas* (2014) and has co-edited the *Routledge Handbook of Spanish Translation Studies* among other books. His essay first appeared in *Across Languages and Cultures* 15, no. 2 (2014): 219–41.